New Perspectives on

DATA-DRIVEN WEB SITES WITH MICROSOFT® ACCESS 2000: TOOLS FOR E-COMMERCE

Advanced

New Perspectives on

DATA-DRIVEN WEB SITES WITH MICROSOFT® ACCESS 2000: TOOLS FOR E-COMMERCE

Advanced

LISA FRIEDRICHSEN

COURSE
TECHNOLOGY

Thomson Learning™

ONE MAIN STREET, CAMBRIDGE, MA 02142

Australia • Canada • Denmark • Japan • Mexico • New Zealand • Philippines
Puerto Rico • Singapore • South Africa • Spain • United Kingdom • United States

New Perspectives on Data-Driven Web Sites with Microsoft Access 2000: Tools for E-Commerce is published by Course Technology.

Managing Editor	Greg Donald	Associate Product Manager	Melissa Dezotell
Senior Editor	Donna Gridley	Editorial Assistant	Jill M. Kirn
Senior Product Manager	Rachel A. Crapser	Developmental Editor	Rachel Biheller Bunin
Product Manager	Catherine V. Donaldson	Text Designer	Meral Dabcovich
Production Editor	Catherine DiMassa	Cover Designer	Douglas Goodman

© 2001 by Course Technology, a division of Thomson Learning

For more information contact:

Course Technology
One Main Street
Cambridge, MA 02142
Or find us on the World Wide Web at: http://www.course.com

For permission to use material from this text or product, contact us by

- Web: www.thomsonrights.com
- WebPhone: 1-800-730-2214
- WebFax: 1-800-730-2215

Trademarks

Disclaimer

Course Technology reserves the right to revise this publication and make changes from time to time in its content without notice.

ISBN 0-619-01948-4

Printed in the United States of America

1 2 3 4 5 6 7 8 9 10 MZR 04 03 02 01 00

PREFACE

The New Perspectives Series

About New Perspectives

Course Technology's **New Perspectives Series** is an integrated system of instruction that combines text and technology products to teach computer concepts, the Internet, and microcomputer applications. Users consistently praise this series for innovative pedagogy, use of interactive technology, creativity, accuracy, and supportive and engaging style.

How is the New Perspectives Series different from other series?

The **New Perspectives Series** distinguishes itself by **innovative technology**, from the renowned Course Labs to the state-of-the-art multimedia that is integrated with our Concepts texts. Other distinguishing features include **sound instructional design, proven pedagogy,** and **consistent quality**. Each tutorial has students learn features in the context of solving a realistic case problem rather than simply learning a laundry list of features. With the **New Perspectives Series**, instructors report that students have a complete, integrative learning experience that stays with them. They credit this high retention and competency to the fact that this series incorporates critical thinking and problem solving with computer skills mastery. In addition, we work hard to ensure accuracy by using a multi-step quality assurance process during all stages of development. Instructors focus on teaching and students spend more time learning.

Choose the coverage that's right for you

New Perspectives applications books are available in the following categories:

Brief
2-4 tutorials

Brief: approximately 150 pages long, two to four "Level I" tutorials, teaches basic application skills.

Introductory
6 or 7 tutorials, or
Brief + 2 or 3 more
tutorials

Introductory: approximately 300 pages long, four to seven tutorials, goes beyond the basic skills. These books often build out of the Brief book, adding two or three additional "Level II" tutorials.

Comprehensive
Introductory + 4 or 5
more tutorials. Includes
Brief Windows tutorials
and Additional Cases

Comprehensive: approximately 600 pages long, eight to twelve tutorials, all tutorials included in the Introductory text plus higher-level "Level III" topics. Also includes two Windows tutorials and three or four fully developed Additional Cases.

Advanced
Quick Review of basics +
in-depth, high-level
coverage

Advanced: approximately 600 pages long, covers topics similar to those in the Comprehensive books, but offers the highest-level coverage in the series. Advanced books assume students already know the basics, and therefore go into more depth at a more accelerated rate than the Comprehensive titles. Advanced books are ideal for a second, more technical course. The book you are holding is an Advanced book.

Office

Quick Review of basics +
in-depth, high-level
coverage

Custom Editions

Choose from any of the
above to build your own
Custom Editions or
CourseKits

Office: approximately 800 pages long, covers all components of the Office suite as well as integrating the individual software packages with one another and the Internet.

Custom Books The New Perspectives Series offers you two ways to customize a New Perspectives text to fit your course exactly: *CourseKits*™ are two or more texts shrinkwrapped together, and offer significant price discounts. *Custom Editions*® offer you flexibility in designing your concepts, Internet, and applications courses. You can build your own book by ordering a combination of topics bound together to cover only the subjects you want. There is no minimum order, and books are spiral bound. Contact your Course Technology sales representative for more information.

What course is this book appropriate for?

New Perspectives on Data-Driven Web Sites with Microsoft Access 2000: Tools for E-Commerce can be used in any course in which you want students to learn all the most important topics of data-driven Web sites with Access 2000, including an introduction to e-commerce, an introduction to Access Data Access Pages, creating Data Access Pages for data entry, creating Data Access Pages for interactive reporting, installing a Web server and publishing Web pages, and an introduction to other Web-enabled database technologies. It is particularly recommended for a full-semester course on data-driven Web sites. This book assumes that students have learned basic Windows navigation and file management skills from Course Technology's *New Perspectives on Microsoft Windows 95— Brief*, or the equivalent book for Windows 98 or NT, and a basic knowledge of Microsoft Access 2000.

Proven Pedagogy

CASE

Tutorial Case Each tutorial begins with a problem presented in a case that is meaningful to students. The case turns the task of learning how to use an application into a problem-solving process.

45-minute Sessions Each tutorial is divided into sessions that can be completed in about 45 minutes to an hour. Sessions allow instructors to more accurately allocate time in their syllabus, and students to better manage their own study time.

1.
2.
3.

Step-by-Step Methodology We make sure students can differentiate between what they are to *do* and what they are to *read*. Through numbered steps—clearly identified by a gray shaded background—students are constantly guided in solving the case problem. In addition, the numerous screen shots with callouts direct students' attention to what they should look at on the screen.

TROUBLE?

TROUBLE? Paragraphs These paragraphs anticipate the mistakes or problems that students may have and help them continue with the tutorial.

Tutorial Tips Page This page, following the Table of Contents, offers students suggestions on how to effectively plan their study and lab time, what to do when they make a mistake, and how to use the Reference Windows, MOUS grids, Quick Checks, and other features of the New Perspectives series.

Read This Before You Begin Page Located opposite the first tutorial's opening page for each level of the text, the Read This Before You Begin page helps introduce technology into the classroom. Technical considerations and assumptions about software are listed to save time and eliminate unnecessary aggravation. Notes about the Data Disks help instructors and students get the right files in the right places, so students get started on the right foot.

Quick Check Questions Each session concludes with meaningful, conceptual Quick Check questions that test students' understanding of what they learned in the session. Answers to the Quick Check questions are provided at the end of each tutorial.

Reference Windows Reference Windows are succinct summaries of the most important tasks covered in a tutorial and they preview actions students will perform in the steps to follow.

Task Reference
Located as a table at the end of the book, the Task Reference contains a summary of how to perform common tasks using the most efficient method, as well as references to pages where the task is discussed in more detail.

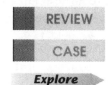

End-of-Tutorial Review Assignments and Case Problems Review Assignments provide students with additional hands-on practice of the skills they learned in the tutorial. These Assignments are followed by four Case Problems that have approximately the same scope as the tutorial case but use a different scenario. In addition, some of the Review Assignments or Case Problems may include Exploration Exercises that challenge students and encourage them to explore the capabilities of the program they are using, and/or further extend their knowledge.

File Finder Chart This chart, located in the back of the book, visually explains how students should set up their Data Disks, what files should go in what folders, and what they'll be saving the files as in the course of their work.

New Perspectives on Data-Driven Web Sites with Microsoft Access 2000: Tools for E-Commerce Instructor's Resource Kit contains:

- Electronic Instructor's Manual
- Data Files
- Solution Files
- Course Test Manager Testbank
- Course Test Manager Engine
- Figure Files
- Sample Syllabus

These supplements come on CD-ROM. If you don't have access to a CD-ROM drive, contact your Course Technology customer service representative for more information.

The New Perspectives Supplements Package

Electronic Instructor's Manual Our Instructor's Manuals include tutorial overviews and outlines, technical notes, lecture notes, solutions, and Extra Case Problems. Many instructors use the Extra Case Problems for performance-based exams or extra credit projects. The Instructor's Manual is available as an electronic file, which you can get from the Instructor Resource Kit (IRK) CD-ROM or download it from **www.course.com**.

Data Files Data Files contain all of the data that students will use to complete the tutorials, Review Assignments, and Case Problems. A Readme file includes instructions for using the files. See the Read This Before You Begin page for more information on Data Files.

Solution Files Solution Files contain every file students are asked to create or modify in the tutorials, Review Assignments, Case Problems, and Extra Case Problems. A Help file on the Instructor's Resource Kit includes information for using the Solution files.

Figure Files Many figures in the text are provided on the IRK CD-ROM to help illustrate key topics or concepts. Instructors can create traditional overhead transparencies by printing the figure files. Or they can create electronic slide shows by using the figures in a presentation program such as PowerPoint.

Course Test Manager: Testing and Practice at the Computer or on Paper Course Test Manager is cutting-edge, Windows-based testing software that helps instructors design and administer practice tests and actual examinations. Course Test Manager can automatically grade the tests students take at the computer and can generate statistical information on individual as well as group performance.

Online Companions: Dedicated to Keeping You and Your Students Up-To-Date Visit our faculty sites and student sites on the World Wide Web at www.course.com. Here instructors can browse this text's password-protected Faculty Online Companion to obtain an online Instructor's Manual, Solution Files, Data Files, and more.

Acknowledgments

Thank you to the fabulous publishing team at Course Technology. You are a very special group of people. Thank you to the reviewers, Anthony Briggs, Lorraine Bergkvist, and Cherylee Kushida, for your good advice. Thank you to my wonderful friend and partner, Rachel Bunin, for all of your work in so many aspects on this book. Special thanks to my awesome husband, Doug, who is always there with an encouraging word.

Lisa Friedrichsen
April 26, 2000

TABLE OF CONTENTS

Tutorial 3   DDWS 3.01

Creating Data Access Pages for Data Entry

Using Web Pages to Update the Aaron Michael Toys Database

Tutorial 4   DDWS 4.01

Creating Data Access Pages for Data Analysis

Using Web Pages to Analyze and Chart Data in the Aaron Michael Toys Database

Reference Window List

Tutorial Tips

These tutorials will help you learn about data-driven Web sites with Access 2000. The tutorials are designed to be worked through at a computer. Each tutorial is divided into sessions. Watch for the session headings, such as Session 1.1 and Session 1.2. Each session is designed to be completed in about 45 minutes, but take as much time as you need. It's also a good idea to take a break between sessions.

To use the tutorials effectively, read the following questions and answers before you begin.

Where do I start?

Each tutorial begins with a case, which sets the scene for the tutorial and gives you background information to help you understand what you will be doing. Read the case before you go to the lab. In the lab, begin with the first session of a tutorial.

How do I know what to do on the computer?

Each session contains steps that you will perform on the computer to learn how to use Access 2000 to create data-driven Web sites. Read the text that introduces each series of steps. The steps you need to do at a computer are numbered and are set against a shaded background. Read each step carefully and completely before you try it.

How do I know if I did the step correctly?

As you work, compare your computer screen with the corresponding figure in the tutorial. Don't worry if your screen display is somewhat different from the figure. The important parts of the screen display are labeled in each figure. Check to make sure these parts are on your screen.

What if I make a mistake?

Don't worry about making mistakes—they are part of the learning process. Paragraphs labeled "TROUBLE?" identify common problems and explain how to get back on track. Follow the steps in a TROUBLE? paragraph only if you are having the problem described. If you run into other problems:

- Carefully consider the current state of your system, the position of the pointer, and any messages on the screen.

- Complete the sentence, "Now I want to…" Be specific, because identifying your goal will help you rethink the steps you need to take to reach that goal.

- If you are working on a particular piece of software, consult the Help system.

- If the suggestions above don't solve your problem, consult your technical support person for assistance.

How do I use the Reference Windows?

Reference Windows summarize the procedures you will learn in the tutorial steps. Do not complete the actions in the Reference Windows when you are working through the tutorial. Instead, refer to the Reference Windows while you are working on the assignments at the end of the tutorial.

How can I test my understanding of the material I learned in the tutorial?

At the end of each session, you can answer the Quick Check questions. The answers for the Quick Checks are at the end of that tutorial.

After you have completed the entire tutorial, you should complete the Review Assignments and Case Problems. They are carefully structured so that you will review what you have learned and then apply your knowledge to new situations.

What if I can't remember how to do something?

You should refer to the Task Reference at the end of the book; it summarizes how to accomplish tasks using the most efficient method.

Before you begin the tutorials, you should know the basics about your computer's operating system. You should also know how to use the menus, dialog boxes, Help system, and My Computer.

Now that you've read the Tutorial Tips, you are ready to begin.

New Perspectives on

DATA-DRIVEN WEB SITES WITH MICROSOFT ACCESS 2000: TOOLS FOR E-COMMERCE

Read This Before You Begin

To the Student

Data Files

To complete the Tutorials, Review Assignments, and Case Problems in Tutorials 2 through 6, you need data files. Your instructor may provide the data files, or you can download them by going to Course Technology's Web site, www.course.com. If you go to www.course.com to get the data files, search for this book in the Academic area of the Web site using the book's ISBN (International Standard Book Number) as the search criterion for the fastest results.

From Course Technology's Web site, the data files will be downloaded to you as a single compressed, executable file. After you download the file, double-click it to extract the actual data files. There are no data files for Tutorial 1, but starting with Tutorial 2, the files will be placed on your hard drive using the following general folder structure:

C:\XXXX\Tutorial.02\Tutorial\data files…

C:\XXXX\Tutorial.02\Review\data files…

C:\XXXX\Tutorial.02\Cases\data files…

(*Note:* XXXX is a number assigned by Course Technology to uniquely identify the data files for each of our books.)

When working with an Access database to create Web pages, the size of the database and number of associated files grows quickly. While it is possible to complete the exercises in Tutorial 2 from a floppy disk (provided you store no more than one Access database on one floppy disk), the exercises in Tutorials 3, 4, 5, and 6 require more space than available on a single floppy disk, and *will not work correctly* if you attempt to complete them from a floppy disk.

Therefore, we recommend that you create the following Solutions folders, and copy the corresponding data files into the Solution folders **before working on Tutorials 2, 3, 4, 5, and 6**:

C:*YourName*\Tutorial.0x\Tutorial\Solutions

C:*YourName*\Tutorial.0x\Review\Solutions

C:*YourName*\Tutorial.0x\Cases\Solutions

All of the screen shots in this book assume that you are using this hard drive folder hierarchy to complete your exercises. All of the instructions instruct you to open and save files to your **Solutions Folder**.

If you are working with data files from other New Perspectives textbooks (and therefore have other Tutorial, Review, and Cases folders to manage), you may wish to modify the folder hierarchy to identify the book you are using as well. For example, the following hierarchy allows you to manage the data files of multiple New Perspectives books from within the *YourName* folder:

C:*YourName*\A2Kweb\Tutorial.0x\Tutorial\Solutions

C:*YourName*\A2Kweb\Tutorial.0x\Review\Solutions

C:*YourName*\A2Kweb\Tutorial.0x\Cases\Solutions

You may also use removable storage media such as Zip or Jaz drives to manage your data files. If you use removable storage media, a good rule of thumb is to not allow the disk to become more than half full because the temporary files created in the steps of this book require as much space as the data files themselves.

If you need to work on these exercises using more than one computer, you can use a compression program such as WinZip to compress and package the files so that they can be transported on a floppy and then decompressed on another machine. See Appendix A for more information on how to use WinZip to help manage the process of working with your data files on more than one computer.

Also note that in Tutorial 5 and in the end-of-tutorial exercises for Tutorial 5, you must be able to publish data files to your computer's Personal Web Server, PWS. By default, files published to the PWS go into the directory c:\Inetpub\wwwroot\ on your hard drive.

To the Instructor

The data files are available on the Instructor's Resource Kit for this title. Follow the instructions in the Help file on the CD-ROM to install the programs to your network or standalone computer. For information on managing data files, see the "To the Student" section above.

You are granted a license to copy the data files to any computer or computer network used by students who have purchased this book.

OBJECTIVES

In this tutorial you will:

- Learn about different types of electronic commerce (e-commerce)

- Tour several types of e-commerce Web sites

- Study the impact e-commerce has on business today

- Learn about supporting Internet technologies

- Set business goals for your own e-commerce Web site

- Learn how different components, such as Web servers, browser software, databases, and Web pages work together to support a Web-enabled database

UNDERSTANDING ELECTRONIC COMMERCE

Evaluating Electronic Commerce for Aaron Michael Toys

CASE

Aaron Michael Toys

As a new employee at Aaron Michael Toys (AMT), a small toy store that specializes in hard-to-find educational toys, you have been given the challenge to determine how e-commerce would benefit the company. First you'll research the existing state of e-commerce and present your preliminary findings to AMT management. Together with management, you'll help develop AMT's e-commerce strategy. Later, you'll design the Web site, build the supporting database and Web pages, and launch the e-commerce Web site. Your research starts by examining a wide variety of existing e-commerce Web sites.

SESSION 1.1

In this session you'll surf the World Wide Web to find how e-commerce is being implemented to support many different business needs, and you'll project the potential impact of e-commerce on Aaron Michael Toys.

Introducing E-Commerce

Electronic commerce (**e-commerce**) means conducting business using the Internet. Some people narrowly define e-commerce as "shopping on the Internet," and refer to other Internet-based business activities such as providing customer support, advertising, or conducting market research with the broader term, **electronic business** (**e-business**). Other popular "e- words" include **e-tailing** (electronic retailing), **e-zine** (electronic magazine), **e-cash**, **e-shopping**, **e-copy**, **e-form**, and of course the mother of all "e" words, **e-mail**. All of these e-terms have one thing in common: they provide an electronic, rather than in-person, way to do business. This new electronic business model provides tremendous advantages in speed, breaks down geographic barriers, and stays open for business 24 hours a day, 7 days a week. You are convinced that e-commerce would provide many opportunities to cut costs and increase sales at AMT and have decided to examine several types of existing e-commerce sites in order to determine which concepts would most benefit AMT.

Search engines are Web sites devoted to indexing and finding other Web sites. You know that your research will be best served by using search engines to find information.

Finding E-Commerce Tutorials

Several good tutorials about e-commerce exist on the Internet today. You could search for them using general Internet search engines such as Yahoo! (*www.yahoo.com*) or Lycos (*www.lycos.com*). However, when you want to find general information on a subject, you may wish to use a special search engine such as About.com (*www.about.com*) that has already reviewed and classified the references it provides.

Using Portals

Search engines that are specifically indexed to provide categories of high-quality information are sometimes called **portal** Web sites. The word "portal" is a relatively new term and may also be used to describe the first page that you are presented with when you connect to the Internet. For example, if you connect to the Internet from your home computer using the Microsoft Network, you may use the associated *www.msn.com* Web site as your personal portal. A good portal site is often customizable so that it presents the information and links you are most likely to be interested in.

If you wish to find more information about portals, or anything related to information systems or telecommunications, there is an excellent glossary of technology-related terms at *www.whatis.com*. Use this site any time during this tutorial when you wish to find additional information on a technical term.

Aaron Michael Toys uses Internet Explorer (IE) to browse the Web. While you can surf the World Wide Web using other browsers, the Web pages that you will later be creating with Access 2000 work best when you use IE version 5.0 or later as your browser. IE is also used in the figures throughout this book.

To use a portal:

1. Connect to the Internet, then load Internet Explorer (IE).

Many of the steps in this book will direct you to go to a specific Web address on the Internet. To do this, you need to type the Web address indicated in the step directly into the Address bar of your browser.

2. Go to **www.about.com**, as shown in Figure 1-1.

Periods (called "dots") are used to separate the parts of the Web address, but Web page addresses never end in a period and never have spaces. Web addresses may be uppercase- and lowercase-sensitive, so always type them exactly as referenced. If you are using Internet Explorer or Netscape Navigator as your browser software, you do not need to type the http:// portion of a Web page address in the Address Bar.

| Figure 1-1 | ABOUT.COM |

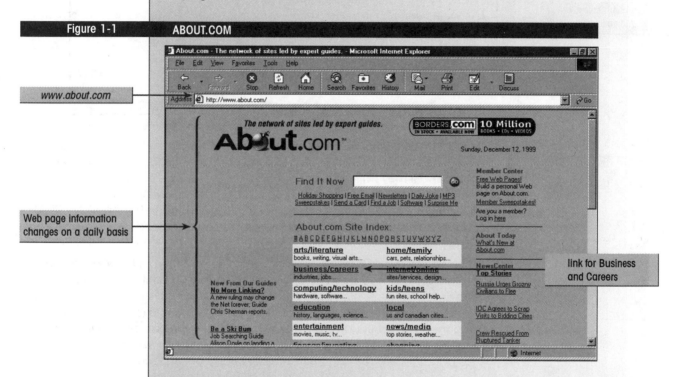

www.about.com

Web page information changes on a daily basis

link for Business and Careers

TROUBLE? If you do not have Internet Explorer, you may use Netscape Navigator as your browser for this exercise. In later tutorials, however, when you use Access to create a Web-enabled database, you'll need to use Internet Explorer as your browser in order to interact with the underlying Access database.

3. Click the **business/careers** link, click the **Electronic Commerce** link in the Business list, and then click the **E-Commerce 101** link to view the e-commerce page shown in Figure 1-2.

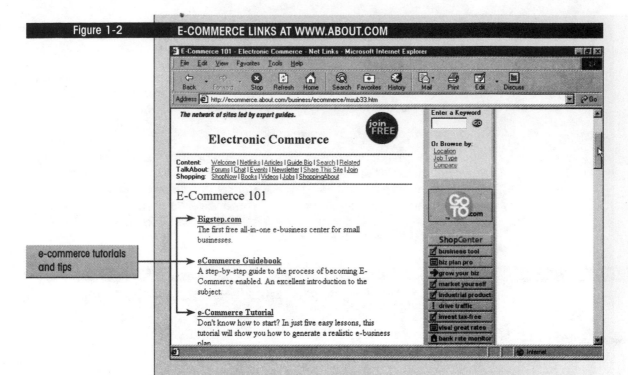

Figure 1-2   **E-COMMERCE LINKS AT WWW.ABOUT.COM**

e-commerce tutorials
and tips

TROUBLE? Web pages and links are constantly changing. While it's safe to
assume that a section on e-commerce exists at *www.about.com*, the specific
links to find it may have changed.

4. Click the **links** to find out more information about e-commerce. Read the articles
on your screen, and then print an article that discusses the ways a small business
can benefit from e-commerce if you want to have a hard copy.

Printing a Web page is fairly simple. If you are using IE as your browser, you can
click File on the menu bar, then click Print. You can set a print range, because
often the first page contains all of the information you really need. Also, if you are
using IE, click File on the menu bar, then click Page Setup to adjust the margins,
header, and footer. Become familiar with the codes you can enter in the header
and footer. The &u code placed in the header or footer, for example, prints the
Web page address (the URL), which is extremely helpful documentation.

5. Print one article from a Web page that discusses small business e-commerce.

TROUBLE? Web pages can be several paper pages long. If your browser supports
a print preview feature, it is well worth your time to first preview a Web page
before printing it.

6. Click the **Back** button ⇐ on the IE Standard Buttons toolbar as many times
as required to return to the *www.about.com* page that references pages on
e-commerce.

General Internet research is often called **surfing**. As you may have already experienced,
a surfing session can last anywhere from a few minutes to several hours, depending on the
amount of time you have available and the value of the information you find.

Benefits of E-commerce

There are an infinite number of ways that electronic commerce can potentially benefit businesses of all sizes. At a minimum, however, your research should have revealed that businesses use e-commerce to improve these general business activities:

- Marketing
- Sales
- Customer service

Marketing

Your business does not need to have a sophisticated Web-enabled database from which customers can locate and order products to benefit from a Web presence. A Web page is a 24-hour, 7-day-a-week, universally available advertisement for your products and services. It's important to have a high-quality Web site, even if it is not used for sales or customer service. Even individuals looking for jobs and career advancement market themselves through the Internet by posting their resumes at places like Monster.com (*www.monster.com*) and Careernet (*www.careernet.com*).

Sales

Providing a way for customers to order products in a 24-hour, 7-day-a-week format from anywhere in the world should be an obvious reason to establish a Web presence. While some products and services are difficult to purchase without the buyer seeing the physical product or visiting with a sales representative, others lend themselves to this type of purchasing. A **virtual store** is a Web site in which you can purchase goods or services. Amazon.com (*www.amazon.com*) and Borders (*www.borders.com*) have been pioneers in developing virtual stores for books and music. At *www.1800flowers.com* and *www.ftd.com*, you can send flower and gift arrangements. The sites of Travelocity (*www.travelocity.com*) and Expedia.com (*www.expedia.com*) have been very successful in selling airline tickets and other travel-related services. You can even save a trip to your local post office by purchasing stamps from the United States Postal Service at *www.stampsonline.com*.

Other types of sales Web sites include **virtual auction houses** such as uBid (*www.ubid.com*) and eBay (*www.ebay.com*) and **virtual malls** such as *www.virtualmall.com*. Webster's Dictionary defines the word **virtual** as "being in essence or in effect, though not in fact." This definition fits well when applied to virtual stores, virtual auction houses, and virtual malls.

The end result of shopping at one of these entities—purchasing a product—is the same as shopping at their "real" counterparts. There are some significant differences, though. With a virtual store, the sales process itself—the interaction between the customer and the seller—is being done via an Internet connection. Delivery of products such as clothes or flowers purchased on the Internet is accomplished via the US mail or a delivery service such as FedEx or UPS. Delivery of other products such as software or tickets may be accomplished over the Internet as well. With e-commerce, the traditional process of visiting a physical store, auction, or mall and carrying the product home is eliminated. This means that the nature of the product, and the customer's attitude about whether he or she can purchase it without physically touching it or talking to a representative, will somewhat dictate its e-commerce success.

Customer Service

Giving customers 24-hour, 7-day-a-week access to product information, updates, and commonly asked questions lowers costs, improves service, and strengthens your relationship with your customers. For example, allowing customers to track the status of their FedEx package at *www.fedex.com*, check the status of a book or music order at *www.bn.com*, check their bank balance at *www.citibank.com*, or find out their grade for a class at Keller Graduate School at *www.keller.edu* are great examples of using the Web to improve customer service. Course Technology, the publisher of this book, provides a tremendous amount of customer service through its Web site at *www.course.com*. The Web site allows a visitor to download student data files, supplemental instructional materials, and supplemental educational activities.

Drilling Down to Research E-commerce on the Web

Many users prefer to use their favorite search engine for general Internet research. The About.com Web site (*www.about.com*) limits the amount of information it presents to specific Web sites that have already been reviewed and deemed valuable by About.com's staff. If you use a general search engine, such as Yahoo! (*www.yahoo.com*) or Lycos (*www.lycos.com*) you will probably see many more links with a wide range of quality and applicability to your issue. General search engines do not screen the quality of the links, and you will find that your search results may not always apply to your needs. Even within a general search engine, however, you can still "drill down" into categories before entering your search criteria. **Drilling down** means clicking on a category heading, and then clicking subcategories within categories before you enter search criteria. Drilling down limits the number of links that you receive to those within the current category and generally improves the speed and quality of your search.

To drill down into a search engine:

1. Connect to the Internet if you are not already connected, load Internet Explorer (IE) if it is not already loaded, and then go to **www.altavista.com**.

   There are many different search engines on the Internet, and almost all of them give you the ability to drill down from the first page of the site. The first page of any Web site is called the **home page**.

2. Click the **Business & Finance** link, click the **E-commerce** link, and then click the **Small Business Solutions** link.

3. Type **database** in the Find this text box, and then click the **Search** button to search for databases within the current category.

   By drilling down into a specific category before entering search criteria, you limited the number of links pertaining to databases you received to those within the Small Business Solutions category. You probably were not presented with links for mainframe database products such as DB2, large database warehousing systems, genealogy databases, or other types of hobbyist databases that would not be discussed within the category of small business e-commerce.

   TROUBLE? If you have entered a Web address correctly, but IE presents a "The page cannot be displayed" message, click the Refresh button 🔄 to request another copy of the Web page from the Web server.

4. Read any Web pages that you find relevant.

5. Go to **www.excite.com** and search for more information on the benefits of e-commerce to small businesses.

6. Go to **www.hotbot.com** and search for more information on the benefits of e-commerce to small businesses.

7. Go to **www.yahoo.com**, and search for more information on the benefits of e-commerce to small businesses.

It is important to understand the benefits of researching a topic by using the drill down method versus entering search criteria on the search engine's initial home page by comparing the number and quality of links that are presented.

To compare search engines:

1. Go to **www.attbusiness.net**. This site provides a good listing of search engines.

2. Click the link for **Search Engines**. Experiment using the drill down method versus entering search criteria on the search engine's initial home page to compare the number and quality of links that are presented.

3. Print one more article on how e-commerce can benefit small businesses.

Exploring Additional Purposes for Web sites

Many company Web sites today provide a variety of business services. Once a company's Web presence is established, selling space on the home page to others is an easy way to make additional revenue from having a Web presence. Your research should have found that, in addition to the most common uses of the Web for marketing, sales, and customer service, e-commerce could also be used as a vehicle for many additional business purposes: These include gathering consumer information, providing a service, linking communities, and entertainment.

Gathering Consumer Information

Some sites require users to fill out consumer information forms before providing requested information. The "get a quote" feature at the Web site *www.chrysler.com* is a good example of this. Some sites can capture limited user information as soon as a user visits the site. Information can be acquired even if the visitor has not explicitly provided information to them in a form. Of particular benefit to e-tailers is your e-mail address. It can be used in targeted mass mailings and can be sold to other businesses. As you might suspect, the practice of gathering consumer information without your explicit knowledge is somewhat controversial. Cookies are another form of electronic consumer information. A **cookie** is a small file stored on your hard disk that contains information about your interaction with a particular Web site. It is often used to help you remember details of your last interaction with the Web site, such as your username or password. It can be used to present a Web page that is tailored to your past preferences and activities. Because of the intrusive and manipulative nature of cookie files, they are still somewhat controversial, although they have become widely used and are usually helpful to the user.

Providing a Service Such as News or Public Information Links

www.greatergood.com connects not-for-profit charities such as Special Olympics, March of Dimes, and the Diabetes Research Institute Foundation, and online retailers such as Wine.com (*www.wine.com*), eToys.com (*www.etoys.com*), and JCPenney (*www.jcpenney.com*) so that at least 5% of any on-line purchase you make is sent back to the charity of your choice at no extra cost to you.

Linking Communities of People with a Common Interest

www.ivillage.com is a Web site whose primary purpose is to bring together groups of people who have common interests or problems. Interests can be as specific and targeted as women breast cancer survivors. The site recently went public, meaning that they were able to sell shares of stock to help fund the site. Even though the site itself does not sell anything and does not have a direct revenue stream, it was able to command a large group of investors because of its wide appeal and audience. Traffic through the site (that eventually translates to e-commerce spending), created value for the Web site on the public stock market.

Entertaining Visitors

Try *www.dilbert.com* for some fun and also for some big business. In addition to providing new daily humor, the site supports a virtual store for Dilbert paraphernalia. The site commands huge advertising fees from other companies with links or banners on the page.

In most cases, especially if there is a sales, customer service, or consumer information purpose for the Web site, a Web-enabled database has been implemented behind the scenes to provide the needed information and interactivity between the Web site and the user. Now that you've had some experience using these amazing technologies, you'll review some of the key terminology underlying e-commerce.

The Internet

The **Internet** is a global public network of computer networks that pass information from one to another using common computer **protocols** (rules that dictate the structure of data and computer-to-computer communication). Although electronic transmission of data from one company's computer to another through **electronic funds transfer** (**EFT**) and **electronic data interchange** (**EDI**) has been common for at least 20 years, these transfers were mainly achieved by building private networks dedicated to the specific business transactions of a few trading partners. Without a public network with the magnitude of the Internet, the term "e-commerce" might not have been born. The Internet has several inherent characteristics that make it an extremely powerful business tool. The Internet is:

- Global
- Accessible 24 hours a day, 7 days a week
- Based on standardized computer protocols so that information you provide via the Internet is accessible by every computer connected to the Internet
- Not yet subject to the same levels of taxation as traditional businesses
- Very inexpensive to use (typical connection fees range from $20/month for individuals to $600/month for small businesses for unlimited usage)

The Internet is Not the World Wide Web

Some people think that the Internet and the World Wide Web are equivalent entities, but they are not. The Internet started as an initiative in the 1960s by the Department of Defense (DoD) to connect computers in different locations. The DoD wanted to tie multiple military computers together so that they could communicate and share information in an effort to minimize the loss of any single computer. Throughout the 1970s and 1980s, the uses for the Internet expanded to support activities such as **electronic mail (e-mail)**, **file transfer protocol (FTP)**, and Telnet. **Telnet** allowed users to log on to computers from remote sites. The Internet also supported **Gopher** as a way to find and retrieve documents by using text menus, and **WAIS** (wide area information servers), another tool used to index and find electronically published material. The World Wide Web had not yet been developed, and Internet activity was restricted to noncommercial activities. At that time, the users of the Internet included government employees, researchers, and university professors and students.

The Internet Today

Several dramatic developments occurred in the 1980s and 1990s that paved the way for today's Internet as summarized below:

- The microcomputer revolution made it possible for an average person to own a computer. The majority of businesspeople use computers on a daily basis.
- Advancements in networking hardware, software, and media made it possible for business PCs to be inexpensively connected to larger networks.
- People are now introduced to computers in kindergarten. Resistance to change, as it relates to applying computers to solve business problems, is no longer an issue for business owners.
- The speed, convenience, and minimal cost of e-mail has made it an incredibly popular tool for business and personal communication.
- The World Wide Web, a technology for linking files located on different Web servers located throughout the Internet, evolved to provide an easy-to-use hypertext navigation system to retrieve Internet resources. World Wide Web technology is used for both the Internet and intranets. Businesses employ intranets. An **intranet** is a computer network that uses Internet and Web technologies, but is used for the internal communication of a business.
- **Browser software** such as Netscape Navigator and Microsoft Internet Explorer gave the end user an easy-to-use **graphical user interface** (**GUI**) by which to locate, find, and display Web pages connected by hyperlinks.
- The **National Science Foundation** (**NSF**), which had funded the early infrastructure of the Internet, eased restrictions on Internet commercial activity.

The World Wide Web

Originally, the World Wide Web (WWW) was conceived as a way to connect and share technical research documents over the Internet. Scientists at CERN (European Laboratory for Particle Physics, located in Switzerland) are given most of the credit for developing **Hypertext Markup Language** (**HTML**). HTML consists of the codes and hyperlinks that determine how Web pages are created as well as how they are linked together. At first, the WWW was just another technology that used the Internet infrastructure. It took its place alongside the other types of Internet tools including FTP, e-mail, Telnet, newsgroups, Gopher, and WAIS. Today, however, almost all new Internet e-commerce initiatives are built for and accessed through the World Wide Web.

The WWW's popularity grew for many reasons:

- Basic Web pages are easy to create.
- Web pages are extremely flexible. Web pages can be connected to many other more complex technologies that can provide an unlimited interface for the user. For example, Web pages can support almost any type of electronic multimedia effect, can be used to interactively query a database, and can provide a screen by which a user can make a secure purchasing transaction.

- Browser software makes Web pages easy to find, download, and display.
- From their initial design, Web pages included **hyperlinks** that provide a fast and easy way to find and move from one page to another. A **hyperlink** is text or a graphic that when clicked, downloads a new Web page.

Creating Web pages

A **Web page** is an **HTML file**. HTML files can be created using popular **HTML editors** such as Microsoft FrontPage or MacroMedia Dreamweaver. Almost all application programs have a "Save as HTML" option that allows you to save a file, such as a word-processed document or spreadsheet in an HTML Web page format. If the final goal is to create a Web page, programs devoted to creating Web pages will probably be easier and better to use for this purpose.

Browsing for Web Pages

HTML files are stored on a special computer called a **Web server**, which is given a special Internet address and connected to the Internet at all times. **Web browser** computer programs, commonly called 'browsers', are used to find Web pages located on the vast network of Web servers located throughout the Internet. A browser downloads and then displays the Web page for the user. Browsers are loaded on the user's machine (commonly called the **client**), and are started just like any other application such as a word processor or a spreadsheet program.

Browsers have to translate requests for Web pages made by the user into the **Hypertext Transfer Protocol (HTTP)** which is used to find and route Web pages over the Internet. Requests for Web pages are made using two general techniques:

- The user may enter the **Web page address**, the **Uniform Resource Locator (URL)**, in a special address bar or location text box in the browser window.
- The user may click a hyperlink that appears as a text or graphic in a Web page that is currently displayed in the browser window.

Netscape Navigator and **Internet Explorer** are currently the two most popular browser programs. Each come bundled with other end-user Internet applications, which are collectively called **Internet software suites**.

The heart of any client Internet software suite is the browser. It is through the browser that a user can easily access the vast resources of the World Wide Web. The E-mail component allows you to write, send, and receive e-mail messages. The HTML Editor allows you to create and publish HTML documents (Web pages). Chat tools are used to communicate in real time by typing messages in a window, with others who are also online. Some of the most popular components of Internet software suites are described in Figure 1-3.

Figure 1-3	INTERNET SOFTWARE SUITES				
COMPANY	**INTERNET SOFTWARE SUITE**	**BROWSER**	**E-MAIL**	**HTML EDITOR**	**CHAT**
Netscape	Netscape Communicator	Navigator	Messenger	Composer	AOL Instant Messenger
Microsoft	Internet Explorer	Internet Explorer	Outlook	FrontPage	Microsoft Chat

Other features such as voice over Internet (VOI), newsgroups, file transfer tools, e-mail address books, and push technology are also components of robust Internet software suites.

Push Technology

Push technology tools such as Channels within IE or Netcaster within Netscape have become very popular. To use push technology effectively, you must customize the type of information you wish to see at regular intervals. You can customize requests for news, weather, sports, or financial updates. The browser does the work of finding and downloading the desired Web pages in the background. In this manner, the push tool "pushes" information in the form of Web pages to you at the interval you define rather than waiting for you to actively "pull" or request the Web page. Push technology can save you a lot of time requesting Web pages and reading Web pages. The pages it has "pushed" reside on your hard drive. This allows you to open and read them much faster because you don't have to wait for them to travel through the Internet.

The first time that you or your business seriously attempts to leverage the incredible power of Internet and the World Wide Web, it can be very challenging. Learning the applicable terminology is a huge task in and of itself! Be patient. Remember that it took several decades for the Internet to become what it is today, and no one understands or uses all of it. Probably one of the most meaningful ways to learn any new technological tool, however, is to have an important business problem or purpose in mind for which the tool will be used. Now that you've explored e-commerce in general and learned about the key components, you're ready to set e-commerce business goals for Aaron Michael Toys.

Setting Up Your E-Commerce Web Site

One of the hardest things about developing a Web site for your business is getting started. Many people let the enormity of "what could be" overwhelm them to the point that nothing gets done! Even though you could strategize with an e-commerce consulting firm about the potential benefits and goals for your Web site, a more practical scenario is for you, as a small business owner, to get started with a basic Web page for marketing purposes, and to grow the site from there. Two key decisions that you must consider at the very beginning are how to secure a domain name and how you will set up the Web server.

Understanding Domain Names

Determining your **Web server address** (also called **domain name**), such as *www.ibm.com*, *www.whitehouse.gov*, or *www.redcross.org*, is one of the first strategic decisions that you must make. This decision is even more important than naming your business because it will have a direct impact upon the ease with which customers can find and remember your Web site. Ideally, your Web site address should be short, descriptive, and easy to remember. For example, it is easy to remember *www.flowers.com* when you want to order flowers over the Internet. You will be able to recall *www.weather.com* when checking the forecast. The Web server address is the telephone number, postal address, and primary advertisement for your business all rolled into one word or phrase. Choosing a good Web address is an incredibly important task.

Depending on the amount of time and expertise you possess, you can tackle the task of applying for a domain name on your own or hire an e-commerce or Internet consulting firm to help you. Many e-commerce consulting firms offer a variety of different services including Web hosting, domain name registration, Web page development, and Web-enabled database development, to name a few. The more you know about these tasks, however, the better you can direct and manage those services that you outsource to others.

Securing a Domain Name

The **Internet Network Information Center (InterNIC)** maintains server addresses on a first-come, first-served basis, but there are some rules. Company trademarked names are reserved, for example, and the domain name extensions must match the actual type of organization to which the address belongs. Figure 1-4 lists many common domain name extensions for US entities.

Figure 1-4	DOMAIN NAME EXTENSIONS
DOMAIN NAME EXTENSION	**DESCRIPTION**
com	Commercial, for-profit company
edu	Educational institution
gov	U.S. government organization
mil	U.S. military organization
net	Network service or networked organization
org	Nonprofit organization

Once commercial traffic was allowed on the Internet, applications for Web server addresses with the "com" extension grew like wildfire. The "net" domain name extension was soon added, and is used for a wide variety of purposes. For example, the Web server address for Johnson County Community College in Overland Park, Kansas, was originally *www.johnco.cc.ks.us*. When established, the address made sense because each part of the address represented a significant piece of information and adhered to a structure for Web server addresses for community colleges across the nation. As the WWW grew in popularity, however, the long address became cumbersome. JCCC applied to InterNIC and was granted the alias Web server address of *www.jccc.net*, which was much easier for the public to remember. An **alias** Web server address translates one address into another, and is one way that companies funnel more "hits" to their Web sites. You may have encountered an alias Web server address before if you have typed an address into your browser and then been automatically rerouted to a different site. Another good example of the use of an alias Web server address is *www.barnesandnoble.com* and *www.bn.com*. Both addresses go to the same Barnes and Noble e-commerce Web site.

To research a domain name:

1. Connect to the Internet if you are not already connected, start Internet Explorer (IE) if it is not already started, and then go to **www.internic.net**, as shown in Figure 1-5.

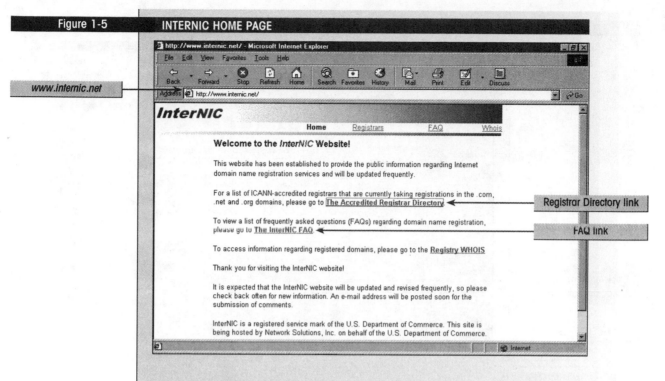

Figure 1-5   INTERNIC HOME PAGE

www.internic.net

2. Click **The Accredited Registrar Directory** link.

   The Accredited Registrar Directory page at the InterNIC site provides links to a list of those businesses that check the availability and handle the actual paperwork of applying for a domain name with a .com, .net, or .org extension.

3. Click the **Back** button ⬅ on the IE toolbar, click **The InterNIC FAQ** link, and then read the Web page.

   FAQ is an acronym for "frequently asked questions." This Web page will print on about three sheets of paper, but it contains a great deal of important information for those applying for a Web site address for the first time.

4. Click the **Back** button ⬅ on the IE toolbar, click **The Accredited Registrar Directory** link, click the **Listing by Location of Registrar** link for a listing of companies, click the **Contact Information** link for *www.register.com*, and then click the **www.register.com** logo (or just enter *www.register.com* into your browser).

   As you have seen, many different domain name registration companies exist. Each business has slightly different charges for helping you establish your Web site identity. The charges range from $50 to $200 to establish the name and are about the same amount per year to maintain it. There is no charge, however, at the *www.register.com* site to check the availability of existing domain names.

   You will check for the availability of the Web site address of *www.amt.com* and *www.amt.net* for Aaron Michael Toys.

5. Type **amt** in the www. search text box, then click both the **.com** and **.net** **Available Domain Name Extensions** check boxes as shown in Figure 1-6.

Figure 1-6 — CHECKING A DOMAIN NAME AT WWW.REGISTER.COM

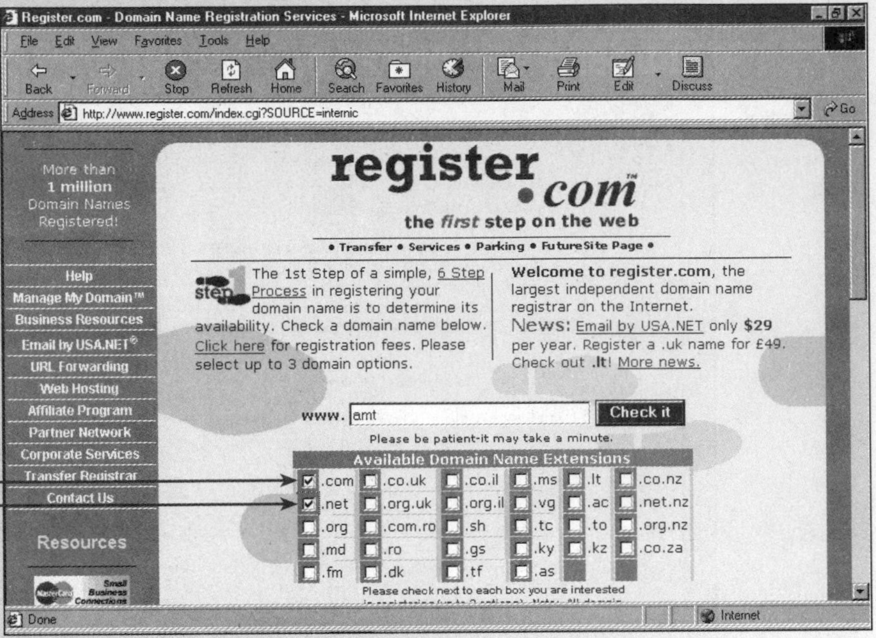

check for .com and .net domain extensions

6. Click the **Check It** button.

You should not be surprised to learn that both *www.amt.com* and *www.amt.net* are taken, as shown on the resulting Web site. The shorter and more obvious the Web server address, the more likely it has already been reserved.

7. Click the **amt.com is taken** link.

The resulting Web page indicates that *www.amt.com* has been reserved for American Manufacturing Technologies in Avondale, PA. An administrative contact and other information is provided as well. Web addresses that have already been reserved or are already in use are generally not easy to change, but if you felt strongly enough about the need to have a particular address, you could buy it (for a very high price, no doubt) from its current owner.

8. Click the **Back** button ← twice, type **amtoys** in the www. search text box, and then click the **Check It** button.

The resulting Web page shown in Figure 1-7 indicates that amtoys.net is available, but amtoys.com is taken.

TROUBLE? If your resulting Web page shows that amtoys.net is also taken it is possible that the name was registered after the publication of this book. New Web addresses are registered every day.

Figure 1-7	FINDING AN AVAILABLE DOMAIN NAME

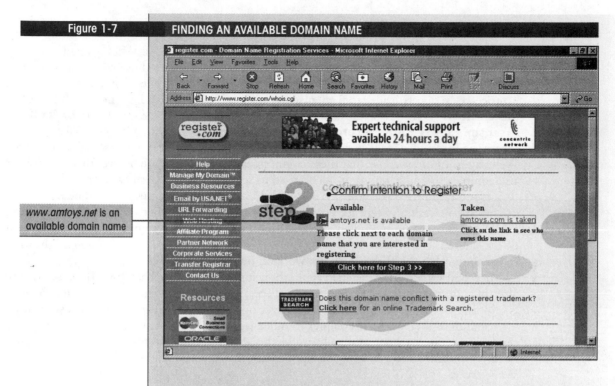

www.amtoys.net is an available domain name

Since this decision is so very important to your e-commerce success, you would probably want to take the time to research all possibilities including the following:

toys.com, toys.net

amtoy.com, amtoy.net

aarontoys.com, aarontoys.net

aaronmichaeltoys.com, aaronmichaeltoys.net

For now, however, proceed as if you wish to register the amtoys.net domain name.

9. Click the **amtoys.net is available** check box (or any other domain name that you'd rather use), then click **Click here for Step 3**.

Step 3 requires that you identify yourself to *www.register.com*.

10. Click the **Continue** button for New Users.

At this point, you would have to fill out a survey indicating contact information for your business. The next step would be to fill out credit card information to pay for the reservation (currently $70 for a two-year registration). Within a few days, you would be notified of the exclusive right to use the domain name. You would give this information to the people who are physically managing your Web server.

11. Click the **Register.com logo** in the upper-left corner of the Web page to return to the home page for *www.register.com*.

12. Check as many potential domain names as you wish.

With the amtoys.net domain name secured for Aaron Michael Toys, you are ready to address the issue of setting up a Web server.

Selecting Server Software

The **Web server** is the computer that will store your Web pages, Web-enabled database, and any other electronic resources you wish to make available to those who surf onto your Web site. The Web server plays a similar role to a file server in a local area network in that it processes requests made from clients, and responds by downloading files (Web pages) to the client. A Web server, however, must process and obey the protocols of **TCP/IP** (**Transmission Control Protocol/Internet Protocol**) used to package and send data across the Internet, as well as the HTTP (Hypertext Transfer Protocol) used specifically for Web pages. It's no surprise that these communication protocols are inherently more robust and complex than the typical protocols used to send data over a local area network.

It is important that you research and understand the complexities involved before deciding on the operating system for your Web Server. Currently, Microsoft Windows NT and UNIX are the two most popular choices. Linux and AIX are versions of UNIX that should be considered. Unfortunately, some of the databases and software tools that you might want to use to develop the Web site do not work on both platforms.

Microsoft Office is the installed application suite at Aaron Michael Toys. Because you are already comfortable with Microsoft Access, you want to use it as your back-end database. It is important to make sure that the Web server operating system can support this software.

Installing a Web server is complex in other ways too. The need for greater security, the requirement for 24-hour availability, and the ability to quickly respond to the changing needs of business are a few key business issues that must be addressed when setting up a Web server.

Selecting a Web Hosting Company

Since installing and administering a Web server often requires the technical and business expertise of several experienced people, it has become popular among small businesses to outsource this business function to a company devoted to Web server issues. These companies are usually called a **Web hosting company**. You know that the Internet is a great resource to explore Web hosting companies.

To research a Web hosting company:

1. Go to **www.zdnet.com**, type **Web hosting** into the Search For text box at the ZDNet site, and then click the **GO** button.

   ZDNet organizes the search results by Hot Links, Product Reviews, Shopping, Consumer, Tech News, Downloads, and several other categories. The search should yield a list of links in each category that match the Web Hosting phrase.

2. Click at least two of the links in the Commentary category, read through the articles, and then click two links in the Product Reviews category to find the most popular information on Web hosting provided by the ZDNet site.

3. Determine the article that is of most interest to you and then click the **Print** button 🖨 to print one page of one article.

4. On the back of the printout, write a sentence or two highlighting the new aspect of Web hosting that you learned about.

5. Go to **www.webhosting.com**, as shown in Figure 1-8.

   Webhosting.com is just one of hundreds of companies devoted to helping businesses get their e-commerce sites up and running.

Figure 1-8 | **WWW.WEBHOSTING.COM**

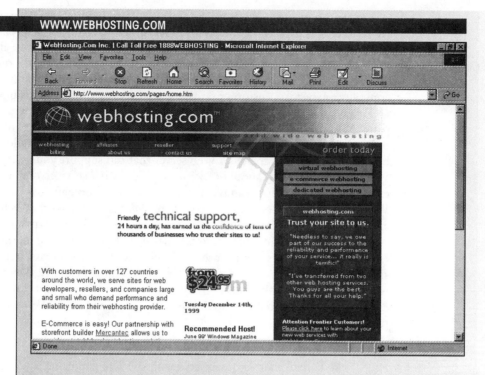

6. Click links on the *www.webhosting.com* site to read about the services they provide.

7. Go to **www.netnation.com**. NetNation is one of many Web hosting and e-commerce solutions companies.

8. Click the links on the *www.netnation.com* site to read about the services they provide.

9. Click the **Technical FAQ link** on the *www.netnation.com* home page, and then click the links to read each FAQ.

   TROUBLE? If you can't find the specific link indicated in the steps, search and find another Web hosting business, and then find a FAQ page about that Web hosting service.

10. Click the **Print** button 🖨 on the Standard Buttons Toolbar to print the FAQ page.

In some ways, finding a Web hosting business is more difficult than determining the appropriate domain name because it involves making more decisions. Each Web hosting business will have different skills, offerings, and strengths. A good Web hosting company should be able to work with your business to help determine your e-commerce goals. The goals in turn determine the technology and tools required to develop your e-commerce Web site. The more expansive your plans and hopes for your Web site are, the more sophisticated the technology and resources required to create the site. Therefore, it's important to go with a company that is easy to communicate with and provides a high level of service. All major cities have Web hosting businesses. Selecting a hometown Web hosting company might be your best alternative so that you can more easily meet with the local representatives of the company.

Perhaps one of the best ways to choose a Web hosting company is to have one of their representatives give you a tour of Web sites they have developed for other businesses. Not only will you get many ideas for your own business, you'll be better able to determine if the Web hosting company has the expertise you'll need to meet your own e-commerce goals. Talk with current customers who use the Web hosting company and ask questions about the company's expertise, customer satisfaction, response time and flexibility.

Finally, be sure to mention any specific requirements that you want your Web hosting company to handle. For example, if you already have a company database developed in Access 2000 that you want to use to drive an interactive Web-based product catalog, be sure that the Web hosting company has created a Web server that can support your software and database. The Web hosting company should make it very clear what services they will provide, and what is expected from you. For example, it is common for a company to develop the Web pages and Web-enabled databases of their e-commerce Web site, and use the Web hosting service merely as the vehicle by which the content is presented, secured, and distributed over the Internet.

Web hosting services run from $25 per month to host basic marketing Web sites to several thousand dollars per month to develop and host sophisticated database-driven Web sites with high levels of redundancy, security, and availability. Most Web hosting services will base their monthly charges on the amount of traffic or "hits" to your Web page.

Your research should have found that at a minimum, most Web hosting businesses provide the following services:

- Domain name registration services
- E-mail addresses associated with your domain name
  (e.g., *YourName*@AMTOYS.net)
- Internet access services
- Web page design services
- E-Commerce consulting such as business planning and marketing
- E-Commerce software such as secure credit card processing and shopping carts
- Web-enabled database development services

Keeping Track of E-Commerce Resources

The ability of a business to manage information effectively has a significant impact upon its success. The same is true of individuals. The more you know and can communicate clearly, the more rapidly you will advance within a company or improve your own business. The Web is indisputably the largest single source for information, and if you can use it effectively, you will have a tremendous personal advantage over those who are uncomfortable with the technology.

Since the key to finding valuable Web-based information is knowing the address of the desired Web site, anything you can do to improve your ability to save and manage URLs will be extremely valuable. If you use Netscape Navigator as your browser, read the Help text that explains how to use **bookmarks** to save and organize URLs. Within IE, you'll want to learn everything you can about the **Favorites** feature, which saves and organizes Web addresses, URLs.

To work with Favorites in IE:

1. Go to **www.webmonkey.com**.

Notice that the actual Web page address, *www.webmonkey.com*, is used as an alias for the actual site, *http://hotwired.lycos.com/webmonkey/*. The Webmonkey Web site is dedicated to providing resources, tutorials, and information about developing Web sites. You will want to come back to this site often as you develop AMT's Web site, so you save it using the favorites feature in IE.

TROUBLE? If the Favorites window is already open, and your IE browser screen already looks similar to Figure 1-9, skip Step 2.

2. Click the **Favorites** button 🔳 on the Standard toolbar to toggle the Favorites window on.

Your screen should look similar to Figure 1-9. Of course each Favorites window will have different Web sites and different folders listed. Favorites are determined by each user. You may have folders for Links, Media, and Channels at the top of the list.

Figure 1-9	FAVORITES WINDOW IN IE

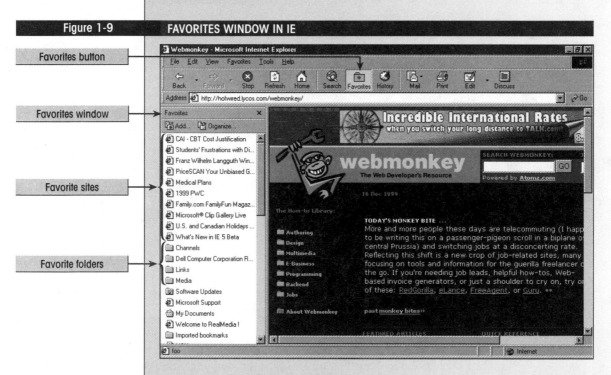

Favorites button

Favorites window

Favorite sites

Favorite folders

3. Drag the **IE icon** 🔳, which is on the left of the Web page address in the Address bar, to the top of the Favorites window, as shown in Figure 1-10.

The Webmonkey URL appears as a link with its own unique icon in the Favorites list. After a time, you will have so many favorite entries stored that you'll want to organize them in folders.

Figure 1-10	CREATING A FAVORITE WEB SITE REFERENCE

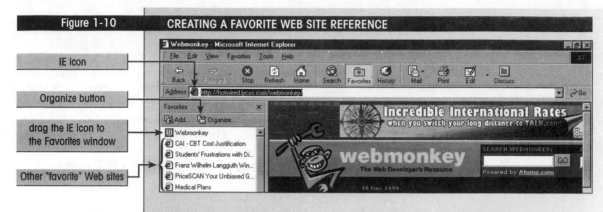

IE icon

Organize button

drag the IE icon to the Favorites window

Other "favorite" Web sites

4. Click the **Organize** button 🔄 in the Favorites window, and then click the **Create Folder** button in the Organize Favorites dialog box.

A New Folder is created and the folder name New Folder is selected. If you are familiar with creating folders in Explorer, this will be a familiar task for you. Folder names should be descriptive.

5. Type **ECOMMERCE**.

TROUBLE? If you are using a shared computer, create the folder with the name ECOMMERCE-*Your Initials* to differentiate it from other ECOMMERCE folders that may have been created.

Your Organize Favorites dialog box will appear similar to Figure 1-11. Now move the Webmonkey URL reference into the ECOMMERCE folder.

Figure 1-11	CREATING A WEB SITE FOLDER

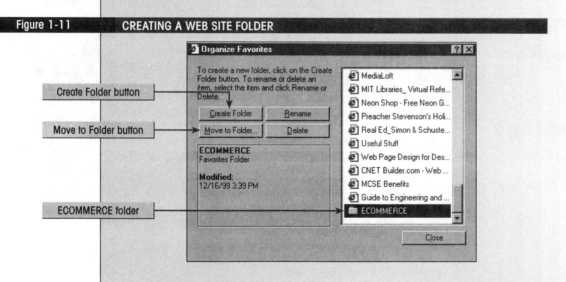

Create Folder button

Move to Folder button

ECOMMERCE folder

6. Click **Webmonkey** in the Organize Favorites dialog box, click the **Move to Folder** button, click the **ECOMMERCE** folder in the Browser for Folder dialog box as shown in Figure 1-12, click the **OK** button, and then click the **Close** button.

Figure 1-12	MOVING A WEB SITE REFERENCE INTO A FOLDER

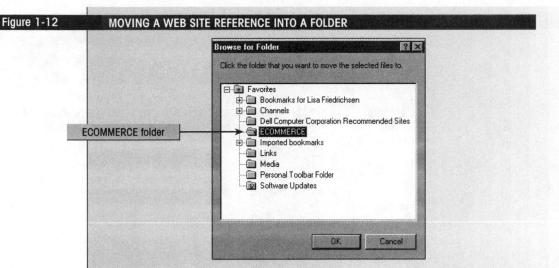

ECOMMERCE folder

Now that your ECOMMERCE folder has been created in the Favorites window, you can add new URLs to it directly.

7. Go to **www.webcom.com**.

This site provides Web hosting services. Most plans include a 30-day free trial. You want to add this URL to your ECOMMERCE folder.

8. Drag the **IE icon** 🗐, which is positioned to the left of the Web page address, to the **ECOMMERCE** folder in the Favorites window.

The reference to the **www.webcom**.*com* site is now stored within the ECOMMERCE folder. Depending on the way the Web page was developed, the description of it in the Favorites window may or may not be appropriate. You can easily change the text associated with the reference.

9. Right-click the **www.webcom.com** reference (the reference may be "Hosting your Web site"), click **Rename**, type **Webcom**, and then press the **Enter** key.

Your Favorites window should look similar to Figure 1-13.

| Figure 1-13 | RENAMING A WEB PAGE REFERENCE |

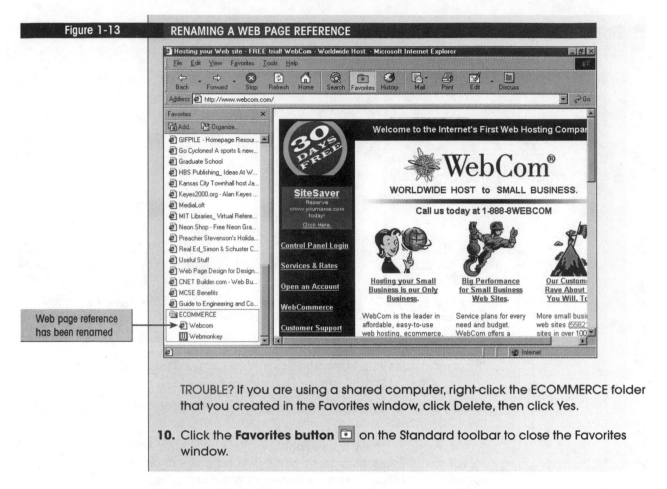

Web page reference has been renamed

TROUBLE? If you are using a shared computer, right-click the ECOMMERCE folder that you created in the Favorites window, click Delete, then click Yes.

10. Click the **Favorites button** 🔲 on the Standard toolbar to close the Favorites window.

Although the favorites feature is one of the most useful ways to document and preserve valuable Web addresses, there are many more features within IE as well as in the other packages within the IE suite that are extremely valuable for anyone who regularly uses the Internet. This tutorial gave you a brief introduction to the Internet, IE, and the e-commerce possibilities for Aaron Michael Toys. Now that you've spent some time learning about the unlimited potential benefits of e-commerce, you're ready to build the underlying Access database that will be a crucial piece of the e-commerce site.

To Exit IE and disconnect from the Internet:

1. Click **File** on the menu bar, and then click **Close** to exit IE.

2. Disconnect from the Internet if you are using a Dial-up system.

For your convenience, Figure 1-14 provides a comprehensive listing of all of the Web addresses referenced in this tutorial, including those referenced in the end-of-unit exercises.

Figure 1-14	E-COMMERCE WEB SITES	
CATEGORY	**WEB ADDRESS**	**DESCRIPTION**
Career	www.careernet.com	Online jobs and resumes
	www.monster.com	
Charity	www.greatergood.com	A connection between charities and e-commerce retailers, who donate a portion of your e-shopping dollars to the charity of your choice
	www.redcross.org	Red Cross
Domain name company	www.register.com	Domain name registration company
E-commerce support	www.bbb.org	Better Business Bureau
	www.cpsc.gov	US Consumer Product Safety Commission
	www.ftc.gov	Federal Trade Commission
	www.globalbizdir.com	Directory of companies with an Internet presence
	www.naag.org	National Association of Attorneys General
	www.scamfreezone.com	Advice, tools, and legitimate home business opportunities for entrepreneurs seeking work-at-home or Internet-based self-employment
E-mail (Web-based)	www.hotmail.com	Provides free Web-based e-mail
Encyclopedia	www.encarta.com	Online encyclopedia
Government	www.whitehouse.gov	White House
Microsoft	www.microsoft.com	Microsoft's Home Page
	www.microsoft.com/access	Microsoft Access Home Page
	www.microsoft.com/windows	Microsoft Windows Home Page
Music	www.mp3.com	Digital music downloads
Portals and search engines	www.about.com	General portal
	www.altavista.com	General portal and search engine
	www.attbusiness.net	General portal; also provides a list of search engines
	www.cnet.com	Web site and search engine; for Web-related and technology issues
	www.devsearch.com	Search engine Web site for computer and Web issues
	www.excite.com	General portal and search engine
	www.google.com	General search engine
	www.goto.com	General portal and search engine
	www.hotbot.com	General portal and search engine
	www.lycos.com	General portal and search engine
	www.msn.com	General portal and ISP service
	www.yahoo.com	General portal and search engine
	www.zdnet.com	Technology-oriented portal and search engine
	www.webmonkey.com	Web-oriented portal and search engine
	www.yahooligans.com	General search engine specifically for children

Figure 1-14	E-COMMERCE WEB SITES (CONTINUED)	
CATEGORY	**WEB ADDRESS**	**DESCRIPTION**
Price comparisons and shopping, for a wide range of consumer products	www.cadabra.com www.mysimon.com www.pricescan.com	Virtual mall and price comparisons Virtual mall and price comparisons Price comparison and shopping guide. Especially strong in consumer electronics.
Schools	www.jccc.net	Johnson County Community College in Overland Park, Kansas
	www.johnco.cc.ks.us	Johnson County Community College in Overland Park, Kansas
	www.keller.edu	Keller Graduate School of Management, headquartered in Oak Brook, Illinois
Technical information	www.whatis.com	Glossary for information systems and telecommunications terms
	www.slashdot.org	News service for technical happenings and gossip
Virtual auction house	www.ebay.com	Electronic auction site for a wide range of consumer goods
	www.ubid.com	Electronic auction site for a wide range of consumer goods
Virtual communities	www.ivillage.com	Electronic community geared toward women's issues
Virtual mall	www.buy.com	Electronic mall for a wide range of consumer goods
	www.virtualmall.com	Electronic mall for a wide range of consumer goods
Virtual store – banks	www.citibank.com	Citibank
Virtual store – shipping and packaging	www.fedex.com	Fedex
Virtual stores – books and music	www.amazon.com www.barnesandnoble.com www.bn.com	Amazon.com, Inc. Barnesandnoble.com Barnes and Noble
Virtual stores – cars	www.chrysler.com	Chrysler Corporation
Virtual stores – computers	www.ibm.com	IBM Corporation
Virtual stores – flowers	www.1800flowers.com	Online florist
	www.flowers.com	Online florist
	www.ftd.com	Online florist
Virtual stores- Post Office	www.stampsonline.com	Online access to U.S. Postal Service
Virtual stores – general merchandise	www.landsend.com www.jcpenney.com	Lands' End JCPenney
Virtual stores – humor-related	www.dilbert.com	Dilbert comics
Virtual stores – publishers	www.course.com	Course Technology
Virtual stores – toys	www.etoys.com	Online toy store
	www.toysrus.com	Online toy store
Virtual stores – travel	www.expedia.com	Online travel agent
	www.travelocity.com	Online travel agent
	www.previewtravel.com	Online travel agent

Figure 1-14	E-COMMERCE WEB SITES (CONTINUED)	
CATEGORY	**WEB ADDRESS**	**DESCRIPTION**
Virtual stores – wine	www.wine.com	Online wine store
Weather	www.weather.com	National weather information; The Weather Channel
Web hosting companies	www.netnation.com	NetNation Communications
	www.verio.com	Verio
	www.Webhosting.com	WebHosting.com
	www.Webcom.com	WebCom
Web pages – personal	www.geocities.com	Hosts millions of personal Web pages

QUICK CHECK

1. What is the difference between a general search engine and a portal Web site?

2. Identify six business reasons to have a Web presence.

3. What characteristics of the Internet make it a great business tool?

4. Why did the World Wide Web become so popular?

5. What are the two major uses for a Web browser?

6. What are the most popular domain name extensions?

7. What organization is ultimately responsible for providing, authorizing, and organizing domain names?

8. What types of services do Web hosting companies provide?

9. What feature do you use within Netscape and IE to log and organize Web page URLs that you plan to visit frequently?

REVIEW ASSIGNMENTS

There is no end to the tutorials, resources, and information made available through the Internet. In this lesson, you'll further explore e-commerce, the World Wide Web, and ways that businesses can participate in e-commerce. You may have to modify the steps slightly because links and Web pages constantly change and improve.

1. Connect to the Internet, load Internet Explorer (IE), go to *www.goto.com*, then click the Web hosting link to drill down into the search engine.

2. Follow the links to find a new Web hosting company, follow the links that describe the company's services, then print that page. Surf around the site and read about the company. On the back of the printout, write down two new things you learned from the site.

3. Click the Back button ⬅ enough times to return to *www.goto.com*, type **educational toys** in the GoTo.com text box, then click the Find It! button.

4. Click links to explore one or two educational toy Web sites, then print the home page for one of them. On the back of the printout, write down two Web site ideas for Aaron Michael Toys.

5. Go to *www.globalbizdir.com*, (a business directory of companies with an Internet presence).

6. Click the links through this site until you find the category for Toys-Retail. How many results did you find?

7. Follow the links to the home page for Toys R Us (*www.toysrus.com*). Print their home page, then surf around the site, looking for educational toys for a 7 year old and a 10 year old. Write two comments on the back of the printout explaining your opinions on the usability and quality of the site.

8. Go to *www.yahooligans.com*. Yahooligans! is a search engine specifically designed for children. Enter **toys** as the search criteria, then click the Search button.

9. Surf through the links in search of an educational toy. Print one page that describes the toy that you found. Write two comments on the back of the printout comparing your experiences with surfing for educational toys at the Toys R Us and the Yahooligans! sites.

10. Go to *www.google.com* and enter **educational toys** as the search criterion.

11. Surf through the links in search of an educational toy. Print one page that describes the toy you found. Write two comments on the back of the printout comparing your experiences with surfing for educational toys at the Google and Yahooligans! sites.

12. Go to *www.devsearch.com* and enter **domain name** as the search criterion, then click Search.

13. Surf, find, and print one page for one article on issues relating to domain names. On the back of the paper, summarize two new things you learned about domain names from the article or your surfing experience.

14. Click the Back button or go to *www.devsearch.com* to start a new search. Enter **Web hosting** as the search criterion, then click Search.

15. Surf, find, and print one page for one article on issues relating to Web hosting. On the back of the paper, summarize two new things you learned about Web hosting from the article or your surfing experience.

16. Click the Favorites button on the IE Standard Buttons toolbar.

17. Click the Organize button within the Favorites window, click the Create Folder button within the Organize Favorites dialog box, and then create a Folder called **SCHOOL**. If you are using a shared computer, name the folder **SCHOOL-*Your Initials***.

18. Using your favorite search engine, find the URLs for three colleges in your area. Drag the IE icon for each URL into the SCHOOL folder that you just created.

19. With the SCHOOL folder and its contents clearly displayed in the Favorites window, press the Print Screen key on the keyboard to put the image of the screen on the Clipboard.

20. Load Word, or any other available word-processing program on your computer, type your name as the first line, the current date as the second line, and then press the Enter key to create a blank line.

21. Click the Paste button on the Standard toolbar of the word processor to paste an image of your IE window with the SCHOOL folder and its contents into the document, then print the document.

22. Close the document without saving your changes, then close IE, and disconnect from the Internet if you are using a dial-up connection.

CASE PROBLEMS

Case 1. E-Commerce Auction Houses   From the largest antique dealer to the smallest coin collector, e-commerce has revolutionized the auction business. Not only can you place a bid in a virtual auction house, but you can also sell your own items without leaving the comfort of your own home. Internet-based electronic auctions are strong in all of the areas where traditional auctions have been popular: jewelry, stamps, coins, antiques, dolls, and collectibles of all types. eBay and uBid, two of the largest virtual auction houses, have extended the concept to a wide range of consumer products. In this case you'll use both sites to experience this form of e-commerce. You may have to modify the steps slightly because links and Web pages constantly change and improve.

1. Connect to the Internet, load Internet Explorer (IE), go to *www.ebay.com* then click the Toys category link.

2. Enter **leapfrog** as the search criterion, to determine if any Leap Pad Deluxe Learning Centers, made by the LeapFrog company, are currently for sale. (This is a phonics-intensive game for new readers. The game currently retails at $89.99.)

3. Click the link that most closely looks like this toy, then print that page. If you wanted to bid on this item, you would have to register with eBay.

4. Surf around the eBay site to find the Register link. (*Hint*: It is found at the bottom of almost every page.)

5. Click the Register link, then begin the registration process.

6. When you get to the part of the registration in which you have to enter your name and other personal information, print that page.

7. Go to *www.ubid.com*. If there is no Toys link, enter **leapfrog** as the search criterion and click the Go button. Did you find any results?

8. Click the Back button to return to the home page for uBid and print the home page. On the back write two statements explaining how uBid appears to differ from eBay.

9. Find and click the link to sign up for a uBid account. (*Hint*: It is found at the bottom of almost every page.)

10. Print the registration page for uBid and compare it to that of eBay. On the back of the registration page for uBid write two statements that differentiate the uBid registration form from the eBay registration form.

11. At either the eBay or uBid site, search for a tutorial or other Help-related information. Research the steps required to sell an item at either site, then print that Web page.

12. Close IE, and disconnect from the Internet if you are using a dial-up connection.

Case 2. E-Commerce Scams and Support   As you would suspect, there are a wide-range of e-commerce scams and ripoffs. They range from annoying e-mail chain letters (which track, record, and then sell your e-mail address) to flagrant destruction of electronic data (viruses, malevolent hackers) to credit card theft. If you are willing to do a little research, however, there are several good resources available to help keep you out of e-commerce trouble. In this case you'll go to a few Web sites that provide e-commerce consumer and business information on a variety of e-commerce scam and support topics. You may have to modify the steps slightly because links and Web pages constantly change and improve.

1. Connect to the Internet, then load Internet Explorer (IE).

2. Go to each of the following Web sites listed below, and print the first page of each home page.

   - *www.bbb.org*
     Better Business Bureau

   - *www.cpsc.gov*
     U.S. Consumer Product Safety Commission

   - *www.ftc.gov*
     Federal Trade Commission

   - *www.globalbizdir.com*
     Directory of companies with an Internet presence

   - *www.naag.org*
     National Association of Attorneys General

   - *www.scamfreezone.com*
     Advice, tools, and legitimate home business opportunities for entrepreneurs seeking work-at-home or Internet-based self-employment.

3. On the back of each page, write two statements about e-commerce advice you learned from the site.

4. Close IE, and disconnect from the Internet if you are using a dial-up connection.

Case 3. Comparing Product Prices on the Internet   The number of e-commerce sites is overwhelming, and no one could possibly be aware of or have the time to search all of them before making a purchase. Fortunately, there are several good sites, such as PriceSCAN.com, cadabra.com, and mySimon, that help you compare prices between different e-commerce sites. In this case, you'll use two of the sites to compare the price for digital cameras. You may have to modify the steps slightly because links and product specifications constantly change and improve.

1. Connect to the Internet, load Internet Explorer (IE), then go to *www.cadabra.com*.

2. Scroll down the home page to find the Product Index listing, then click the necessary links for Digital Cameras. Since you are fond of Kodak products, you'll limit your search to that manufacturer.

3. Click the Kodak check box in the Manufacturer area, then observe how many known models and exact matches cadabra.com offers. Also observe how many items and stores are being searched.

4. Click the price list arrow for the bottom of your price range, and click the dollar value closest to $500. Click the price list arrow for the top of your price range, and click the dollar value closest to $1500. Observe how many models and exact matches cadabra.com offers.

5. Click the link to compare the models selected with these preferences.

6. Use the Sort features to sort the matches in different orders other than price. Print that Web page.

7. Go to *www.pricescan.com*, click the Electronics link, and then click the links to drill down into the digital camera area.

8. Choose Kodak as the manufacturer and enter a maximum price of $1500 as search criteria. Click the Search button.

9. Click the link for the Kodak DC260 Zoom, then print the Web page that lists the vendors and prices for this product. If available, click the price trend graph link, then print that page as well.

10. On the back of the PriceSCAN.com printout, write two statements that identify differences between the two price comparison Web sites.

11. Write a one-page paper identifying the benefits of using price comparision Web sites to do your shopping.

12. Close IE and disconnect from the Internet if you are using a dial-up connection.

Case 4. Renting Space at a Virtual Mall   Securing an appropriate domain name and setting up a Web server are requirements for any e-commerce venture that intends to use a back-end database, is of significant size, or anticipates growth. However, there is a very low-cost and exciting way for the hobbyist or home-based business to start selling products on the Internet—renting space at a virtual mall. You can advertise and sell a nominal number of products at an existing virtual mall, and not have to worry about the technical details of the transaction. In this case, you'll learn about virtual malls, using the *www.cnet.com* Web site. You may have to modify the steps slightly because links and Web pages constantly change and improve.

1. Connect to the Internet, load Internet Explorer (IE), then go to *www.cnet.com*.

2. Enter the search criterion **Web store**, then click the Search button.

3. Surf through the links to find a site that allows you to rent their Web server to start selling your product. Two sites that allow you to do this are: *http://store.yahoo.com/vw/howitwor.html* and *http://www.icat.com/services/store/*

4. Find the documentation on how to build a rental space at a virtual mall and print one page of it.

5. Go back to *www.cnet.com* and search for **Web store** again (or use your Back button). Surf through the links to find free software to build your Web site. Print one page that describes the software.

6. For fun, surf around the CNET.com site and try to search for their recommendations by using **top 10** as the criteria. Most search engines and portals have a what's cool, what's hot, or what's new list to help you stay on top of exciting developments on the Web.

7. For more fun, surf the top 10 CNET.com recommendations described in Figure 1-15.

Figure 1-15

RANK	URL	DESCRIPTION
1	www.yahoo.com	Serves as a comprehensive portal and search engine. Provides additional services such as free e-mail, auctions, investment portfolios, and GeoCities.
2	www.microsoft.com	Provides Microsoft product info and downloads. Enter www.microsoft.com/productname to quickly go to the homepage for any Microsoft product. (www.microsoft.com/access is the home page for Access, and www.microsoft.com/windows is the home page for Windows.)
3	www.geocities.com	Used for personal Web pages. Millions of people have home pages here. It was recently purchased by Yahoo.
4	www.hotmail.com	Provides free Web-based e-mail
5	www.amazon.com	Sells books, CDs, videos, toys, and consumer electronics
6	www.ebay.com	Supports a person-to-person auction site. There are around two million ongoing auctions available on a daily basis.
7	www.encarta.com	Provides encyclopedic information. For a small annual subscription fee, you can access many articles, links, and digital images.
8	www.previewtravel.com	Sells tickets, reservations, and other types of travel agency products
9	www.mp3.com	Provides tens of thousands of free digital music downloads
10	www.slashdot.org	Serves as a news service for those technonerds who just can't get enough gossip

8. Close IE and disconnect from the Internet if you are using a dial-up connection.

QUICK | CHECK ANSWERS

Session 1.1

1. Search engines that are specifically indexed to provide categories of high-quality information are sometimes called portal Web sites. General search engines do not filter the number or quality of links that are found but usually do provide a category drill-down capability.

2. Common business uses for the Internet include: marketing, sales, customer service, gathering consumer information, providing a service, linking communities of people with common interests, and entertainment.

3. The characteristics of the Internet that make it a great business tool include the fact that it is:

    ■ Global

    ■ Accessible 24 hours a day, 7 days a week

    ■ Based on standardized computer protocols so that information you provide via the Internet is accessible by every computer connected to the Internet

    ■ Not yet subject to the same levels of taxation as traditional businesses

    ■ Very inexpensive to use

4. The WWW's popularity grew for many reasons:

    ■ Basic Web pages are easy to create.

    ■ Web pages are extremely flexible. Web pages can be connected to many other more complex technologies that can provide an unlimited interface for the user. For example, Web pages can support almost any type of electronic multimedia effect, can be used to interactively query a database, or can provide a screen by which a user can make a secure purchasing transaction.

    ■ Browser software makes Web pages easy to find, download, and display.

    ■ From their initial design, Web pages include hyperlinks that provide a fast and easy way to find a page and move from one page to another.

5. The Web browser is used to:

    ■ Display Web pages for the user

    ■ Translate requests for Web pages made by the user into the Hypertext Transfer Protocol (HTTP), which used to find and route Web pages over the Internet

6. | Domain Name Extension | Description |
    |---|---|
    | com | Commercial, for-profit company |
    | edu | Educational institution |
    | gov | U.S. government organization |
    | mil | U.S. military organization |
    | net | network service or networked organization |
    | org | nonprofit organization |

7. Internet Network Information Center (InterNIC)

8. Web hosting companies provide the following services:

   - Domain name registration services
   - E-mail addresses associated with your domain name (e.g. *YourName*@AMTOYS.net)
   - Internet access services
   - Web page design services
   - E-Commerce consulting such as business planning and marketing
   - E-Commerce software such as secure credit card processing and shopping carts
   - Web-enabled database development services

9. Netscape uses Bookmarks to keep track of URLs. IE uses the Favorites feature to document Web page URLs. You organize the URLs in folders using the Favorites feature in IE similarly to how you organize files in folders using Windows Explorer.

OBJECTIVES

In this tutorial you will:

- Review key Access terminology and concepts

- Explore table datasheets, subdatasheets, and Table Design view

- Work with table relationships and relational design concepts

- Explore query datasheets and Query Design view

- Explore query features such as sorting, criteria entries, calculated fields, and aggregate calculations

- Use Form View, work with form controls, and explore Form Design view

- Preview reports, work with report controls, and explore Report Design view

UNDERSTANDING
ACCESS 2000

Working with the Access 2000 Database for Aaron Michael Toys

CASE

Aaron Michael Toys

Now that you've explored e-commerce and understand the benefits that e-commerce can bring to a small business, you've decided to build a Web-enabled database for Aaron Michael Toys. You know that creating a Web site for AMT will provide immediate marketing and customer service benefits. Later, as your knowledge and skills in developing Web-enabled information grows, you'll expand the capabilities of the Web site for sales, consumer research, and community service purposes too.

The toy inventory database currently being used for Aaron Michael Toys is an Access 2000 database. You'll use the Web-enabled capabilities provided by Access 2000 to help build your e-commerce site. Your first step, therefore, is to become thoroughly familiar with the existing Access 2000 Aaron Michael Toys database.

SESSION 2.1

In this session you will review key Access 2000 terminology and concepts, explore the tables within an Access 2000 database, and study the relational design of the Aaron Michael Toys database.

A Review of Access Terminology and Concepts

Access is a powerful relational database program that runs on microcomputers. A **relational database** is a collection of related tables that share information. The goals of a relational database are to satisfy dynamic information management needs and to eliminate duplicate data entry wherever possible. In order to become proficient with Access, it is important for you to understand the key terminology listed in Figure 2-1.

Figure 2-1	KEY ACCESS TERMINOLOGY	
TERM	**DEFINITION**	**EXAMPLE AT AARON MICHAEL TOYS**
field	A category of information about an item in the database	A field describing one characteristic. Fields for a toy would include the toy name, color, manufacturer, quantity on hand, and price. Fields describing a customer would include the customer name, contact information, and telephone number.
key field	A field that contains unique information for each record	The product number would be a good key field for a toy since every product number for every toy is different. The product name would be a poor key field choice, since multiple toys could potentially have the same name.
record	A group of related fields for an item	One record consists of all of the fields for one toy.
table	A collection of records for a single subject	The Products table consists of all of the records for all of the toys.
datasheet	A logical view of the fields and records of a single table or query, in which a field appears as a column and a record as a row	When you open a table or query in an Access database, the data is presented as a datasheet.
database	A broad collection of data associated with a topic	The Aaron Michael Toys database consists of all of the tables stored about the business, such as product, sales, customer, and vendor information.

To start Access, open an existing database, and view the Products table:

1. Start Access 2000, then open the **AMToys-2** database from the Tutorial\Solutions Folder for Tutorial 2, click the **Tables** button 🔲 on the Objects bar if it isn't already selected, and then click the **Categories** table.

   The database opens and presents the table objects as shown in Figure 2-2. The tables are listed in alphabetical order in the Database window. You will review key Access terminology using the Aaron Michael Toys database.

Figure 2-2	AMTOYS ACCESS DATABASE

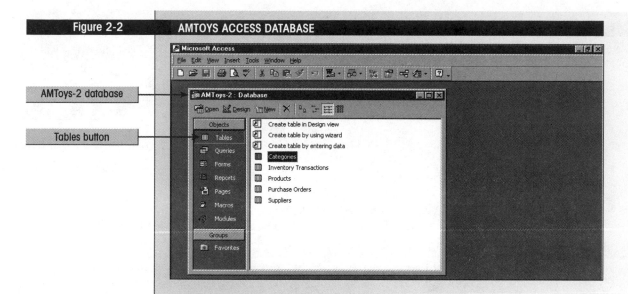

There are five tables of information within the Aaron Michael Toys database.

2. Double-click the **Products** table to open it, and then maximize the datasheet as shown in Figure 2-3. You will use the Products table to review key Access terminology by viewing actual data.

Figure 2-3	PRODUCTS DATASHEET

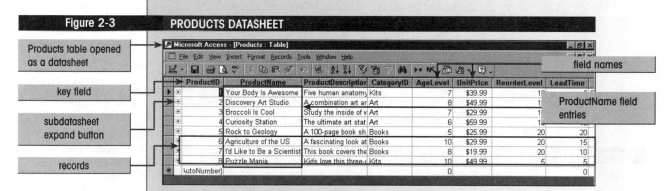

The Products table contains eight records, but not all of the fields are visible at the same time. You can press either the Tab key or Enter key to move through the fields of a record.

3. Press the **Tab** key seven times to move through the fields of the first record.

You can use the Navigation buttons in the lower-left corner of the datasheet window to navigate through the records of a datasheet. The Navigation buttons are shown in Figure 2-4.

TROUBLE? If you cannot see all of the data in a field, you can quickly resize the width of a given column by pointing to the vertical line that separates field names in the column header and dragging the ↔ left or right to narrow or widen a field. You can also double-click the line to widen it to fit the widest entry.

Figure 2-4 NAVIGATION BUTTONS

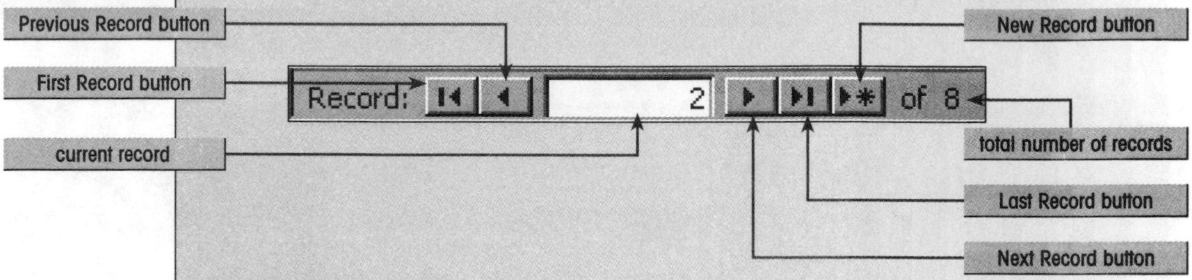

4. Click the **Last Record** button in the Navigation buttons, and then click the **Previous Record** button in the Navigation buttons six times to navigate to the second record.

The **current record** is the record that is selected in the datasheet. A current record symbol looks like a black triangle and appears in the **record selector** to the left of the current record. When you enter or update data, this symbol changes to an **edit record symbol**.

The records of this table may be related in a **one-to-many** relationship with the records of another table. *One* record from this table may have *many* related records in another table. In this case, one product record has many inventory transaction records. The **Subdatasheet Expand** button allows you to view the "many" related records from within the datasheet of the table on the "one" side of the relationship.

5. Click the **Subdatasheet Expand** button for ProductID 1, the first record.

Your screen should look like Figure 2-5. The Expand button changes to a Collapse button. The subdatasheet from the Inventory Transactions table shows that there are three related records for the first product.

Figure 2-5 EXPANDING THE INVENTORY TRANSACTION SUBDATASHEET FOR THE FIRST PRODUCT

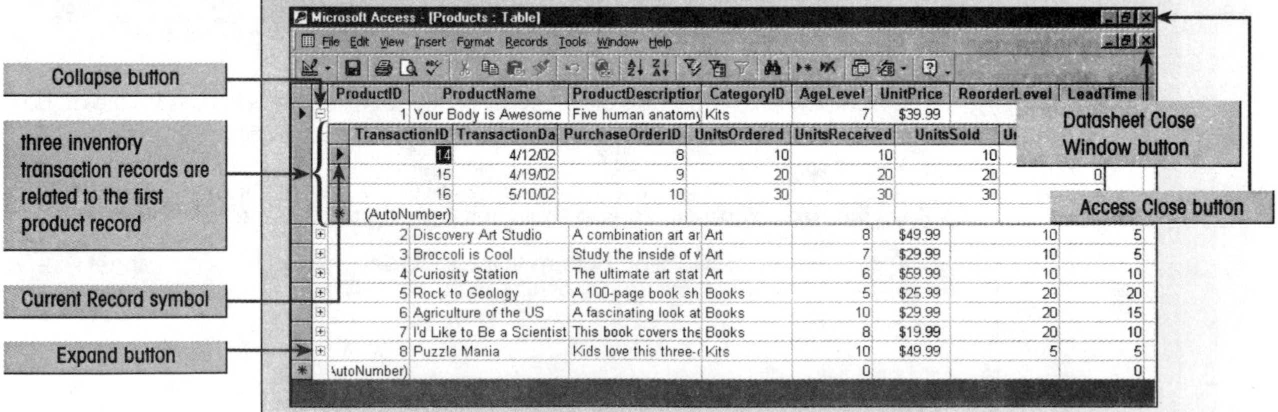

6. Click the **Datasheet Close Window** button to close the Products datasheet. Click **Yes** if prompted to save changes.

TROUBLE? If you exited Access rather than just closing the table, you probably clicked the Access Close button in the top-right corner and closed the entire Access program. To close an object within Access, always click the lower Close button in the upper-right corner. The lower Close button is called the Close Window button when that window is maximized.

Access Objects

The objects in an Access database are **tables**, **queries**, **forms**, **reports**, **pages**, **macros**, and **modules**. These seven basic object types provide all of the functions of the database and are summarized in Figure 2-6.

Figure 2-6	OBJECTS IN AN ACCESS DATABASE
OBJECT	**PURPOSE**
Table	Contains all of the raw data within the database, organized by fields and records in a spreadsheet-like view called a datasheet. Tables can be linked by a common field to share information and therefore minimize data redundancy.
Query	Creates a datasheet that displays a subset of fields and/or records from one or more tables. Queries are created when a user has a "question" about the data in the database. Queries can also be used to create calculated fields and summarized information.
Form	Provides an easy-to-use data entry screen that generally shows only one record at a time.
Report	Provides a professional printout of data, which may contain enhancements such as headers, footers, and calculations on groups of records. Mailing labels can also be created from report objects.
Page	Creates Web pages from Access objects and provides Web page connectivity features to an Access database.
Macro	Stores a collection of keystrokes or commands to automate a task such as printing several reports or displaying a toolbar when a form opens.
Module	Stores Visual Basic programming code that extends the functions and automated processes of Access.

Naming Objects

Even though object names can be up to 64 characters long, you want to keep them short yet descriptive. There are a few special characters that you cannot use in an object name. These include the period (.), exclamation point (!), accent grave (`), and square brackets ([ ]). Some database designers use the **Leszynski Naming Convention**. This popular naming convention uses a three-letter tag to identify the object type in the object name (see Figure 2-7).

Figure 2-7	LESZYNSKI NAMING CONVENTION FOR OBJECTS

OBJECT	TAG	EXAMPLE
Table	tbl	tblEmployees
Form	frm	frmEmployeeEntry
Query	qry	qryIncome2000
Report	rpt	rptAccount1Qtr
Macro	mcr	mcrHRToolbar

The Relationship Between Access Objects

Having an overall idea of how the objects function together to create the entire database is important to your success with the database. Tables are the most important object within an Access database because they contain all of the data within the database. Query objects are based on tables. Form, page, and report objects can be based on either tables or queries. Data can be entered and edited through four of the objects, tables, queries, pages, and forms, but is only stored in tables. The relationships between the objects are shown in Figure 2-8.

Figure 2-8 **THE RELATIONSHIP BETWEEN ACCESS OBJECTS**

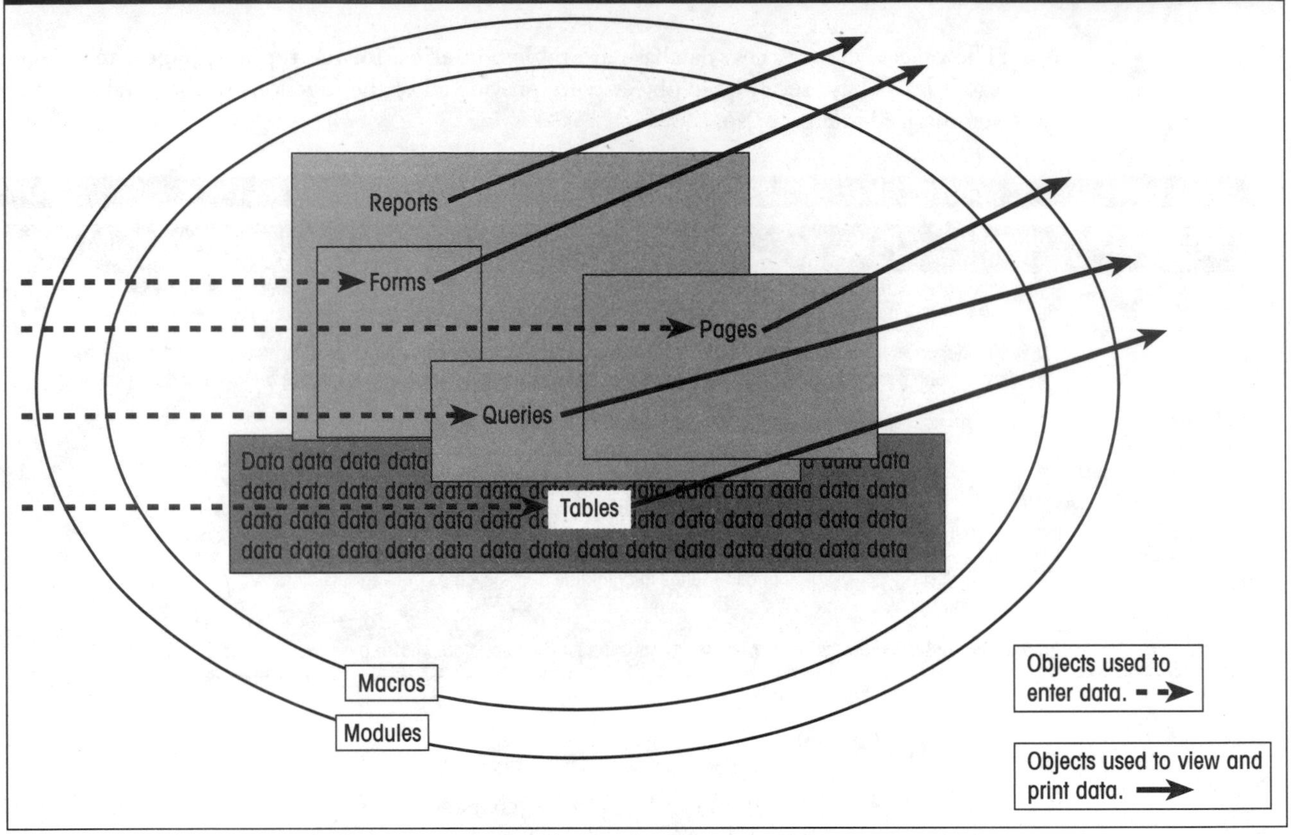

Unlike the other five objects of the database, the macro and module objects are not used to view or edit data, but rather to provide additional database productivity and automation features. For example, you may build a macro or Visual Basic module to execute a series of actions when a command button is clicked. Command buttons are commonly placed on forms to help a user navigate through the database or mask the complexity of a calculation. Regardless of how many objects of the various types you create, they are all stored in one database file that can grow up to a 2-GB size limitation.

The Objects Bar and Objects Toolbar

The database window organizes the objects by type of object. To display the objects of one type, click the corresponding object button in the **Objects Bar** identified in Figure 2-9. To open a specific object, double-click it or click it and then click the Open button on the Objects toolbar. Click an object and then click the Design button to modify an existing object.

Figure 2-9	ELEMENTS OF THE OPENING ACCESS DATABASE WINDOW

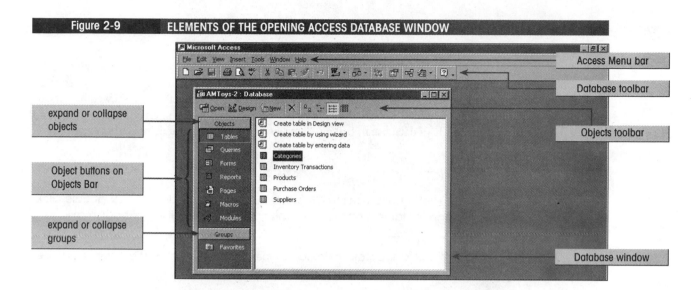

The buttons on the **Objects toolbar** are explained in Figure 2-10. The buttons on the Objects toolbar work with the objects in the database, not with the database as a whole. For example, if you wanted to create a new query object, you would click the Query button on the Objects Bar, then click the New button on the *Objects toolbar*. The New button on the *Database toolbar* is used to build an entirely new database file.

Figure 2-10	BUTTONS ON THE OBJECTS TOOLBAR		
BUTTON NAME	**USED FOR WHICH OBJECTS?**	**ICON**	**DESCRIPTION**
Open	Tables, Queries, Forms, Pages		Opens the selected object in datasheet, form, or page view
Preview	Reports		Previews the selected report
Run	Macros, Modules		Runs the selected macro or module
Design	Tables, Queries, Forms, Reports, Pages, Macros		Opens the selected object in design view
Design	Modules		Opens the selected module code window
New	Tables		Opens the New Table dialog box
New	Queries		Opens the New Query dialog box
New	Forms		Opens the New Form dialog box
New	Reports		Opens the New Report dialog box
New	Pages		Opens the New Data Access Page dialog box
New	Macros		Opens a new Macro window
New	Modules		Opens a new Code window
Delete	All		Deletes the selected object
Large Icons	All		Displays the objects as large icons in the database window
Small Icons	All		Displays the objects as columns of small icons in the database window
List (Default View)	All		Displays the objects as a single column in the database window
Details	All		Displays five columns of details about the objects in the database window

Tables

Table objects contain all of the raw data in the database and are therefore the first objects created within the database. Without table objects, the rest of the objects are meaningless because the database contains no data. You have already opened the Products table and viewed its datasheet. The datasheet is where you can view, enter, and edit data. Now open the other tables of the Aaron Michael Toys database to become familiar with the data contained within them.

To explore tables:

1. Click the **Tables** button on the Objects bar if it is not already selected, double-click the **Categories** table, and then maximize the datasheet (if not already maximized).

   The datasheet for the Categories table opens. The Categories table contains three records.

2. Click the **Subdatasheet Expand** button [+] for the record for CategoryID 1.

   The records for the two toys in the Products table, ProductID 1 and ProductID 8, expand for that CategoryID.

3. Click the **Subdatasheet Expand** button [+] for the record for CategoryID 2, and then click the **Subdatasheet Expand** button [+] for the record for CategoryID 3.

   Each of the three records has its subdatasheet expanded, and you can view the toys within each category, as shown in Figure 2-11.

| Figure 2-11 | EXPANDING THE SUBDATASHEETS FOR THE CATEGORIES TABLE |

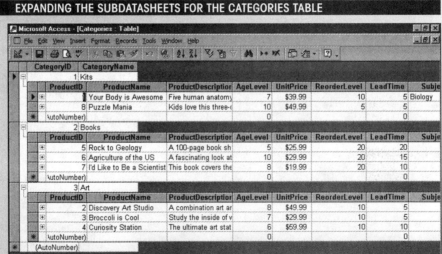

Clicking a Subdatasheet Expand button shows related records. In this case, one CategoryID record has many related records in the Products table.

4. Click the **Subdatasheet Expand** button [+] for the ProductID 1 record (Your Body Is Awesome).

   This subdatasheet shows that the first Product record has three related records in the Inventory Transaction table.

Understanding the one-to-many relationships between the tables of your database is fundamental to your success with the database. These relationships will be explored in more depth later in this tutorial.

5. Click the **Close Window** button to close the Categories table (if asked if you want to save your changes, click the No button). You return to the database window. The Table objects are still visible in the window.

6. Double-click the **Suppliers** table to open its datasheet.

   There are four records in the Suppliers table. The first record is for the JB Toy Factory.

7. Press the **Enter** key three times to move to the ContactLName field.

   Jennifer Brown's name has changed to Jennifer Best. You can make this change directly in the datasheet.

8. Type **Best**, press the **Enter** key nine times to move to the E-mail field, type **jbest@jbtoyfactory.net** as the new E-mail field entry, then press the **Enter** key.

   Notice that entries in the last field, Web, appear as hyperlinks. A **hyperlink** on a datasheet responds exactly like a hyperlink on a Web page. When clicked, it will open the default browser such as Netscape Navigator or Internet Explorer on your computer and then find and display the associated Web page.

   TROUBLE? If you click the hyperlink in the Web field in error, you may receive an "Unable to open ..." message. The hyperlinks in this database are fictitious. If clicked, they will attempt to find, download, and display the associated Web page, but since the page does not exist, you will most likely get an error message window, which you will have to close.

9. Click the Suppliers table **Close Window** button.

10. Double-click the **Inventory Transactions** table to open that table, then press the **Enter** key seven times to move through and view the fields of that table.

    Notice that date and numeric entries are right-aligned in the columns of the datasheet and that text entries are left-aligned in the columns.

11. Close the Inventory Transactions datasheet.

12. Double-click the **Purchase Orders** table to view its datasheet.

13. Click the **Subdatasheet Expand** button ⊞ for PurchaseOrderID 4.

    The three inventory transaction records for that PurchaseOrderID 4 appear in the subdatasheet.

14. Close the Purchase Orders table.

Table Design View

Every object has at least two views, which are used for very distinct purposes. So far, you have been using the Datasheet view of a table, which allows you to work with the data contained within the table. The **Design view** of an object is where you create and modify the object's structure. Think of the Design view as an object's blueprint. The Design view of a table is where you define the fields for that table. For example, if you wanted to add a new field to the Products table that identified which school subject (math, science, geography) the toy would support, you would add that field in the table's Design view. As you would suspect, understanding the Design view of the Table object is very important to your ability to work with the database.

To add a field in the Design view of a table:

1. Click the **Products** table, then click the **Design** button 🖺 on the Objects toolbar.

   The Design view of the Products table appears as shown in Figure 2-12.

Figure 2-12	DESIGN VIEW OF THE PRODUCTS TABLE

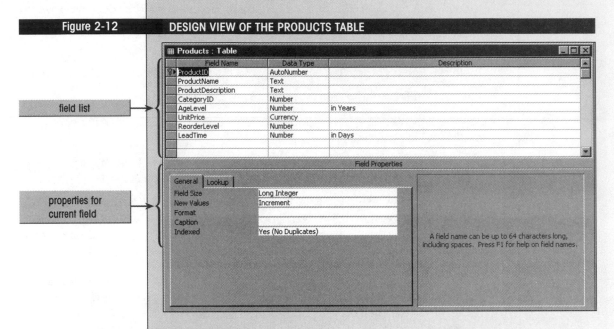

The Design view of a table is divided into two sections. The upper section shows all of the field names and corresponding data types. The upper section also allows you to enter a description for each field if you wish. The lower section shows you the properties for the currently selected field. **Properties** are characteristics that further define the field. Not all properties require an entry. If the property is required, Access will provide a default value. You decide to add two fields to the Products table, one to track the toy's subject area and the other for a numeric customer satisfaction value.

2. Click in the first blank Field Name cell below the LeadTime field name, type **Subject**, then press the **Tab** key.

   The subject field data type is Text, the default, and you do not need to enter a description.

3. Click in the next blank Field Name cell just below the Subject field name, type **Rating**, press the **Tab** key, and click the **Data Type** list arrow, click **Number**, press the **Tab** key, and then type **Overall Customer Satisfaction Rating from 1 (lowest) to 10 (highest)**.

   Field descriptions are optional, but the text that you enter in the Description cell will appear in the Status bar when you edit that field in Datasheet view.

Field Names

Field names follow the same rules as object names (they must be 64 characters or less and cannot contain the period, exclamation point, accent grave, or square bracket characters). Spaces are allowed in object and field names, but many database designers do not like to use spaces because they often require extra programming syntax if the object or field name is referenced in a Visual

Basic programming statement in a module. The Leszynski Naming Convention can also be applied to field names. See Figure 2-13.

Figure 2-13	LESZYNSKI NAMING CONVENTION FOR FIELD NAMES	

FIELD DATA TYPE	TAG	EXAMPLE
Currency	cur	CurRetail
Date/Time	dtm	DtmSaleDate
Number (Integer)	int	IntDistrictNo
Number (Double)	dbl	DblMicrons
Number (Single)	sng	SngMillimeters
Memo	mem	MemComments
OLE Object	ole	OlePicture
Text	str	StrFName
Yes/No	ysn	YsnGoldClub

Data Types

By default, all new fields are given a Text data type, the most common one. The field **data type** is extremely important because it determines the type of data that the field will accept. Data type choices are further defined in Figure 2-14.

Figure 2-14	DATA TYPES	

DATA TYPE	USED FOR THIS TYPE OF DATA:	FIELD NAME EXAMPLES
Text (default)	Text or a combination of text and numbers up to 255 characters in length. Also used for numeric entries that will not be used in calculations.	FirstName Phone ZipCode
Memo	Text entries that are beyond 255 characters in size	Notes Comments
Number	Numeric data that may be used in a mathematical calculation later	Quantity GradePoint
Date/Time	Date or time values	BirthDate BillingDate
Currency	Numeric data that represents money	SalePrice RetailPrice Salary
AutoNumber	An automatic field entry that increments the field value by one for each new record. The user cannot type into an AutoNumber field, and numbers cannot be reused if a record is deleted.	RecordNumber
Yes/No	When only one of two values are possible for the field (yes/no, true/false, or on/off)	SetupRequired BatteriesNeeded
OLE Object	A linked or embedded file created outside of Access such as an Excel spreadsheet, Word document, graphic, or sound clip	Resume Picture
Hyperlink	Web page addresses or links to other files or objects	HomePage

Field Properties

Table Design view is also used to modify field **properties**, the characteristics that further define the field such as field size, caption, format, and validation rule. Properties vary depending on the data type for the field. For example, the Decimal Places property is part of a Number or Currency field, but is not needed and therefore not provided for a Text field. Field Size is a property associated with a Text field, but not with a Date/Time field, since Access controls the size of all entries in a Date/Time field.

You do not need to memorize all of the properties for each data type. Access presents the available properties for the current field in the bottom portion of the Table Design view. Access also provides a default value for properties that require an entry.

To modify the properties of a field in the Design view of a table:

1. Click the **Subject** field name, double-click **50** in the Field Size text box in the Field Properties section, and then type **12** as shown in Figure 2-15.

   A description of the property that you are modifying appears to the right of the Field Properties in Table Design view.

Figure 2-15	MODIFYING FIELD PROPERTIES IN TABLE DESIGN VIEW

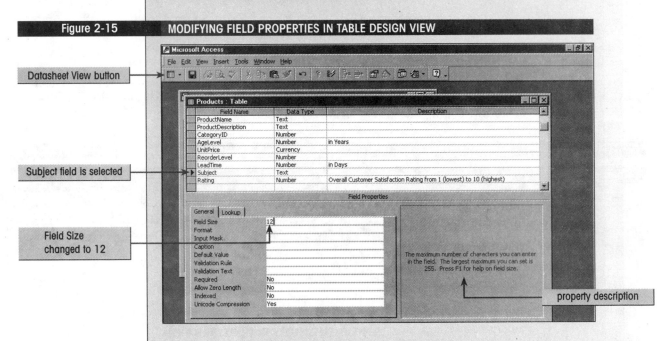

2. Click the **Rating** field name.

   Field properties vary depending on the field's data type.

3. Click the **Field Size** text box, click the **Field Size** list arrow, and then click **Integer**.

   If you wanted even more explanation for a particular property, you could press the F1 key to open the Help manual to the specific location that describes that property.

4. Click the **Save** button 🖫 on the Table Design toolbar, and then click the **Datasheet View** 🔲 button on the Table Design toolbar.

5. Press the **Tab** key eight times to move into the Subject field for the first record, type **Biology**, press the **Tab** key to move into the Rating field, and then type **8** as shown in Figure 2-16.

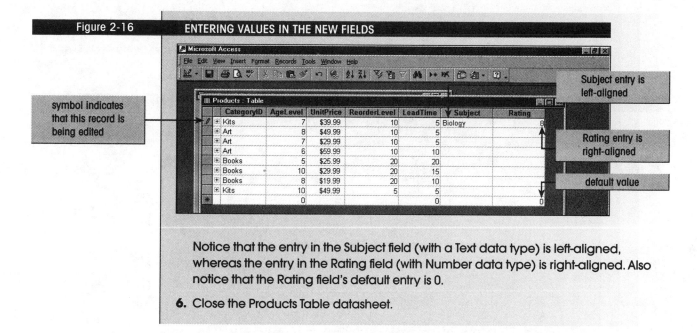

Figure 2-16   **ENTERING VALUES IN THE NEW FIELDS**

symbol indicates that this record is being edited

Subject entry is left-aligned

Rating entry is right-aligned

default value

Notice that the entry in the Subject field (with a Text data type) is left-aligned, whereas the entry in the Rating field (with Number data type) is right-aligned. Also notice that the Rating field's default entry is 0.

6. Close the Products Table datasheet.

You do not have to save data that you have entered into an Access database. Access automatically saves the data as you move to a new record, or when you print or close an object.

Relationships

An Access database is a **relational database**, which means that more than one table can share information, or "relate." The major benefit of organizing your data into a relational database is that this minimizes redundant data. This leads to other benefits including more accurate data, less data entry, more flexible report capabilities, and a faster, more efficient database. In the AMToys database you enter the description and name of a product once in a Products table. The product is linked to many records in the Inventory Transactions table. When viewing the datasheet of the Products table, you see related subdatasheets of Inventory Transaction records.

The One-to-Many Relationship

The synchronization between tables is accomplished by defining a common field that connects the records between the tables. In the most common relationship between tables, the **one-to-many** relationship, the common linking field is the **key field** in the table on the "one" side, and is linked to the **foreign key field** in the table on the "many" side of the relationship. The key field is also called a **primary key field**. In the AMToys database, to link the Products table to the Inventory Transactions table, the ProductID field was used in both tables to make the connection. The ProductID field is the primary key field in the Products table, and a foreign key field in the Inventory Transactions table. The process of designing a relational database is called **normalization**, and involves determining the appropriate fields, tables, and table relationships.

To explore existing relationships between tables:

1. Click the **Relationships** button 🔡 on the Database toolbar, and then maximize the window as shown in Figure 2-17.

Figure 2-17	RELATIONSHIPS BETWEEN THE TABLES OF THE AMTOYS DATABASE

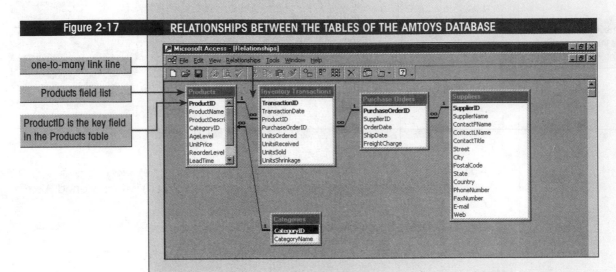

The fields of each table in the AMToys database are displayed as a field list. The table name is in the title bar for each field list. The key field for each table is bold and always serves as the "one" field of a one-to-many relationship between tables. The infinity symbol points to the "many" field of a one-to-many relationship. If a scroll bar is visible within the field list, it means that the table contains more fields than are currently visible. You can examine an existing relationship by double-clicking the link line.

2. Double-click the **one-to-many link line** between the Products and Inventory Transactions tables.

The Edit Relationships dialog box opens as shown in Figure 2-18. It is used to define and edit relationships between tables.

TROUBLE? If the Edit Relationships dialog box didn't open, be sure to double-click the link line, and not the "one" or "infinity" (many) symbols.

Figure 2-18	EDIT RELATIONSHIPS DIALOG BOX

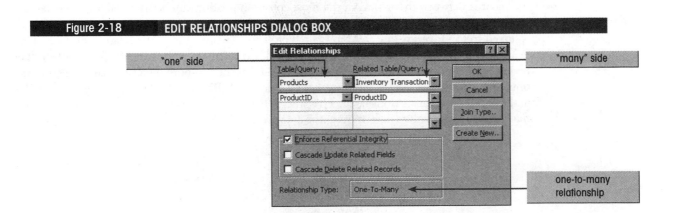

The Edit Relationships dialog box clearly shows which field in which table forms the "one" and "many" side of the relationship. The linking field does not have to have the same name within each table, but often the linking fields have the same name.

The Enforce Referential Integrity Option

Enforce referential integrity is an important option that you can choose within the Edit Relationships dialog box. It helps you maintain the accuracy of your data. It prevents a value from being entered into the foreign key field that isn't first entered into the primary key field of the related table. In other words, you can't enter an Inventory Transaction record for a product that doesn't first exist in the Products table. Referential Integrity also prevents you from deleting a record on the "one" side of a relationship (e.g., a product) that has related records (e.g., inventory transactions) in the "many" table, a condition that creates "**orphaned records.**" If the Enforce Referential Integrity check box is not checked, the link line will not appear with the "one" and "many" symbols on the ends.

To explore the enforce referential integrity option:

1. Click the **Enforce Referential Integrity** check box to clear it, and then click the **OK** button in the Edit Relationships dialog box.

   The link line between the Products and Inventory Transactions tables no longer appears with "one" and "many" symbols, even though the relationship type is still "one-to-many."

2. Double-click the **link line** between the Products and Inventory Transactions tables to reopen the Edit Relationships dialog box, and then click the **Enforce Referential Integrity** check box.

   The Relationship Type area in the bottom of the Edit Relationships dialog box continues to indicate that the relationship is "One-To-Many." When Enforce Referential Integrity is checked, the Cascade Update Related Fields and Cascade Delete Related Records options are also available. These options should be used cautiously, however, since in both cases they automatically change data in the "many" table simply because you made a change in the "one" table of the relationship.

3. Click the **OK** button in the Edit Relationships dialog box.

Join Properties

The relationship line between the Products and Categories tables has an additional arrow on the "many" side of the link line. This indicates a variation of the default one-to-many relationship link.

To explore join properties:

1. Double-click the **one-to-many link line** between the Products and Categories tables. The Edit Relationships dialog box opens.

   CategoryID is the linking field. It is the primary key field in the Categories table, the "one" side of the relationship. It is the foreign key field in the Products table, the "many" side of the relationship.

2. Click the **Join Type** button in the Edit Relationships dialog box. The Join Properties dialog box opens with additional information about the link as shown in Figure 2-19.

Figure 2-19 | JOIN PROPERTIES DIALOG BOX

default join property →

Join Properties   [?] [X]

○ 1: Only include rows where the joined fields from both tables are equal.

◉ 2: Include ALL records from 'Categories' and only those records from 'Products' where the joined fields are equal.

○ 3: Include ALL records from 'Products' and only those records from 'Categories' where the joined fields are equal.

[OK]   [Cancel]

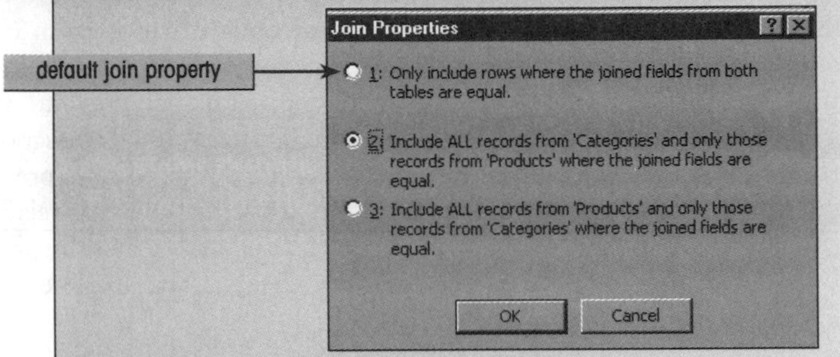

By default, a one-to-many relationship joins two tables according to the first option, which only shows the records from both tables when the same field value appears in both the "one" and "many" sides of the link (in both the primary key field and the foreign key field). The join properties for this relationship have been modified so that *all* of the records in the Categories table, regardless of whether they have any matching records in the Products table, will always appear in the datasheet of a query. This modification in the join property will become more meaningful when you create queries and experience how the modification affects the data that appears on the resulting datasheet.

3. Click the **OK** button in the Join Properties dialog box, and then click **OK** in the Edit Relationships dialog box.

To delete an existing relationship between two tables, right-click the link line and then click Delete from the shortcut menu. To create a new relationship, drag the linking field from one table to the linking field of the next, and then make the appropriate relationship choices in the Edit Relationships dialog box.

Printing the Relationships Window

Since the Relationships window shows a listing of table names, fields within tables, and table relationships, it is an extremely valuable picture of your database. It is an especially handy reference document when you are trying to create a new query, form, page, or report, and do not have the field names and tables memorized.

To print the Relationships window:

1. Click **File** on the menu bar, and then click **Print Relationships**.

Access 2000 creates a report with a picture of your Relationships window. Each field list is expanded to show all of the fields for each table. The report also contains the filename for the database and the current date.

2. Click the **Print** button 🖶 on the Print Preview toolbar, close the report, and then click **No** when prompted to save the changes to Report1.

Access returns to the Relationships window.

You can move the field lists within the Relationships window by dragging their title bars, and you can resize the field lists to make the relationships easier to read.

3. Drag the bottom edge of the **Products** table down so that all of the fields are visible within this field list, close the Relationships window, and then click **Yes** when prompted to save the changes to the layout of Relationships.

Relationship Types

The majority of all table relationships are "one-to-many," but the "one-to-one" and "many-to-many" relationships deserve to be mentioned as well. You may run into these relationships in someone else's database or need to use them when designing your own database from scratch. Relationship types are summarized in Figure 2-20.

Figure 2-20	RELATIONSHIP TYPES		
RELATIONSHIP	**DESCRIPTION**	**EXAMPLE**	**CONSIDERATIONS**
One-to-One	A record in Table X has no more than one matching record in Table Y.	A supplier may have no more than one set of survey results. So a Supplier table may have a one-to-one relationship with a Survey table.	One-to-one relationships are not common because all fields related in this way could be stored in one table. Sometimes, however, this relationship is used to separate rarely used fields from a table or to improve the overall performance of the database by splitting up a table with an extremely large number of fields into two tables.
One-to-Many	A single record in Table X has many records in Table Y.	One category can be referenced by several products, one purchase order can order several products, and one supplier can receive several purchase orders.	This is the most common type of relationship.
Many-to-Many	A record in Table X has many records in Table Y, and a record in Table Y has many records in Table X.	One product can be ordered several times. One purchase order can order several products. (In the AMToys database, the Inventory Transactions table serves as the junction table between the Products and the Purchase Orders tables.)	It is impossible to directly create many-to-many relationships in Access. Instead, a third table, called a **junction table**, must be established between the original tables. The junction table contains foreign key fields that link to the primary key fields of each of the original tables, and thus establishes separate one-to-many relationships with them, with the junction table serving as the "many" side of each relationship.

Session 2.1 QUICK CHECK

1. Use the words field, record, table, and database in one sentence that describes the relationship of each to the others.

2. What are the seven Access objects and what is the major purpose of each?

3. What is the most important Access object and why?

4. Data can be edited through which of the Access objects?

5. Where do you create new field names?

6. What does a field's data type determine?

7. What data types are available and what is the purpose of each?

8. What are field properties?

9. What is the role of the primary key field and the foreign key field in a one-to-many relationship?

10. Explain the relationship between the Categories and Products table in the AMToys-2 database by identifying the relationship type, the primary key field, and the foreign key field.

SESSION 2.2

In this session you will explore the query object's capabilities within the Aaron Michael Toys database.

Queries

Queries represent a subset of fields and records from one or more tables. They are not a duplication of data, but rather, a logical view of data. All physical data is stored in tables in an Access database, so queries can be created and deleted without destroying any data. The primary purpose of a query is to collect a subset of data to answer a particular question. For example, you might want to show all of the toys that are within the "Kit" category, or all of the orders placed since a certain date. If your question is asked on a regular basis, you would save the query object and **run** it (open it) whenever you needed the information. A query will always display the most updated view of the data you have requested.

To explore queries:

1. If Access is not already running, start Access, and then open the **AMToys-2** database from the Tutorial\Solutions folder for Tutorial 2.

2. Click the **Queries button** on the Objects Bar.

   Currently, the AMToys-2 database contains one query object called Product OnHand. You can use the options in the database window to create a new query object in Design view from scratch, or you can use a wizard. Queries are used to combine a subset of fields and records from one or more tables into a single **recordset**. When you open a query, the recordset is presented as a datasheet.

3. Double-click the **Product OnHand** query object to open the Product OnHand query datasheet, and then maximize it as shown in Figure 2-21.

Figure 2-21 **PRODUCT ONHAND QUERY**

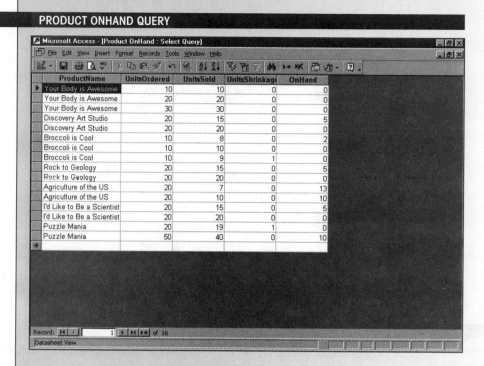

This query pulled 16 records from the database and presents the Product Name field from the Products table, and the UnitsOrdered, UnitsSold, and UnitsShrinkage fields from the Inventory Transactions table. Behind the scenes, a query actually creates **SQL** (structured query language) that is used to gather the data requested from the specified tables.

Even though data is physically stored in a table object, it can be entered or edited using a query object.

4. Click to the right of **US** in any one of the **Agriculture of the US** ProductName fields (the first field value in record 11 or 12), type **A**, and then click another record.

Moving from record to record automatically saves the data you entered or edited in the previous record. The ProductName value for this product is physically stored only once in the Products table, but logically it appears twice in this query, since there were two Inventory Transactions for this product. Changing either occurrence of that field value to "Agriculture of the USA" changes both occurrences of this data simultaneously.

Since you can enter and edit data in a query datasheet just as you can in a table datasheet, it is easy to mistake a query's datasheet for a duplicate copy of the data. Remember, the only object that contains the actual data is the table object. Queries merely represent new ways to display and edit the data stored in underlying tables.

The most common type of query is called a **select query** because it selects fields and records to display in a datasheet. The other types of queries include the **crosstab query**, which provides a pivot table arrangement of data, and four **action queries** that are used to update or change data. The action queries are the **make-table query**, **append query**, **delete query**, and **update query**.

Because a query can show fields from more than one table in a single datasheet, and because those tables have one-to-many relationships with one another, you will often see the same field value appear twice in a query's datasheet even though it is physically stored only once. It is easier to understand this powerful object when you examine query Design view.

Query Design View

The Design view of a query object is where you describe what fields and records you want to display in the resulting datasheet. Using a query, fields may be collected from one or more tables into a single datasheet, sort orders can be saved, and limiting criteria can be entered so a subset of records is displayed in the datasheet.

To explore the query Design view:

1. Click the **Design View** button ⊠ on the Query Datasheet toolbar. The Design view of the Products OnHand select query opens as shown in Figure 2-22.

Figure 2-22	THE DESIGN VIEW OF A QUERY

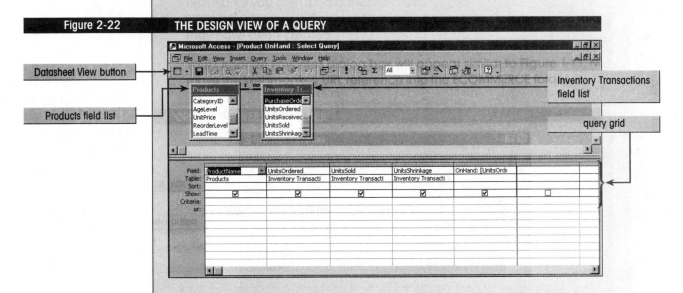

The View button on the toolbar changes so that you can easily move between the two views of an object. When viewing a query's datasheet, the View button appears as the Design View button. When viewing a query's Design view, the View button appears as the Datasheet View button.

The Query Design view is divided into an upper section, which displays field lists, and a lower section, the query grid. The **query grid** displays the fields that will appear in the resulting datasheet. To add a field to the query grid, you can drag it from its field list to the desired query grid column or you can double-click it to place it in the next free column.

2. Drag the **TransactionDate** field from the Inventory Transaction field list to the **second column** in the query grid as shown in Figure 2-23.

TROUBLE? If you don't see TransactionDate in the field list, you may have to scroll through or resize the Inventory Transaction field list to find it. TransactionDate is the second field from the top of the list.

| Figure 2-23 | ADDING A FIELD TO THE QUERY GRID |

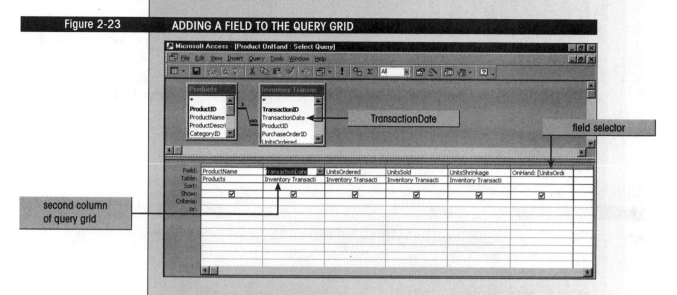

If you add a field to the query grid, the existing fields move to the right to make room for the new addition. You can delete fields by clicking the **field selector** in the query grid, then pressing the Delete key. You can move fields in the query grid by clicking the field selector, then dragging the fields left or right in the grid.

3. Click the **field selector** for the OnHand field (it is the last one in the grid).

   The OnHand column is selected.

4. Drag the **OnHand** field selector to the left until it is positioned as the third field, between the TransactionDate and the UnitsOrdered fields.

   TROUBLE? Once you click the field selector to select a field, you must release the mouse button, then point, click, and drag the field selector to move the field. If you fail to release the mouse button after selecting the field, the drag motion will simply select more fields rather than move the first one that is selected.

5. Click the **Datasheet View** button 📖 on the Query Design toolbar.

   Now it's a little more obvious why the "Your Body is Awesome" ProductName appears three times on this datasheet. Each record represents an inventory transaction for a different date for that product.

Sorting

You can sort the records of a query on one field by using the Sort Ascending button 🔼 or Sort Descending button 🔽 on the Query Datasheet toolbar. To use these buttons, first click any value in the field by which you want to sort, then click the desired sort button. If you want to use more than one sort order you have to enter the sort criteria for the query in Design view.

To sort a query:

1. Click any entry in the **ProductName** field, and then click the **Sort Ascending** button on the Query Datasheet toolbar.

   The records are sorted in ascending order based on the values of the ProductName field. Since there are several records with the same ProductName, however, you would like to specify a secondary sort.

2. Click the **Design View** button on the Query Datasheet toolbar, click the **Sort cell** for the ProductName field, click the **Sort cell** list arrow, click **Ascending**, click the **Sort cell** list arrow for the TransactionDate field, and then click **Ascending** as shown in Figure 2-24.

   TROUBLE? The Sort cell list arrow does not appear unless you click in the Sort cell first.

| Figure 2-24 | SPECIFYING SORT ORDERS IN QUERY DESIGN VIEW |

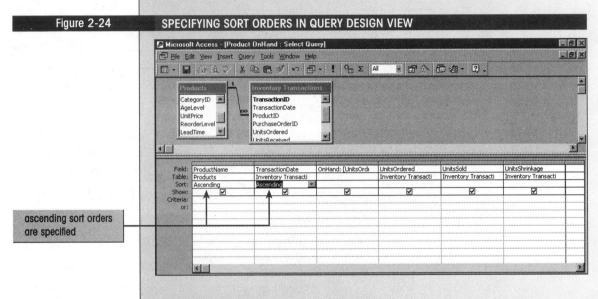

ascending sort orders are specified

Sort orders are evaluated in a left-to-right order when specified in Query Design view.

3. Click the **Datasheet View** button on the Query Design toolbar.

   The records are now listed in alphabetical order by ProductName. Records with the same ProductName value are further sorted by the TransactionDate. The last sort order you apply to the query is saved with the query object.

Criteria

You can limit the number of records that appear on the resulting datasheet to a certain subset by adding **criteria** to Query Design view. Criteria determine which records will appear on the datasheet and are entered in the Criteria and subsequent "or" rows of the grid. The data type of the field for which you are entering the criteria as well as the comparison operator (e.g., greater than, less than, equal to) determine the syntax of the entry. Fortunately, Access 2000 provides much assistance in this area.

To enter limiting criteria into a query:

1. Click the **Design View** button 🔲 on the Query Datasheet toolbar, click the **Criteria** cell for the OnHand field, and then type **>0** as shown in Figure 2-25.

Figure 2-25

| Figure 2-25 | ENTERING CRITERIA IN QUERY DESIGN VIEW |

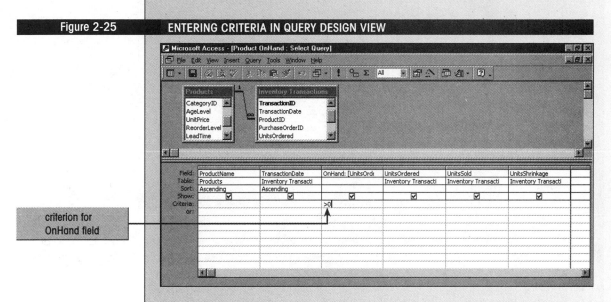

criterion for OnHand field

Aaron Michael Toys orders most of its products for immediate delivery and keeps very little inventory on hand. This criterion will determine what products they currently have in local storage.

2. Click the **Datasheet View** button 🔲 on the Query Design toolbar.

Only seven records now appear in the datasheet, each with an OnHand field value greater than zero. Criteria can be entered for more than one field. In this case, you want to find which products in the Art category are in local storage.

3. Click the **Design View** button 🔲 on the Query Datasheet toolbar.

To find just those products in the Art category, you'll need to add criteria for the Category field to the query grid. The Products table contains the CategoryID field, but you are not familiar with the field entries in that field. You need to add the Category table to this query so that you can use the CategoryName field that contains descriptive text such as "Art" and "Books."

4. Click the **Show Table** button 🔲 on the Query Design toolbar to open the Show Table dialog box.

5. Click **Categories** if it is not already selected, click the **Add** button, and then click the **Close** button to close the Show Table dialog box.

The Categories table is added to the Query Design view. You can drag the title bars of the field lists to better organize them.

6. Drag the title bar of the **Inventory Transactions** field list to the right, drag the title bar of the **Products** field list to the middle, and drag the field list of the **Categories** table to the left to better arrange them as shown in Figure 2-26.

| Figure 2-26 | REARRANGING FIELD LISTS IN QUERY DESIGN VIEW |

Show Table button

drag the title bar to move the field list

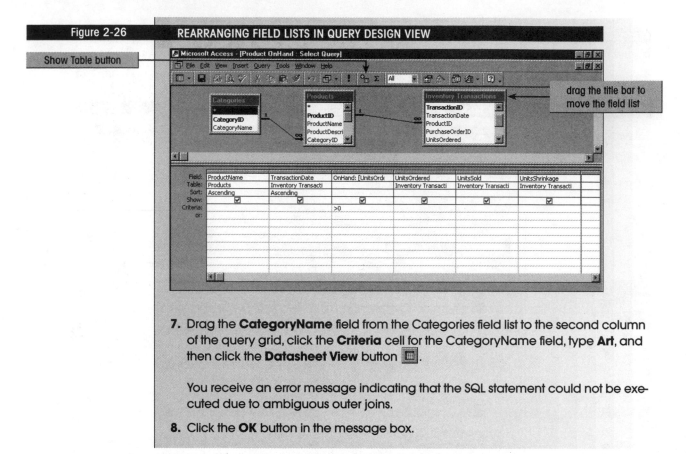

7. Drag the **CategoryName** field from the Categories field list to the second column of the query grid, click the **Criteria** cell for the CategoryName field, type **Art**, and then click the **Datasheet View** button ⊞.

   You receive an error message indicating that the SQL statement could not be executed due to ambiguous outer joins.

8. Click the **OK** button in the message box.

The query couldn't run because of the special join property between the Categories and Products tables defined in the Relationships window. As you recall, the special join property between the Categories and Products tables indicates that *all* records from the Categories table should appear in the resulting datasheet. This join property conflicts with the criterion in your query, which specifies that only *Art* records should appear. Fortunately, you can modify the join properties between two tables for a single query.

To modify the join properties for a query:

1. Double-click the **link line** between the Categories and Products tables to open the Join Properties dialog box.

   TROUBLE? If the Query Properties dialog box opens rather than the Join Properties dialog box, close it, point directly at the link line, then double-click again.

2. Click the option **1** option button to change the join property so that only those records in which fields from both tables are equal will appear, click the **OK** button, and then click the **Datasheet View** button ⊞ on the Query Design toolbar.

   The relationship modification affects only this query.

   The two records shown in Figure 2-27 appear on the resulting datasheet. In both cases, "Art" is the category name, and the OnHand values are greater than zero.

| Figure 2-27 | DATASHEET WITH CRITERIA IN ONE ROW |

CategoryName is Art *and* OnHand values are greater than zero

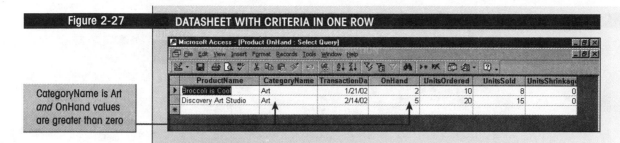

Now compare the effect of using criteria on the *same* line of the query grid with that of putting the criteria on *different* rows of the query grid.

3. Click the **Design View** button 📐, delete **"Art"** in the Criteria cell of the CategoryName field, click the *or* **Criteria** cell for the CategoryName field, and then type **Art** as shown in Figure 2-28.

| Figure 2-28 | USING TWO CRITERIA ROWS |

criterion added to *or* row

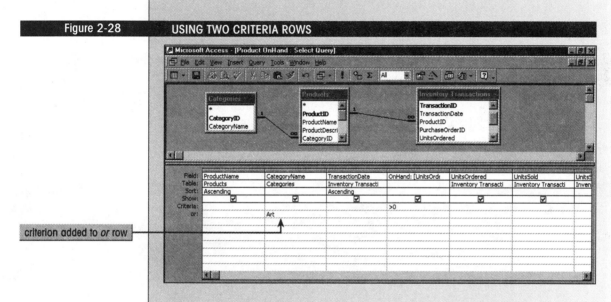

Criteria added to different rows are evaluated in separate processes. Any record that has a CategoryName equal to Art *or* an OnHand value greater than zero will be displayed in the resulting datasheet. When the criteria was on the same row, both criteria were evaluated in the same process, and the record had to have a CategoryName equal to Art *and* an OnHand value greater than zero. For this reason, adding new criteria to *separate* rows *increases* the number of records displayed in the resulting datasheet, because you are adding more opportunities for the record to "match" the criteria. Adding new criteria to the *same* row *decreases* the number of records displayed in the resulting datasheet, because the record must simultaneously match more criteria within one record.

4. Click the **Datasheet View** button 🔲 on the Query Design toolbar.

Ten records are displayed as shown in Figure 2-29. In each case, the CategoryName field is either equal to "Art," or the OnHand value is greater than zero. Both conditions, however, do not need to be true because the criteria was placed on separate rows in the query grid.

Figure 2-29 | DATASHEET FOR CRITERIA ON TWO ROWS

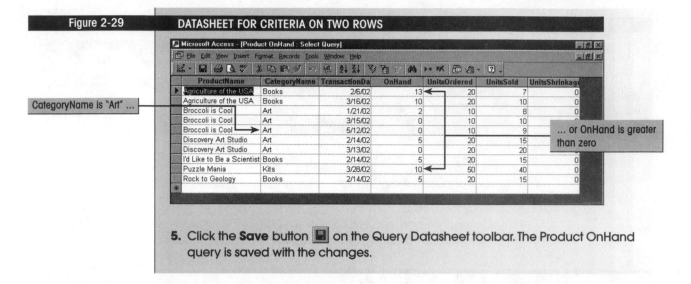

CategoryName is "Art" ...

... or OnHand is greater than zero

5. Click the **Save** button 🖫 on the Query Datasheet toolbar. The Product OnHand query is saved with the changes.

Specifying Criteria: Comparison Operators and Wildcards

You may have noticed that Access 2000 automatically added quotation marks around criteria in fields with a Text data type. Figure 2-30 identifies how criteria are displayed in the query grid for fields of various data types. Fortunately, you do not need to memorize the delimiter characters for each data type. Access 2000 will automatically help you with criteria syntax as soon as you finish entering the criteria or attempt to display the resulting datasheet.

Figure 2-30 | QUERY GRID CRITERIA ENTRIES FOR DIFFERENT DATA TYPES

DATA TYPE	CRITERIA ENTERED BY THE USER	DELIMITING CHARACTER	FINAL SYNTAX
Text	Art	"Quotation Marks"	"Art"
Date/Time	1/1/02	#Pound Signs#	#1/1/02#
Yes/No	Yes	(NA)	Yes
Number	5	(NA)	5
Currency	100	(NA)	100
AutoNumber	10	(NA)	10

If criteria are entered without a **comparison operator**, Access assumes that you want the records to be equal to the criteria. Therefore, you never need to type the equal sign (=) in a criteria entry. If you want the criteria to be compared to the value in the field in any other way, however, you must enter the comparison operators shown in Figure 2-31 into the criteria entry.

Figure 2-31	COMPARISON OPERATORS USED IN QUERY CRITERIA		
COMPARISON OPERATOR	**DESCRIPTION**	**EXAMPLE**	**RESULT**
>	Greater than	>50	Value exceeds 50
>=	Greater than or equal to	>=50	Value is 50 or greater
<	Less than	<50	Value is less than 50
<=	Less than or equal to	<=50	Value is 50 or less than 50
<>	Not equal to	<>50	Value is any number other than 50
Between...And	Finds values inclusive and between two numbers or dates	Between #2/2/95# And #2/2/98#	Dates between 2/2/95 and 2/2/98, including 2/2/95 and 2/2/98
In	Finds a value that is one of a list	In("IA","KS","NE")	Value equals IA or KS or NE
Null	Finds values that are blank	Null	No value has been entered
Is Not Null	Finds values that are not blank	Is Not Null	Any value has been entered
Like	Finds values that match the criteria	Like "*A"	Value equals all text that ends in the letter A
Not	Finds values that do not match the criteria	Not "2"	Numbers other than 2

In addition to using comparison operators, you may wish to use a **wildcard** to further expand the capabilities of your criteria. The asterisk (*) is the most common wildcard character and is used to represent any number of characters. The criteria 1/*/02 in a date field, for example, would find all records with a date in the month of January for the year 2002. The criteria A* in a text field would find all entries that start with the letter A. The ? question mark character is used to match any single alphanumeric character.

Calculated Fields

You may have noticed that the OnHand field in the Product OnHand query is a **calculated field**. It was created using the following expression: [UnitsOrdered]-[UnitsSold]-[UnitsShrinkage]. An **expression** is a combination of fields, values, functions, and mathematical operators that calculates a single value. Mathematical operators that you can use in an Access expression are shown in Figure 2-32.

Figure 2-32	MATHEMATICAL OPERATORS
OPERATOR	**DESCRIPTION**
+	Addition
-	Subtraction
*	Multiplication
/	Division
^	Exponentiation

When a field is referenced in an expression, the field name is surrounded by [square brackets]. In order to maximize productivity and eliminate errors, data that can be calculated should never be defined as a field in a table and entered manually. Rather, use the power of Access to create an expression that automatically generates this data for you. To create a calculated field in Access, enter the new field name, a colon (:), and the expression that calculates the new value, in the Field name cell of the query grid.

To evaluate a calculated field in a query:

1. Click the **Design View** button 🖾, right-click the **OnHand** field in the query grid, click **Zoom**, and then click the **Zoom window** to deselect the entry. The Zoom dialog box for that field appears as shown in Figure 2-33.

| Figure 2-33 | ZOOM DIALOG BOX |

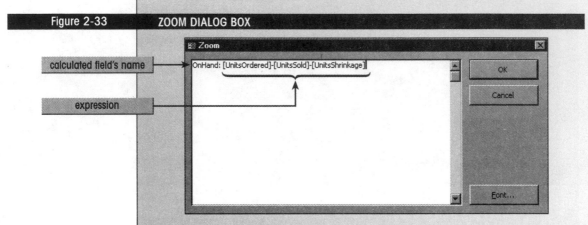

calculated field's name

expression

The Zoom dialog box gives you a much larger area to work with than the Field Name cell in the query grid.

2. Click the **OK** button, and then click the **Datasheet View** button 🎛 on the Query Design toolbar.

   A calculated field creates a new value for each record. In this case, the OnHand field is calculated by subtracting the values of the UnitsSold and UnitsShrinkage fields from the UnitsOrdered field.

3. Double-click the **0** value record in the **UnitsShrinkage** field for 2/6/02 Agriculture of the USA, type **5**, and then click another record.

   Changing the data in any field that is referenced in an expression automatically updates the calculated field. In this case, the OnHand value for the record changed to 8.

4. Click the **Undo** button 🔄 on the Query Datasheet toolbar to undo the change to the UnitsShrinkage field.

   The Undo button undoes only your last action in Access 2000.

Aggregate Calculations

Sometimes you want to create a calculation based on the values of *several* records rather than create a new calculated field for *each* record. A calculation created by using the field values of several records is called an **aggregate calculation**. To accomplish this, you use an **aggregate function**, as defined in Figure 2-34, that determines how the values will be totaled.

Figure 2-34	AGGREGATE FUNCTIONS

AGGREGATE FUNCTION	USED TO FIND THE:
Sum	Total of values in a field
Avg	Average of values in a field
Min	Minimum value in the field
Max	Maximum value in the field
Count	Number of values in a field (not counting null values)
StDev	Standard deviation of values in a field
Var	Variance of values in a field
First	Field value from the first record in a table or query
Last	Field value from the last record in a table or query

In Query Design view, you specify aggregate functions by using the Total row of the query grid. For example, you may want to see a summed value for the OnHand, UnitsOrdered, UnitsSold, and UnitsShrinkage fields for each category of toy in the database.

To build an aggregate calculation:

1. Click the **Design View** button 🔲 on the Query Datasheet toolbar, then click the **Totals** button Σ on the Query Design toolbar.

   The Total row appears in the query grid just above the Sort row. You specify the aggregate function in the Total row. The default value in the Total row for each field is Group By. The **Group By** value specifies which field values will be grouped to develop the aggregate totals. In this case, you want to group the records by CategoryName, and sum the quantity fields. You don't need the ProductName or TransactionDate fields, so you'll delete them from the query grid.

2. Click the **field selector** for the ProductName field, press the **Delete** key, click the **field selector** for the TransactionDate field, and then press the **Delete** key.

   You do not want to specify any limiting criteria.

3. Delete the **"Art"** criteria for the CategoryName field, and then delete the **>0** criteria for the OnHand field.

   Now that you have the fields you need and the unwanted criteria have been deleted, you are ready to choose the Sum aggregate function for the quantity fields.

4. Click the **Group By list arrow** for the OnHand field, and then click **Sum**.

   TROUBLE? The Group By list arrow does not appear unless you click the Group By cell.

5. Click the **Group By list arrow** for the UnitsOrdered field, click **Sum**, click the **Group By list arrow** for the UnitsSold field, click **Sum**, click the **Group By list arrow** for the UnitsShrinkage field, and then click **Sum** as shown in Figure 2-35.

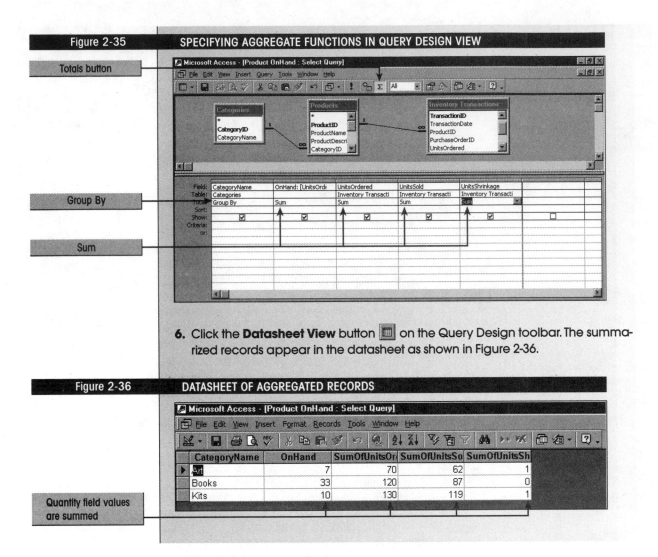

Figure 2-35 — SPECIFYING AGGREGATE FUNCTIONS IN QUERY DESIGN VIEW

Totals button

Group By

Sum

6. Click the **Datasheet View** button 🔲 on the Query Design toolbar. The summarized records appear in the datasheet as shown in Figure 2-36.

Figure 2-36 — DATASHEET OF AGGREGATED RECORDS

CategoryName	OnHand	SumOfUnitsOr	SumOfUnitsSo	SumOfUnitsSh
Art	7	70	62	1
Books	33	120	87	0
Kits	10	130	119	1

Quantity field values are summed

Since there are only three CategoryNames in the AMToys-2 database, there are three records displayed on the datasheet—one for each grouped category. The other values in the datasheet represent summarized values of all of the records within each category. Sometimes it is nice to see not only a total value for a category, but also a count of records that are within that category. You can easily add a Count aggregate function to this datasheet using Query Design view.

To add a Count aggregate function:

1. Click the **Design View** button 🔲 on the Query Datasheet toolbar, and then drag the **CategoryName** field from the Categories field list to the second column of the query grid.

A field name can be used multiple times in the query grid. In this case you want both to group the records by CategoryName and to count the records within each CategoryName.

2. Click the **Group By list arrow** for the CategoryName field in the second column, and then click **Count**.

3. Click the **Datasheet View** button 🔲 on the Query Design toolbar to view the resulting datasheet as shown in Figure 2-37.

| Figure 2-37 | **UPDATED DATASHEET OF AGGREGATE RECORDS** |

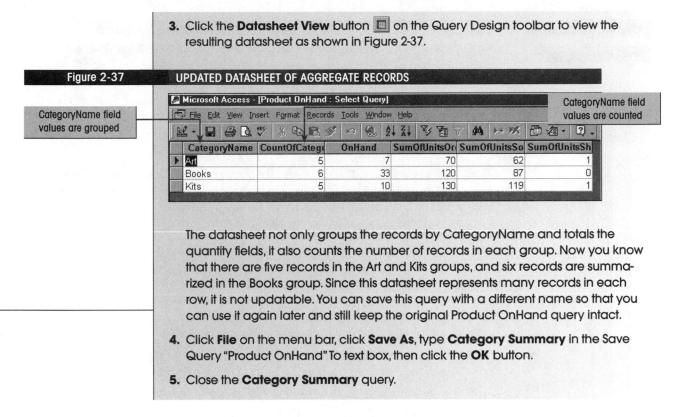

CategoryName field values are grouped

CategoryName field values are counted

The datasheet not only groups the records by CategoryName and totals the quantity fields, it also counts the number of records in each group. Now you know that there are five records in the Art and Kits groups, and six records are summarized in the Books group. Since this datasheet represents many records in each row, it is not updatable. You can save this query with a different name so that you can use it again later and still keep the original Product OnHand query intact.

4. Click **File** on the menu bar, click **Save As**, type **Category Summary** in the Save Query "Product OnHand" To text box, then click the **OK** button.

5. Close the **Category Summary** query.

The AMToys-2 database now has two query objects in the database window.

SQL (Structured Query Language)

As you know, a query object doesn't contain any real data. A query object is simply a set of instructions that collects certain fields and records from one or more tables, and displays them in a single datasheet. The set of instructions you actually create by designing your query in Query Design view uses a special programming language called SQL (structured query language). **SQL** is a *de facto* (by fact, not by law) standard database programming language. In other words, SQL has become the programmers' language of choice for extracting data from a relational database. Today's relational database programs must be written so that SQL programming code can extract the data, or they won't have much of a chance of gaining any market credibility. Access was developed so that you do not have to be an SQL programmer to extract data. The Query Design view, in fact, is simply a **GUI** (graphical user interface) screen that allows you to build SQL code without knowing all of the rules of SQL. You can view the SQL code you create in any query.

To view the SQL code created by a query object:

1. Double-click the **Product OnHand** query to open its datasheet.

2. Click the **View button list arrow** 🔲, and then click **SQL View**. The SQL window opens, displaying the SQL code as shown in Figure 2-38.

Figure 2-38	SQL VIEW

View button list arrow

SQL code

```
SELECT Products.ProductName, [Inventory Transactions].TransactionDate, [UnitsOrdered]-[UnitsSold]-[UnitsShrinkage] AS OnHand, [Inventory
Transactions].UnitsOrdered, [Inventory Transactions].UnitsSold, [Inventory Transactions].UnitsShrinkage
FROM Products INNER JOIN [Inventory Transactions] ON Products.ProductID = [Inventory Transactions].ProductID
ORDER BY Products.ProductName, [Inventory Transactions].TransactionDate;
```

SQL Code starts with the SELECT statement and ends with a semicolon (;). Even if you have never seen SQL before, you will recognize other parts of the instructions such as table names and field names.

3. Close the SQL window.

Query Tips

Once the database is designed, the tables are built, and the data is entered, queries become the focal point of your database efforts. In summary, queries are used to:

- Select a subset of fields and records from one or more tables to view as a datasheet or upon which to build a form, page, or report
- Modify and change data through action queries
- Create calculated fields of data for each record
- Create aggregated calculations across groups of records

The following list clarifies some of the most common misunderstandings about queries:

- Query objects create SQL code that selects data from underlying tables. Queries themselves do not store any data.
- Every time you open a query, you are viewing the most up-to-date data in the database.
- You enter criteria to limit the number of records in the resulting datasheet. The row in which you enter criteria is significant. Criteria in the same query grid row are evaluated in one process (sometimes called an *And* query). Criteria in different rows are evaluated in separate processes (sometimes called an *Or* query), resulting in more records being displayed in the datasheet, since a record must be "true" for only one row in the query grid.
- If you do not precede query criteria with a comparison operator, an equal sign (=) is assumed.
- The datasheets of most queries can be used to enter and edit data. When you enter or edit data in a query datasheet, every other table, form, page, and report object in the database automatically displays the update as well.
- Some datasheets are not updatable, such as the datasheet of a query in which an aggregate function is used or the datasheet of a crosstab query. In those datasheets, every row represents more than one underlying record.
- You can create calculated fields in queries to create a new field of data for each record. You can also create an aggregate calculation in a query that calculates a statistic for a group of records.

■ Action queries change data in a batch update process. You change a select query into an update query by choosing the appropriate action query using the Query Type list arrow ▣ ▾ in Query Design view. The update does not occur, however, until you click the Run button ❗ .

■ In Query Design view, the field lists are related in the same way that the relationships were previously defined between tables in the Relationships window. You can change a relationship between two tables within a query by double-clicking the link line and making the appropriate change in the Edit Relationships dialog box. If you change a relationship in the Query Design view, the change is only applied to that query.

Session 2.2 QUICK CHECK

1. What is the purpose of the query object?

2. What character is used as a delimiter for text criteria in the query grid? For date criteria?

3. What comparison operators can you use with query criteria? Describe each.

4. What is the benefit of creating a calculated field in a query?

5. What is the difference between calculated fields and aggregate calculations?

6. Describe the aggregate functions available in the Query Design view.

7. What is SQL, and why is it important?

8. How do you view SQL code?

SESSION 2.3

In this session you will explore the form and report objects within the Aaron Michael Toys database.

Forms

The form object is the primary tool used to enter and edit data in an existing database. The form object contains no data itself, but rather acts as a formatted "window" by which a user can view, enter, and update data that is stored in underlying tables. A form can be based on the fields and records of a single table, or more commonly, it is based on a query that collects a subset of fields and records from multiple tables for a specific data entry purpose.

Since fields can be placed on a form in almost any arrangement, forms can be designed to look like actual documents used in your business. Forms can also contain GUI elements, such as command buttons, list boxes, option buttons, and check boxes, that facilitate fast and accurate data entry. Any data that is entered or updated through a form is, of course, stored in the appropriate table object. **Form view** is used to enter and update the data in the underlying tables. **Form Design view** is used to modify the structure or formatting of the form object.

To explore forms:

1. Click the **Forms** button 🗐 on the Objects Bar.

   Currently, the AMToys-2 database contains five forms.

2. Double-click the **Products** form. It opens in Form View as shown in Figure 2-39.

Figure 2-39	PRODUCTS FORM

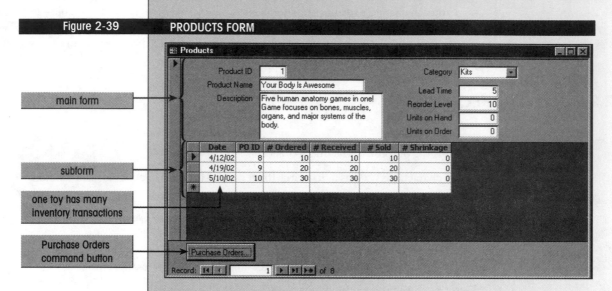

The Form view of the Products form displays data for one toy in the upper portion, and the inventory transactions for that toy as a datasheet in the lower portion. This is a common arrangement of records with a one-to-many relationship (one toy has many inventory transactions). The fields on the "one" side of the relationship create the **main form**. The fields in the datasheet that constitute the "many" side of the relationship are called the **subform**.

3. Click the **Purchase Orders** command button in the lower-left corner to open the Purchase Orders form as shown in Figure 2-40.

Figure 2-40	PURCHASE ORDERS FORM

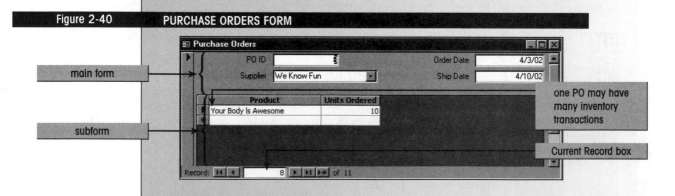

Command buttons are buttons used on a form to initiate common actions such as closing the form, printing the current record, or in this case, opening another form. The Purchase Orders form opened to the eighth record, the first in which the "Your Body Is Awesome" toy was ordered.

4. Click the **Next record** button ▶ in the Purchase Orders form twice. You moved through the three purchase orders in which the "Your Body Is Awesome" toy was ordered from the supplier, We Know Fun. .

5. Select **10** in the Current Record box on the Purchase Orders form, type **3**, and then press the **Enter** key. You navigate to the third record in the Purchase Orders form.

   This purchase order is from the supplier, KidSense, and three products were ordered. The ship date was incorrectly entered for this PO, so you'll edit the value in the form.

6. Double-click **12** within 2/12/02 to select the day in the ShipDate field, type **11** as the new day value, press the **Page Down** key to move to the fourth purchase order record, then press the **Page Up** key to move back to the third purchase order record.

   TROUBLE? If your computer formats the date as 2/12/2002, you may have to enter 02 as the year. In this case the input mask (2 digit year) is different from the format property (4 digit year).

   Edits and entries to data made through a form are stored in underlying table objects. The form is simply a tool used to present data in a certain format and arrangement.

7. Close the Purchase Orders form, and then close the Products form.

Form Design View

The **Design view** of a form is where you make structural and formatting changes to the form object itself. Each item on the form is called a **control**. A control may be bound, unbound, or calculated. **Bound controls** are used to display actual data from a field of the underlying record source. Common bound controls include the text box, combo box, list box, and check box. The entry displayed by the bound control will change as you move from record to record. **Unbound controls** exist only to clarify or enhance the appearance of the form. Common unbound controls are labels, lines, tabs, and clip art. Unbound controls do not change as you move through different records in a form. **Calculated controls** are actually text boxes that contain expressions such as page numbers, dates, or other calculated values based on data from other controls. Figure 2-41 shows many types of controls on a sample form.

Figure 2-41	A FORM WITH MANY DIFFERENT TYPES OF CONTROLS

You will see many different mouse pointers in Form Design view. The shape of each mouse pointer gives you information about what will happen if you click or drag that pointer. Form Design view mouse pointers are summarized in Figure 2-42.

Figure 2-42	FORM DESIGN VIEW MOUSE POINTERS

MOUSE POINTER SYMBOL	MOUSE POINTER NAME	DISPLAYED WHEN YOU POINT TO:	DESCRIPTION
⬉	Arrow	Any control that isn't currently selected	Click a control with this mouse pointer to select it. Click away from a selected control with this mouse pointer to deselect it.
↔	Horizontal resizing	A middle sizing handle on the left or right side of the selected control	Drag this mouse pointer to narrow or widen a control.
↕	Vertical resizing	A middle sizing handle on the top or bottom side of the selected control	Drag this mouse pointer to make a control taller or shorter.
⬊ and ⬈	Diagonal resizing	A corner sizing handle on a selected control	Drag this mouse pointer to change both the width and height of a control at the same time for proportional resizing.
✋	Move selected controls	The edge of a selected control (between sizing handles)	Drag this mouse pointer to move all selected controls.
☝	Move single control	The large sizing handle in the upper-left corner of a selected control	Drag this mouse pointer to move only a single control, even if several are selected.
↓	Down selection arrow	The horizontal ruler at the top of the form	Click or click and drag this mouse pointer across the horizontal ruler to select all controls that touch the selection line.
→	Right selection arrow	The vertical ruler at the left side of the form	Click or click and drag this mouse pointer up and down the vertical ruler to select all controls that touch the selection line.

To explore the Design view of a form:

1. Double-click the **Suppliers** form, and then maximize the form in Form view.

   The Suppliers form currently contains only two types of controls, labels in the first column and text boxes in the second column. Labels are the most common type of unbound control, and text boxes the most common bound control.

2. Press the **Page Down** key three times to move through the records.

   Notice that the labels are unbound. They do not change as you move from record to record. The information in the text boxes, however, is bound to a field in the Suppliers table and displays data that changes from record to record.

3. Click the **Design View** button 📖 on the Form View toolbar. The Suppliers form appears in Design view as shown in Figure 2-43.

| Figure 2-43 | DESIGN VIEW OF THE SUPPLIERS FORM |

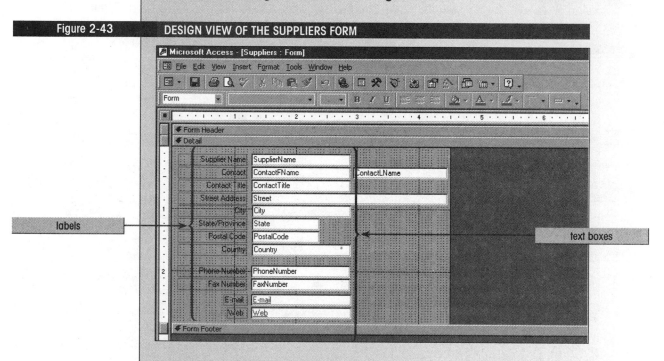

labels

text boxes

The Design view of a form is where you add, delete, move, resize, or format controls as well as modify the properties of the form object. The first step in manipulating a control is selecting it. You select a control with a single click. A selected control will display **sizing handles** that appear as black boxes in the corners and middle edges of the control.

4. Click the **Supplier Name** label.

   Dark gray sizing handles appear on a selected control.

   TROUBLE? Be sure to select the Supplier Name label on the left and not the SupplierName text box on the right.

   In Form Design view, text boxes display the field name to which they are bound. The first text box, therefore, is bound to the SupplierName field, the second to the ContactFName field, and so forth. Once a control is selected, it can be formatted using the Formatting (Form/Report) toolbar.

5. Click the **Font/Fore Color list arrow** ▲ on the Formatting (Form/Report) toolbar.

6. Click the **bright blue square** in the second row, click the **Fill/Back Color list arrow** 🔾 on the Formatting (Form/Report) toolbar, and then click the **bright yellow square** in the fourth row. You can see the formatting applied to the label.

   In addition to formatting controls, you may want to move or resize them.

7. Click the **Street** text box to select it, point to the **middle sizing handle** on the right edge so that your mouse pointer changes to ↔, and then drag to the left so that the Street text box is the same size as those above and below it.

   The Street text box should look as shown in Figure 2-44.

Figure 2-44	FORMATTING AND RESIZING CONTROLS

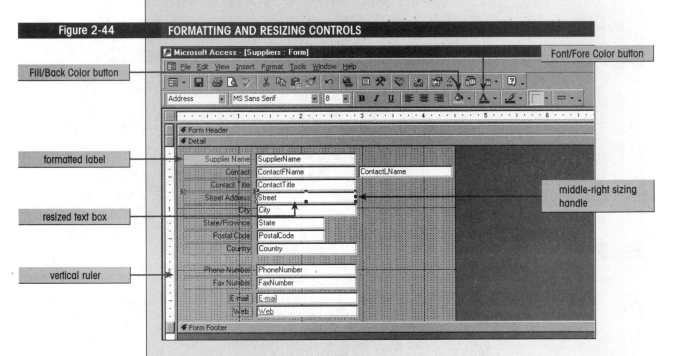

TROUBLE? If you make a mistake, it's very easy to select, move, resize, or otherwise modify the wrong control in a busy screen in Form Design view. Don't forget to use the Undo button 🔄 to correct your last action, if needed.

8. Point to the edges of the **Street** text box to observe the mouse pointers described in Figure 2-42.

9. Drag the mouse pointer from the top to the button in the **vertical ruler**, and then release the mouse button to observe how multiple controls can be selected at the same time.

   You can also select multiple controls by dragging the mouse pointer through the horizontal ruler. Yet another way to select multiple controls at the same time is to click the first one, then hold the Shift key down while clicking subsequent controls.

10. Click outside the edge of the form to deselect all controls.

11. Click the **Save** button 🖫 on the Form Design toolbar to save your changes, and then click the **Form View** button 🖽 to observe the changes.

Controls

You add controls to a form in Form Design view using the buttons on the **Toolbox toolbar**. Figure 2-45 describes controls found on the Toolbox toolbar.

Figure 2-45	SUMMARY OF CONTROLS ON THE TOOLBOX		
NAME OF CONTROL	**TYPE OF CONTROL**	**TOOLBOX TOOLBAR BUTTON**	**HOW IT IS USED ON A FORM**
Label	Unbound	*Aa*	To add descriptive text
Text box	Bound	ab|	To display the contents of a Text, Number, Currency, Memo, or Date/Type field
Option group	Bound		To organize the options available for a field with only a few possible entries such as Gender field
Option button	Bound	⊙	To provide the mutually exclusive choices within an bound option group. For example, Option buttons within an option group bound to a Gender field would provide a male or female field entry.
Toggle button	Bound		To display a "yes" or "no" answer for a Yes/No field in the form of a toggled button
Check box	Bound	✔	To display a "yes" or "no" answer for a Yes/No field in the form of a checked or unchecked box
List box	Bound		To provide a lengthy list of mutually exclusive choices for a field such as a State field. The user clicks the choice for the field from the list.
Combo box	Bound		To provide a control that is a combination of both the text box and list box controls. The combo box provides a list of field entry choices plus the ability for the user to enter a new value for the field from the keyboard. A field such as City that contains a group of common entries that cannot be reduced to a single list is a good choice for a combo box.
Command button	Unbound		A button that, when clicked, initiates a macro or other action
Image	Unbound		To add a clip art image
Unbound object frame	Unbound		To add a sound, movie, spreadsheet, document, or other type of object from another application to a form
Bound object frame	Bound		To display the contents of an OLE field
Tab control	Unbound		To create a three-dimensional aspect to a form so that other controls can be organized and displayed in Form view by clicking the tabs
Subform	Bound		To insert a subform that displays the fields and records on the "many" side of a one-to-many relationship for the recordset on which the form is based. The data in a subform is usually organized as a datasheet.
Line	Unbound	\	To insert a line
Rectangle	Unbound	▭	To insert a rectangle
Page break	Unbound		To force a page break on a printed copy

Unbound Controls

Unbound controls do not change from record to record and exist only to clarify or enhance the appearance of the form.

To add a control to a form:

1. Click the **Design View** button 📝 on the Form View toolbar, and then click the **Toolbox** button 🛠 on the Form Design toolbar to toggle this toolbar on the screen, if it isn't already displayed.

2. Click the **Label** button *Aa* on the Toolbox toolbar, click in the free space to the right of the State text box in the form, type **Supplier Entry Form**, and then click outside the control as shown in Figure 2-46.

Figure 2-46   **ADDING A LABEL TO A FORM**

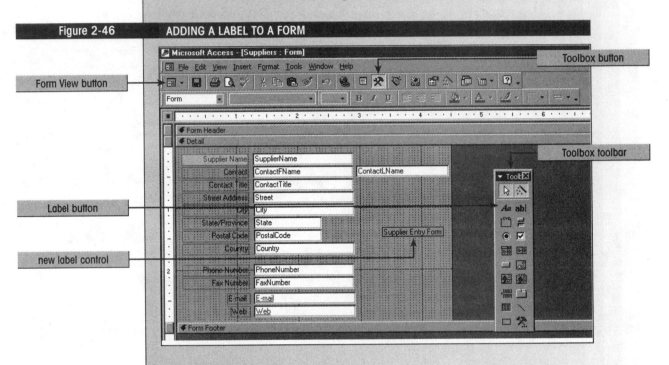

TROUBLE? Don't worry about making your label exactly match Figure 2-46, but if it isn't positioned to your satisfaction, go ahead and practice your skills at moving or resizing the control.

Some controls have wizards associated with them that help guide your actions as you add the control to the form. The Command Button Wizard is particularly helpful. To use the wizards, make sure that the Control Wizards button 🖄 on the Toolbox is selected.

3. Verify that the **Control Wizards** button 🖄 is selected, click the **Command Button** button ⬜ on the Toolbox, and then click to the right of the E-mail text box in the lower-right corner of the form.

The Command Button Wizard appears, and presents a listing of possible actions for your new command button.

4. Click **Record Operations** in the Categories list, click **Print Record** in the Actions list, and then click the **Next** button.

5. Click the **Next** button to accept the default button picture, type **Print This Record** as the name for the button, and then click the **Finish** button.

6. Click the **Save** button 🖫 on the Form Design toolbar, and then click the **Form View** button 🖭 on the Form Design toolbar.

The new label and command button are shown in Figure 2-47.

Figure 2-47 **FORM VIEW OF UPDATED SUPPLIERS FORM**

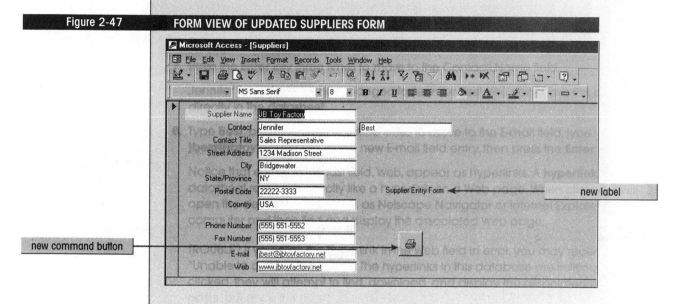

7. Click the **Print** command button that you just created to print the current record.

TROUBLE? Don't click the Print button 🖨 on the Form View toolbar unless you want to print *every* record in the underlying recordset (which is generally a very long printout).

8. Close the Suppliers form.

Both the label and command button controls that you added to this form are unbound. Even though the command button is more exciting because it initiates an action when clicked, neither the label nor the command button have any dynamic connection with the underlying data in the Suppliers table. Neither change as you move from record to record within this form.

Bound Controls

Bound controls, those that display data from an underlying field, are inherently more complex than unbound controls because they are used to display, enter, and update actual data. They change as you move from record to record in a form. In later tutorials you will be working extensively with bound controls on a page object because the page object is used to create corresponding HTML files that can be viewed using browser software. The page object is used to make your database "Web-enabled." Bound and unbound controls work similarly on the form, report, and page objects, however, so there is a great deal of overlap in the skills and knowledge needed for working with these three objects.

Reports

The report is the primary object used to print data from an Access database. You cannot enter data into the database using a report object; it is used strictly for output purposes. A report object can be based on the fields and records of a table, or more commonly, on a query that has collected a subset of fields and records into one object for a specific reporting purpose. Although you can print data from many objects such as the datasheet of a table, the datasheet of a query, or the Form view of a form, the report object gives you many more capabilities by which to tailor the printout. In a report object, for example, you can customize multiple headers and footers, add clip art, and format different sections of the report.

In addition, the report object allows you to group records and create group calculations. **Grouping** means to sort records and create a section on the report that prints before and after the group. It is an extremely powerful reporting feature that is best understood by examining an actual report. The report in Figure 2-48 groups the inventory transaction records by the ProductName field, and provides a total for the ordered, received, sold, and shrinkage fields for each product. Previously, when you viewed these types of aggregate totals through the query object, you were able to view either the grouped totals or the individual records that created the total, but not both at the same time. In a report object, you can see both individual records and summary statistics on a group of records in one printout.

| Figure 2-48 | SAMPLE REPORT |

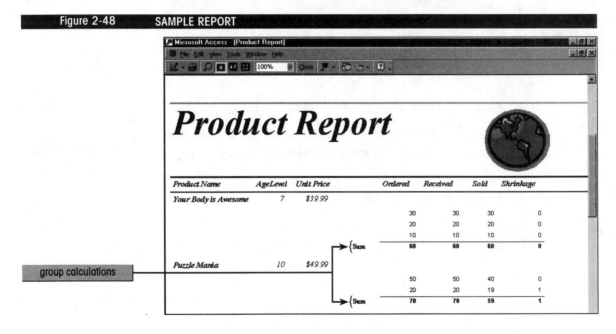

To explore reports:

1. Click the **Reports** button on the Objects bar, and then double-click the **Products On Hand Report** to preview it as shown in Figure 2-49.

Figure 2-49   PRODUCTS ON HAND SUMMARY REPORT

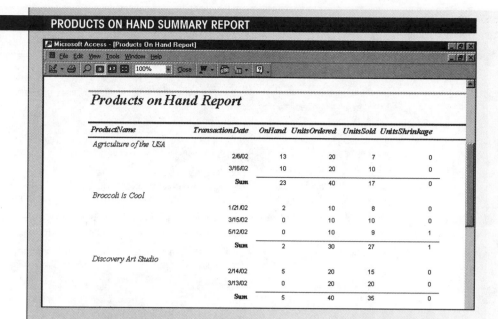

The Products on Hand report groups records by product name and provides on hand, ordered, sold, and shrinkage totals at the end of each group.

TROUBLE? If you want to have your name on the printout, add a Label control with your name to the report in Design view.

TROUBLE? Depending on your printer, you may need to modify the layout to Landscape in order for the report to print as shown. Click File on the menu bar, click Page Setup, click the Page tab, click the Landscape Orientation option button, and then click the OK button in the Page Setup dialog box.

2. Click the **Print** button 🖨 on the Print Preview toolbar.

The report prints. You can see that the report provides totals for the groups. You also can see that the report printed on two pages and needs some modification. These changes are done in Design view.

Sections and Report Design View

Similar to forms, every element on a report is called a control. Bound controls display data from an underlying field, unbound controls, such as labels and lines, are added to improve the report's clarity, and calculated controls are used to total a group of records. Controls are placed in sections. **Sections** are areas of the report that determine where and how often a control will print. The different sections of a report are summarized in Figure 2-50.

Figure 2-50	REPORT SECTIONS		
SECTION NAME	**WHERE DOES THIS SECTION PRINT?**	**HOW OFTEN DOES THIS SECTION PRINT?**	**WHAT TYPES OF CONTROLS ARE GENERALLY PLACED IN THIS SECTION?**
Report header	At the top of the first page	Once for the report	Labels, lines, and other unbound controls
Page header	At the top of each page, but below the report header on the first page	Once at the top of each page of the report	Labels, lines, and other unbound controls
Group header	At the beginning of each group of records	Once for every new group of records	A text box bound to the field by which the records are grouped
Detail	In the middle of the report (or between the group header and group footer sections)	Once for every record in the underlying recordset	Text boxes bound to the fields in the underlying recordset
Group footer	At the end of each group of records	Once for every group of records	Text boxes that contain expressions calculate totals for the preceding group of records
Page footer	At the bottom of each page	Once at the bottom of each page of the report	Labels, lines, and calculated controls that contain the date or page number
Report footer	After the last detail record or group footer section in the report	Once for the report	Text boxes that contain expressions and calculate totals for the entire report

To explore Report Design view:

1. Click the **Design View** button 📖 on the Print Preview toolbar. The report opens in Design view as shown in Figure 2-51.

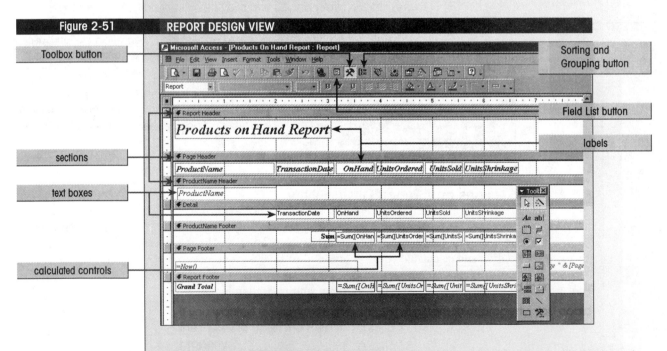

Figure 2-51	REPORT DESIGN VIEW

The sections of the report are identified with gray bands. All of the controls placed under that gray band print according to the rules of that section. There are several buttons on the Report Design toolbar that toggle additional information on and off the screen.

2. Click the **Field List** button 📄 on the Report Design toolbar to toggle the field list on if it is not already visible.

   The **field list** contains all of the fields that are available in the underlying recordset (table or query) for this report. You can drag field names out of the field list to create text box controls bound to that field.

3. Click the **Field List** button 📄 on the Report Design toolbar to toggle it off, click the **Toolbox** button 🔧 on the Report Design toolbar to toggle it off if it is currently visible, and then click the **Sorting and Grouping** button ≣ on the Report Design toolbar.

   The Sorting and Grouping dialog box opens as shown in Figure 2-52.

Figure 2-52   SORTING AND GROUPING DIALOG BOX

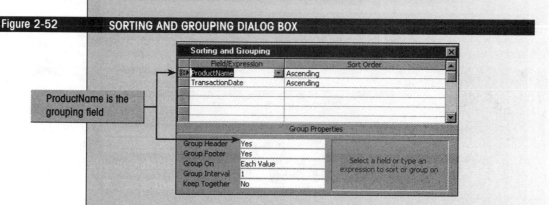

ProductName is the grouping field

The Sorting and Grouping dialog box helps clarify how the records within the report are organized. It shows that the records are first sorted by ProductName. The secondary sort is TransactionDate. The Sorting and Grouping dialog box further shows that the ProductName field is used as a grouping field. The grouping icon is displayed to the left of the field name. The Group Header and Group Footer properties are set to "Yes" in the Group Properties section of the dialog box for the ProductName field.

4. Click the **Sorting and Grouping** button ≣ on the Report Design toolbar to toggle it off.

5. Click the **ProductName** text box in the ProductName header section, and then click the **Properties** button 📄 on the Report Design toolbar.

   The property sheet for the ProductName text box control opens as shown in Figure 2-53.

| Figure 2-53 | PROPERTY SHEET FOR THE PRODUCTNAME TEXT BOX |

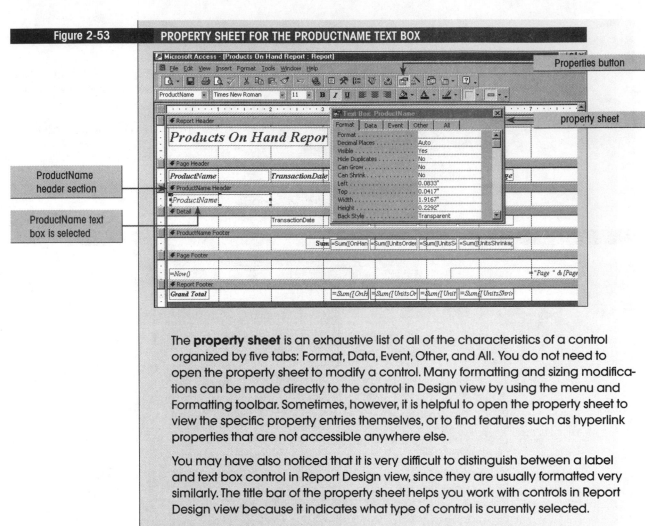

ProductName header section

ProductName text box is selected

The **property sheet** is an exhaustive list of all of the characteristics of a control organized by five tabs: Format, Data, Event, Other, and All. You do not need to open the property sheet to modify a control. Many formatting and sizing modifications can be made directly to the control in Design view by using the menu and Formatting toolbar. Sometimes, however, it is helpful to open the property sheet to view the specific property entries themselves, or to find features such as hyperlink properties that are not accessible anywhere else.

You may have also noticed that it is very difficult to distinguish between a label and text box control in Report Design view, since they are usually formatted very similarly. The title bar of the property sheet helps you work with controls in Report Design view because it indicates what type of control is currently selected.

6. Click the **Data** tab in the property sheet.

The most important property of any bound control is the **Control Source** property. It determines which field will be displayed within the control. This property "binds" the control to the underlying field.

7. Click the **Properties** button 📄 on the Report Design toolbar to toggle off the property sheet.

8. Click the **Print Preview** button 🔍 on the Report Design toolbar, and then practice zooming in and out of the preview screen by clicking in different locations on the report.

9. Close the report and save changes if prompted. Close the database and exit Access.

The better you understand the existing Access 2000 database for Aaron Michael Toys, the easier it will be for you to expand it into a Web-enabled database. Data-driven Web sites do not replace existing databases, but rather build upon them.

Session 2.3 QUICK CHECK

1. Use the words main form, subform, and one-to-many relationship in a sentence that describes their relationship to one another.

2. Distinguish between bound, unbound, and calculated controls.

3. List several common bound and unbound controls.

4. What does grouping records on a report mean?

5. What do sections on a report determine?

6. Identify four buttons on the Report Design toolbar that function as "toggles."

REVIEW ASSIGNMENTS

You work in the business office of a graduate school, Adair Graduate School, that offers several degrees, including a Master of Business Administration (MBA), Master of Telecommunications Management (MTM), and Master of Information Systems Management (MISM). You have developed an Access database called AdairGS-2 to help the faculty track students, classes, assignments, grades, and instructors. You'll use this database to become familiar with Access concepts and the table, query, form, and report objects.

1. Start Access and open the **AdairGS-2** database from the Review\Solutions folder for Tutorial 2.

2. Click the Tables button on the Objects bar, then double-click the Students table to open its datasheet. On a piece of paper, record how many records as well as how many fields are in this table.

3. Open the Students table in Design view, then change the Field Size property for the StateOrProvince field to 2.

4. Save the table and click Yes when prompted that you may lose some data. You won't lose any data because none of the entries in the StateorProvince field are longer than 2.

5. Rename the PostalCode field to **Zip**. Rename the StudentNumber field to **SSN**, and save the table.

Explore 6. Write down why the data type of this field should be Text as opposed to Number, even though a social security field would contain only numeric data.

7. Write down the key field and its data type.

Explore 8. Write down why names should always be entered in at least two fields, which represent the first and last names. Save and then close the Students table.

9. Click the Relationships button on the Database toolbar, write down and describe the relationships the Students table has with any other tables. Be sure to describe the tables involved, the relationship type, the primary key field, and the foreign key field in each relationship.

10. Resize or move the field lists so that all of the field names are visible and all of the relationships are clearly displayed.

11. Click File on the menu bar, then click Print Relationships. Preview the resulting report. If the report is longer than one page, close it without saving changes, move the field lists in the Relationships window so that they are closer together, then create the report again. Once the report fits on one page, click the Design View button, add your name as a label in the right side of the Report Header section, print it, then close it without saving it. You may want to keep this report handy to help you understand the relationships between the tables of the AdairGS databases for the rest of the Review Assignments in this book. If it is still open, close the Relationships window and save the changes.

12. Click the Queries button on the Objects Bar.

Explore 13. Double-click the Create query by using wizard option and then choose the following fields from the following tables below, in the order shown:

   Table: Classes
   Fields: ClassName, ClassDescription, Term, Day, and Time
   Table: Instructors
   Fields: InstructorFName, InstructorLName

14. Click the Next button, then title the query **Instructor Roster**. Click the Finish button.

15. In the resulting datasheet, change Brad Reneau's last name to *your last name*.

16. Sort the datasheet in ascending order based on the ClassName entry, click File on the menu bar, click Page Setup, click the Page tab, and then change the orientation to Landscape. Preview, print, and then save the datasheet. The printout should fit on one page.

17. Close the datasheet, then click the Design button on the Objects toolbar to open the Instructor Roster query in Design view.

18. In the first Criteria cell for the ClassName, enter **TM*** to indicate that you want to view all classes whose name starts with the TM prefix. Click the Datasheet button to view the records. There should be three.

19. Claire Lightfoot has changed her last name to Ankeny. Double-click Lightfoot in either one of Claire's records, type **Ankeny**, then click a different record. Both occurrences of Claire's last name should have been updated, since her last name is actually only stored once in the Instructors table.

20. Click File on the menu bar, then click Save As. Enter **TM Roster** as the new query name, and then click the OK button.

21. Open the Page Setup dialog box, change the page orientation to Landscape, print the datasheet, and close the TM Roster query.

22. Click the Forms button on the Objects Bar, double-click the Create form by using wizard option, then choose the following fields from the following tables below, in the order shown:

   Table: Departments:
   Fields: DepartmentName
   Table: Instructors:
   Fields: InstructorFName, InstructorLName
   Table: Classes:
   Fields: ClassName, ClassDescription

23. Click the Next button; click the Next button again to view the data by Department. Select the Datasheet layout for the subform, click the Next button, select the Standard style and then click the Next button. Accept the default titles, and then click the Finish button to open the form in Form view.

Explore   24. Double-click the small black vertical bars that separate field names in the subform to automatically resize them to fit the widest entry.

25. Navigate to the second record of the main form (Business is the DepartmentName), then change Sara Eidie's last name to **Johnson**.

26. Click the Design View button, and then use the Command Button Wizard to add a command button to the upper-right corner. It should automatically appear when you create a command button if the Control Wizards button is selected on the toolbox. In the Wizard, choose the Print Record action from the Record Operations category. Specify that the text **Print Record** be placed on the button, and give the button the meaningful name of PrintCurrentRecord.

27. Save the form, then click the Form View button. There are five records in the main form. Navigate to the last department (Human Resource Management), change Brad's name to *your first name*, and then click the Print Record command button.

28. Close the form.

Explore   29. Click the Reports button on the Objects Bar, double-click the Create report by using wizard option, and then choose the following fields from the tables below, in the order shown:

Table: Students:
Fields: FirstName, LastName, Major
Table: Classes:
Fields: ClassName, Term, Credits

Be sure to view the data by Students, but do not add any more grouping levels, sort the records in ascending order by ClassName, use a Stepped layout, a Portrait orientation, and a Corporate style. Title the report **Student Roster**.

30. Preview the report, then click the Design View button and add your name as a label to the right side of the Report Header section.

31. Save, preview, print, and then close the report.

32. Close the **AdairGS-2** database.

CASE PROBLEMS

Case 1. Tracking Clients and Projects at Premier Consulting You work for a Web hosting business called Premier Consulting that rents Web server space to small businesses, as well as providing a variety of Web consulting services such as Web page design and creation, Web-enabled database development, and Web programming. You have developed an Access database, called **PremierConsulting-2**, that tracks clients, projects, payments, and employees. You'll use this database to become familiar with Access concepts and the table, query, form, and report objects.

1. Start Access and open the **PremierConsulting-2** database from the Cases\Solutions folder for Tutorial 2.

2. Click the Tables button on the Object bar, double-click Employees to open the datasheet, click the Expand button for Kim Chin, and then click the Expand button for ProjectID. Write down the relationships between the Payments, Projects, and Employees tables, based on your observation of the subdatasheets.

3. Close the **Employees** datasheet.

4. Click the Queries button on the Objects Bar, then double-click Create query in Design view.

5. Double-click Clients, double-click Projects, and double-click Payments, then click Close in the Show Table dialog box.

6. Add the following fields to the query grid in the order shown:

   Table: Clients:
   Field: CompanyName
   Table: Projects
   Field: ProjectName
   Table: Payments
   Field: PaymentDate, PaymentAmount

7. Click the Datasheet View button, enter *Your Name's* Company in the Company Name field for any White Clover Markets record, and print the datasheet. Save and close the query as **Company Payment Activity**.

8. Click the Design View button, click the Totals button in the Design view toolbar, delete the PaymentDate field, change the Group By function to Sum for the PaymentAmount field, and then view the datasheet.

9. Write down why there are two records for both Lazy K Kountry Store and *Your Name's* Company.

10. Click the Design View button, delete the ProjectName field, then display and print the datasheet again.

11. Use the Save As command on the File menu to save the query as **Sum of Payments** and then close the query datasheet.

Explore 12. In Query Design view, create a new query with the following fields in the order shown:

   Table: Employees
   Fields: FirstName, LastName
   Table: Projects
   Fields: ProjectName, ProjectBeginDate, ProjectEndDate

Explore 13. In the first free field cell, create a new calculated field by typing the following expression: **Length: [ProjectEndDate]-[ProjectBeginDate]**. Then view the datasheet.

14. Something is wrong with the first two records, since the length is negative. Change the ProjectEndDate to the year **2003** for records one and two. Change Kim to *your first name*, and print the datasheet.

15. Save the query as **Project Length**, then close it.

16. To help prevent incorrect dates from being recorded in the Project table again, you will create a form to enter the data, and then modify the ProjectEndDate control's properties so that the entry must be greater than the ProjectBeginDate value. Click the Forms button in the Objects bar, and then click the New button in the Objects toolbar.

Explore 17. Click AutoForm: Columnar, choose Projects as the table or query where the object's data comes from, and then click the OK button.

Explore ▶ 18. Click the Design View button, maximize the window, double-click the ProjectEndDate field text box to open its property sheet, click the Data tab, click the Validation Rule property text box, and then type >**[ProjectBeginDate]** to make sure that the end date is at least one day greater than the date in the ProjectBeginDate field.

Explore ▶ 19. Click the Validation Text property text box, and then type **The project end date must be at least one day later than the project begin date**. Close the **Property** Sheet.

20. Save the form, click the OK button when prompted to save the form with the name **Projects**, and then click the Form View button.

Explore ▶ 21. Test the validation rule by typing **5/31/02** in the ProjectEndDate field of the first record, then press the Enter key. Click the OK button when you are prompted with the Validation Rule, then press the Esc key to remove the inappropriate entry in the ProjectEndDate field.

22. Close the **Projects** form.

Explore ▶ 23. Click the Reports button on the Objects Bar, double-click Create report by using wizard, and then choose all of the fields in the Company Payment Activity query. View the data by Clients, sort in ascending order by PaymentDate, click the Summary Options button, and then click the Sum check box to Sum the PaymentAmount field. Use an Outline 2 Layout, a Portrait Orientation, a Casual style, and title the report **Client Activity Report**.

24. View the report in Print Preview mode. Scroll through the report to see all the sections and summary statistics.

25. Click the Design View button.

Explore ▶ 26. In Report Design view, delete the long calculated field that starts with **="Summary for"** in both the ProjectNameFooter and CompanyNameFooter sections.

Explore ▶ 27. Move the remaining controls in the ProjectNameFooter and CompanyNameFooter footers to the top of those sections.

Explore ▶ 28. Double-click the Sum label in the ProjectNameFooter section to open the property sheet. Change the Caption property text on the Format tab to **Sum for Project**. Change the Sum label in the CompanyNameFooter section to **Sum for Company**. Resize the labels as needed to display all the text.

29. Save, preview, print, and then close the report.

30. Click the Relationships button, then use the Print Relationships command on the File menu to create a report from this window.

31. Add a label to the Report Header section of the report with your name in it, then print it. You may want to save this printout for reference in future tutorials.

32. Close but do not save the report, and close the Relationships window.

33. Close the **PremiereConsulting-2** database and exit Access.

Case 2. Tracking Events and Expenditures at Dyslexia Organization You are the director of a charitable organization dedicated to the education of and support services for those who suffer from dyslexia. You have created an Access database called **Dyslexia-2** that currently tracks contributors and pledges. You wish to expand the database to also track events and expenditures. You'll build the tables, relationships, and queries necessary to accomplish this.

1. Start Access and open the **Dyslexia-2** database from the Cases\Solutions folder for Tutorial 2.

2. Click the Relationships button, and then resize the field lists so that you can clearly see all fields and their names within each list. After reviewing the fields in each table, save and then close the Relationships window.

3. In order to track events and expenditures, you'll have to build two more tables. Click the Tables button in the Objects bar, click the New button in the Object toolbar, click Design view in the New Table dialog box, and then click the OK button.

Explore

4. Add the following field names and data types to the Design view of the new table, then save it with the name **Events**. (Use the default properties for each field.)

Field Name	Data Type
EventID (Primary Key Field)	AutoNumber
EventName	Text
EventDate	Date/Time

5. Open the **Events** table in Datasheet view, add the following records, and then print and close the datasheet. Use your own elementary school name in the second record if you wish to uniquely identify your printout.

EventID	EventName	EventDate
1	Blue Valley District Teacher Meeting	9/5/00
2	Oak Hill Elementary School Screening	9/6/00

6. Close the **Events** table, click the New button in the Object toolbar, click Design View in the New Table dialog box, then click the OK button.

Explore

7. Add the following field names, data types, and descriptions to the Design view of the new table, make PaymentID the primary key field, then save it with the name **Payments**. (Use the default properties for each field.)

Field Name	Data Type	Description
PaymentID (Primary Key Field)	AutoNumber	
EventID	Number	Foreign key field
PaymentDate	Date/Time	
PaymentAmount	Currency	
PaymentDescription	Text	
Payee	Text	

8. Open the **Payments** table in Datasheet view, add the following records, and then print and close the datasheet. Use your own name as the Payee in the last record if you wish to uniquely identify your printout.

PaymentID	EventID	PaymentDate	PaymentAmount	PaymentDescription	Payee
1	1	9/5/00	$100.50	handouts	Kinko's
2	1	9/5/00	$200.50	refreshments	Bagel & Bagel
3	2	9/6/00	$300	supplies	OfficeMax
4	2	9/6/00	$200	refreshments	HyVee
5	2	9/6/00	$40	posters	Alphagraphics

9. The Events and Payments tables have a one-to-many relationship based on the EventID field. Click the Relationships button on the taskbar, click the Show Table button on the Relationship toolbar, double-click Events, double-click Payments, and then click the Close button to close the Show Table dialog box.

10. Resize the field lists in the Relationships window so that all fields and field names are visible.

Explore 11. Drag the EventID field from the Events table to the EventID field in the Payments table, click the Enforce Referential Integrity check box in the Edit Relationships dialog box, and then click Create. You should see "one" symbols beside the EventID field in the Events, and the "many" symbol beside the EventID field in the Payments table. If you had any trouble creating this relationship, it probably means that you either incorrectly set the primary key fields in the tables, or made a keying error when entering data in the datasheets. Review Steps 4 through 8 and then try to reestablish the one-to-many relationship. (*Hint*: You can delete or edit a relationship by right-clicking the link and choosing Edit Relationship or Delete from the shortcut menu.)

12. Once the relationship between the Events and Payments tables is properly established, click File on the menu bar, then click Print Relationships. In the Relationships for Dyslexia-2 report, add *your name* as a label to the upper-right corner of the report then print the report. On the printout, identify the primary key field for each table. Identify the foreign key fields for each table, if one exists in that table. (*Hint*: Foreign key fields are only used in the table on the "many" side of a one-to-many relationship.) You may want to keep this printout for reference in future tutorials.

13. Close the **Relationships for Dyslexia-2** report without saving changes, and then save and close the Relationships window.

14. Even though payments (expenses) are attached to a particular event, in this database, there is no direct relationship between the Pledges and Payments tables. In other words, when pledges are received, they are made to the organization as a whole, and are not earmarked for a particular event. Still, the organization needs to be aware of how much money has been pledged and received in order to plan for and cover their payments. They can accomplish this through a query.

15. Click the Queries button in the Objects bar, click the New button, click Design View in the New Query dialog box, and then click the OK button.

16. Add the Payments and Pledges tables to the Query design window, then close the Show Table dialog box.

17. Add the following fields to the query grid in the order shown:

    Table: Payments
    Field: PaymentAmount
    Table: Pledges
    Field: AmountPledged and Paid

18. Click the Datasheet button. One hundred twenty-five records appear. When tables are added to Query Design view without a relationship, the program attempts to link *each* record from one table with *each* record from the other. In this case, there are 5 records in the Payments table and 25 records in the Pledges table; 5 x 25 = 125. When you observe an unrealistically large number of records in a datasheet, the problem is often due to an inappropriate relationship.

19. Fortunately, you can establish a relationship between records in the Query Design view that overrides the relationship created in the Relationships window for that query. Return to the Query Design view. Drag the PaymentID field in the Payments table to the PledgeID field in the Pledges table, then double-click the link line to open the Join Properties dialog box.

20. Since there are so many more pledges than payments, click option 3 "Include ALL records from 'Pledges' and only those records from 'Payments' where the joined lines are equal," then click the OK button.

21. Click the Datasheet View button. You should see 25 records (since there are 25 pledges), as well as the 5 payments in the PaymentAmount field.

22. Click the Design View button, click the Criteria cell for the Paid field, type **Yes,** then click the Datasheet View button. Twenty-four records should appear.

23. Save the Query as **Detailed Payments and Pledges** – *Your Initials*, then print the datasheet.

Explore ▶ 24. Open **Detailed Payments and Pledges** – *Your Initials* in Design view, then uncheck the Show check box for the Paid field so that it doesn't appear on the datasheet.

25. Now that you have details of all payments and pledges on one datasheet, you wish to summarize them. Click the Totals button on the Query Design toolbar, then change the Group By function to Sum for both the PaymentAmount and AmountPledged fields. Click the Datasheet button. The summarized payment field should equal $841.00, and the summarized pledge field should equal $1,965.00. If your payment value is different, check the accuracy of the payment values you typed in Step 8, then rerun this query.

26. Click File on the menu bar, click Save As, then change the word Detailed to **Summarized**, and click the OK button.

27. Print, then close the **Summarized Payments and Pledges-***Your Initials* query.

28. Close **Dyslexia-2** and exit Access.

Case 3. Tracking Clients and Workouts at Ship Shape You work in the business office of a health club called Ship Shape. You have developed an Access database that tracks clients, workouts, and exercises, called **ShipShape-2**. You'll use this database to become familiar with Access concepts and the table, query, form, and report objects.

1. Start Access and open the **ShipShape-2** database from the Cases\Solutions folder for Tutorial 2.

2. Click the Relationships button, then move and resize the field lists so that all fields are visible, and so that when you print the relationships report, it fits on one page. To print the relationships report, click File on the menu bar, and then click Print Relationships.

3. In the Design view of the Relationships for ShipShape-2 report, add *your name* as a label in the right side of the report header section, and then print the report. Close the report without saving changes. You may want to save a copy of this report to refer to during this and future tutorials.

4. Close the Relationships window, saving the changes.

5. You want to create a data entry form to help clients log the details of their workouts. Since you'll need fields from multiple tables in the form, you'll create an intermediary query object to help you collect the fields and records desired in the final form. Click the Queries button on the Objects Bar, click the New button, click Design view in the New Query dialog box, and then click the OK button.

6. Add the following tables to the query in order:

Clients, Workouts, WorkoutDetails, Exercises, and Units.

7. In the query grid, add the following fields in the order shown:

   Table: Clients
   Fields: ClientFName, ClientLName
   Table: Workouts
   Fields: WorkoutDescription, DateEntered
   Table: Workout Details
   Fields: Sets, RepsOrDuration, and WeightOrSetting
   Table: Exercise
   Field: ExerciseName
   Table: Units
   Field: Units

8. Click the Datasheet button, then change the ClientLName entry in the first record to *your last name* and print the datasheet.

9. Save the query as **Client Workout Details** and close it.

10. Click the Forms button on the Objects bar, then double-click Create form by using wizard.

11. In the Form Wizard dialog box, select the Client Workout Details query from the Tables/Queries list, select all available fields, and then click the Next button.

12. View the data by Clients, then click the Next button.

13. Choose a Datasheet style for both subforms, a Standard style for the main form, accept the default form titles, and open the resulting form in Form view.

14. Print the first record for Rachel. On the printout, describe why there are two subforms.

Explore

15. Going back and forth between Form view and Design view, resize both subforms so that they can both comfortably display four or more records at a time. The subforms, when selected, have sizing handles and can be resized just like any other control. Enlarge the form to make room for the expanded subforms by dragging the form footer down. Delete the labels in the upper-left corner of both subforms to provide more vertical space in which to resize the subforms.

16. In Form view, double-click the gray line that separates field names within each subform, so that all fieldnames and field entries are clearly displayed.

17. Print the first record again and answer the following questions on the printout. How many workouts are recorded for Rachel? How many exercises are recorded for Rachel's Ju-Jitsu Lesson workout?

18. Move through the client records. Write down the name of the most active client and explain why you came to this conclusion.

19. Save and close the **Clients** form.

20. Click the Reports button on the Objects Bar.

21. Double-click Create report by using wizard, choose the Client Workout Details query from the Tables/Queries list, then select all of the fields, view the data by Workouts, do not add any more grouping levels, and do not sort or summarize the detail records. Use a Block layout, a Landscape orientation, and a Bold style. Title the report **Workouts**, then preview the report.

22. Zoom in and out of the report, observing the records for Rachel. The exercises for each workout are not listed together. Print this report, and on the printout, write down the probable cause for this problem. (*Hint*: If you don't know the reason for this problem, work ahead to correct it, then come back and write down your answer.)

23. Click the Design View button, then click the Sorting and Grouping button on the Report Design toolbar.

24. The Sorting and Grouping dialog box shows that the records are grouped by ClientFName, but no further group or sort orders were used. Click the second Field/Expression cell, click the list arrow, and then click WorkoutDescription.

25. With the WorkoutDescription field still selected, click the Group Header property, then click Yes, to not only sort the fields but also to group them by WorkoutDescription. Click the Sorting and Grouping button on the Report Design toolbar to close the dialog box.

26. You will close the WorkoutDescription Header, since you don't want to place any controls there. Drag the top edge of the Detail section up to the bottom edge of the WorkoutDescription Header section to close that area of the report.

Explore ▶ 27. Click the WorkoutDescription text box in the Detail section, click the Properties button, and then click the Format tab. Make sure that the Hide Duplicates property is set to "Yes" to make the field "appear" grouped on the final report even though it prints in the Detail section. Close the property sheet.

28. Click the Save button, then click the Preview button on the Report Design toolbar.

Explore ▶ 29. Use formatting, sizing, editing, and moving skills to clarify the labels in the Page Header section.

30. Save and print the report, then close it.

31. Close **ShipShape-2**, then exit Access.

Case 4. Tracking Events and Attendees at Distinctive Meetings Distinctive Meetings is an event management company that organizes corporate seminars for such areas as sales, communication, and computer training. They have developed an Access database called **DistinctiveMeetings-2**, which tracks events, event registration, attendees, and internal employees. You'll use this database to further explore Access terminology and objects.

1. Start Access and open the **DistinctiveMeetings-2** database from the Cases\Solutions folder for Tutorial 2.

2. Click the Tables button on the Objects Bar, then double-click the Attendees table to open its datasheet.

3. Click the Expand button for the fourth attendee, Dava Einstone, to see what meetings she has signed up for. Change the address for her record to your own address, change the page layout to landscape, then print the datasheet with Dava's subdatasheet expanded. (It will print on two pages because of the width.)

4. Close the **Attendees** datasheet.

5. Click the Relationships button on the Database toolbar.

6. Click File on the menu bar, then click Print Relationships. Make sure that the printout will fit on one page. If it will not, close the report without saving the changes, resize the field lists in the Relationships window, then create the report again.

7. Click the Design View button on the Preview toolbar and add your name as a label in the upper-right corner of the report. Print the report. You may want to save this as a guide to the design of this database for future tutorials.

8. Close the report without saving it, then close the Relationships window. Save changes to the Relationships window.

9. On the back of the Relationships report, explain why the Employees table is linked to both the Events and Registration tables in one-to-many relationships.

10. Click the Queries button on the Objects bar, then double-click the Attendee Count by Event query object. This is a summary, or aggregate query, in that it shows a total number of attendees for each meeting.

11. Click the Design View button on the Datasheet toolbar.

12. Double-click the RegistrationFee field to add it to the next location in the query grid, then change the "Group By" entry in the Total cell for that field to "Sum." View the resulting datasheet to make sure that the RegistrationFee field was summed correctly. The entry for the first record, Public Speaking Skills, should be $1,500.00.

Explore 13. To uniquely identify your printout, change one of the field names to a name that includes your initials in Query Design view. To do this, click to the left of the RegistrationFee field name in the Field cell in the query grid and rename the field using the NewFieldName: Expression syntax. Use your initials in the new field name. The field name entry will look similar to this: LF-FEE: RegistrationFee

14. Click the Datasheet View button to view the resulting datasheet then print it.

15. Save the Attendee Count by Event query, then close it.

16. Click the Forms button on the Objects Bar, click the New button on the Objects toolbar, click AutoForm: Columnar in the New dialog box, choose the Events table as the table where the object's data will come from, and then click the OK button.

Explore 17. Notice that two combo boxes were automatically created for you for the EventTypeID and EmployeeID fields. On a piece of paper, explain why. (*Hint*: Click the Database Window button, click the Tables button on the Objects Bar, then open the Events table in Design view. Check out the lookup properties for both the EventTypeID and EmployeeID fields to see what information is automatically "looked up" for both of these fields. The Display Control and Row Source properties determine why these fields appear as combo boxes and what entries they display when you click their list arrows.)

18. Click the Design View button on the Form View toolbar, then resize the StartTime, EndTime, RequiredStaff, and Confirmed text boxes so that they are the same width as the StartDate and EndDate text boxes above them.

Explore 19. Select all six text boxes from StartDate down to Confirmed, click Format on the menu bar, point to Align then click Right to align the right edges of all six text boxes.

20. Save the form with the name **Event Entry Form**, then click the Form View button.

21. Click the New Record button on the navigations buttons. Add a new record with the event name of **Strategy Development**. The EventTypeID is **Leadership Seminars**. Enter reasonable data for the rest of the record. In the Event Description field, enter **Develop your corporate strategy using *your last name's* proven method**.

22. Click File on the menu bar, click Print, click the Selected Record option, and then click the OK button to print only that record.

23. Save the form, then close it.

24. Open the Attendee Count by Event query in Design view, click the Show Table button, double-click the Events table to add it to Design view, close the Show Table dialog box, and then click the Datasheet button.

25. Write down your answer to the following question: "Why doesn't the new event that you just added "Strategy Development" appear on the datasheet?"

26. Click the Design View button, double-click the link line between the tables to open the Join Properties dialog box, then click option 2, "Include ALL records from 'Events' and only those records from 'Registration' where the joined fields are equal," and then click the OK button.

27. To make sure that the EventName field is pulled correctly from the Events table, change the first field (the Group By field) to the EventName field in the Events table, and then click the Datasheet button. You should see two events (E-Commerce Fundamentals and the Strategy Development event you just added) with no registrations or associated fields in the resulting datasheet. Print this datasheet then close the query.

28. Click the Reports button on the Objects bar, then double-click the Create report by using wizard option.

29. Base the report on the following fields:

    Table: Events:
    Fields: EventName, StartDate, EndDate, StartTime, EndTime, RequiredStaffing, AvailableSpaces
    Table: Employees:
    Fields: FirstName, LastName

30. View the data by employees. Group by StartDate. Do not add any sorting fields, but click the Summary Options button, and sum the AvailableSpaces field.

31. Use an Align Left 1 layout, and a Landscape orientation. Use a Compact style and title the report **Employee Responsibilities**.

32. Click the Design View button, then delete all of the controls in the StartDate and EmployeeID footers, except for the calculated control that sums up the AvailableSpaces field.

Explore 33. Add a 2 pt red line at the bottom of the EmployeeID footer to differentiate between groups of records within each employee on the report.

34. Save and preview the report.

35. Delete the two name labels (LastName and FirstName) as well as the two name text boxes (LastName and FirstName) in the EmployeeID Header.

36. Click the Text Box button in the toolbox, then click in the EmployeeID Header in the same location as the deleted name controls.

37. Click the Unbound text box and type the expression

    =[FirstName]&" "&[LastName]

    so that the text box displays the employee's first and last names with a space in between them as one entity.

38. Change the accompanying label to display the text **Name**, then format, resize, and move the controls as desired.

Explore 39. Preview the report and make sure that the entire employee's name appears in the new text box control you just added. Return to Design view and make further formatting enhancements as desired.

40. In Design view, add your name as a label on the right side of the Report Header, then print the first page of the report.

41. Save and close the report, then close the **DistinctiveMeetings-2** database.

QUICK | CHECK ANSWERS

Session 2.1

1. All of the fields of one item constitute a record, all of the records of one subject constitute a table, and all of the tables of one business constitute a database.

2. The seven Access objects and their purposes are as follows:

   ■ Table: Contains all of the raw data within the database in a spreadsheet-like view called a datasheet. Tables can be linked with a common field to share information and therefore minimize data redundancy.

   ■ Query: Creates a datasheet that displays a subset of fields and/or records from one or more tables. Queries are created when a user has a "question" about the data in the database. Queries can also be used to create calculated fields and summarized information.

   ■ Form: Provides an easy-to-use data entry screen that generally shows only one record at a time.

   ■ Report: Provides a professional printout of data that may contain enhancements such as headers, footers, and calculations on groups of records. Mailing labels can also be created from report objects.

   ■ Page: Creates Web pages from Access objects, and provides Web page connectivity features to an Access database.

   ■ Macro: Stores a collection of keystrokes or commands such as printing several reports or displaying a toolbar when a form opens.

   ■ Module: Stores Visual basic programming code that extends the functions and automated processes of Access.

3. Tables are the most important object within an Access database because they contain all of the data within the database.

4. Data can be entered and edited through four of the objects: tables, queries, pages, and forms.

5. You create new field names in the Design view of the appropriate table.

6. The field's data type determines the type of data that the field will accept.

7. The following data types are available:

Data Type	Used for This Type of Data:
Text (default)	Text or a combination of text and numbers up to 255 characters in length; also used for numeric entries that will not be used in calculations
Memo	Text entries that are beyond 255 characters in size
Number	Numeric data that may be used in a mathematical calculation later
Date/Time	Date or time values
Currency	Numeric data that represents money
AutoNumber	An automatic field entry that increments the field value by one for each new record. The user cannot type into an AutoNumber field, and numbers cannot be reused if a record is deleted.
Yes/No	When only one of two values are possible for the field (yes/no, true/false, or on/off)
OLE Object	A linked or embedded file created outside of Access such as an Excel spreadsheet, a Word document, a graphic, or a sound clip.
Hyperlink	Web page addresses or links to other files or objects

8. Field properties are the characteristics that further define the field, such as field size, caption, format, and validation rule.

9. In the one-to-many relationship, the common linking field is a key field, also called a primary key field in the table on the "one" side and the foreign key field in the table on the "many" side of the relationship.

10. The Categories and Products tables are linked by a one-to-many relationship, using the CategoryID field. The CategoryID field is the primary key field in the Categories table (the "one" side of the relationship) and is the foreign key field in the Products table (the "many" side of the relationship).

Session 2.2

1. Query objects are used to:

■ Select a subset of fields and records from one or more tables to view as a datasheet or upon which to build a form, page, or report

■ Modify and change data through action queries

■ Create calculated fields of data for each record

■ Create aggregated calculations across groups of records

2. The quotation mark (") is used to surround text criteria in the query grid. Date criteria is surrounded by pound signs (#).

3. The following table describes the comparison operators you can use with criteria in the query grid.

Comparison Operator	Description
>	Greater than
>=	Greater than or equal to
<	Less than
<=	Less than or equal to
<>	Not equal to
Between...And	Finds values between two numbers or dates
In	Finds a value that is one of a list
Null	Finds records that are blank
Is Not Null	Finds records that are not blank
Like	Finds records that match the criteria
Not	Finds records that do not match the criteria

4. Creating calculated fields in a query maximizes productivity and eliminates errors because the data is automatically created for you.

5. A calculated field creates a new field value for each record. An aggregate calculation groups several records together to find a value for a group of records.

6.

Aggregate Function	Used to Find the:
Sum	Total of values in a field
Avg	Average of values in a field
Min	Minimum value in the field
Max	Maximum value in the field
Count	Number of values in a field (not counting null values)
StDev	Standard deviation of values in a field
Var	Variance of values in a field
First	Field value from the first record in a table or query
Last	Field value from the last record in a table or query

7. SQL, structured query language, is the de facto (by fact, not by law) standard database programming language. SQL has become the programmers' language of choice for extracting data from a relational database. You wouldn't want to invest in a database that could not be accessed by using SQL, since that would severely limit the flexibility of the data.

8. Open a query, click the View button list arrow, and then click SQL.

Session 2.3

1. When the records of a form are related in a one-to-many relationship, a main form is used to show the fields from the table on the "one" side of the relationship, and a subform is used to show the fields from the table on the "many" side of the relationship.

2. Bound controls are used to display actual data from a field of the underlying record source. The entry displayed by the bound control will change as you move from record to record. Unbound controls exist only to clarify or enhance the appearance of the form. They do not change as you move through different records in a form. Calculated controls are actually text boxes that contain expressions such as page numbers, dates, or other calculated values based on data from other controls.

3. Common bound controls include the text box, combo box, list box, and check box. Common unbound controls are labels, lines, tabs, and clip art.

4. Grouping means to sort records and additionally to provide a section on the report that prints before and after the group.

5. Sections are areas of the report that determine where and how often a control will print.

6. The Field List, Toolbox, Sorting and Grouping, and Properties buttons are all located on the Report Design toolbar and work as toggles.

OBJECTIVES

In this tutorial you will:

- Learn the purpose for the page (data access page) object and how it is related to Web pages and Internet Explorer

- Use the AutoPage tool to create pages for data entry

- Use the Page Wizard to create pages for interactive reporting

- Use Page view

- Use Internet Explorer to view, enter, and update Access data

- Modify data access pages using Page Design View

- Create and use hyperlink fields and controls

- Learn about other Access Web and Internet connectivity tools

CREATING DATA ACCESS PAGES FOR DATA ENTRY

Using Web Pages to Update the Aaron Michael Toys Database

CASE

Aaron Michael Toys

Now that you've explored e-commerce and the existing Access 2000 database for Aaron Michael Toys, you're ready to use the features of Access 2000 to make the database accessible through Web technologies.

In this tutorial you will learn about Web connectivity to an Access 2000 database. You'll use the page object within Access 2000 to create Web pages that are dynamically connected directly to an Access database. Using Page View and the Navigation toolbar, you'll learn how to navigate, sort, filter, and edit data using Web pages. You'll also learn how the page object differs from the form and report objects. Using Internet Explorer, you will open and view Web pages, and use them to enter, edit, delete, and manipulate the data in the underlying Access database. You'll also learn about hyperlinks, both as a field data type and as a text or image hotspot control. Finally, you'll explore Page Design View and learn about some of the other Access Web and Internet connectivity tools beyond the data access page and hyperlink features.

SESSION 3.1

In this session you will explore ways that Access 2000 provides Web connectivity through the page object.

The Relationship Between the Page Object, Web Pages, and Internet Explorer

There are several features within Access 2000 that enable your database to work with the World Wide Web, the most significant of which is the page object. The **page** object, also called the **data access page (DAP)**, is a special Access object that creates Web pages used to view, enter, and analyze Access data. Because the page object can be used both for data entry and data reporting, it functions as a combination of the form and report objects. The page object's interactive pivot tables and graphs allow you to analyze data in new ways that go beyond the capabilities of the form and report objects.

The page object's major purpose is to create dynamic **HTML (Hypertext Markup Language)** files. These HTML files are Web pages that can be opened in Internet Explorer to change, enter, and analyze the database. By creating Web pages that are dynamically connected to the database, the page object expands the benefits of the database to anyone at any location who has Internet Explorer and the authorization to locate and download these Web pages.

In order to use all of the data entry and interactive reporting features of the page object, you must use Internet Explorer version 5.0 or later as your browser. IE 5.0 was used for the figures in this book.

Figure 3-1 shows the typical way that the Access 2000 database and the HTML files created by the page object are organized.

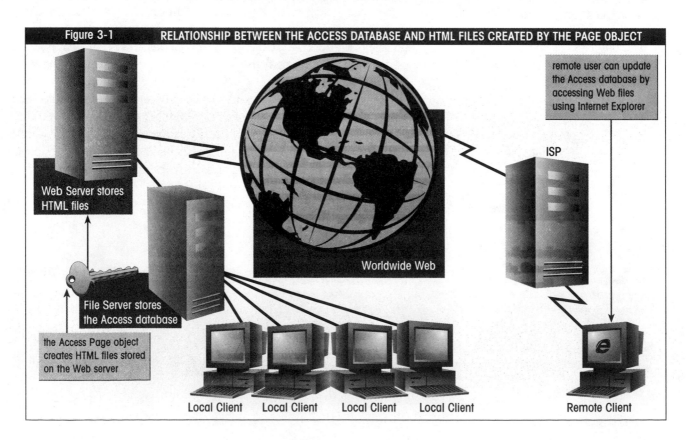

Figure 3-1   RELATIONSHIP BETWEEN THE ACCESS DATABASE AND HTML FILES CREATED BY THE PAGE OBJECT

remote user can update the Access database by accessing Web files using Internet Explorer

ISP

Worldwide Web

Web Server stores HTML files

File Server stores the Access database

the Access Page object creates HTML files stored on the Web server

Local Client   Local Client   Local Client   Local Client   Remote Client

Usually, a company will store an Access 2000 database on a **file server**, a powerful micro-computer that stores data files and software that will be shared by multiple users in a **local area network, (LAN)**. Unlike other Microsoft Office files that allow only one person to write to a file at a time, Access allows multiple people to read from and write to the database simultaneously provided that the users have the proper security clearance for that database file. An Access database file is sometimes described as a **record-locking** file because it allows multiple people to simultaneously update the same database (but not the same record).

In contrast, Excel spreadsheets, Word documents, and PowerPoint files are **file-locking** files because they do not allow more than one person to update the same file at the same time. It is important to note, however, that there are some new **collaboration tools** within the Office 2000 suite of products such as online meetings, shared workbooks, and document discussions that are starting to address the need for multiple people to be actively working with the same data at the same time.

Reviewing Web Servers

You will recall from Tutorial 1 that a **Web server** is a special type of file server dedicated to managing Web pages. The Web server and file server may be the same physical computer, but most businesses separate the two in order to separate the functions of, improve the speed of, maximize the capabilities of, and increase the security of both machines. A medium-sized or large business would have many file servers and many Web servers networked together to provide the needed services to their large community of users. A **client** can be defined as any computer used to access the services provided by a **server** computer. Local clients that have direct access to the database file will probably use the traditional Access objects (tables, queries, forms, and reports) to enter, update, and analyze data, just as you explored in Tutorial 2. Remote clients that do not have direct access to the database file, however, can still update and analyze data using their Internet Explorer browser to view Web pages created by the page object.

A remote user may have the ability to call into and connect to the company Web server directly, or may use an **Internet service provider (ISP)** to provide a connection to the Internet, which in turn routes information back and forth between the remote user and the corporate Web server.

Building the infrastructure for a local area network and readying a Web server to communicate with the Internet involve an understanding of several technologies. Those who work with these technologies are often called **network administrators** or **Webmasters**. The infrastructure required to support a Web-enabled database will be explored more in a later tutorial. For now, you'll focus on the page object itself.

Purposes for the Page Object

The three major purposes for the page object are described in Figure 3-2.

Figure 3-2	PURPOSES FOR THE PAGE OBJECT	
PURPOSE	**DESCRIPTION**	**EXAMPLE**
Interactive reporting	To publish summaries of information using sorting, grouping, and filtering techniques. You can't edit data on this type of page.	To publish summaries of the products from each supplier. Expand and collapse buttons provide interactivity so that you can view as much or little detail within each supplier as desired.
Data entry	To view, add, and edit records.	To enter new products, purchase orders, or suppliers.
Data analysis	To analyze the data using pivot tables and charts. You can't edit data on this type of page.	To determine inventory trends by analyzing the quantity of a product sold over time.

Each page object that you create is stored within the Access database file, just as every other object is stored within the Access database file. Existing page objects are accessed by clicking the Pages button 🖼 on the Objects bar.

Creating **Page Objects**

Page objects can be created in several ways. Figure 3-3 lists four major techniques for creating a page object.

Figure 3-3	WAYS TO CREATE A PAGE OBJECT	
TECHNIQUE	**CONSIDERATIONS**	**OTHER SIMILAR TOOLS**
AutoPage	The fastest way to create a page object is to use the AutoPage tool. The only information required by the AutoPage tool to create a page object is the name of the query or table that contains the recordset for the resulting page.	AutoForm and AutoReport
Page Wizard	One of the easiest ways to create a page object but still retain some control over the page development process is by using the Page Wizard. The Page Wizard asks questions about the design of the resulting page, such as which fields are to be displayed, how the records are to be grouped and sorted, and what title you wish to use for the page.	Form and Report Wizards
Page Design view	Creating a page object from scratch in Page Design view provides the maximum amount of control over the resulting object. As you would suspect, however, it also requires a high level of knowledge of objects and properties. Often, Page Design view is used to modify a page that was initially created by the AutoPage or Page Wizard tools.	Form and Report Design View
Use an existing Web page	You can create a page object from an existing Web page. Access creates a shortcut to the HTML file in the database window. You may want to use this technique to reference existing Web pages that you wish to quickly locate from within your Access database.	

AutoPage Tool

The **AutoPage Tool** is the fastest way to create a new page object in a column style, but doesn't provide you with any choices other than the initial decision regarding which table in a column style or query will supply the recordset for the page. You can access the AutoPage tool by clicking the New Object button list arrow 🖾 on the Database toolbar, or by clicking the Pages button 🖼 on the Objects Bar.

REFERENCE WINDOW	RW
<u>Creating a Page Object using the AutoPage Tool</u> ■ Click the Pages button on the Objects Bar and then click the New button on the Database Window toolbar to open the New Data Access Page dialog box. ■ Click the AutoPage: Columnar option and choose the table or query where the page object's data comes from. ■ Click the OK button in the New Data Access Page dialog box.	

To create a page object using the AutoPage tool:

1. Start Access 2000, and then open the **AMToys-3** database from the Tutorial\Solutions folder for Tutorial 3.

   The database window for the AMToys-3 database opens.

   TROUBLE? Starting with this tutorial, you will not be able to work off a floppy disk. The "Read This Before You Begin" section at the front of this book provides recommendations on how to organize your hard drive and copy the data files into *Solutions folders* so that you won't run into speed or space problems. Appendix A contains information on how to use Winzip to compress and package the files so that they can be transported on a floppy if you need to work on them on more than one computer.

2. Click the **Pages** button 📄 on the Objects Bar, and then click the **New** button 📄 on the Database Window toolbar to open the New Data Access Page dialog box as shown in Figure 3-4.

   You base page objects on tables and queries similarly to how reports and forms are created.

Figure 3-4	NEW DATA ACCESS PAGE DIALOG BOX

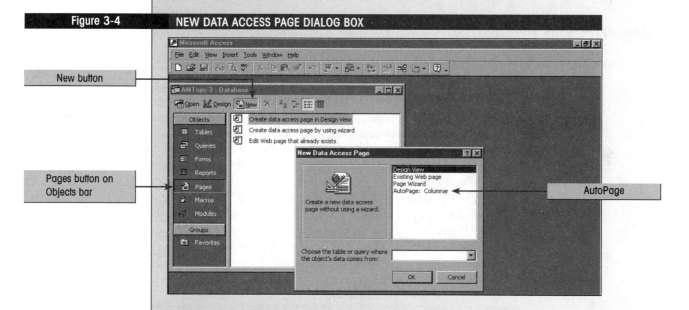

New button

Pages button on Objects bar

AutoPage

3. Click **AutoPage: Columnar**, click the **Choose the table or query where the object's data comes from** list arrow, click **Suppliers**, and then click the **OK** button.

   The page object is automatically created and displayed in Page view.

4. Maximize the new Suppliers page object window.

   Your page should look like Figure 3-5. It displays the record for SupplierID 1, JB Toy Factory.

Figure 3-5	PAGE VIEW OF NEW PAGE OBJECT

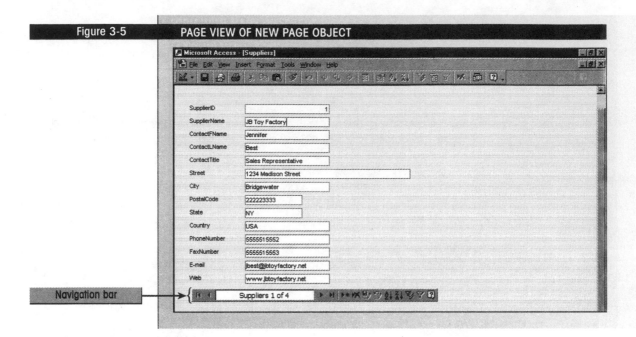

Navigation bar →

Working in Page View

Page view is where you view how the Web page will appear within IE. It can also be used to view, enter, edit, and work with data, just as Form view is used when working with data within a form object. The **Navigation bar** is used to find, filter, sort, delete, edit, and move between records. In a page object, the Navigation bar and its buttons are part of the page itself so that you can use these buttons when you view the associated Web page from within IE. Since this page was based on the Suppliers table, each field of the Suppliers table is visible. The Navigation bar allows you to scroll through the four records of the Suppliers table.

When you save a page object, you're actually saving two parts at the same time: a Web page (an HTML file), and a link to the Web page. Links to the Web pages are part of the Access database. They appear as a listing of page objects in the database window when you click the Pages button on the Objects bar. The Web page files can be stored in any folder you specify. To simplify the file management issues in this book, you'll save the Web pages in the same folder as the database file itself.

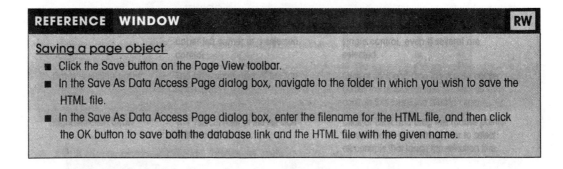

REFERENCE WINDOW **RW**

<u>Saving a page object</u>
- Click the Save button on the Page View toolbar.
- In the Save As Data Access Page dialog box, navigate to the folder in which you wish to save the HTML file.
- In the Save As Data Access Page dialog box, enter the filename for the HTML file, and then click the OK button to save both the database link and the HTML file with the given name.

To save a page object:

1. Click the **Save** button 🖫 on the Page View toolbar.

The Save As Data Access Page dialog box opens as shown in Figure 3-6.

| Figure 3-6 | SAVE AS DATA ACCESS PAGE DIALOG BOX |

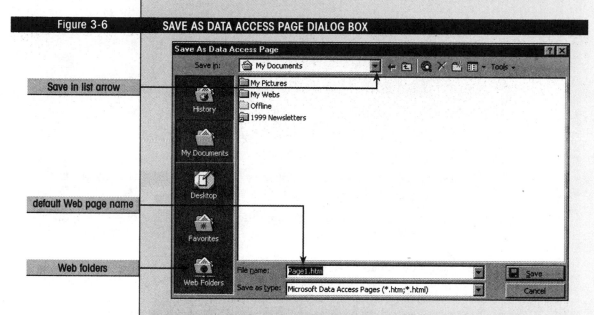

If your business had prepared a **Web folder** (a special shared folder located on a Web server that manages Web pages), you would save the HTML file there so that a remote client could easily access it later. For now, however, you'll save the HTML files to your Tutorial\Solutions folder for Tutorial 3, the same folder that stores your Aaron Michael Toys database.

2. Click the **Save in** list arrow, navigate to the Tutorial\Solutions folder for Tutorial 3 that contains the **AMToys-3** database, double-click the **Page1.htm** default file-name, type **Suppliers**, and then click the **Save** button.

Both the Suppliers link within the **AMToys-3** database and its associated HTML file have been saved to your Tutorial\Solutions folder. You do not need to give links and their related HTML files the same name, but it makes them easier to manage if they have the same name.

3. Close the Suppliers page object.

The page link in the database window does not have to have the same name as the HTML file, and you can change the name of the link after it is created. You change the name of a link by right-clicking it within the database window, clicking Rename, and entering the new name. Be very careful about renaming or moving the HMTL file. If you rename or move HTML files, the path from the link to the file is broken and has to be reestablished. The last part of this tutorial explains how to restore broken links.

Entering and Editing Data in Page View

You see the Suppliers page link within the database window. If you double-click the link, you will open the page object in Page view. Although Page view can be used to enter and update data, you normally wouldn't use it for this purpose. Forms still provide more flexible and user-friendly data entry screens than pages. Page view presents the HTML file just as it would appear in IE. In other words, Page view is actually a browser within Access that displays the HTML file just as it will be displayed within IE.

> *To enter and edit data in Page view:*
>
> 1. Double-click the **Suppliers** page object to open it in Page view.
>
>   Edit the first record because Jennifer Best is actually the Marketing, not the Sales, Representative for JBToy Factory.
>
> 2. Double-click **Sales** in the ContactTitle field for the first record, type **Marketing**, press the **Spacebar**, and then press the **Tab** key.
>
> 3. Press the **Tab** key 10 times to move through all of the fields of the record.

Page view does not handle all keystrokes in the same way as Form view, and if you are an experienced Access user and regularly work with forms, you'll want to be aware of the differences. For example, pressing the Tab key in the last field of Page view moves you to the first field of the same record. In Form view, pressing the Tab key in the last field moves you to the first field of the next record. Also, you cannot press the Enter key to move from field to field in Page view as you can in Form view. In addition, some of the field properties (for example input masks in the PostalCode, PhoneNumber, and FaxNumber fields) are not automatically applied to the controls in Page view as they are on a form. The reason for many of these differences has to do with the restrictions of the HTML code that the page object creates.

Remember, the page object's main purpose is to develop a Web page that can be used with the Internet Explorer browser, not to create an object that is equivalent to an existing form or report within Access. IE and Web pages have their own set of rules and programming limitations, which the page object must obey in order to work with Internet technologies.

Navigation Toolbar

A great way to work with the data in Page view is to become familiar with the buttons on the Navigation toolbar. There are no ScreenTips available when you point to the buttons on the Navigation toolbar, so you have to become familiar with them without relying on that visual cue. Figure 3-7 describes the buttons on the Page Navigation toolbar.

Figure 3-7   **BUTTONS ON THE PAGE NAVIGATION TOOLBAR**

BUTTON IMAGE	BUTTON NAME	CLICK THIS BUTTON TO
◀	First Record	Move to the first record
◀	Previous Record	Move to the previous record
▶	Next Record	Move to the next record
▶▌	Last Record	Move to the last record
▶✶	New Record	Add a new record
✗	Delete Record	Delete the current record
🖫	Save Record	Save the current record
↺	Undo Last Change	Undo the last edit
⬇	Sort Ascending	Sort the records in ascending order, based on the values in the current field
⬇	Sort Descending	Sort the records in descending order, based on the values in the current field
▽	Filter by Selection	Filter the records so that only those with the same entry in the current field are displayed
▽	Remove Filter	Removes the filter
?	Microsoft Access Data Pages Help	Displays a window for the Microsoft Access Data Pages Help system

To use the buttons on the Navigation toolbar:

1. Click the **Next Record** button ▶ on the Navigation toolbar to move to the second supplier, We Know Fun.

2. Click the **Last Record** button ▶▌ on the Navigation toolbar to move to the last supplier, Totally Amazing.

3. Click the **New Record** button ▶✶ on the Navigation toolbar.

   A blank page appears in which you can enter a new record.

4. Click in the **SupplierName** field, type **Toy Warehouse**, press the **Tab** key, enter your own first and last name in the ContactFName and ContactLName fields, type **Sales Manager** in the Contact Title field, and then fill out the rest of the fields (except for the SupplierID field) with reasonable entries.

5. Click the **Save Record** button 🖫 on the Navigation toolbar.

   Saving the record causes the SupplierID field to be automatically updated because it was created with an AutoNumber data type. Moving to a new record also saves all changes in the previous record, just as it did in Form view.

6. Click the **Print** button 🖨 on the Page View toolbar to print the current record with your name.

   TROUBLE? If some or all of the text boxes appear blank, you need to increase the size of the text box controls in Page Design view in order for the data to appear on the printout. This problem occurs with some print drivers.

Printing a page highlights another difference between the form and page object. If you click the Print button 🖨 in Page view, only the current record is printed. If you click the Print button 🖨 in Form view, all records are printed. To print only the current record in Form view, click File on the menu bar, click the Print option, click Selected Record in the Print dialog box, then click OK.

To review your changes in Page view:

1. Click to the left of the "**T**" in Toy Warehouse in the SupplierName field, type **Mega**, and then press the **Spacebar**.

   Notice that the Save Record button 🖫 and Undo Last Change buttons 🔄 on the Navigation toolbar are not available until you start editing a value.

2. Press the **Tab** key, then click the **Undo Last Change** button 🔄 on the Navigation toolbar.

   You can only undo your last action in Page view. The SupplierName is back to Toy Warehouse.

3. Click the **SupplierName** field, then click the **Sort Ascending** button 🔼 on the Navigation toolbar.

   All of the records are sorted in ascending order, based on the entry in the SupplierName field, and JB Toy Factory should be the first record.

4. Click the **Sort Descending** button 🔽.

   All of the records are sorted in descending order, based on the entry in the SupplierName field, and therefore We Know Fun should be the first record. You can use Page view to delete records from the database.

5. Click the **Next Record** button ▶ on the Navigation toolbar to move to the Toy Warehouse record, and then click the **Delete Record** button ⊠ on the Navigation toolbar.

   You cannot undo the deletion action, so Access provides a confirmation dialog box to be sure that you want to complete the action.

6. Click **Yes** to delete the record.

7. Click the **Previous Record** button ◀, click **IA** in the State field, and then click the **Filter by Selection** button 🔽 on the Navigation toolbar.

   The Filter by Selection button works the same way as it did in Form view. The two suppliers from Iowa are shown in Figure 3-8.

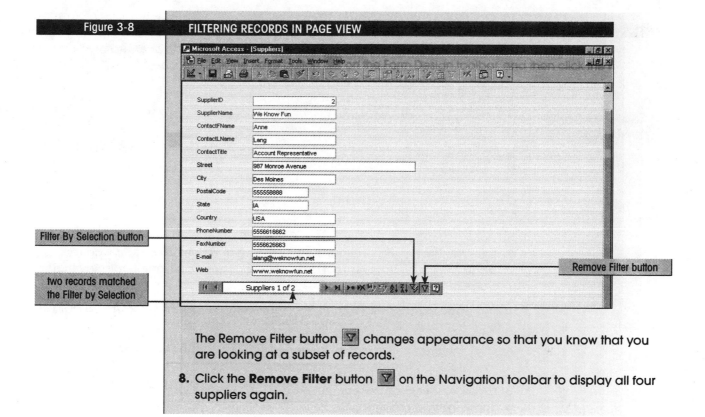

Figure 3-8 · FILTERING RECORDS IN PAGE VIEW

Filter By Selection button

two records matched the Filter by Selection

Remove Filter button

The Remove Filter button ▽ changes appearance so that you know that you are looking at a subset of records.

8. Click the **Remove Filter** button ▽ on the Navigation toolbar to display all four suppliers again.

Microsoft Access Data Pages Help System

There is a great amount of useful material on the page object in the Access Help system as well as in the Data Pages Help system, which is available by clicking the Microsoft Access Data Pages Help button ⚿ on the Navigation toolbar. This Help button is provided on the Navigation toolbar because once you are viewing the DAP as a Web page within Internet Explorer, you will no longer have the regular Access menus and toolbars available.

To use the Microsoft Access Data Pages Help system:

1. Click the **Microsoft Access Data Pages Help** button ⚿ on the Navigation toolbar.

2. Maximize the Help screen, and then click **Troubleshoot data access pages** in the Contents window as shown in Figure 3-9.

Figure 3-9	MICROSOFT ACCESS DATA PAGES HELP SYSTEM

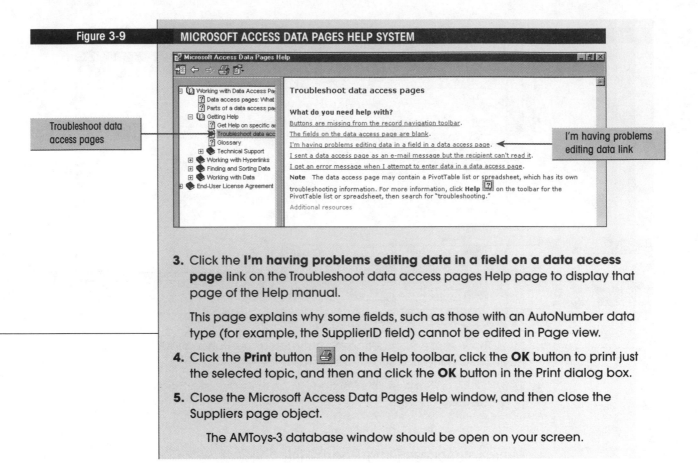

Troubleshoot data access pages

I'm having problems editing data link

3. Click the **I'm having problems editing data in a field on a data access page** link on the Troubleshoot data access pages Help page to display that page of the Help manual.

   This page explains why some fields, such as those with an AutoNumber data type (for example, the SupplierID field) cannot be edited in Page view.

4. Click the **Print** button 🖨 on the Help toolbar, click the **OK** button to print just the selected topic, and then and click the **OK** button in the Print dialog box.

5. Close the Microsoft Access Data Pages Help window, and then close the Suppliers page object.

   The AMToys-3 database window should be open on your screen.

Page Wizard

The **Page Wizard** is a tool that can be used to quickly create a page object, but unlike the AutoPage tool, it allows the user to make some basic choices about the design of the page by presenting a series of dialog boxes. As with all Access wizards, you can click the Next and Back buttons within the Page Wizard to move forward and backward through the choices you have made. Whether you create a page object using the AutoPage tool, the Page Wizard, an import process, or Page Design view, the resulting page object can be used and modified just like any other object in the database.

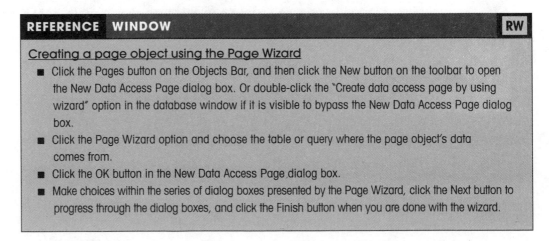

REFERENCE WINDOW | **RW**

Creating a page object using the Page Wizard

- Click the Pages button on the Objects Bar, and then click the New button on the toolbar to open the New Data Access Page dialog box. Or double-click the "Create data access page by using wizard" option in the database window if it is visible to bypass the New Data Access Page dialog box.
- Click the Page Wizard option and choose the table or query where the page object's data comes from.
- Click the OK button in the New Data Access Page dialog box.
- Make choices within the series of dialog boxes presented by the Page Wizard, click the Next button to progress through the dialog boxes, and click the Finish button when you are done with the wizard.

To create a page object using the Page Wizard:

1. Double-click **Create data access page by using wizard** in the database window.

   TROUBLE? If the "Create data access page by using wizard" option is not visible in the database window, click Tools on the menu bar, click Options, click the View tab, click the New object shortcuts check box, and then click the OK button.

   The first dialog box presented by the Page Wizard opens, prompting you to choose information for the resulting data access page. This dialog box is just like the first dialog box presented by the Form Wizard and Report Wizard. You have to select the fields from the tables and queries in the database that you want to include in the page object.

2. Click **CategoryName**, click the **Select Single Field** button ⊳ , click the **Tables/Queries** list arrow, click **Table:Products**, click **ProductName**, click the **Select Single Field** button ⊳ , click **AgeLevel**, click the **Select Single Field** button ⊳ , click **UnitPrice**, and then click the **Select Single Field** button ⊳ as shown in Figure 3-10.

| Figure 3-10 | FIRST DIALOG BOX OF THE PAGE WIZARD |

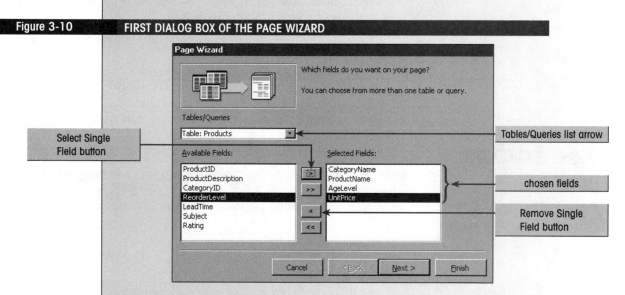

Select Single Field button

Tables/Queries list arrow

chosen fields

Remove Single Field button

   TROUBLE? If you choose the wrong field or the wrong order for the fields, click the Remove Single Field button ⊲ to remove the field from the chosen list, and then try again.

3. Click the **Next** button.

   The second dialog box presented by the Page Wizard is very similar to that of the Report Wizard. You are asked whether you wish to display any grouping levels and warned that if you do, you will create a read-only page. You cannot update or enter data in a read-only page.

   Grouping refers to sorting records in such a way that the grouping field is listed once, and all records with the same value in that field are presented within that group.

4. Click **CategoryName** if it is not already selected, then click the **Select Single Field** button ⊳ .

Grouping by CategoryName means that this field will print only once for each group of records with the same CategoryName value. The Page Wizard dialog box presents the CategoryName field in blue in a group header position in the dialog box so that you can visualize what the final page will look like. The ProductName, AgeLevel, and UnitPrice fields will be listed within each CategoryName.

5. Click the **Next** button.

The third dialog box is also familiar because it is used in both the Form and Report Wizards. You are asked whether you wish to sort the records in any particular order within each group.

6. Click the **first sort order** list arrow, click **UnitPrice**, and then click the **Sort Ascending** button 〔🔼〕 to toggle it into the Sort Descending button.

This will list the most expensive toys within each category first.

7. Click the **Next** button.

The last question presented by the Page Wizard asks for a title for the Web page.

8. Type **Products within Categories** in the text box, click the **Open the page** option button, and then click the **Finish** button.

The page is created and displayed in Page view as shown in Figure 3-11.

TROUBLE? If your page object opened in Design view, click the Page View button 〔🔳〕 on the Page Design toolbar. If your page opened in Page view, but all of the controls are not completely displayed, click the Design View button 〔🔳〕, and then click the Page View button 〔🔳〕 to refresh the screen.

Figure 3-11	PRODUCTS WITHIN CATEGORIES PAGE OBJECT

Even though it takes extra effort to create a page object using the Page Wizard (compared to the AutoPage tool), the additional choices you were able to make regarding the data and presentation of the data on the resulting page makes the Page Wizard extremely valuable. Because this page groups data by CategoryName, you cannot use this page for data entry, but you can still use it for interactive reporting by selectively expanding and collapsing data as well as by using the filter and sort buttons on the Navigation toolbar.

Using Page Objects for Interactive Reporting

Interactive reporting is valuable because the user can interact with the data that is published. Examples of this interaction include expanding or collapsing grouped records, sorting, and filtering. The page object presents these interactive options by providing an expand button 〔➕〕 or collapse button 〔➖〕 to the left of a grouping field as well as by providing sort and filter buttons on the Navigation toolbar. The Access report object, on the other hand, is a *noninteractive* presentation of the data. The user cannot modify the way the data is grouped, sorted, or filtered while reviewing a regular report. Note, however, that the information prepared by *both* the report and page objects is *dynamic* because in both cases the information changes as the data in the database changes. Both objects present up-to-date information as of the moment they are opened.

To explore interactive reporting on a page object:

1. Click the **expand** button 🔲 to the left of the GroupOfProducts-CategoryName label.

   TROUBLE? If the field text boxes do not appear properly, click the Design View button 🔲 and the Page View button 🔲 to refresh the view, and then click the Expand button again.

   Your screen should look like Figure 3-12.

Figure 3-12	EXPANDING GROUPED RECORDS

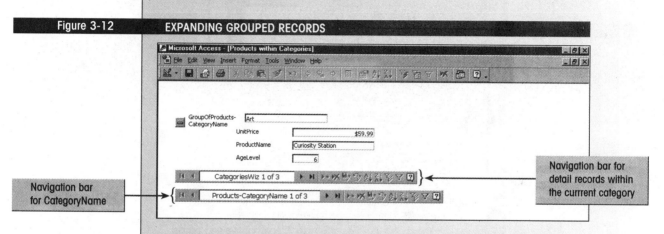

Navigation bar for CategoryName

Navigation bar for detail records within the currrent category

Two navigation bars are visible. The upper bar is used to work with the detail records, and the lower bar is used to work with the grouping field.

2. Click the **Last Record** button 🔲 on the lower navigation bar to move to the last group of records (Kits), then click the **expand** button 🔲 to the left of the GroupOfProducts-CategoryName label as shown in Figure 3-13.

Figure 3-13	EXPANDING THE KITS GROUP

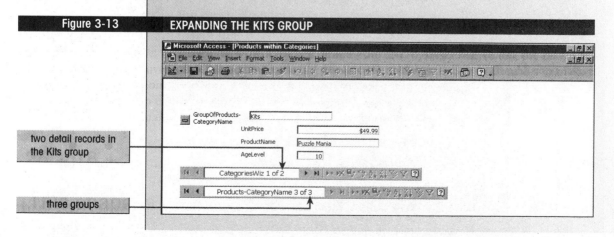

two detail records in the Kits group

three groups

The upper navigation bar shows the number of the current record and total number of records in that category. Puzzle Mania is the first record, and there are two products in the Kits group. The lower navigation bar shows the current category number and the total number of category groups. Kits is the third category, and there are three different categories or groups of toys (Art, Books, Kits).

3. Double-click **Mania** in the ProductName field, and then try to type **Fun**.

   You cannot edit, add, or delete records on a page object that groups records. You can, however, sort and filter grouped records.

4. Click the **Previous Record** button ◄ on the lower navigation bar to move to the Books group, and then click the **expand** button ➕ for the Books group.

5. Click **$29.99** in the UnitPrice field, and then click the **Sort Ascending** button ⬆ in the upper Navigation toolbar.

   The records are sorted in ascending order, placing the $19.99 record first as shown in Figure 3-14.

Figure 3-14	SORTING DETAIL RECORDS

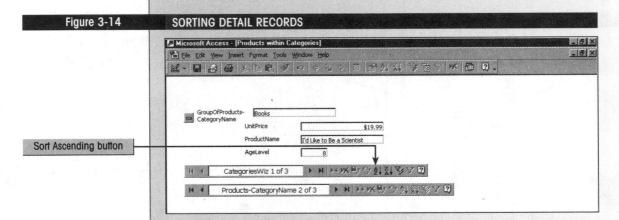

The three detail records in the Books group are now sorted from the smallest unit price to the highest unit price.

Since you cannot edit data in a page that also groups records, you will not see the blinking I-beam in the selected field. The Navigation bar itself, however, gives you some clues as to which field is selected.

6. Click **Books** in the grouped CategoryName field, and then view the Navigation bars.

   Notice that the Sort and Filter by Selection buttons for the lower Navigation bar are active, but the Sort and Filter buttons for the upper Navigation bar, which works with detail records, are not. The buttons that allow you to enter, delete, save, and undo an edit are dim on both toolbars because grouped data cannot be edited.

7. Click **$19.99** in the UnitPrice field, and then view the Navigation bars again.

   Now the Sort and Filter by Selection buttons for the upper Navigation bar are active.

8. Click the **Save** button 💾 on the Page View toolbar.

   The Save as Data Access Page dialog box opens.

You see that Access has created a folder called Suppliers_files in the Tutorial-Solutions folder. As you build certain types of Page objects, Access will build supporting files behind the scenes and place them in folders within the appropriate Solutions folder.

9. If the appropriate Solutions folder for Tutorial 3 is not the selected folder, click the **Save in list arrow**, navigate to the Tutorial\Solutions folder for Tutorial 3 that contains the **AMToys-3** database, double-click the **Page1.htm** default filename, type **Products within Categories**, and then click the **Save** button.

   Both the Products within Categories link within the AMToys-3 database and its associated Web page have been saved.

10. Close the Products within Categories page object.

   You see the two page objects that you created in the database window.

11. Close the **AMToys-3** database.

When you use the Page Wizard to create a page object, you choose the fields, grouping levels, sort orders, and name for the object. The wizard determines all of the other choices for the page such as the way that it is formatted, the size and placement of the field text boxes, the label captions, and even the text displayed in the Navigation toolbars. You can modify the properties of any page control in Page Design view by working with the control's property sheet, just as you could modify the controls created by the Report Wizard and the Form Wizard. For now, however, you'll accept the default options provided by the Page Wizard and continue learning more about how to create and use pages.

Session 3.1 QUICK CHECK

1. What is another name for the page object?

2. How is the page object similar to the form and report objects? How is it different?

3. What is the purpose for the page object?

4. Why is an Access database called a "record-locking" file?

5. In a typical corporate setting, where would the Access database and dynamic HTML files used by remote users be located?

6. Within a company, what are the typical titles for those whose job is it to develop the file server and Web server network infrastructures?

7. What are the three general purposes for the page object?

8. What are four ways to create a page object?

9. What is the purpose of Page view?

10. What is the purpose of the Navigation toolbar?

11. What is the difference between creating a page object using the AutoPage tool and using the Page Wizard?

12. What does interactive reporting mean?

SESSION 3.2

In this session you will use IE to update the AMToys-3 database, work with hyperlinks, and learn about other Access Web-enabling tools.

Using Internet Explorer to Update an Access Database

Now that you've created two page objects and become familiar with the page object's navigation toolbar, it's time to open the associated HTML files using Internet Explorer and work with the Access data from within IE. You'll see that viewing Web pages created by an Access page object from within Internet Explorer is very similar to using Page view within Access. The Navigation toolbar on the Web page will provide the functions you can use when viewing Access data from within IE.

To open the page in Internet Explorer:

1. Click the **Start** button on your taskbar, point to **Programs**, and then click **Internet Explorer**.

   Depending on how you last used IE, you may see a Search, Favorites, or History window in the left part of the IE screen.

2. If a Search, Favorites, or History window is open, click the corresponding button on the Standard Buttons toolbar to close it.

   Depending on the options set within IE and whether or not you are connected to the Internet, a default home page may load when you start IE. You don't need to be connected to the Internet to open the Suppliers Web page you created from within Access within this browser window. Since the Suppliers Web page file is located on your local computer, you'll open it directly within this IE browser window.

3. Click **File** on the menu bar, click **Open**, click the **Browse** button, click the **Look in** list arrow in the Microsoft Internet Explorer dialog box, navigate to your Tutorial\Solutions folder for Tutorial 3, double-click **Suppliers.htm**, then click the **OK** button in the Open dialog box.

   The Web page opens within IE as shown in Figure 3-15.

Figure 3-15	SUPPLIERS WEB PAGE IN IE

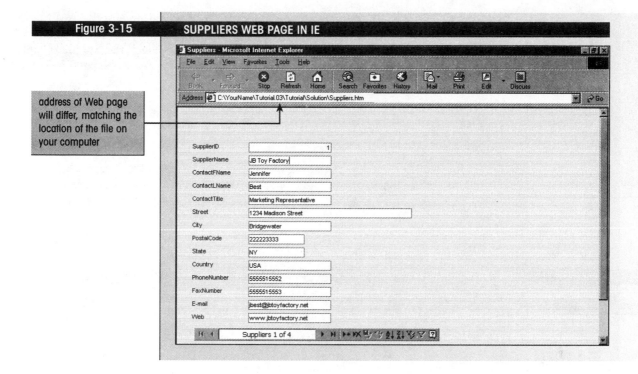

address of Web page will differ, matching the location of the file on your computer

The IE Address bar indicates that the address of this Web page is a local drive—that it was not downloaded from the World Wide Web. Another way to open the Suppliers.htm Web page in IE would be to type the local address of the Web page, such as C:\YourName\Tutorial.03\Tutorial\Solution\Suppliers.htm, into the Address bar rather than browsing for it using the File and Open menu options. Had the Web page been located on a Web server, you would have entered the appropriate URL (Uniform Resource Locator) such as *www.amtoys.net/suppliers* into the Address bar to download the Web page. You'll learn how to publish Web pages to a Web server in a later tutorial.

You can use the Web page within Internet Explorer to edit and enter Access data, just as you did when you were viewing the Web page within Page view in Access.

To use Internet Explorer for data entry:

1. Double-click **Jennifer** in the first record, and then type **Jen**.

2. Click the **Next Record** button ▶ in the Navigation bar, click to the left of the "D" in the City field, type **West**, and then press the **Spacebar**.

3. Click the **Save Record** button in the Navigation bar, then click the **New Record** button ▶✳ in the Navigation bar.

   A new, blank Suppliers record appears awaiting your input.

4. Click the **SupplierName** field, type **Test**, and then click the **Save Record** button.

   At the moment that the record is saved, the SupplierID field should be updated because it was created with an AutoNumber data type. The next sequential number for the SupplierID field is 5.

5. Close Internet Explorer.

Now that you've used IE to open the Suppliers Web page and update the AMToys-3 database, you see that working with a Web page within IE is extremely similar to using the Page view within Access. Now open the AMToys-3 database to check the Suppliers table and make sure that the edits made through the Suppliers Web page were actually incorporated into the database.

To check the data updates made from within IE:

1. Open the **AMToys-3** database.

2. Click the **Tables** button 🔲 on the Objects bar, double-click the **Suppliers** table, maximize the Suppliers table window, and then resize the fields as necessary so that you can see the three edits to the table you made through the Suppliers Web page.

   Your screen should look like Figure 3-16.

Figure 3-16 **SUPPLIERS TABLE**

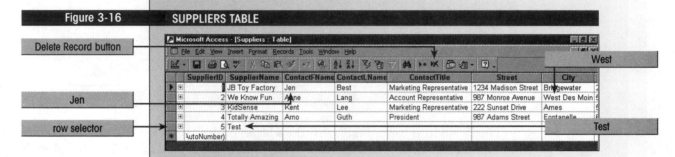

Delete Record button

West

Jen

row selector

Test

3. Click the **row selector** for the **Test** supplier record, click the **Delete Record** button ⬛ on the Table Datasheet toolbar, and then click **Yes** when prompted to confirm the deletion.

4. Close the **Suppliers** table and click **Yes** if prompted to save changes.

Data that is edited, added, or deleted in an Access database is automatically saved as you work within the database, and you will not lose any edits if you click "No" when prompted to "save changes." When you close an object, Access prompts you to "save changes" if you made any structural changes to the object. In this case, you were prompted to "save changes" if you resized any of the field widths. Clicking "Yes" saved the new column width structure for the next time you open the table.

Using **IE** for Interactive Reporting of an Access Database

Any Web page you create with Access works the same way in IE that it does in Page view, regardless of whether the page is used for data entry, interactive reporting, or data analysis. Still, it's good to open your Web pages within IE and work with them as a user would experience the Web page just to make sure that everything is working properly.

To use Internet Explorer for interactive reporting:

1. Right-click the **Start** button on the taskbar, and then click **Explore**.

2. Navigate to your Tutorial\Solutions folder for Tutorial 3 using the folder tree on the left side of the Exploring window, and then double-click **Products within Categories.htm**.

The Web page should open within IE as shown in Figure 3-17.

TROUBLE? If your computer used Netscape Navigator to open the Products within Categories.htm file instead of IE, you'll quickly see that Netscape Navigator is capable of opening the file, but not capable of providing live connectivity back to your Access 2000 database. If the file opens in Netscape Navigator, it is because the .htm file extension on your computer is associated with Navigator instead of IE. To quickly force this page into IE, you can copy and paste the path to the file from Netscape to IE using the following steps: Click to the right of the file entry in the Navigator Address bar so that the entire path is selected, click the Edit menu, click Copy, open an IE window, click in a blank Address bar, click the Edit menu, click Paste, and then press the Enter key. The Products within Categories Web page should now be opened within IE. You can also open the file directly within IE using the File and Open menu options. Refer to Appendix B for information on how to change file type associations if you want to automatically associate .htm files with IE.

Figure 3-17 | **PRODUCTS WITHIN CATEGORIES WEB PAGE IN IE**

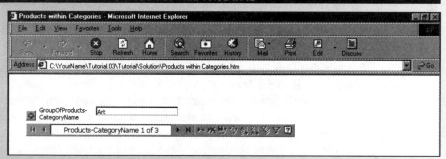

3. Click the **Expand** button for the Art category, click the **AgeLevel** field, then click the **Sort Descending** button in the upper Navigation bar.

   The product with the highest AgeLevel value within the Art category is the Discovery Art Studio.

4. Click the **Next Record** button twice in the upper Navigation bar to move to the second and third detail records within the Art category and to make sure that the sort worked correctly.

5. Click the **Next Record** button in the lower Navigation toolbar to move to the second category of toys (Books), and then click the **expand** button.

   The Books category also has three detail records.

6. Click **10** in the AgeLevel field, and then click the **Filter by Selection** button in the upper Navigation bar.

   Only one record in the Books category matched the selection of "10" in the AgeLevel field as shown in Figure 3-18.

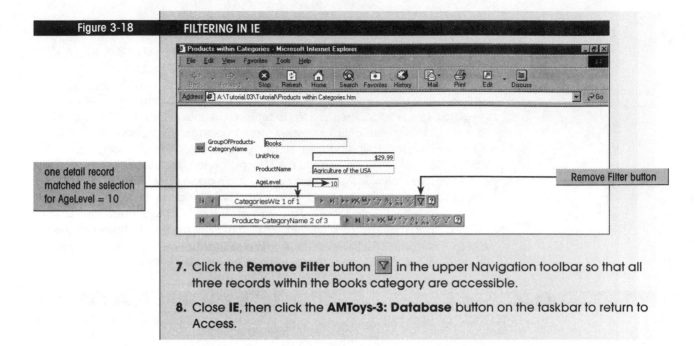

Figure 3-18   **FILTERING IN IE**

one detail record matched the selection for AgeLevel = 10

Remove Filter button

7. Click the **Remove Filter** button in the upper Navigation toolbar so that all three records within the Books category are accessible.

8. Close **IE**, then click the **AMToys-3: Database** button on the taskbar to return to Access.

At this point you are saving all of your Web pages to the same local Tutorial\Solutions folder for Tutorial 3 where your AMToys-3 database is located. You are opening these Web pages directly within IE instead of using Internet technologies such as Web servers and communication protocols to transfer the page to the browser. Even though there is obviously much more complexity involved in storing Web pages on a secure Web server and downloading them through an Internet connection, the way that the user works with the Web page once it is opened within IE is the same. Some of the issues involved with setting up a Web server and shared Web folders will be discussed in later tutorials. For now, however, as you're becoming more familiar with the page object, you'll store your Web pages (HTML files) in the same folder as the Access database files for convenience.

As discussed at the beginning of this tutorial, a corporate Access database is generally stored in a shared folder on a file server so that multiple local users can work directly with the Access database file using traditional Access objects such as queries, forms, and reports. Remote users who do not have direct access to the database file will have the ability to enter, edit, and interactively report on information through the use of Web pages downloaded to IE. These Web pages are generally stored in special Web folders located on a Web server. Later on you'll learn how to publish your Web pages to a Web server and open them as if you were a remote user.

Hyperlinks

The term hyperlink refers to two different things within an Access database, the hyperlink data type and the hyperlink control.

Hyperlink Data Type

The **hyperlink data type** indicates that the field entry is either a **URL** (Uniform Resource Locator) more commonly known as a Web page address, or a **UNC** (Universal Naming Convention). UNC is a naming convention used to locate a file on a local area network. The structure of a UNC is *servername**sharedfoldername**filename*. Clicking a URL or UNC within a hyperlink field—regardless of whether that address appears on a datasheet, within Form view, within Page view, or on a Web page—opens the linked Web page or file.

To explore a field with a hyperlink data type:

1. Click the **Tables** button 🔲 on the Objects Bar, double-click **Suppliers**, then press the Tab key 13 times to move to the Web field.

   The entries in the Web field are all URLs. Their blue color and underline make them appear as hyperlinks.

2. Point to the *www.totally.com* hyperlink in the fourth record.

   When you point to a hyperlink, the hyperlink mouse pointer 🖑 appears as well as a ScreenTip with the actual address. Since the URLs entered in this database are fictitious, you'll enter an actual URL to see how a hyperlink entry is really supposed to work.

3. Press the **Down Arrow** key three times so that the *www.totally.com* hyperlink is selected, then press the **Delete** key to delete the entry.

4. Type **www.toysrus.com** in the Web field, press the **Enter** key, press ←, and then click **www.toysrus.com**.

   If you are connected to the Internet, the home page for the Toys R Us company will appear within IE.

   TROUBLE? If you are not connected to the Internet, you may be prompted to connect to the Internet to continue, or Access may present an "Unable to open" message. If you get the "Unable to open" message, click the OK button, connect to the Internet, then click the *www.toysrus.com* link again to open that page.

5. Explore the Toys "R" Us page, and then close IE.

6. Click the **Suppliers : Table** button in the taskbar to return to that window if you're not already viewing it, and then click the **Undo** button 🔄 on the Standard toolbar to undo *www.toysrus.com* and restore the previous fictitious entry, *www.totally.com*.

7. Close the Suppliers table.

The hyperlink data type is a great way to store Web page addresses or file locations that are associated with the individual records of a table.

Hyperlink Controls

Within Access, **hyperlink** also refers to a control in the form of a label, button, or image placed on a form that when clicked, automatically opens another object, document, e-mail message, or Web page. These types of hyperlinks can be placed on a form or page object. For example, as you develop the page objects within a database, you'll probably want to provide connectivity between them. A hyperlink placed on one Web page that links it to another would support this additional navigation need.

To add a text hyperlink to a page object:

1. Click the **Pages** button 🖺 on the Objects Bar, click the **Products within Categories** page object, click the **Design View** button 🔏 on the toolbar, and then maximize the window if it is not already maximized to display the Products within Categories page object in Page Design view.

2. Move and resize the field list and close extra toolbars and windows so that your screen matches Figure 3-19.

Figure 3-19	PAGE DESIGN VIEW OF PRODUCTS WITHIN CATEGORIES OBJECT

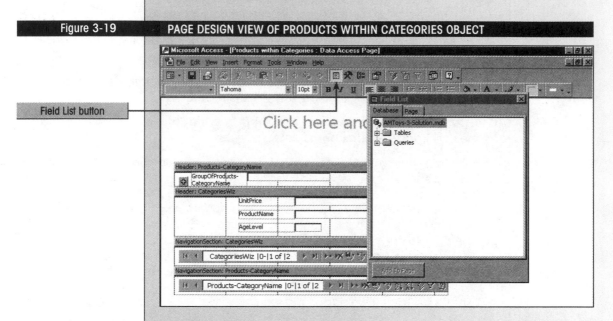

There are many similarities between Page Design view and Form or Report Design view such as the field list, Toolbox toolbar, and Sorting and Grouping dialog box. The page object has its own unique components such as sections for Navigation bars and many new controls that are particularly useful in analyzing Access data from within IE. You'll work more with Page Design view and some of these advanced controls in the next tutorial. To add a hyperlink control, you need to open the Toolbox toolbar. You don't need the field list, so you'll close it.

3. Click the **Field List** button 🗐 on the Page Design toobar to close the field list, and then click the **Toolbox** button 🛠 on the Page Design toolbar if the tool- box is not already visible..

The toolbox opens as shown in Figure 3-20.

Figure 3-20	WORKING WITH THE TOOLBOX TOOLBAR IN PAGE DESIGN VIEW

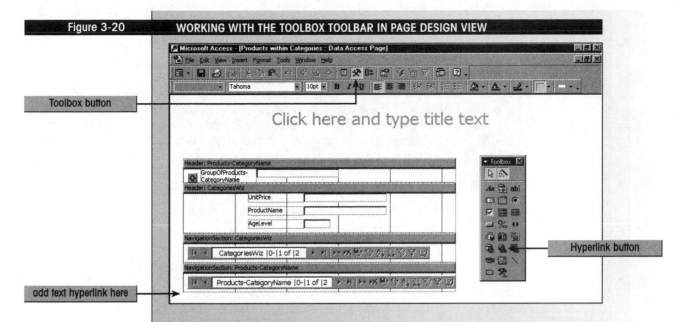

The hyperlink can be text or a graphic image. In this case, you'll make a text hyperlink with the phrase "Enter Suppliers" so that it describes the page that you are linking to.

4. Click the **Hyperlink** button 🖫 on the Toolbox toolbar, and then click just below the left corner of the lower navigation section.

The Insert Hyperlink dialog box opens requesting information about the link as shown in Figure 3-21.

Figure 3-21	INSERT HYPERLINK DIALOG BOX

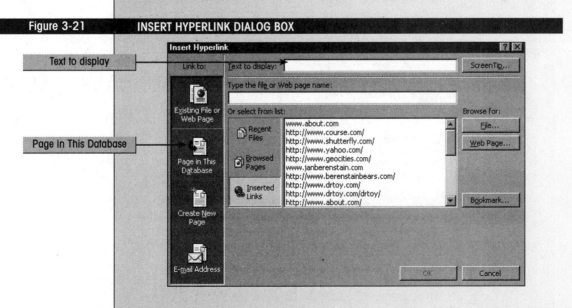

5. Type **Enter Suppliers** in the Text to display text box, click the **Page in This Database** button in the Link to list, click the **Suppliers** page entry, and then click the **OK** button.

The hyperlink is added to the page. Now view it in Page view to make sure it works.

6. Click the **Page View** button 🔲 on the Page Design toolbar, and then click the **Enter Suppliers** hyperlink.

IE should automatically load with the Suppliers Web page open.

TROUBLE? If Netscape opened the page instead of IE, you'll have to force the page into IE by copying and pasting the address from the Netscape address bar into the IE address bar, or by using the File and Open menu options within IE. Refer to Appendix B for how to change file type associations if you want to associate .htm files with IE rather than Netscape on your computer.

7. Close IE, then click the **Products within Categories** button in the taskbar.

8. Close the **Products within Categories** page, and then click **Yes** when prompted to save changes.

If you would prefer to have the hyperlink control appear as an image rather than as text, Access provides a control called the **hotspot image** control, which looks like a piece of clip art but behaves like a hyperlink.

Hotspot Hyperlinks

To add a hotspot hyperlink to a page object:

1. Click the **Suppliers** page object, and then click the **Design View** button 🔲 on the toolbar to open the object in Page Design view.

The Toolbox toolbar should still be displayed, since you did not toggle it off the last time you were working in Page Design view.

2. Click the **Hotspot Image** button 🔲 on the Toolbox, and then click just above the left edge of the Suppliers header section.

The Insert Picture dialog box opens, prompting you for an image choice for the hyperlink.

3. Click the **Look in** list arrow, navigate to the Tutorial\Solutions folder for Tutorial 3, and then double-click **block.bmp** to use this file as the hotspot image.

The Insert Hyperlink dialog box opens, prompting you for information on what the hyperlink will link to.

4. Click the **Page in This Database** button in the Link to list, click **Products within Categories** page, and then click the **OK** button.

The hyperlink is added as an image hotspot in Page Design view. Check to make sure that it works by using Page view.

5. Click the **Page View** button 🔲 on the Page Design toolbar. The Suppliers page opens in Page view as shown in Figure 3-22.

| Figure 3-22 | HOTSPOT HYPERLINK |

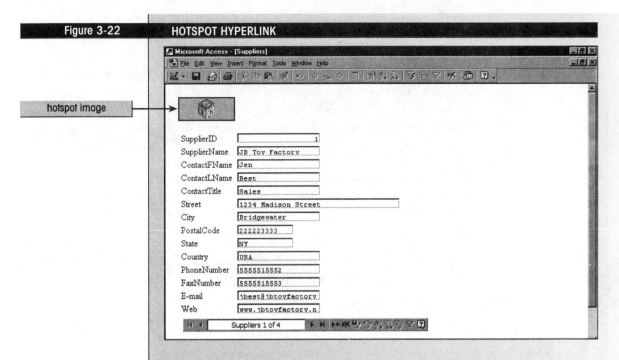

hotspot image

6. Point to the **block** image so that the pointer changes to the hyperlink pointer 🖑 and then click the **block** hotspot.

   If the hyperlink works correctly, IE should automatically load with the Products within Categories Web page showing.

   TROUBLE? If Netscape opens the Web page instead of IE, force the page into IE by copying and pasting the Web page address from one browser to another. Refer to Appendix B on how to associate .htm files with IE so that they automatically open within IE.

7. Close IE and then click the **Suppliers** button on the taskbar.

8. Close the Suppliers page, click **Yes** when prompted to save changes, and then close the **AMToys-3** database.

Broken Links

You may have experienced broken links when surfing the World Wide Web. The following common problems will cause Internet Explorer to indicate that "The page cannot be displayed" when you enter a URL or click a hyperlink on a page.

- You typed the URL (Web page address) into the Address box incorrectly.
- The URL/hyperlink is valid, but the Web page has been deleted.
- The URL/hyperlink is valid, but the Web page has moved.
- The URL/hyperlink is valid and the Web page exists, but there was a network problem (extremely heavy traffic, for example) in delivering the Web page to your browser.
- Your browser settings (security, content, and other default options) prevent you from displaying that page.
- The Web page contains content that your browser is incapable of displaying.

The specific solutions to these problems range from easy to extremely technical, but provided you have a working connection to the Internet, many of these problems can be solved with these troubleshooting tips:

■ If you type the URL into the Address box, make sure that it is entered correctly. There are never any spaces in URLs, the slashes are always forward slashes (/), and some URLs are case sensitive. A URL never ends in a period.

■ If you are sure that you have typed the URL into the Address box correctly but are still receiving an error from IE, click the Refresh button 🔁 on the IE Standard Buttons toolbar to reload the Web page.

■ Keep your browser updated. Staying at the most current level of Internet Explorer will automatically eliminate certain surfing problems that result from advanced Web page content that older browsers cannot handle.

■ If none of these options work, and it appears that you have been given an incorrect URL or the Web page appears to be missing, click the Back button ⬅ on the Standard Buttons toolbar to reload the previous page, then click a new hyperlink or type a new URL.

When working with the page object within Access, there is one more type of broken link message that you should be aware of. You receive the message shown in Figure 3-23 when you try to open a page object in Page view, but Access cannot find the corresponding HTML file.

Figure 3-23	LOST HTML FILE MESSAGE

This error message means that the **path** (the folder, drive, and server location) to the associated HTML file stored within the page object does not work. This happens when you move either the HTML file or the Access database file to a new location or rename any part of the path. To reestablish the link between the page object and its HTML file, click the Locate button in the error message, and then use your navigation skills to find and select the HTML file.

As you know, the page object as presented within Access is just a link to the HTML file. Therefore if the HTML file is deleted, the page object link itself is useless and should be deleted as well. When you view the page object within Access in Page View, you are actually using a very special browser provided by Access that opens the HTML file within Access. Page Design view is analogous to a Web page editor program. It allows you to edit the actual HTML file with features and controls that provide connectivity to an Access database.

Other Access Web and Internet Connectivity Tools

Although data access pages and hyperlinks are two of the most exciting ways to connect an Access database to Web and Internet technologies, there are a few other related tools that you should know about. These are described in Figure 3-24.

Figure 3-24	OTHER ACCESS WEB AND INTERNET CONNECTIVITY TOOLS
TOOL	**DESCRIPTION**
Create server-generated HTML files in ASP or IDC/HTX format, using the Export option on the File menu	A table, query, or form object can be exported to the Active Server Pages or older IDC/HTX format. The data is displayed in a datasheet format but can be viewed from any browser (not just IE) and retains a live link to the data.
Create static HTML files using the Export option on the File menu.	A table, query, form, or report object can be exported to a static HTML file format. The data is displayed in a datasheet format for tables, queries, and forms, and appears in a report format for reports. These files can be viewed from any browser (not just IE), but do not retain a live link to the data.
Import or link an HTML table or list into an Access database, using the Get External Data option of the File menu.	Data in the form of a list or a table on an existing Web page can be imported or linked to an Access database. Once the process is started, the Import HTML Wizard and Link HTML Wizard provide additional instructions on how to import or link the data.
Transfer or share data, or collaborate over the Internet using NetMeeting.	Using Microsoft NetMeeting, an Internet communications application that is part of Windows 98, you can transfer or share files, or collaborate within an Access database with anyone in your current meeting. Performing a file transfer is similar to sending a file attached to an e-mail message. Everyone gets a copy of the database. Sharing allows others to see the database, but only you can work in it. This is handy for demonstration or teaching purposes. Collaborating allows others to work directly within the application file, too.

Session 3.2 QUICK | CHECK

1. Compare working with an HTML file created from an Access page object in IE to working with the associated Page view in Access.

2. The term "hyperlink" refers to two different things in an Access database. What are they?

3. A field with a Hyperlink data type stores what type of data?

4. How does a hyperlink control placed on a page object appear?

5. Why might you receive the error message "The page cannot be displayed" from within IE?

6. What steps would you take to resolve message "The page cannot be displayed" from within IE?

7. What will happen if you move the location of either the Access database or a HTML file created by the page object?

8. How do you reestablish a link between a page object and its associated HTML file?

9. You can export Access objects in what other Web-oriented formats?

10. You can import data from an HTML file into an Access database, provided the data is in a certain structure on the HTML page. What is that structure?

11. How does NetMeeting allow you to expand the capabilities of an Access database via the Internet?

REVIEW ASSIGNMENTS

You work in the business office of a graduate school, Adair Graduate School, that offers several master's degrees, including Master of Business Administration (MBA), Master of Telecommunications Management (MTM), and Master of Information Systems Management (MISM) degrees. You have developed an Access database called **AdairGS-3** to help the faculty track students, classes, assignments, grades, and instructors. You'll use this database to build data access pages for data entry and interactive reporting.

1. Start Access and open the **AdairGS-3** database from your Review\Solutions folder for Tutorial 3.

2. You want to develop a data access page to enter new students into the database via the Web. Click the Pages button on the Objects Bar, then double-click Create data access page by using wizard.

3. Select all fields from the Students table. Do not add any grouping or sorting levels, accept the default title of Students, and open the page in Page view. There are seven records, and the first student is Nancy Gray.

4. Change the address for the first student to a unique address that you can identify. Be sure to delete the existing apartment information in the Street field. (*Hint*: The apartment information is hidden in the text box because it is the second row of the Street field.) Print that page by clicking the Print button on the Page View toolbar. When you print a record from Page view, only that record is printed. Navigate to the second record to save the changes.

   Note: If some or all of the text boxes appear blank, you will need to slightly increase the size of the text box control in Page Design view in order for the data to appear on the printout.

5. Save the data access page object and corresponding HTML file to the appropriate Solutions folder with the name **Students**. Close the page object and close the **AdairGS-3** database.

6. Start IE, click File on the menu bar, click Open, click the Browse button, click the Look in list arrow and navigate to the Review\Solutions folder where you saved the file. Find and double-click the **Students.html** file to open it within IE.

7. Sort the records in ascending order by LastName. On a piece of paper, write the last name entry for the first record.

8. Filter for all students who live in the state of Washington. On a piece of paper, write the number of students who live in the state of Washington and then remove the filter.

9. Click the New Record button in the Navigation toolbar and enter your own information into the eighth record. Note that input mask property for the PhoneNumber field was not retained for the text box. (This may come as a surprise because input mask properties added to fields in Table Design view are automatically applied to text boxes added to form objects.) Therefore, enter just the numbers of the phone number without parentheses or dashes. The entry for your student number can be any alphanumeric value.

10. Navigate to the previous record to force your information to be saved to the database, and then navigate back to the last record with your information. Print the new record with your information.

11. Find the record for Marcus Dunn and change the Street number from 14 to **1400**. Navigate to the next record to save that change, then close IE.

12. Open the **AdairGS-3** database from your Review\Solutions folder for Tutorial 3, and then open the datasheet for the Students table. Your record should appear as record eight. Adjust the column widths and margins so that the printout will fit on one page in landscape orientation. Preview, print, then close the datasheet. On the printout, circle the change to the record for Marcus Dunn made in Step 10.

13. Create a new query in Design view using the Instructors and Classes tables. Create a new field in the first column of the query grid that combines the instructor's first and last names as follows:

    Instructor: [InstructorFName] & " " & [InstructorLName]

    Then add the following three fields from the Classes table to the query grid.

    ClassName, Term, and Day

14. Save the query with the name **Instructor Assignments**, view the datasheet, and then close it.

15. Click the Pages button in the Objects bar, and then double-click the Create data access page using wizard option. Choose all of the fields from the Instructor Assignments query.

16. Use the Instructor field as the grouping level, sort the records in ascending order by ClassName, title the page **Instructor Assignments**, and then view the new page in Page view.

17. Navigate to Sara Eidie's record, then click the expand button to the left of her name. Print this page. On the printout, circle the number that identifies how many class assignments are made to Sara Eidie. On the printout, circle the number that identifies the total number of instructors.

Explore 18. Click the Instructor field, then sort in ascending order. On your printout from Step 16, identify the first instructor when the records are sorted in this way. On your printout, identify which database field is used to determine the order of the values in the calculated Instructor field.

19. Save the data access page object and corresponding HTML file with the name **Instructor Assignments** in the same Review\Solutions folder as your AdairGS-3 database, then close the Instructor Assignments page object.

20. You decide to compare the differences between a text and image hyperlink. Open the Students page in Design view, open the Toolbox toolbar if it is not already visible, click the Hyperlink button in the toolbox, and then click just above the upper-left corner of the Header: Students section.

21. Click the Page in This Database button in the Link to list in the Insert Hyperlink dialog box, and then double-click the Instructor Assignments entry in the Select a page in this database list.

22. Click the Hotspot Image button on the Toolbox, then click just above the upper-right corner of the Header: Students section.

23. In the Insert Picture dialog box, click the Look in list arrow and navigate to your Solutions folder. Find and double-click the **teaching.bmp** file, and then double-click the Instructor Assignments entry in the Select a page in this database list.

24. Click the Page View button to view the page and hyperlinks, and then click the Instructor Assignments text link to make sure that it loads the Instructor Assignments Web page within IE.

25. Close IE and the Instructor Assignments Web page, then click the Academic Teaching image and make sure that it also loads the Instructor Assignments Web page.

Explore ▶ 26. Now that you experienced both types of hyperlinks, you have decided to keep the image link and not the text link. Click the Design View button on the Page View toolbar, click the Instructor Assignments text link, and then press the Delete key.

27. Save the page and click the Page View button to view your final data access page.

28. Print the first record, close the Students page, close the **AdairGS-3** database, then exit Access.

CASE PROBLEMS

Case 1. Building Web Pages for Premier Consulting   You work for a Web hosting business called Premier Consulting that rents Web server space to small businesses as well as provides a variety of Web consulting services such as Web page design and creation, Web-enabled database development, and Web programming. You have developed an Access database that tracks clients, projects, payments, and employees, called **PremierConsulting-3**. You'll use this database to build data access pages for data entry and interactive reporting.

1. Start Access and open the **PremierConsulting-3** database from your Cases\Solutions folder for Tutorial 3.

2. You want to develop a data access page to enter and edit employee information in the database via your intranet, which is built on Web technologies. Click the Pages button on the Objects Bar, then double-click Create data access page by using wizard.

3. Add all of the fields from the Employees table, do not add any grouping levels, do not add any sort orders, title the page **Employees**, and view it in Page view.

Explore ▶ 4. Maximize the page, then click the Design View button to view the page in Design view. Click in the Click here and type title text area (above the Header: Employees section) and type **Employee Update Screen.** View the page in Page view.

5. Add your own name as the sixth record and enter **Project Manager** in the Title field, then navigate to the previous record to save the entry. Return to your record and print it.

   If some or all of the text boxes appear blank, you will need to slightly increase the size of the text box control in Page Design view in order for the data to appear on the print-out. This problem occurs when you use Windows 95 or 98 and printers using the Printer Control Language (PCL) driver.

6. Navigate to Kim Chin's record, then filter for those employees with a title of Project Manager. On your printout, write down how many records are displayed after filtering. Remove the filter.

7. Sort the records in descending order based on the BillingRate field. On your printout, write down the highest value in the BillingRate field.

8. Save the Web page as **Employee Update Screen** to your Cases\Solutions folder, then close the page object.

Explore ▸ 9. You wish to develop another Web page, which groups projects by client, for use on your intranet. Create a query in Design view using the Employees, Projects, and Clients tables. Add the following fields in the order shown to the query grid:

> **Table:** Employee
> > Fields: FirstName and LastName

> **Table:** Projects
> > Fields: ProjectName, ProjectTotalBillingEstimate, ProjectBeginDate, and ProjectEndDate

> **Table:** Clients
> > Fields: CompanyName

10. Display the datasheet, save the query as **Project Activity**, then close the datasheet.

11. Click the Pages button in the Objects toolbar, then double-click Create data access page by using wizard. Select all of the fields from the Project Activity query.

12. Group the records by CompanyName, then sort in ascending order by ProjectName. Title the page **Project Activity**, then view the page in Page view.

13. Navigate between the two company records. There should be two projects for each company. Save the page with the name **Project Activity** to your Cases\Solutions folder for Tutorial 3, then close it.

Explore ▸ 14. You have decided to add more fields to the Project Activity page. The easiest way is to add more fields to the underlying query that the page is based on. Open the Project Activity Query in Design view, then double-click the BillingRate field to add it to the last column in the query grid.

Explore ▸ 15. Add a calculated field in the next free column of the query grid with the following expression that estimates the number of days that the project is estimated to last: PotentialRevenue:([ProjectEndDate]-[ProjectBeginDate])*5/7*[BillingRate]

The expression determines the number of days between the beginning and end of the project, multiplies by 5/7 to estimate the number of working days, then multiplies that amount by the billing rate. (*Hint*: Right-click the Field cell and click Zoom from the shortcut menu if you need more room to enter the expression.)

16. Display the datasheet to make sure that the new field and calculated field are working correctly. You see that the calculated field is not formatted appropriately.

Explore ▸ 17. Return to Query Design view, right-click the new PotentialRevenue field, then click Properties. In the Field Properties dialog box, choose Currency for the Format property, then save and close the query.

Explore ▸ 18. Open the **Project Activity** page object in Design view, open the Field List window, expand the Queries folder, and then expand the Project Activity query.

Explore ▸ 19. Drag both the BillingRate and PotentialRevenue fields from the Field List window to the right side of the Header:Project Activity section, and then close the Field list window.

20. Move and format the new controls to improve the layout and clarity of the page.

21. Save the page, and then click the Page View button. Expand the Lazy K Kountry Store records and note that the Currency format was not retained for the calculated field. Save and close the **Project Activity** page.

Explore

22. In order to eliminate the numeric remainders on the PotentialRevenue field in the Page object, open the **Project Activity** query in Design view, then modify the PotentialRevenue field with the Int function, which returns the integer portion of the value as follows:

     PotentialRevenue: Int((([ProjectEndDate]-[ProjectBeginDate])*5/7*[BillingRate])

23. Display the **Project Activity** datasheet. The PotentialRevenue field still appears with the currency format, but all values are rounded to the nearest integer. The Page object does not retain the field's Format property, but since the value is now an integer, you have eliminated the remainders.

24. Close the **Project Activity** datasheet, then open the **Project Activity** page object in Page view and expand the first record. The PotentialRevenue field for the Lazy K Kountry Store's first project should be 24292.

25. Click the PotentialRevenue field, then click the Sort Ascending button on the upper Navigation toolbar. The Web Advertising project's potential revenue for Lazy K Kountry Store is 11942.

26. Save the **Project Activity** page, print this record, and then close the **Project Activity** page object.

27. Close the **PremierConsulting-3** database and exit Access.

Case 2. Building Web Pages for Dyslexia Organization   You are the director of a charitable organization dedicated to providing educational and support services for those who suffer from dyslexia. You have created an Access database called **Dyslexia-3** that currently tracks contributors and pledges. You wish to expand the database to also track events and expenditures. You'll use this database to build data access pages for data entry and interactive reporting.

1. Start Access and open the **Dyslexia-3** database from the Cases\Solutions folder for Tutorial 3.

2. You want to develop a data access page to enter and edit contribution information in the database via your intranet, which is built on Web technologies. Click the Pages button on the Objects Bar, then double-click Create data access page by using wizard.

3. Add all of the fields in the Contributors table, do not add any grouping levels, do not add any sort orders, title the page **Contributors**, and open it in Page view.

4. Sort the records in ascending order by MemberLName and print the first record.

5. Add your own information in a new, sixth, record. The ContributorID field has an AutoNumber data type, so you won't be able to (or need to) make an entry for that field.

6. Change the MemberFName value for John (Thumb) to **Tom**.

7. Save the page with the name **Contributors** in your Cases\Solutions folder, and then close the page.

8. Double-click Create data access page by using wizard, and then add all of the fields from the Pledges table. Accept the natural grouping by ContributorID, do not add any more grouping levels, do not add any sort orders, title the page **Pledges**, and open it in Page view.

9. Print the page for the first contributor, then use the navigation buttons to write down how many different pledges each of the five contributors made.

10. Save the page as **Pledges** in your Cases\Solutions folder, and then close the **Pledges** page object.

Explore

11. You are interested in the total amount pledged per contributor, so you'll build a query to summarize this value, then build a page on that query. Click the Queries button on the Objects bar. Double-click Create query in Design view, then add both the Contributors and the Pledges tables to Query Design view.

12. Create a calculated field in the first column with the following expression:

    Member:[MemberFName]&" "& [MemberLName]

Explore

13. Add the AmountPledged field twice (to the second and third columns) of the query grid.

Explore

14. Click the Totals button on the Query Design toolbar, then change the Group By option in the Total row to Sum for the AmountPledged field in the second column. Change the Group By option to Count for the AmountPledged field in the third column.

15. View the datasheet, save it as **Total Contribution**, and then print it and close it.

16. Click the Pages button on the Objects bar, double-click Create data access page by using wizard, and then choose all of the fields in the Total Contribution query. Do not add any grouping levels, but sort the records in descending order by SumOfAmountPledged. Title the page **Total Contribution**, then open it in Page view.

17. Navigate through the five records in the database. The CountofAmountPledged field should match the answer you wrote in Step 9 regarding how many pledges each contributor had made.

Explore

18. Click the Page Design View button, and then make the following formatting changes to the page:

    ■ Move the three text boxes in the Total Contribution section to the right.

    ■ Resize the three labels in the Total Contribution section so that all of the text is visible.

    ■ Edit the SumOfAmountPledged and CountOfAmountPledged labels so that there are spaces between the words.

19. Open the Toolbox toolbar and add a Hyperlink control to the lower-left corner of the page that links to a Page in This Database, the Pledges page.

20. Save the page with the name **Pledge Summary** to your Cases\Solutions folder, then open it in Page view.

21. Print the page for Helvetius Greco, click the Pledges hyperlink to make sure that it works, then close IE.

22. Return to the Pledge Summary page within Access, and observe the title bar. The caption Total Contribution (the name of the query that the page was originally based on) appears in the page's title bar, even though the Web page is actually saved with the name Pledge Summary. To change this, you must change the Title property of the page itself.

Explore

23. Click the Design View button, click Edit on the menu bar, click Select Page, then click the Properties button on the Page Design toolbar. Click the Other tab in the Page property sheet, delete **Total Contribution** from the Title property text box and enter **Pledge Summary** in its place.

24. Save and view the **Pledge Summary** page in Page view to observe the change in the title bar, close the **Pledge Summary** page, close the **Dyslexia-3** database, and exit Access.

Case 3. Exploring the Help System on Data Access Pages   You work in the business office of a health club called Ship Shape. You have developed an Access database that tracks clients, workouts, and exercises, called **ShipShape-3**. You'll use this database to learn more about data access pages using the Help system.

1. Start Access and open the **ShipShape-3** database from your Cases\Solutions folder for Tutorial 3.

2. You want to develop a data access page to enter and edit employee information in the database via your intranet, which is built on Web technologies. You decide to thoroughly explore the Help system on data access pages.

3. If the Office Assistant is not already visible on your screen, click the Microsoft Access Help button on the Database toolbar. Type **data access page** in the text box, then click Search.

4. Click the Data access pages: What they are and how they work link, and then maximize the Help window.

5. All Microsoft Office Help windows are built with similar features. Blue words are glossary words. Click page Design view in the first sentence in the Designing different types of data access pages section. A window appears that defines and sometimes provides pictures for that item. Click within the data access page Design view window to close it.

6. Blue underlined words are hyperlinks. They will automatically link you to a different page or section within the current page of the Help manual. Click the link for Using data access pages in Internet Explorer.

7. Sometimes you want to get an overview of what is available in the Help manual rather than ask a specific question. Click the Show button on the Microsoft Access Help toolbar. Click the Contents tab (short for Table of Contents). Click the expand button to the left of Working with Data Access Pages. Click the expand button to the left of Data Access Page Basics, click the expand button to the left of Creating Data Access Pages, and then click the entry titled Create a data access page to read the description on the right. The book icons in the Contents window indicate that there are many subbooks or pages within that section. The page/question mark icons indicate a page topic heading.

8. Click the Should I use a form, report, report snapshot, or data access page? topic heading. Click the Print button in the Microsoft Access Help toolbar to print this page. It helps differentiate between the features of forms, reports, and pages.

9. Spend some time expanding more book icons in the Contents window within the Working with Data Access Pages section. When you find a page that you find particularly helpful, print it, then write a sentence or two explaining why you chose that page on the printout.

10. Click the Answer Wizard tab in the left panel of the Help window. The Answer Wizard provides an area to create a natural language question. Type **How do I open a data access page in IE?** and then click the Search button. You can enter a natural language question in either the Answer Wizard or the Office Assistant prompt.

11. Click the Open a data access page topic in the list, then read the information on the right. Toward the bottom of the Help page, two methods of opening a page in IE are explained.

12. Click the Index tab in the left panel of the Help window. You want to find out more information about how to use Netscape Navigator with an Access database. Type **Netscape** in the Type keywords text box. You see the entries of NetMeeting and network. Netscape should be between those entries, so you know that there is not a page in the help manual indexed with this word. If you do not find a "hit" in the index, you might try to search for the word using the Answer Wizard, since it works more like a "full text search" tool, attempting to find the search words anywhere within the page (rather than just as an indexed keyword). Of course the more pages that the search tool "finds," the more pages you'll have to wade through before finding the specific answer to your question.

13. Since software versions are constantly changing, you decide to look for the latest information on Access and Netscape on the Microsoft Web site. Close the Microsoft Access Help window, connect to the Internet (if not already connected), click the Help menu option, and then click Office on the Web.

14. This Help menu option takes you to a Microsoft-supported Web page that offers additional help for Access. As of this writing, the URL was
http://officeupdate.microsoft.com/welcome/access.asp

15. Scroll through the page, find and click the Technical Support link for Access. Scroll through the links for hot issues, general information, and frequently asked questions. Click the links to learn about Access, then print a page that is particularly interesting to you. On the printout, write one or two sentences about why you chose to print that article. (*Note*: The goal of Steps 15 and 16 is to find up-to-date Web-based information about how to use Netscape and Access software together. If the Microsoft Help Web pages have been changed and do not match these steps, modify your steps to find the information needed using the new Web site design.)

16. Find the Search button, and click it. Enter **Netscape Navigator Access** as the search criteria, use **All Words** to further define your search, and search only the Support & Knowledge Base database. Scroll through the hits, reading the ones of interest, then print the one that was most interesting to you.

17. Disconnect from the Internet, close IE, close the **ShipShape-3** database, and then exit Access.

Case 4. Building Web Pages for Distinctive Meetings   Distinctive Meetings is an event management company that organizes corporate seminars for such areas as sales, communication, and computer training. They have developed an Access database, called **DistinctiveMeetings-3**, that tracks events, event registration, attendees, and internal employees. You'll use this database to build data access pages for data entry and interactive reporting.

1. Start Access and open the **DistinctiveMeetings-3** database from your Cases\Solutions folder for Tutorial 3.

2. You want to develop a data access page to enter and edit attendee information in the database via your intranet, which is built on Web technologies. Click the Pages button on the Objects Bar, then double-click Create data access page by using wizard.

3. Add all of the fields from the Attendees table, do not add any grouping levels, do not add any sort orders, title the page **Attendees**, and then open and maximize the page in Page view.

4. Sort the names in ascending order by AttendeeLastName. On a piece of paper, write down the last name of the first record in this sort order.

5. Find and filter for those attendees who live in Kansas. On your piece of paper, write down how many attendees are from this state. Remove the filter.

6. Add a new record with your own information. The AttendeeID field has an AutoNumber data type, so you won't be able to (or need to) make an entry for that field. Give yourself a Title of President and use the address for your school or business. Click the Save Record button on the Navigation toolbar to save the changes.

7. Save the page with the name **Attendees** to the Cases\Solutions folder for Tutorial 3 and then close the page.

8. Start IE, click File on the menu, click Open, click Browse, click the Look in list arrow and navigate to your Cases\Solutions folder for Tutorial 3. Double-click the Attendees HTML file and then click OK. Find your record, and then change your title from President to **CEO**.

9. Fred Rubble has been promoted to Regional Sales Manager. Update the Title field of his record with the new title.

10. Click the Save Record button in the Navigation toolbar, and then close IE.

Explore ▶ 11. In the DistinctiveMeetings-3 database window, click the Reports button in the Objects Bar, and then double-click Create report by using wizard. Choose the AttendeeFirstName, AttendeeLastName, Title, and CompanyName fields from the Attendees table for the report. Do not add any grouping levels, and sort the records in ascending order on AttendeeLastName.

12. Use a Tabular layout, Landscape Orientation for the report, and a Compact style. Title the report **Attendees**, print, and close it. Circle the changes you made in Steps 8 and 9 on the printout.

13. You want to build a data access page that displays sales information for each registration and also displays summarized attendee information. You need to build two queries to support the page. Build the first query in Query Design view using the Attendees, Registration, and Events tables. Create a calculated field in the first column that combines the first and last name of the attendee as follows:

    Attendee:[AttendeeFirstName]&" "&[AttendeeLastName]

    Add the RegistrationFee field from the Registration table and the EventName field from the Event table as the second and third columns.

14. Save the query with the name **Sales**, then display the datasheet.

Explore ▶ 15. Return to Query Design view, then click the Totals button. Change the Group By function to Sum for the RegistrationFee, and change the Group By function to Count for the EventName.

16. Display the datasheet, click File on the menu bar, click Save As, enter **Sales Summary** as the query's name, click the OK button in the Save As dialog box, and then close the **Sales Summary** query.

17. With both queries created, you are ready to build the page object. Click the Pages button in the Objects Bar, double-click Create page by using a wizard, and then choose all of the fields from the Sales query. Group the records by Attendee, and sort them in ascending order by RegistrationFee. Title the page **Sales**, and open it in Design view.

Explore ▶ 18. You wish to add the summary information from the Sales Summary query to the same page. Open the Field List if it is not already opened, and then expand the Queries folder. Drag the Sales Summary query to the right side of the Header: Sales section. The Layout Wizard dialog box opens.

Explore ▶ 19. In the Layout Wizard dialog box, click the Individual Controls option button, then click the OK button. The New Relationship dialog box helps determine how the records between the two queries will be related. Access guesses that the queries are related through the Attendee field, which is a correct assumption. Click the OK button.

20. Move the text box controls in the Header: Sales section so that the EventName and RegistrationFee text boxes are on the left, and the SumOfRegistrationFee and CountOfEventName text boxes are on the right. Delete the Attendee1 label and text

box, since that information is already displayed in the Header: Sales-Attendee section and does not need to be repeated. Continue to move and resize the controls in the Header: Sales section until they are all clearly visible.

21. Click the Page View button to view the new page. Navigate to Fred Rubble's record, then expand it. Navigate to the third event that Fred has registered for (Public Speaking Skills), then watch what happens to the SumOfRegistrationFee and CountOfEventName fields. Since they are summary values, they should not change as you move between the individual events that Fred has registered for. Print this page.

22. Save the page with the name **Sales Summary** to your Cases\Solutions folder for Tutorial 3, close the **Sales Summary** page, close the **DistinctiveMeetings-3** database, and then exit Access.

QUICK | CHECK ANSWERS

Session 3.1

1. The page object is also called the data access page.

2. The page object functions as a combination of the form and report objects in that the page object can be used both for data entry and data reporting. The page object also has some capabilities that go beyond those of the existing form and report objects such as interactive pivot tables and graphs that allow you to analyze data in new ways.

3. The major purpose of the page object is to create dynamic HTML (Hypertext Markup Language) files.

4. An Access database is sometimes described as a record-locking file because it allows multiple people to simultaneously update the same database (but not the same record).

5. In a typical setting, the Access database would be located in a shared folder on a file server. HTML files that dynamically update the Access database would be located in a Web folder on a Web server.

6. Network administrators and Webmasters are typical job titles for those who set up and develop local area networks, file servers, and Web servers.

7. The three general purposes for HTML files created by the page object are data entry, interactive reporting, and data analysis.

8. Four ways to create a page object are by using the AutoPage tool, by using the Page Wizard, from scratch in Page Design view, or by converting an existing Web page into an Access page object.

9. Page view is where you view, enter, and work with data using a page object, just as in Form view you modified the data using a form object.

10. The Navigation bar is used to find, filter, sort, delete, edit, and move between records in Page view.

11. The Page Wizard is a tool that can be used to quickly create a page object, but unlike the AutoPage tool, it allows the user to make some basic choices about the design of the page by presenting a series of dialog boxes.

12. Interactive reporting means that the user can interact with the presentation of the data. Examples of this interaction include expanding or collapsing grouped records, sorting, and filtering.

Session 3.2

1. Working with a Web page within IE is extremely similar to using the Page view within Access.

2. The term hyperlink refers to two different things within an Access database, the hyperlink data type and the hyperlink control.

3. The Hyperlink data type indicates that the field entry is either a URL (Uniform Resource Locator more commonly known as a Web page address) or a UNC (Universal Naming Convention).

4. A hyperlink control placed on a page object can appear as text, an image, a button, or any other graphic. When a graphic is used, it is called a Hotspot control.

5. You receive the "The page cannot be displayed" message when:
   - You typed the URL (Web page address) into the Address box incorrectly.
   - The URL/hyperlink is valid, but the Web page has been deleted.
   - The URL/hyperlink is valid, but the Web page has moved.
   - The URL/hyperlink is valid and the Web page exists, but there was a network problem (extremely heavy traffic, for example) in delivering the Web page to your browser.
   - Your browser settings (security, content, and other default options) prevent you from displaying that page.
   - The Web page contains content that your browser is incapable of displaying.

6. Many problems associated with displaying a Web page can be solved with these easy steps.
   a. If you type the URL into the Address box, make sure that it is entered correctly. There are never any spaces in URLs, the slashes are always forward slashes (/), and some URLs are case sensitive. A URL never ends in a period.
   b. If you are sure that you have typed the URL into the Address box correctly but are still receiving an error from IE, click the Refresh button 🔄 on the IE Standard Buttons toolbar to reload the Web page.
   c. Keep your browser updated. Staying at the most current level of Internet Explorer will automatically eliminate certain surfing problems that result from advanced Web page content that older browsers cannot handle.

7. If you move the Access database or HTML file, you will receive an error message when you try to open the page object from within Access.

8. To reestablish the link between the page object and its HTML file, click the Locate button in the error message, then use your navigation skills to find and select the HTML file.

9. You can export Access objects in the following Web-oriented formats: ASP, IDC/HTX, and static HTML.

10. You can import HTML data into an Access database provided that it is in a list or table structure on the Web page.

11. NetMeeting allows you to perform a file transfer, share files, or collaborate within an Access database.

In this tutorial you will:

- Work with controls, sections, themes, and properties in Page Design view

- Use the PivotTable list control to create data access pages for data analysis

- Modify a PivotTable both as a user and as a designer

- Use charts to analyze and compare data trends and patterns

- Use the Chart Property Toolbox to modify a chart

- Build formulas with an Office Spreadsheet control

- Add and modify a scrolling text control

- Add background sound

CREATING
DATA ACCESS PAGES
FOR DATA ANALYSIS

Using Web Pages to Analyze and Chart Data in the Aaron Michael Toys Database

CASE

Aaron Michael Toys

Now that you have created some basic data access pages to be used for data entry and interactive reporting of data within the Aaron Michael Toys Access database, you're ready to work with data access pages for more complex data analysis functions. In this tutorial you will learn how to create and modify PivotTable lists, graphs, and spreadsheet controls on a data access page. These types of controls will help you interact with data in new ways in order to make faster comparisons, spot new trends, and summarize data within multiple categories. You'll become more familiar with Page Design view by expanding your knowledge of the controls, sections, themes, and properties specific to the page object. You'll also learn how to add controls created in other applications, such as charts, HTML code, or sound clips, to a data access page.

SESSION 4.1

In this session you will explore Page Design view in depth. You'll also use the PivotTable list control to group and summarize data in many ways.

Page Design View

When you create a page using the AutoPage Tool or Page Wizard, most of the design work is automatically completed by Access. Unless you want to make a lot of modifications to the resulting page object, you don't need to have extensive knowledge of Page Design view. When building a page object for sophisticated data analysis purposes, however, you will have to use Page Design view and its accompanying features. For example, three powerful controls used for data analysis—the PivotTable List, Office Chart, and spreadsheet control—can only be added to a page from within Page Design view. Page Design view is also where you apply formatting changes to the page object, such as changing the theme or background, and where you can access the property sheet for any control or section. Figure 4-1 reviews Page Design view terminology, much of which is similar to Form or Report Design view terminology.

Figure 4-1	PAGE DESIGN VIEW TERMINOLOGY
TERM	**DEFINITION**
Body	The basic design surface of the data access page. It displays text, controls, and sections. When viewed in Page view or IE, the content in the body automatically adjusts itself to fit the size of the browser.
Field list	A list that contains all of the field names that can be added to an object in Design view. The Field List window within a page object displays *all* tables, queries, and associated fields within them. The Page tab of the Field List displays the bound controls and grouping choices within the Details section.
Toolbox toolbar	A toolbar that contains all of the controls that can be added to the object in Design view. Several controls in the Toolbox toolbar are specific to page objects, including the Office PivotTable, Office Chart, Office Spreadsheet, Expand, and Record Navigation controls.
Control	Each individual element that can be added, deleted, or modified in an object's Design view.
Bound controls	Control that displays data from an underlying recordset. Common bound controls are text boxes, list boxes, and PivotTable lists.
Unbound controls	Control that does not display data from an underlying recordset. Common unbound controls for a page are labels, lines, and toolbars.
Sections	Areas of the object that contain controls. Sections determine where and how often a control will appear or print. New sections within a page object include the **record navigation section**, which is used to display the navigation toolbar, and the **caption section**, which is used to display text. Neither of these two new sections can contain bound controls.
Properties	Characteristics that further describe the selected object, section, or control.
Positioning	The position of text, sections, and other elements in the body of a page relative to one another.

The Page Design view screen can get crowded with the many toolbars and small windows that you'll be using. You'll find that manipulating the windows and toolbars within Page Design view is similar to working in Form and Report Design views, even though elements with the same name as those in Form and Report Design views do appear differently in Page Design view. For example, the Field List window in Page Design view shows all of the fields in all of the tables and queries within the database, not just the fields upon which the object has been based.

The Toolbox toolbar has different controls in Page Design view than it did in Report or Form Design view, and therefore it has a different appearance. It is also important to review the fact that the toolbars may be positioned in many different areas of the window. When a toolbar is positioned at the edge of the screen, it is a **docked** toolbar. When a toolbar is positioned in the middle of the screen, it is a **floating** toolbar and can be resized. Resize a floating toolbar by dragging its edges. Move a floating toolbar (or small window) by dragging its title bar. Move a docked toolbar by dragging the gray bar on the left edge of the toolbar.

Yet another important toolbar issue is the new **More Buttons** button at the end of most Office 2000 toolbars. The More Buttons button provides users with a way to customize their toolbars to display those buttons that they most frequently use. While it is not recommended that you modify the toolbars of a computer that others will use, you should know about the More Buttons button in order to personalize your own computer as well as find buttons on shared computers that appear to be "lost." Because Page Design view presents so many new windows and toolbars, it's important that you know how to manipulate and position the parts of Page Design view easily.

To explore Page Design view:

1. Start Access, open the **AMToys-4** database from the Tutorial\Solutions folder for Tutorial 4, click the **Pages** button 📄 on the Objects Bar, double-click **Create data access page in Design view**, and then maximize the window.

   Your screen should look similar to Figure 4-2, although you may have more toolbars or other small windows open.

Figure 4-2   PAGE DESIGN VIEW

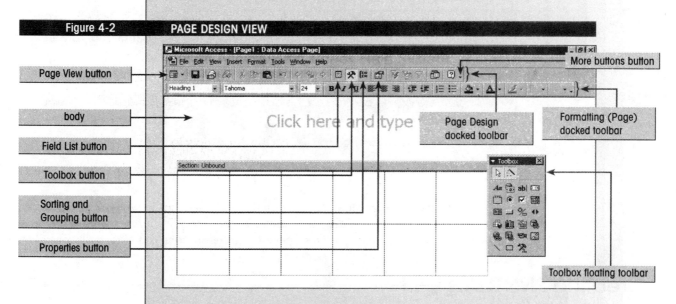

Several buttons on the toolbars are used to toggle toolbars, lists, and dialog boxes. The Field List is used to add bound controls to the form. The Sorting and Grouping dialog box is used to create groups of records for interactive reporting. The Property Sheet is used to modify all of the characteristics of the selected object, section, or control. The Toolbox toolbar contains all of the controls you can place on the page in Design view.

2. Click the **Field List** button 📋 to show the Field List, click it again to turn it off, click the **Sorting and Grouping** button 📑 to open the Sorting and Grouping dialog box, and then click 📑 again to close the dialog box.

3. Click the **Properties** button 🗗 to open the property sheet, and then click it again to close the property sheet.

   The property sheet displays all of the properties and the current value for each property of the selected control. A **property** is a characteristic of the control. Using the property sheet, you can make new choices for various properties to manipulate how the control appears and works on the page.

4. Right-click any visible toolbar, then click **Alignment and Sizing** to toggle that toolbar on.

5. Right-click any **visible toolbar**, click **Web**, right-click any **visible toolbar** and then click **Clipboard**.

   The **Clipboard** toolbar, a new toolbar for the Office 2000 suite of products, saves the last 12 items that have been cut or copied, so that you can selectively paste any of these 12 items within or between application windows.

   You can close toolbars either by right-clicking and toggling them off the list of toolbars or by clicking the close button on the toolbar's title bar. You can also turn toolbars on and off by clicking the View menu option, pointing to Toolbars, and clicking the appropriate toolbar choice.

6. Close all toolbars except the Page Design, Formatting (Page), and Toolbox toolbars, and then resize and move the Toolbox toolbar so that your screen matches Figure 4-2.

7. Click the **Page View** button 📧 on the Page Design toolbar.

   Since there are no controls on this data access page, it is blank when viewed in Page view.

8. Click the **Design View** button 📐 on the Page View toolbar to return to Design view.

By default, Page Design view appears with the same toolbars, windows, and arrangement left by the previous user. Feel free to manipulate the screen either to match the figures in this book or to accommodate your own personal preferences as you work with page objects.

Creating PivotTables

The **PivotTable list** control is a powerful bound control that summarizes data within an interactive table. Crosstab queries in Access and pivot table presentations of data in Excel present data in a similar way. Typically, a PivotTable list control is used to summarize three fields: a numeric field in the middle that is summarized and two non-numeric fields, used as the row and column headings. A sample PivotTable is shown in Figure 4-3.

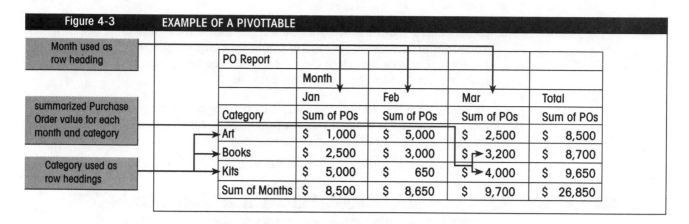

Figure 4-3   **EXAMPLE OF A PIVOTTABLE**

Month used as row heading

summarized Purchase Order value for each month and category

Category used as row headings

PO Report				
	Month			
	Jan	Feb	Mar	Total
Category	Sum of POs	Sum of POs	Sum of POs	Sum of POs
Art	$ 1,000	$ 5,000	$ 2,500	$ 8,500
Books	$ 2,500	$ 3,000	$ 3,200	$ 8,700
Kits	$ 5,000	$ 650	$ 4,000	$ 9,650
Sum of Months	$ 8,500	$ 8,650	$ 9,700	$ 26,850

In this example, the data within the PivotTable list represents the total purchase order value for each category of toy (row heading field) for each month (column heading field). The field being summarized in the middle can be subtotaled or counted. Although the basic PivotTable list displays only one field for the column heading and one for the row heading, you can use more than one field in either location to create subcategories. For example, you might want to summarize purchase orders for each different toy *within* each different category in the row heading area. The organization of the PivotTable data is limited only by the actual fields of information tracked by the database, and by your ability to work with the control. Since the data within a PivotTable list is a summarization of many records, it cannot be edited.

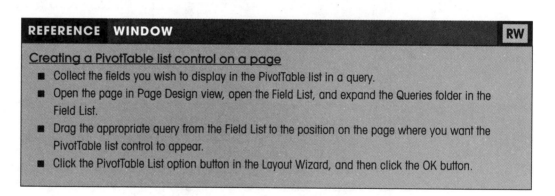

REFERENCE WINDOW   **RW**

Creating a PivotTable list control on a page
- Collect the fields you wish to display in the PivotTable list in a query.
- Open the page in Page Design view, open the Field List, and expand the Queries folder in the Field List.
- Drag the appropriate query from the Field List to the position on the page where you want the PivotTable list control to appear.
- Click the PivotTable List option button in the Layout Wizard, and then click the OK button.

You want to create a PivotTable control to subtotal the number of toys ordered from each supplier within each toy category.

To create a PivotTable list control:

1. If the Toolbox is visible, click the **Toolbox** button ![toolbox icon] to toggle it off, click the **Field List** button ![field list icon] to toggle it on, and then click the **expand** button to the left of the Queries folder to display all of the queries within the **AMToys-4** database.

   The database contains two queries that were previously created. The Supplier Analysis query contains the SupplierName, UnitsOrdered, ProductName, and CategoryName fields you want to use in this PivotTable list.

2. Be sure that the **Control Wizards** button 🔲 on the Toolbox is selected, drag the **Supplier Analysis** query to the upper-left corner of the Section:Unbound section of Page Design view, click the **PivotTable List** option button in the Layout Wizard dialog box, and then click the **OK** button.

TROUBLE? If the Layout Wizard dialog box did not appear, delete the control, then make sure the Control Wizards button 🔲 is selected before dragging the query to the unbound section of Page Design view.

Your screen should look like Figure 4-4.

Figure 4-4	ADDING A PIVOTTABLE LIST CONTROL TO PAGE DESIGN VIEW

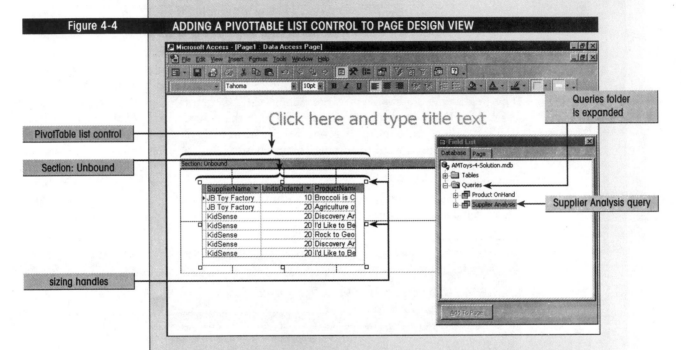

Frequently displaying a partially completed page in Page view will help you see exactly how each new control and modification appears to the user. Feel free to click the View button at any time during the construction of a new page object to switch between Page and Design view to see what the page looks like as you build it.

3. Click the **Page View** button 🔲 on the Page Design toolbar.

Right now, the PivotTable list control is not summarizing any data. The PivotTable list control is displaying the data just as it would appear in the underlying Supplier Analysis query. No fields are used as row or column headings to help the PivotTable list control determine how to group and summarize data.

A horizontal scroll bar appears because not all of the fields are visible. A vertical scroll bar appears because not all of the records are visible. Use Page Design view to modify and resize the PivotTable list control.

4. Click the **Design View** button 🔲 on the Page View toolbar, click the **Field List** button 🔲 to toggle it off, and then click the **PivotTable list** control to select it.

Sizing handles appear on a control that is selected. If the PivotTable list control does not display sizing handles, single-click it to select it.

5. Drag the **middle-right sizing handle** of the PivotTable list control to the far-right edge of the Section: Unbound section, and then drag the **middle-bottom sizing handle** of the PivotTable list control to the bottom edge of the Section: Unbound section.

   If you drag the sizing handles of the PivotTable list control beyond the section edges, you will enlarge the section too.

   Now that the control is larger and easier to see, you can more easily work with the organization of the fields within the PivotTable list control. The Supplier Analysis query on which this PivotTable is based included extra fields that you don't need in the PivotTable list control. You need to open the PivotTable list control for editing in order to delete or otherwise manipulate the fields within the control.

6. Click the selected **PivotTable list control** so that a hashed border appears around the control. The hashed border indicates that you are editing the control and not just selecting it to move, resize, or delete it.

   TROUBLE? If you opened the PivotTable list control's property sheet, you have to close it, then single-click the control again. Opening a PivotTable list control for editing is tricky because it involves two single-clicks. The first single-click selects the control. If the control is already selected, the second single-click will open it for editing. A double-click opens the control's property sheet.

   You don't want the ProductName field on the final PivotTable control.

7. Right-click the **ProductName field** as shown in Figure 4-5, and then click **Remove Field** from the shortcut menu.

Figure 4-5	EDITING A PIVOTTABLE LIST CONTROL

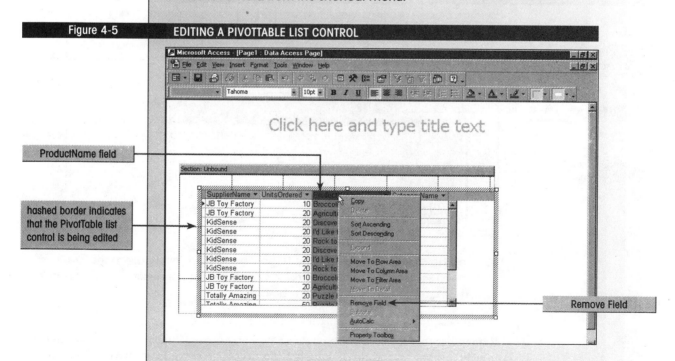

You could also delete the field by clicking the ProductName field heading and pressing the Delete key on the keyboard. However, when you right-click the field name, you are presented with a shortcut menu of other options that you want to become familiar with because you'll use them later.

Three fields remain in the PivotTable list control: SupplierName, UnitsOrdered, and CategoryName. You want to use the CategoryName as the row heading field, sum the UnitsOrdered field within the middle of the PivotTable list control, and use the SupplierName as the column heading field.

8. Right-click the **CategoryName** field, and then click **Move to Row Area**.

The PivotTable list control is recalculated and the CategoryName field is placed in the left side of the PivotTable list control. Each different category creates a single row.

TROUBLE? You may have to click the PivotTable list control again to open it for editing.

9. Right-click the **SupplierName** field, and then click **Move to Column Area**.

The PivotTable list control is recalculated again and the SupplierName field is placed at the top of the PivotTable list control. Each different supplier name creates a single column heading.

10. Right-click the **UnitsOrdered** field, point to **AutoCalc**, and then click **Sum**.

This adds a total value for each intersection of CategoryName and SupplierName to the PivotTable.

11. Click the **Page View** button 🔲 to observe your final PivotTable list control in Page view as shown in Figure 4-6. Use the scroll bars to move through the categories and suppliers to view all of the PivotTable.

Figure 4-6	THE PIVOTTABLE LIST CONTROL IN PAGE VIEW

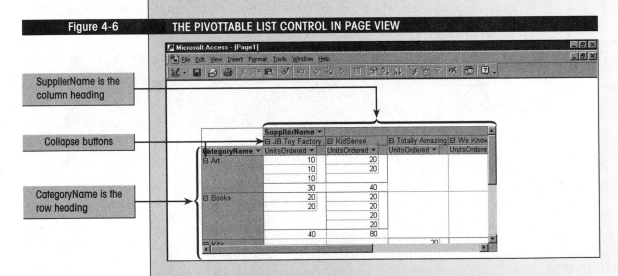

12. Click the **Save** button 🔲 on the Page View toolbar, navigate to the Tutorial\Solutions folder for Tutorial 4, type **Supplier Analysis** in the File name text box, and then click the **Save** button.

Remember that the first time you save a data access page, you are actually saving both the Web page (.htm file) and the link within the Access database. Both parts of the data access page are given the same name, the name that you gave the .htm file in the Save As dialog box.

Now that you have created the PivotTable list control in Page Design view, you'll learn how to work with it for data analysis in Page view. Remember that working with a data access page in Page view gives you the same experience that the users have when they open the associated HTML file in IE. Therefore you can think of Page view as a special type of browser that displays these special Web pages within Access itself. The benefit of learning how to analyze data using the PivotTable list control in Page view rather than opening the Web page in IE is that you have quick access to Page Design view, should you wish to modify the Web page object.

Collapsing, Expanding, and Filtering Data Within a PivotTable

As a user of a PivotTable list control, you can analyze the data by using the expand and collapse buttons for the row and column headings to display or hide details. By default, both the row headings and column headings displayed within the PivotTable list control are expanded, which shows the UnitsOrdered value for every detail record in the underlying Supplier Analysis query. However, seeing the specific number of units ordered for each order may not be important for an overall analysis of supplier activity within toy category.

To collapse or expand the amount of detail shown within the PivotTable List Control:

1. Click the **collapse** button to the left of the **Art** category. The details for that category are collapsed for each supplier, but within that category only.

   You still know that a total of 30 Art units were ordered from JB Toy Factory and that a total of 40 Art units were ordered from KidSense.

2. Click the **collapse** button to the left of the **JB Toy Factory** supplier as shown in Figure 4-7.

Figure 4-7	COLLAPSING DETAIL IN A PIVOTTABLE LIST CONTROL

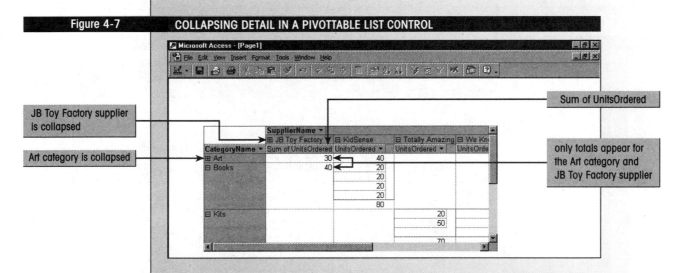

JB Toy Factory supplier is collapsed

Art category is collapsed

Sum of UnitsOrdered

only totals appear for the Art category and JB Toy Factory supplier

   Now the values in all other categories for the JB Toy Factory are collapsed as well. The heading for the UnitsOrdered field for the JB Toy Factory column changed to "Sum of UnitsOrdered", indicating that all of the numbers in this column are subtotaled.

3. Click the **collapse** button to collapse the details for all of the other suppliers; use the horizontal scroll bar as necessary.

   Collapsing the detail records more clearly shows you the overall activity for each supplier. You can also see that neither JB Toy Factory nor KidSense supply any toys in the Kits category. Since there are only four suppliers, you will try to widen the PivotTable list control in Page Design view so that you won't have to scroll in Page view.

4. Click the **Design View** button 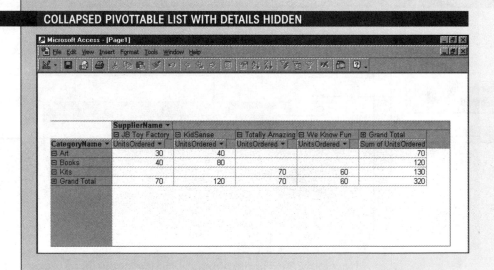, drag the **middle-right sizing handle** of the PivotTable list control to the right edge of the screen, drag the **middle-left sizing handle** of the PivotTable list control to the left edge of the screen, drag the **middle-bottom sizing handle** down to the bottom of the screen, and then click the **Page View** button.

When you switch from Design view to Page view, the PivotTable control appears in Page view as it appeared in Design view, not as it was left by the user manipulating it in Page view (or within an IE window).

Another way to hide or display details is to double-click the summarized value.

5. Double-click the summarized Art category value of **30** for the JB Toy Factory supplier, and then double-click it again.

Double-clicking the subtotal toggles the details on and off for that subtotal. Double-clicking works as a toggle in other parts of the PivotTable control too.

6. Double-click **Art** in the CategoryName column, then double-click it again.

7. Double-click **Totally Amazing** in the SupplierName row, then double-click it again.

8. Double-click **subtotals** within the PivotTable list control until your screen looks like Figure 4-8.

Grand totals are automatically added as the far-right column and bottom row of the PivotTable control to subtotal each category row and supplier column.

Figure 4-8	COLLAPSED PIVOTTABLE LIST WITH DETAILS HIDDEN

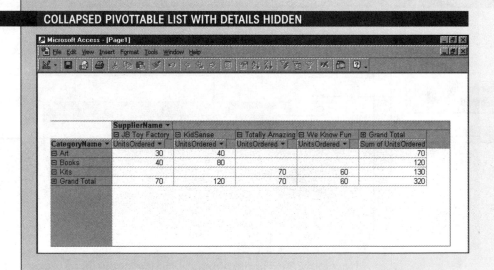

In addition to expanding or collapsing detail values within the PivotTable list, you can use the **filter arrows** to display or hide certain categories, suppliers, or orders. For example, you might only be concerned with the data for the JB Toy Factory and KidSense suppliers. Using the filter arrows, you can easily choose which suppliers will appear on the PivotTable.

To filter within the PivotTable List control:

1. Click the **SupplierName field** filter arrow.

A list of suppliers appears with check boxes. If a box is checked, that supplier will appear in the PivotTable.

2. Click the **Totally Amazing** check box, click the **We Know Fun** check box to clear both boxes as shown in Figure 4-9, and then click the **OK** button.

Figure 4-9	USING THE FILTER ARROWS

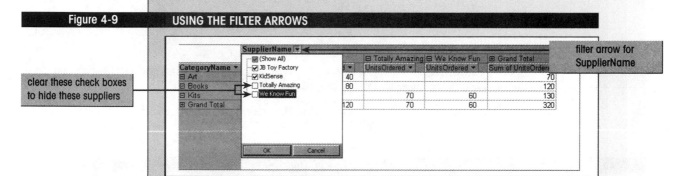

The Totally Amazing and We Know Fun suppliers are not removed from the PivotTable list, but they are hidden from view. Since neither of the remaining suppliers had any data in the Kits category, it was also removed from the PivotTable.

3. Click the **SupplierName field** filter arrow, click the **Show All** check box, and then click the **OK** button to display all of the suppliers and categories again.

4. Click the **CategoryName** filter arrow, click the **Kits** check box to clear it, and then click the **OK** button.

Since neither the Totally Amazing nor We Know Fun suppliers have been used to order any product in the Art or Books categories, they were removed from the PivotTable.

5. Click the **CategoryName** filter arrow, click the **Show All** check box twice to clear all categories, click the **Art** check box, and then click the **OK** button.

Now the grand total for the supplier is the same as the grand total for the Art category because there is only one category displayed on the PivotTable.

6. Click the **CategoryName** filter arrow, click the **Show All** check box to show all categories, and then click the **OK** button.

You can also filter for values within the PivotTable list. For example, suppose that you are looking for any order that contained 50 units.

7. Click the **UnitsOrdered** filter arrow.

It doesn't matter which column you choose since this field is displayed in all columns.

8. Click the **Show All** check box to clear all check marks, click the **50** check box, and then click the **OK** button.

The only order for 50 units was for a product in the Kits category placed with the Totally Amazing supplier. The subtotal is still 70, and the grand totals are still valid, even though you have filtered the PivotTable to show only those orders where the UnitsOrdered field equals 50. This tells you that the subtotals always calculate a value for all of the records, even when part of the data is filtered out.

9. Double-click the **70** subtotal for the Totally Amazing supplier in the Kits category to collapse that section.

10. Click the **UnitsOrdered** filter arrow, click the **Show All** check box to restore all check marks, and then click the **OK** button.

    All of the records are restored.

11. Double-click the **70** subtotal for the Totally Amazing supplier in the Kits category to expand that section.

    You can now see why the subtotal was correctly calculated as 70, even when one of the detail records was filtered out.

12. Double-click the summary values to collapse the details so that your PivotTable looks like Figure 4-10.

Figure 4-10	PIVOTTABLE WITH NO FILTERS AND DETAILS COLLAPSED

		SupplierName ▾			
		⊟ JB Toy Factory	⊟ KidSense	⊟ Totally Amazing	⊟ We Know Fun	⊞ Grand Total
CategoryName ▾		UnitsOrdered ▾	UnitsOrdered ▾	UnitsOrdered ▾	UnitsOrdered ▾	Sum of UnitsOrdered
⊟ Art		30	40			70
⊟ Books		40	80			120
⊟ Kits				70	60	130
⊞ Grand Total		70	120	70	60	320

13. Click the **Save** button 🖫 on the Page View toolbar, and then close the page.

    The PivotTable control is saved according to how it was last modified in Page Design view.

Remember that the PivotTable is saved according to the level of detail that is displayed in Page Design view, not Page view. The manipulations to the PivotTable control made in Page view emulate how a user would modify the control when viewing it as a Web page in IE, and you wouldn't want those modifications saved to the Web page because they will be specific to the data analysis needs of that user. As the designer of the page, you'll want to set the level of detail and filters for the PivotTable control in Page Design view so that every user who opens the page in IE will start with the same PivotTable control.

Collapsing, expanding, and filtering are three common and easy ways to analyze data using the PivotTable list. As the user of this PivotTable, however, you may find yourself wanting an entirely different presentation of the PivotTable data. For example, you may want to sort the information; calculate a different statistic, such as a count instead of a subtotal; or change the organization of the fields. You may want to use an entirely different field. All of these types of analysis tasks can be accomplished from Page view (which means that all of these tasks can also be accomplished by using the Web page within IE too).

Manipulating the Structure of the PivotTable

Your success in manipulating the structure of the PivotTable depends on your knowledge of PivotTable terminology. While the most basic PivotTable consists of three fields to fill the row, column, and detail areas, multiple fields can be used in each of these areas to create more complex PivotTables. Figure 4-11 shows a PivotTable with two row fields. When multiple fields are used in the same area, they should be ordered in a general-to-specific manner. For example, each supplier provides many products so that's why the SupplierName field is listed as the first row field, and the ProductName field is the second row field.

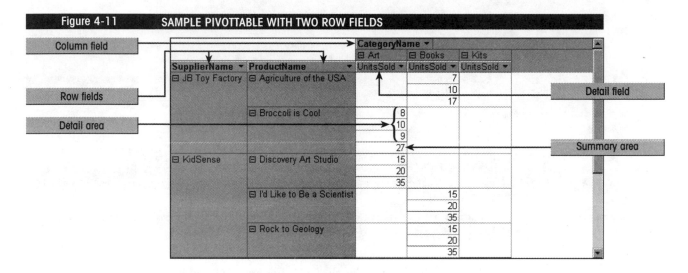

Yet another way to enhance a PivotTable control is to use a field in the **Filter field** position. If you are familiar with Excel pivot tables, you will recognize this as the "Page field position" in Excel. The Filter field is a way to filter out records based on a criteria in a field other than the fields in the row, column, and detail areas. Figure 4-12 shows how the same PivotTable would appear with the ProductName field moved to the Filter field position.

Do not let the term "Filter field" trick you into thinking that it is the only field that can be filtered. Any field added to a PivotTable, including the row, column, detail, and filter fields, can be used to filter the records that are displayed.

Figure 4-13 describes the terminology of a PivotTable.

Figure 4-13	PIVOTTABLE TERMINOLOGY
TERM	**DEFINITION**
Row field	A field in the row area (the leftmost edge of the PivotTable). You can specify more than one row field. For example, you may want the PivotTable to organize information by ZipCode within State. In this case, the State field would be the leftmost row field and the ZipCode field the second row field.
Column field	A field in the column area (the top edge of the PivotTable). You can specify more than one column field. For example, you may want the PivotTable to organize information by Month within Year. In this case, the Year would be the top column field, and the Month would be the second column field.
Detail field	A field that is placed in the intersection of the column and rows, and which contains individual or summary values from the underlying recordset. The underlying recordset can be determined with a table name, a query name, or SQL commands.
Filter field	A field in the filter area (the upper-left corner of the PivotTable).
Field filter arrow	The arrow at the right side of each type of field. When clicked, it presents a list of entries for that field from which you can choose to selectively hide or display in the PivotTable.
Detail area	The part of a PivotTable that shows detail (nonsummarized) data. A PivotTable can show detail and summary data simultaneously.
Summary area	The part of a PivotTable that shows summarized data. A PivotTable can show detail and summary data simultaneously.

You'll create the PivotTables shown in Figures 4-11 and 4-12 to analyze sales and learn more about how to manipulate a PivotTable. The first step will be to create a query that gathers the fields you wish to use in the PivotTable.

To create the underlying query for the PivotTable:

1. Click the **Queries** button 🔲 on the Objects Bar, double-click **Create query in Design view**, and then add the following tables in the order shown: **Suppliers, Purchase Orders, Inventory Transactions, Products, Categories**.

2. Close the **Show Table** dialog box, then add the following fields to the query grid in the order shown:

    SupplierName from the Suppliers table
    UnitsSold from the Inventory Transactions table
    ProductName from the Products table
    CategoryName from the Categories table

3. Click the **Datasheet View** button 🔲 to display the datasheet, save the query with the name **Sales Analysis**, and then close the **Sales Analysis** datasheet.

Now that you have created a query object with the specific fields that you want to analyze in the PivotTable list control, you're ready to create the page object itself.

To create a PivotTable with multiple row fields:

1. Click the **Pages** button 🔲 on the Objects Bar, double-click the **Create data access page in Design view** option, and then maximize the window.

2. Click the **Field List** button 🔲 on the Page Design toolbar, expand the **Queries** folder, drag the **Sales Analysis** query to the upper-left corner of the Section: Unbound section, click the **PivotTable List** option button, and then click the **OK** button.

As you experienced before, the PivotTable control starts out looking just like the datasheet of the query it is based on.

3. Click the **Field List** button 🔲 on the Page Design toolbar to toggle it off, and then drag the **lower-right corner sizing handle** of the new PivotTable list control to the lower-right corner of the screen to enlarge the control.

You should be able to see all four columns. The last record should be for JB Toy Factory and Broccoli Is Cool. Note that the left and top edges of the Section: Unbound section are fixed, so you cannot enlarge a PivotTable list in those directions.

4. Click the **Page View** button 🔲 to view the PivotTable list.

Currently, no fields have been specified for the row or column headings. You can do this directly from Page view or the IE browser.

5. Right-click the **SupplierName** field heading as shown in Figure 4-14, and then click **Move to Row Area**.

Figure 4-14	MOVING FIELDS IN A PIVOTTABLE

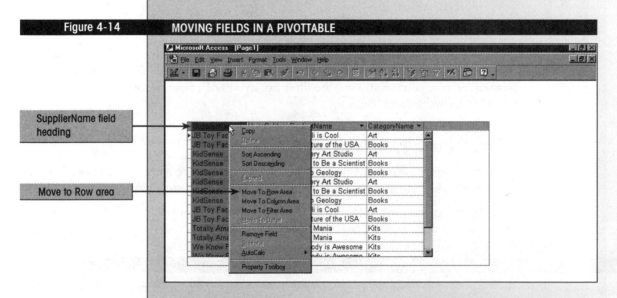

SupplierName field heading

Move to Row area

The PivotTable is recalculated with the SupplierName in the row area.

6. Right-click the **ProductName** field heading, and then click **Move to Row Area**.

Since each supplier provides multiple products, it was important to list the supplier field first, so that the products would be grouped within supplier in the row area.

7. Right-click the **CategoryName** field heading, and then click **Move to Column Area**.

The PivotTable is recalculated with the CategoryName in the column area.

8. Click the **Save** button 🖫 on the Page Design toolbar, navigate to the Tutorial\Solutions folder for Tutorial 4, enter **Sales Analysis** as the filename, and then click the **Save** button.

Once again, the page object was saved *as of the last change made in Design view*. Changes you made to the Page object in Page view *were not* saved in the object, since this view simulates the actions of an individual user of the associated Web page. If you wish to display the PivotTable list control in a particular arrangement, make and save the changes in Page Design view before further manipulating it in Page view. Rebuild your PivotTable in Design view so that you can save it in that arrangement.

9. Click the Design View button 🖾 on the Page View toolbar, single-click the **PivotTable** control twice to open it for editing, right-click the **SupplierName** field heading, click **Move to Row Area**, right-click the **ProductName** field heading, click **Move to Row Area**, right-click the **CategoryName** field heading, and then click **Move to Column Area**.

Now that the PivotTable control has been developed in Design view, when you save it and open this page, every user will see the PivotTable control in this arrangement.

10. Click the **Save** button 🖫 to save this as the permanent arrangement of data within the PivotTable.

Now you'll create a filter field within the PivotTable. The filter field is nothing more than a field in the filter field position. Whether your PivotTable uses fields in the filter field position or not, you can still use the filter list arrows of a field in any PivotTable field position (filter, row, column, detail).

To create a PivotTable with a filter field:

1. In Design view, right-click the **ProductName** field heading, click **Move to Filter Area**, click the **Save** button 🖫, and then click the **Page View** button 🖽.

The ProductName field moves to the upper-left corner of the PivotTable, and its filter is currently set to "All" as shown in Figure 4-15.

Figure 4-15   CREATING A FILTER FIELD

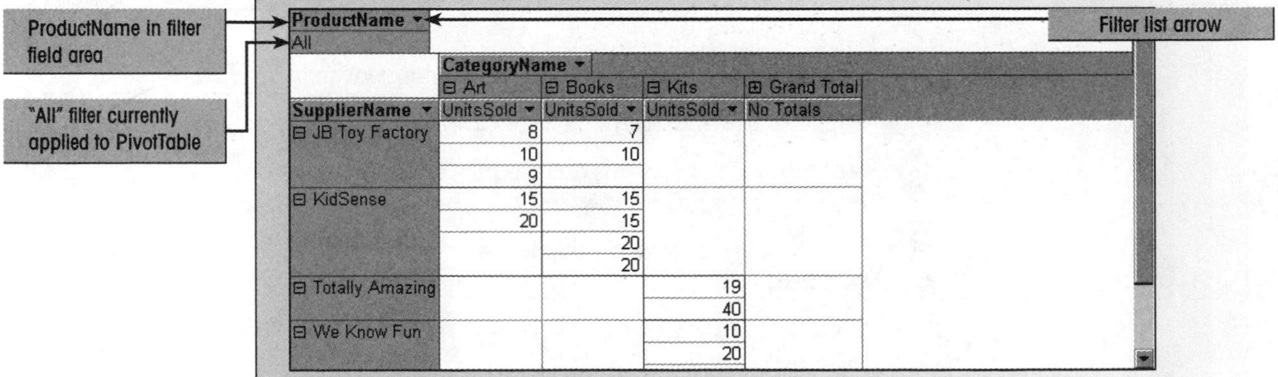

2. Click the **ProductName filter** list arrow, click the **Agriculture of the USA** check box, and then click the **OK** button in the filter window.

This quickly filters out all products except for Agriculture of the USA from the PivotTable.

3. Click the **ProductName filter** list arrow, click the **(All)** check box, and then click the **OK** button in the filter window to display all of the data.

Moving the fields to new locations within the PivotTable provides a fast and powerful way to view and analyze the data. No matter how the data is organized, however, you can still use the expand and collapse buttons as well as the filter list arrows to further customize the amount of detail you wish to show. In addition, you can choose sort options.

To sort a PivotTable:

1. Right-click the **CategoryName** field heading, click **Sort Descending**, and then click in the blank area to the right of the PivotTable so that nothing is highlighted.

Now the categories are listed in reverse alphabetical order: Kits, Books, Art.

2. Right-click the **CategoryName** field heading, and then click **Sort Ascending**.

The categories are sorted in alphabetical order: Art, Books, Kits. You can sort on the detail field as well.

3. Right-click the **UnitsSold** field heading, click **Sort Ascending**, and then click in the blank area to the right of the PivotTable so that nothing is highlighted. Your screen should look like Figure 4-16.

| Figure 4-16 | SORTING A PIVOTTABLE |

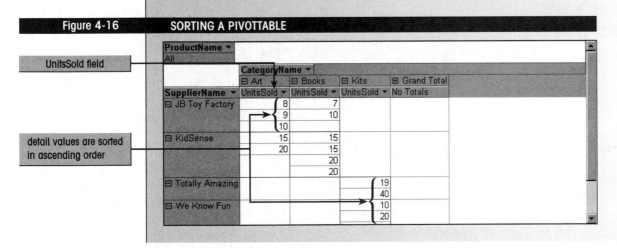

UnitsSold field

detail values are sorted in ascending order

Changing PivotTable Calculations

When you create a PivotTable control, Access makes some assumptions about the default subtotals and other summarized calculations that it will create. For example, the PivotTable control you just created from the Sales Analysis query automatically created a Grand Total column as the last column in the PivotTable to summarize each SupplierName. It automatically created a Grand Total row as the last row to summarize each CategoryName. You may not, however, want this extra column and extra row to appear on your PivotTable.

To work with the PivotTable subtotal column or row:

1. Right-click the **CategoryName** field heading, then click **Subtotal**.

   The Subtotal column on the far-right edge of the PivotTable was removed.

2. Scroll **down** so that you can view the last row of the PivotTable, the Grand Total row.

3. Right-click the **SupplierName** field heading, and then click **Subtotal**.

   The Subtotal row at the bottom of the PivotTable was removed.

4. Right-click the **SupplierName** field heading, and then click **Subtotal** to redisplay the last row.

5. Right-click the **CategoryName** field heading, and then click **Subtotal** to redisplay the last column.

   Right now, the last column and last row aren't that useful, because they are not expanded, so you cannot see the detail values in those areas.

6. Click the **expand** button for the Grand Total column, then scroll down and click the **expand** button for the Grand Total row, as shown in Figure 4-17.

Figure 4-17	EXPANDING GRAND TOTALS

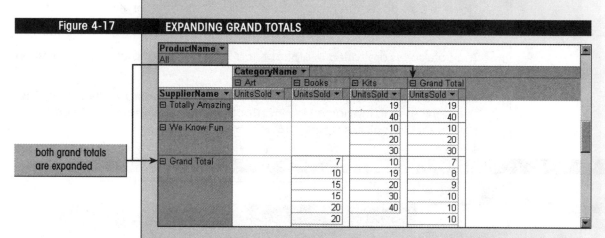

both grand totals are expanded

Expanding either the Grand Total column or the Grand Total row expands the cell in the lower right-hand corner of the PivotTable.

By default, the Grand Total column and row repeat each individual entry in the detail field section of the PivotTable. While this presentation of data may work for small amounts of data, as your database grows, you'll be less interested in individual values, and more interested in summarizations of them. You can easily change the presentation of detailed values to summarized values by working with the calculation options for the detail field.

To change the calculation options for the detail field:

1. Right-click the **UnitsSold** field heading, point to **AutoCalc**, and then click **Sum**.

   The PivotTable is recalculated, adding subtotals to the PivotTable as shown in Figure 4-18.

Figure 4-18	ADDING CALCULATIONS FOR THE DETAIL FIELD

calculated "sums" for the UnitsSold field

ProductName ▾
All

	CategoryName ▾			
	⊟ Art	⊟ Books	⊟ Kits	⊟ Grand Total
SupplierName ▾	UnitsSold ▾	UnitsSold ▾	UnitsSold ▾	UnitsSold ▾
⊟ JB Toy Factory	8	7		7
	9	10		8
	10			9
				10
				10
	27	17		44
⊟ KidSense	15	15		15
	20	15		15
		20		15
		20		20
				20

You already know that by double-clicking any calculation within the PivotTable, you can show or hide the details of that calculation. You can show or hide the details of an entire column or row by double-clicking the column or row heading.

TROUBLE? If you add the Sum of UnitsSold field, delete it, and add it back again, the field will appear with a sequential number after it such as Sum of UnitsSold (2). The number refers to how many times you created the field. Later, you'll learn how to edit this default caption or create an entirely different caption for this summarized field.

2. Double-click the **Grand Total** column heading, and then click to the right of the PivotTable so that nothing is selected.

Your screen should look like Figure 4-19.

Figure 4-19	HIDING THE DETAILS OF A CALCULATION

double-click the column or row heading to show or hide the details within the calculation

ProductName ▾
All

	CategoryName ▾			
	⊟ Art	⊟ Books	⊟ Kits	⊞ Grand Total
SupplierName ▾	UnitsSold ▾	UnitsSold ▾	UnitsSold ▾	Sum of UnitsSold
⊟ JB Toy Factory	8	7		44
	9	10		
	10			
	27	17		
⊟ KidSense	15	15		105
	20	15		
		20		
		20		
	35	70		
⊟ Totally Amazing			19	59
			40	

3. Double-click the **Art** column heading, double-click the **Books** column heading, double-click the **Kits** column heading, and then click below the PivotTable so that nothing is selected.

Your screen should look like Figure 4-20.

Figure 4-20 | SHOWING ONLY SUMMARY INFORMATION WITHIN A PIVOTTABLE

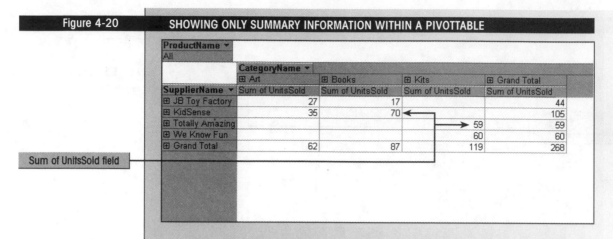

Sum of UnitsSold field

You can show more than one calculation within a PivotTable at the same time. For example, you may want to show Sum and Count functions for the UnitsSold field so that you know how many records are represented within the sum value. You cannot add new statistics when all of the details are hidden, though, because you do not have access to the detail field heading, UnitsSold.

4. Right-click the **SupplierName** field name, and then click **Expand**.

Using the Expand option for either the row or column field, you can show or hide all of the details at one time. Now that the UnitsSold field name is visible, you can add another statistic to the PivotTable, using this field.

5. Right-click the **UnitsSold** field name, point to **AutoCalc**, and then click **Count**.

With the new statistic added, you want to hide the details of the UnitsSold field again.

TROUBLE? If you add the wrong calculation or a duplicate calculation to a PivotTable, you can easily delete it by clicking any value that it has created within the detail area and pressing the Delete key.

6. Right-click the **SupplierName** field name, click **Expand**, and then click below the PivotTable so that nothing is selected.

Your screen should look like Figure 4-21.

Figure 4-21 | SHOWING BOTH A SUM AND COUNT STATISTIC WITHIN A PIVOTTABLE

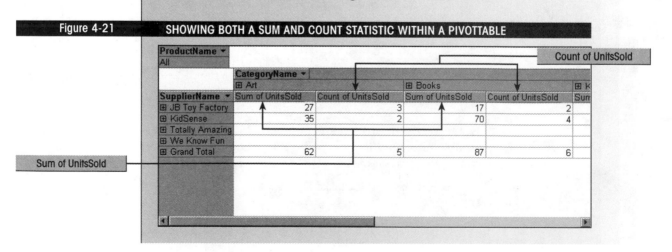

Sum of UnitsSold

The other two calculations that appear on the AutoCalc menu are **Min** (minimum value) and **Max** (maximum value). When values are sorted in an ascending order, the Min value will be the smallest value and the Max value will be the greatest value. All four calculations can be used on a detail field with a Number or Currency data type.

Formatting a PivotTable

Now that you know how to organize, summarize, and sort the data within a PivotTable, you'll probably want to work on some formatting issues as well. Remember that any changes you make in Page view are simulating the activities of an individual user, and will not be saved with the object itself. If you want to make a permanent formatting change, you need to work in Page Design view. Formatting changes include color, number formats, font, and font size changes, as well as column widths and captions.

You cannot make formatting changes to parts of the PivotTable by using the Formatting toolbar. The Formatting toolbar is intended to help you make formatting changes to controls themselves, but not necessarily to the individual parts of a complex control such as the PivotTable list control. You must open the **PivotTable Property Toolbox** to format the individual fields and elements within the PivotTable list control. The sections of the PivotTable Property Toolbox are divided by bars that when clicked, expand or collapse the properties within that section.

To explore the PivotTable Property Toolbox:

1. Click the **Design View** button 📊.

   Your PivotTable returns to the state that it was last saved in Design view.

2. Click the **PivotTable** to select it, click the **PivotTable** a second time to edit it, right-click the **PivotTable**, and then click **Property Toolbox**.

   The PivotTable Property Toolbox window opens as shown in Figure 4-22.

| Figure 4-22 | PIVOTTABLE PROPERTY TOOLBOX |

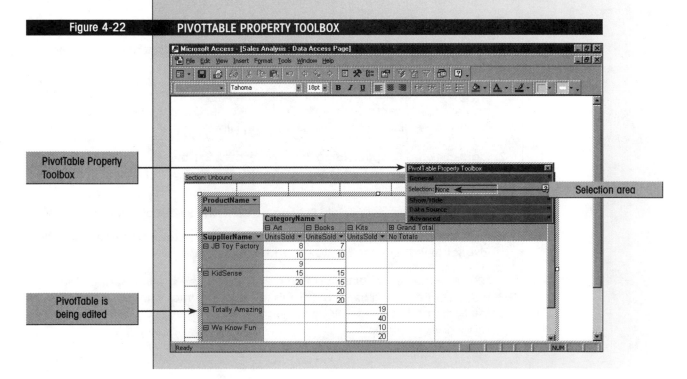

The PivotTable Property Toolbox is analogous to the property sheet within Form Design view or Report Design view because it shows the properties (characteristics) of the currently selected item within the PivotTable. The PivotTable itself has a property sheet just like any other control. The difference between the property sheet for the PivotTable and the PivotTable Property Toolbox is that the latter is for elements *within* the PivotTable. The PivotTable Property Toolbox cannot be opened unless you are *editing* the PivotTable. The selection area of the PivotTable Property Toolbox tells you which item you are currently inspecting. By clicking on different parts of the PivotTable list control, you can observe the change in the selection area and other parts of the PivotTable Property Toolbox.

3. Click the **ProductName** field heading and observe the change in the selection area of the PivotTable Property Toolbox.

4. Click the **CategoryName** field heading, review the changes to the PivotTable Property Toolbox, click the **SupplierName** field heading, review the changes to the PivotTable Property Toolbox, and then click the **UnitsSold** field heading.

Properties and property choices vary as you move from item to item. You can specify a number format for the UnitsSold field, for example, but that option is not available for other non-numeric fields. The bars in the PivotTable Property Toolbox are used to expand and collapse the sections of the toolbox.

5. Click the **Format** bar in the PivotTable Property Toolbox to collapse the section, and then click several other bars to expand and collapse the properties within those sections.

Now that you are comfortable with how the PivotTable Property Toolbox works, you'll use it to modify the PivotTable. You'll make your changes in Page Design view so that they are saved with the page object and presented to all who use this Web page.

To format a PivotTable in Page Design View:

1. Right-click the **UnitsSold** field name, point to **AutoCalc**, and then click **Sum**.

TROUBLE? If there is no AutoCalc option on the shortcut menu, it probably means that you are either pointing to something other than the UnitsSold field name, or are not currently editing the PivotTable. Open the PivotTable list control for editing by slowly single-clicking it twice.

2. Right-click the **SupplierName** field name, click **Expand** to hide all of the detail, right-click the **CategoryName** field, and then click **Expand** to hide all of the detail.

Rename the Sum of UnitsSold field name using the PivotTable Property Toolbox.

3. Click the **Sum of UnitsSold** field name, then click the **Total Caption** bar in the PivotTable Property Toolbox to expand that section.

TROUBLE? The Sum of UnitsSold field name may appear with a sequential number after it such as (2) or (3). This refers to how many times you created the field and is irrelevant since you can replace this caption with something more meaningful.

4. Triple-click the **Sum of UnitsSold** in the Caption text box to select it, type **Subtotal**, and then press the **Enter** key.

Figure 4-23   **USING THE PIVOTTABLE PROPERTY TOOLBOX**

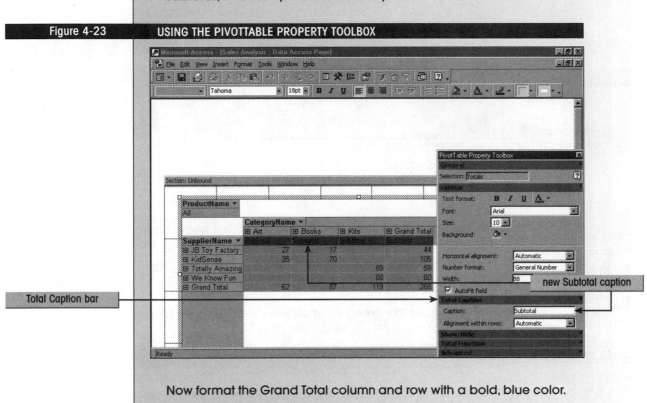

Now format the Grand Total column and row with a bold, blue color.

5. Click the **Grand Total** column heading, click the **Format bar** in the PivotTable Property Toolbox to open the Format section as shown in Figure 4-23, click the **Bold** button B in the Text Format section of the PivotTable Property Toolbox, click the **Font Color** list arrow ⬛▾ in the PivotTable Property Toolbox, and then click the **blue** square in the second row.

With the Grand Total values formatted bright blue, you'll now format the Grand Total row to match the Grand Total column.

TROUBLE? Be sure to move and size the PivotTable Property Toolbox in a way that allows you to observe changes you make to the PivotTable as you make them in the toolbox.

6. Click the **Grand Total** row heading, click the **Bold** button B in the Format section of the PivotTable Property Toolbox, and then click the **Font Color** button.

You don't have to click the Font Color list arrow ⬛▾ because it is currently set to **Blue** as a result of your choice in the previous step.

7. Click the **Save** button 🖫 on the Page Design toolbar, and then click the **Page View** button 🖾.

Your final PivotTable should look like Figure 4-24.

Figure 4-24   FORMATTED PIVOTTABLE

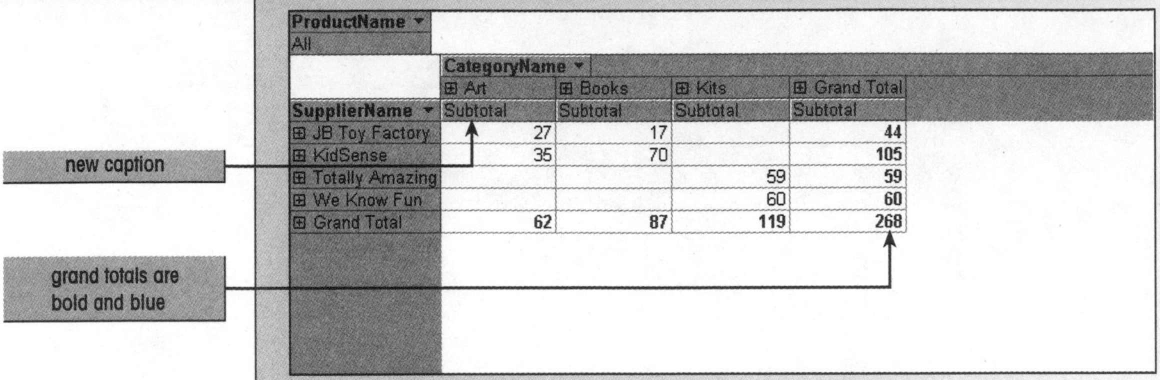

ProductName ▼				
All				

new caption

grand totals are bold and blue

SupplierName ▼	CategoryName ▼			
	⊞ Art	⊞ Books	⊞ Kits	⊞ Grand Total
	Subtotal	Subtotal	Subtotal	Subtotal
⊞ JB Toy Factory	27	17		44
⊞ KidSense	35	70		105
⊞ Totally Amazing			59	59
⊞ We Know Fun			60	60
⊞ Grand Total	62	87	119	268

You can access the PivotTable Property Toolbox from Page view too, but of course any changes made in Page view to the PivotTable are for the temporary purpose of that moment.

To format a PivotTable in Page view:

1. Right-click the **Grand Total** column heading, click **Property Toolbox**, click the **Size** list arrow [10 ▼], and then click **12**.

   Repeat the font size change so that the characters in the Grand Total row also increase in size and are easier to read.

2. Click the **Grand Total** row heading, click the **Size** list arrow [10 ▼] in the Format section, and then click **12**.

3. Click the **Design View** button [⬛] to return to Design view.

Showing and Hiding PivotTable Items

Besides formatting and captioning options, there are other useful options within the PivotTable Property Toolbox that you might want to use when working with a PivotTable. The Show/Hide section of the PivotTable Property Toolbox presents five items that can be toggled on and off: Title bar, Toolbar, Field list, Expand indicators, and Drop areas.

- The **Title bar** button [⬛] displays a title bar above the PivotTable. The text within the title bar can be changed using the PivotTable Property Toolbox.

- The **Toolbar** button [⬛] displays a special PivotTable toolbar above the title bar that can be used for such functions as moving, filtering, and sorting. If you are comfortable with the right-click technique, you might find the extra toolbar redundant. New users, however, may appreciate this extra support on the associated Web page.

- The **Expand indicators** button [⬛] determines whether the expand/collapse buttons are visible.

- The **Field list** button [⬛] toggles on the PivotTable Field list window that is used to add new fields to an existing PivotTable. It contains all of the fields in the underlying recordset (in this case, the Sales Analysis query) as well as the fields you created using the AutoSum feature.

■ The **Drop areas** button ▣ displays the different drop areas (filter field, row field, column field, data field) when you are building a PivotTable from scratch.

To use the Show/Hide section of the PivotTable PropertyToolbox:

1. Click the **white area** of the PivotTable to the right of ProductName to change the Selection choice to "None."

   The Show/Hide section of the PivotTable Property Toolbox is available no matter which PivotTable item is selected, but when the Selection choice is "None," the choices within the PivotTable Property Toolbox are simplified so that the Show/Hide section is easier to use.

2. Click the **Show/Hide** bar to expand that section of the toolbox as shown in Figure 4-25.

Figure 4-25   **USING THE SHOW/HIDE SECTION OF THE PIVOTTABLE PROPERTY TOOLBOX**

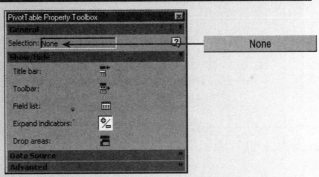

All five of the buttons within this section are toggles. By default, only the **Expand indicators** button is turned "on" when you create a new PivotTable.

3. Click the **Title bar** button ▣ in the PivotTable Property Toolbox.

   A title bar is added above the PivotTable control with the name of the query object on which it was based.

4. Click the **Toolbar** button ▣ in the PivotTable Property Toolbox.

   The toolbar with PivotTable feature is added above the title bar of the PivotTable control. These buttons represent the same features as the shortcut menus that appear when you right-click a PivotTable item.

5. Click the **Field list** button ▦ in the PivotTable Property Toolbox.

   The PivotTable Field list opens, showing you the fields that are available for the PivotTable. You could use this window to add, remove, or rearrange the fields in your PivotTable control instead of right-clicking a field name and choosing an option such as Move to Column Area.

6. Click the **Expand indicators** button ▨ to toggle it off.

   The expand and collapse indicators have been removed from your PivotTable fields.

7. Click the **Expand indicators** button ▨ to toggle it on, and then click the **Drop areas** button ▣.

The Drop areas button toggles on and off the "column," "row," and "filter," areas of the PivotTable Control. If fields are already in those positions, the drop areas are already covered with a field name. If you were building a PivotTable control from scratch, however, you might want to toggle on the Drop areas so that you could drag fields from the Field list into the various field positions of the PivotTable.

8. Click the **Drop areas** button ▦.

Adding New Detail Calculations to a PivotTable

The right-click technique is a handy way to move fields to new areas within the PivotTable control or to remove them from the PivotTable. It can also be used to create new detail calculations within a PivotTable, using the Count, Min, and Max functions.

To add a field to a PivotTable:

1. Click the **Totals** expand button in the PivotTable Field List (if not already expanded).

   TROUBLE? If some of the AutoCalc options are dim, it means that you are not pointing to the UnitsSold field when you right-click. All four calculations should be available for a field that is defined with a Number data type.

2. Click an **expand** button for a CategoryName field, right-click the **UnitsSold** field, point to **AutoCalc**, and then click **Count**.

   You can calculate more than one statistic within the PivotTable. In this case you are both subtotaling the UnitsSold and counting them. Once a calculation is created, it is always available in the Field List (just like any other fields in the underlying query that are not chosen for the PivotTable), even if it is deleted from the PivotTable.

3. Click the **Count of UnitsSold** field, press the **Delete** key, and then click the **Page View** button ▦.

   In Page view, you can use many of the same tools that you used in Page Design view. Remember, though, that any changes made in Page view are not saved with the object. They are for your temporary needs.

4. Right-click the **PivotTable**, and then click **Property Toolbox** to toggle it on (if it isn't already visible).

   TROUBLE? If the Property Toolbox option is not available on the shortcut menu, it means that you were pointing to a specific field when you right-clicked rather than to a white space on the PivotTable. Right-clicking a white space on the PivotTable opens the shortcut menu for the PivotTable as a whole.

   The **PivotTable Field List** can be used to add fields in Page view. It contains just the fields and total calculations available for this PivotTable (as opposed to the Field List, which contains all of the fields from all tables and queries in the database). The fields are from the query upon which the PivotTable was originally based.

5. Click the **collapse** button for the CategoryName field that you expanded in Step 2, click the **Totals** expand button in the PivotTable field list (if not already expanded), and then drag the **Count of Units Sold** value (created earlier) to the data area as shown in Figure 4-26.

Figure 4-26	ADDING A NEW FIELD TO A PIVOTTABLE

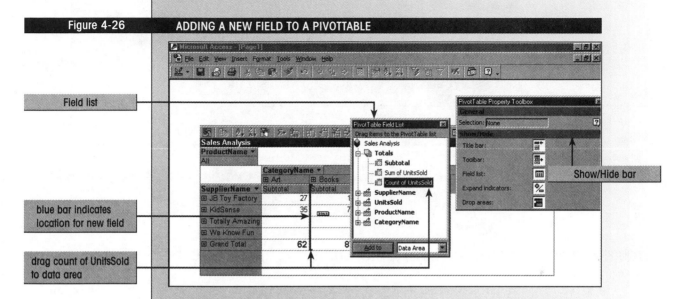

When creating a PivotTable using this drag-and-drop technique, Access gives you an indication of where the field will appear on the PivotTable with a large blue bar.

6. Close the **PivotTable Field List** by clicking its small Close button.

If the PivotTable Property Toolbox also disappeared it means that it is not available because the PivotTable control is not selected.

7. Click anywhere on the **PivotTable** to select it.

The PivotTable Property Toolbox and PivotTable Field List appear and disappear according to whether the PivotTable is active or not.

You decide that you don't want to add the extra statistic to the PivotTable after all. There is no undo feature within the PivotTable control, but you can easily delete any field within a PivotTable by clicking it and pressing the Delete key. By allowing users to add and delete fields from the PivotTable, you give them a tremendous amount of control over what data they can analyze.

8. Click the **Count of UnitsSold** column heading, then press the **Delete** key.

The calculation is deleted from the PivotTable, but is still available in the PivotTable Field List should you want to add it back at a later time. Your final PivotTable should look like Figure 4-27. The buttons on the PivotTable toolbar become available as you click on a field for which they apply.

| Figure 4-27 | FINAL PIVOTTABLE |

9. Save and close the Sales Analysis page. Close the AMToys-4 database and exit Access.

Restricting Access to PivotTable Features for IE Users

At Aaron Michael Toys, you'll want to make sure that each Web page that you produce contains all the fields the users need, but not more. Limiting the number of fields within a PivotTable not only helps secure the data, but also simplifies users' interaction with the page. The user of a PivotTable control in IE has no ability to access the rest of the objects and fields in the database—only those made available through the PivotTable object.

The following list contains the automatic PivotTable restrictions that apply to the PivotTable control when working with it from within IE. An IE user of a Web page with a PivotTable control cannot:

- Change the size of the PivotTable list
- Change the size of the detail area
- Add fields from the database that are not part of the PivotTable's Field List
- Format the title bar or drop area captions
- Display information about fields and source data

Furthermore, you can apply the following additional restrictions when using a PivotTable within IE by using the Advanced properties in the PivotTable Properties Toolbox. The designer can:

- Make the PivotTable Property Toolbox unavailable
- Prevent row and column fields from being added or moved
- Prevent detail data from being displayed
- Block filters

Final PivotTable Considerations

PivotTables are a powerful way to analyze data. They have been available within Excel for some time, and have a small but very dedicated following among Excel users. As these advanced data analysis features gain popularity, people will ask for this functionality regardless of the tool they are using to work with the data. The PivotTable list control and the ability to create dynamic Web pages using the Access page object, make this powerful functionality available to any user of the database. The following list includes some final considerations that may help you use this exciting tool.

■ Before adding a PivotTable to any page, collect the fields and records you want to analyze in a query object upon which the PivotTable will be based. It is far easier and faster to first collect the fields and records you need in a query than to later filter and delete unwanted data from within a PivotTable. Later, if you want to view more data in your PivotTable, simply add the field to the underlying query object. The new field will automatically appear in the PivotTable Field List.

■ Realize that PivotTables are not dynamically updated when underlying data changes. Right-click the PivotTable and choose Refresh Data from the shortcut menu to make sure that all values are updated.

■ If you are using the right-click technique to manipulate the PivotTable and don't see the option that you want on the shortcut menu, this probably means that you have not right-clicked the appropriate item.

■ If you are using the PivotTable toolbar and a button is not available that you want to use, this probably means that you have not selected the appropriate item before attempting to change it.

■ You can copy and paste PivotTable data to Excel by right-clicking the PivotTable and choosing Export to Excel. Excel's pivot table features are more extensive than those within Access. For example, Excel pivot tables can automatically use a Date/Time field in the column or row area to analyze detail fields in a variety of day, week, month, quarter, and year groupings. Excel pivot tables also provide many automatic reporting features that quickly provide detailed information on summarized calculations within the pivot table. Excel also has a more powerful graphing tool than Access.

Session 4.1 QUICK | CHECK

1. What sections in the page object are not contained in either the report or form object?

2. What type of query within Access organizes data in a similar way to the PivotTable list control on a page object? What feature within Excel is similar to the PivotTable list control?

3. Write a brief description of the typical structure of a PivotTable. Be sure to explain where the data field, column field, and row field are positioned.

4. What is the benefit of working with a PivotTable list control in Page view as compared to using it on a Web page opened within IE?

5. Identify five types of analysis activities that you could perform using a PivotTable.

6. Which special window do you use to format the items within a PivotTable control?

7. In Page Design view, describe how you open a PivotTable for editing. What happens if you double-click the PivotTable?

8. How do you update the data in a PivotTable?

SESSION 4.2

In this session you will learn about Access charts, and how to create a chart on a page object so that it can be viewed and manipulated from a Web page.

Chart Types

Charts are popular because they make it easy to compare numeric values and see trends. The **Office Chart control** within the page object allows you to create interactive charts that are dynamically updated when underlying data in the Access database changes. Access provides a variety of chart types that can be used to graphically represent data. In this context, the word **chart** is defined as one of twelve types of business graphs, the most common of which are summarized in Figure 4-28. In this text, the word "chart" does not include general charts such as flow charts, organization charts, or other types of business diagrams.

Figure 4-28	CHART TYPES	
CHART TYPES	**BEST USE:**	**SPECIAL CONSIDERATIONS:**
Area	To show change over time for a cumulative group	■ Does not clearly show the relationship of individual components to one another ■ Since it is generally used to show growth over time, the x-axis is usually a measurement of time.
Column	To show comparisons among items	■ Most common type of business graph ■ Variations include the stacked column chart and horizontal column chart (**bar** chart)
Line	To show trends over time	■ Since it is generally used to show trends over time, the x-axis is usually a measurement of time.
Pie	To show parts of a whole in relationship to one another	■ The pie chart only graphs one series of numbers at a time (unlike the column or line charts that can support multiple series on the same chart). ■ The wedges of the pie (the values that they represent) should add up to 100% of a whole. ■ Sometimes it is difficult to compare differences in wedge sizes. If a close comparison is required, consider using the column chart in which the bar height sizes can be easily compared. ■ Variations include the stacked pie and doughnut pie charts, which can graph more than one series at a time.
XY (scatter)	To show relationships between two numeric values	■ An excellent tool to show correlation (or lack of correlation) between two separate numeric measurements such as sales and demographic statistics (age, education, income level). When a high correlation is found between two measurements, the scatter diagram can be used to predict future values with a high level of confidence.

Creating the actual chart within the page object is the easy part of publishing a graph to a Web page. Deciding what data to graph in the first place, and then choosing the right chart type is much more difficult, but obviously required before you dive into the tools provided by Access to create a chart. Fortunately, the Access Help system provides a summary of chart types with a picture of each.

To explore chart types using the Access Help system:

1. Start Access, open the **AMToys-4** database from the Tutorial\Solutions folder for Tutorial 4, click the **Help** menu, click **Show the Office Assistant**, click the Office Assistant to open the dialog balloon, type **chart types** into the Assistant's text box, click **Search**, and then click **Examples of chart types for charts for the Web**.

   The topic includes reference information for chart types as shown in Figure 4-29.

Figure 4-29	EXAMPLES OF CHART TYPES FOR CHARTS FOR THE WEB

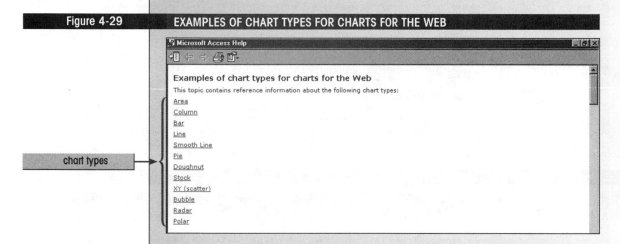

chart types

---

2. Maximize the Help window, right-click the **Office Assistant**, click **Hide**, and then click the **Microsoft Access Help** button on the taskbar.

3. Click the **Area** link to display a sample picture for that chart type.

   Read the description of the area chart. Notice how the area chart clearly shows cumulative growth over time, but does not provide a good comparison of the states to one another.

4. Click the **Return to top** link on the right side of the page, and then click the **Column** link.

   Read the description of the column chart. The column chart is probably the most popular chart type, since it does a great job of comparing individual values. There are many variations of column charts such as the stacked column chart. Many people call the column chart a "bar chart." Note that Microsoft uses the phrase "bar chart" to refer to a different chart type altogether. To Microsoft, a **bar chart** is a column chart with horizontal (rather than vertical) bars.

5. Scroll through the Help page or click the **Return to top** link to get quick access to a link for each chart type. When you are finished exploring chart types, close the Help window.

6. If you want a copy of the Examples of chart types for charts for the Web help section, click the **Print** button 🖨 on the Help toolbar, then click the **OK** button in the Print dialog box to print the Help pages for this topic. (*Note*: This help topic prints on five pages.)

Figures 4-30 through 4-34 show pictures of the most common chart types as presented in the Help system.

Figure 4-30	SAMPLE AREA CHART

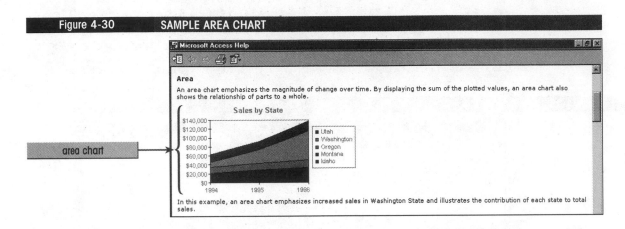

area chart

Figure 4-31	SAMPLE COLUMN CHARTS

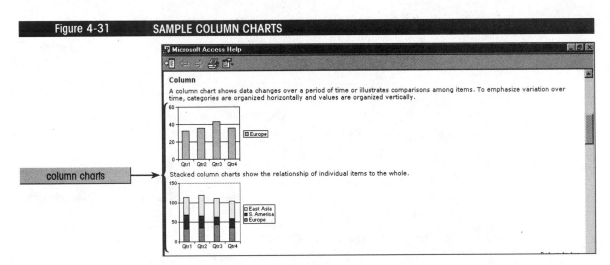

column charts

Figure 4-32	SAMPLE LINE CHART

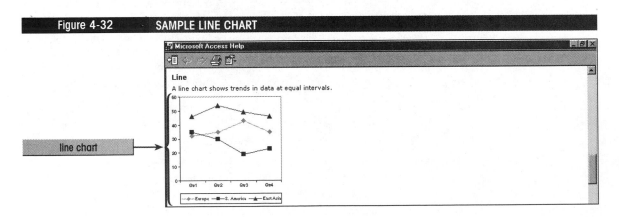

line chart

Figure 4-33	SAMPLE PIE CHARTS

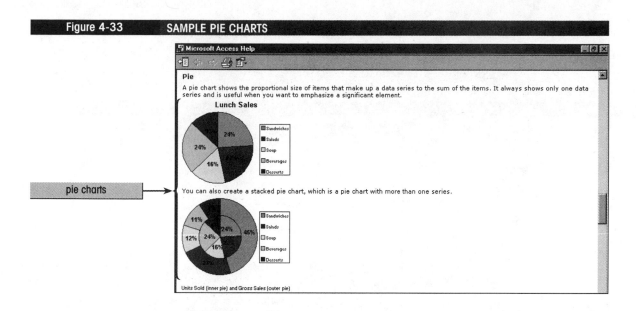

pie charts

Figure 4-34	SAMPLE XY (SCATTER) CHART

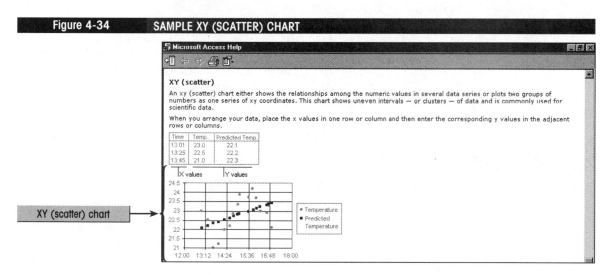

XY (scatter) chart

Chart **Terminology**

If you are an experienced user of charts, you are already familiar with much of the terminology associated with a graph. As you create and modify a chart, however, it will help if you know the specific terms used by Microsoft to identify the various parts of the graph. For example, Microsoft refers to the x-axis as the "category axis." Not knowing this phrase may cause some problems when you attempt to add, delete, or otherwise modify information on the x-axis.

> *To explore chart terminology using the Access Help system:*
>
> **1.** Click the **Help** menu, click **Show the Office Assistant**, click the **Office Assistant** to open the dialog balloon, type **chart types** into the Assistant's text box, click **Search**, and then click **Elements of a chart for the Web**.

2. Maximize the Help window, right-click the **Office Assistant**, click **Hide** and then click the **Microsoft Access Help** button on the taskbar.

3. Study the terminology for data in a column chart as shown in Figure 4-35.

Figure 4-35	TERMINOLOGY FOR DATA IN A COLUMN CHART

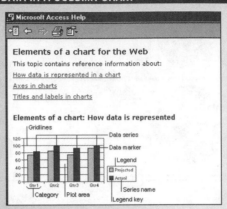

Some of the items, such as the gridlines, plot area, and legend, are fairly intuitive, but other terms used to describe chart elements are not so obvious. For example, each item on the x-axis is called a **category**. A set of bars that graph the same type of data across all categories is called a **data series**. An individual bar is called a **data marker**.

4. Scroll down and study the terminology for axes as shown in Figure 4-36.

Figure 4-36	TERMINOLOGY FOR AXES IN A COLUMN CHART

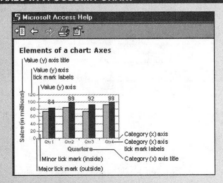

In this figure, the x-axis and y-axis are identified both by their traditional x- and y- names, as well as by the less common Microsoft terms. Microsoft refers to the x-axis as the **category axis**. They call the y-axis the **value axis**.

5. Scroll down and study the terminology for titles and labels as shown in Figure 4-37.

Figure 4-37	TERMINOLOGY FOR TITLES AND LABELS IN A COLUMN CHART

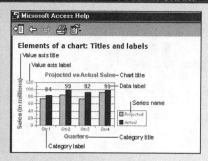

Labels and titles can clarify the information in your chart. Once again, however, notice that Microsoft uses the "category axis" and "value axis" terminology when referring to labels in the x- and y-axis locations.

6. Close the Help window when you are finished reading through the help screens.

Creating a Chart

When building a PivotTable, you first create a query that organizes the fields and records of data that you want to analyze within the PivotTable. The same process applies to charts. You start a chart by first creating a query object, which collects the specific data that you want to summarize in the chart. You can also create a chart based on the data in a table object, in a PivotTable, or from external data such as an Excel spreadsheet.

The second step in creating a chart is choosing an appropriate chart type. You can always change and modify a chart, including its chart type, after you have created it. The more planning you put into a new chart up front, however, the more productive the entire chart creation process will be.

After preparing the source of the data and identifying the chart type, you're ready to use the **Chart Wizard** to create the actual chart object. The Chart Wizard is a special tool that walks you through the process of creating a chart object on a page.

You have decided to create your first chart on the Sales Analysis query. You will use a column chart type to clearly display how the suppliers compare to each other.

REFERENCE WINDOW   **RW**

Creating a Chart
- Create a query that has the fields and records you wish to chart.
- Open Page Design View.
- Click the Office Chart button on the Page Design toolbar and then click the page.
- Complete the steps of the Microsoft Office Chart Wizard to create the chart. The chart can be based on the query you created or on a PivotTable based on the query.

To create a chart:

1. Click the **Pages** button 📄 on the Objects bar if it is not already selected, then double-click **Create data access page in design view**.

2. Click the **Toolbox** button 🛠 to toggle it on, click the **Office Chart** button 📊 on the Toolbox, and then click the upper-left corner of the Section:Unbound section.

The Microsoft Office Chart Wizard – Step 1 of 3 dialog box opens as shown in Figure 4-38. In step one you choose a chart type. The Column chart has three subtypes.

Figure 4-38	THE MICROSOFT OFFICE CHART WIZARD – STEP 1 OF 3

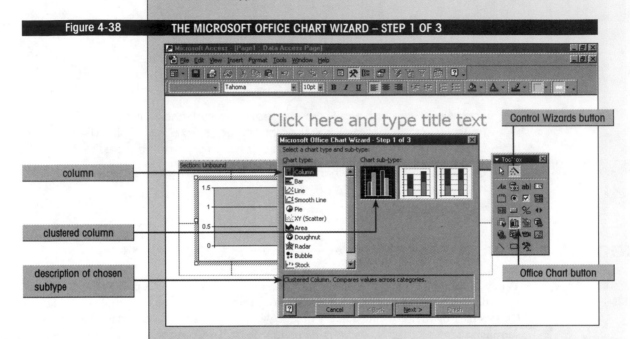

TROUBLE? If the Office Chart Wizard dialog box does not open on your screen, you probably did not have the Control Wizards button 🔧 on the Toolbox toggled on.

3. Click several of the **Chart types** in the Chart type list to observe the available Chart subtypes. When you are finished viewing the chart types, click **Column** in the Chart type list, click **Clustered Column** in the chart sub-type area (the first one), and then click the **Next** button.

In the second step of the Chart Wizard you choose the data source for the chart.

4. Click **Sales Analysis** as shown in Figure 4-39, and then click the **Next** button.

Figure 4-39	SELECTING THE DATA SOURCE FOR THE CHART

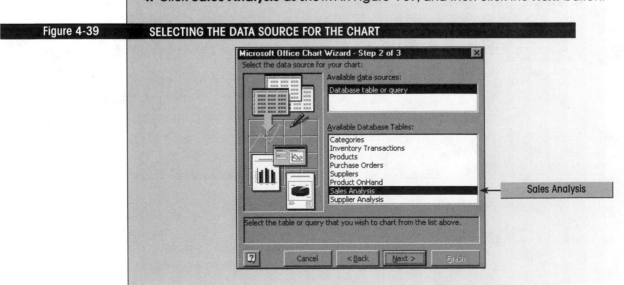

The fields in the Sales Analysis query are now available for this graph. The third step of the Chart Wizard asks how the entries for the legend are organized. Since the source of your data is a query, not a PivotTable that organizes field values in multiple columns, all of the legend entries are organized in a single column.

5. Click the **Next** button.

The second part of the third step requests that you build the chart by specifying the series, value data, and Category (X) axis labels.

6. Click the **Series names** list arrow, click **CategoryName**, click the **Values** list arrow, click **UnitsSold**, click the **Category (X) axis labels** list arrow, and then click **SupplierName**.

A preview of the final chart shows you how the information will appear as a column chart as shown in Figure 4-40.

Figure 4-40	SELECTING THE FIELDS AND PREVIEWING THE CHART

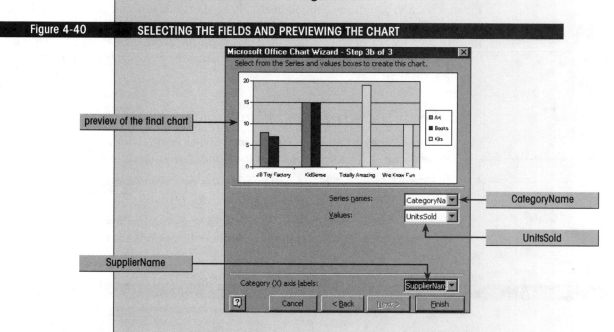

7. Click the **Finish** button, and then click the **Page View** button on the Page Design toolbar.

The final chart appears in Page view as shown in Figure 4-41.

Figure 4-41	FINAL CHART IN PAGE VIEW

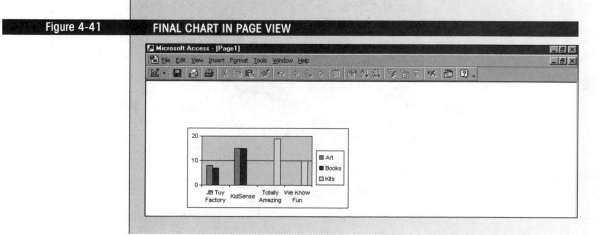

8. Click the **Design View** button 📐, click the "Click here and type title text" area, type **Your Name**, click the **Page View** button 🔲, print the page, and then close it without saving the changes.

The column chart shows a comparison of volume among the four suppliers within three categories. At a glance you can see that KidSense leads JB Toy Factory in both the Art and Book categories, and that Totally Amazing leads We Know Fun in the Kits category. It also shows that JB Toy Factory and KidSense do not currently supply any kits nor does Totally Amazing or We Know Fun supply any art or books.

Creating a Chart from a PivotTable

You may want to give the user the ability to filter out or change the presentation of the data and the chart. For example, the user may only be interested in the suppliers in the Kits category. You can give users this type of flexibility by basing the chart on a PivotTable with filter list arrows. Using their PivotTable skills, they can change the PivotTable to automatically update the chart.

To create a chart from a PivotTable:

1. Click the **Sales Analysis** page object in the database window, click the **Design View** button 📐 on the Object toolbar, and then maximize the window.

The ChartWizard will guide you through the process of creating a chart based on a PivotTable.

2. Click the **Office Chart** button 📊 in the Toolbox toolbar, then click above the center of the PivotTable (above the Section: Unbound) section as shown in Figure 4-42.

| Figure 4-42 | ADDING A CHART TO A PAGE WITH A PIVOTTABLE |

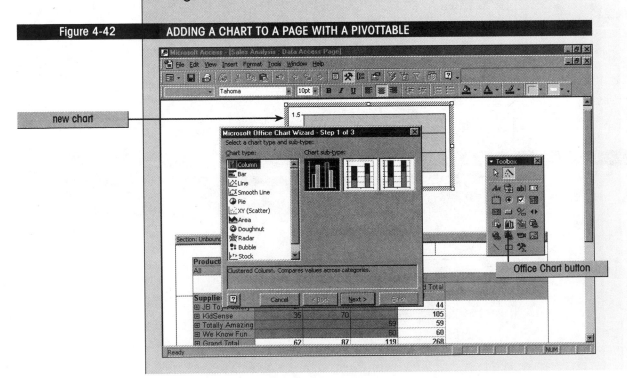

You'll create the same Clustered Column chart as before, but use the PivotTable control to manipulate the chart.

3. Click the **Next** button, then click **Microsoft Office PivotTable** in the Available data sources list in Step 2 of 3.

Each PivotTable list control on the page is sequentially numbered, starting with zero. Since there is only one PivotTable on this page, there is only one option, PivotTable0, in the Available Microsoft Office PivotTable list. If you wanted to give the PivotTable a more descriptive name, you could do this by changing the ID property in the PivotTable's property sheet. In this case, however, since there is only one PivotTable on this page, it's obvious what the name PivotTable0 represents.

4. Click the **Next** button.

Step 3 of 3 shows you a preview of the chart. You wish to switch the legend and x-axis category labels so that Art, Books, and Kits are listed in the legend and the suppliers are used for the x-axis labels. You switch the legend and x-axis entries by choosing the other Series option button.

5. Click the **Columns** option button, click the **Finish** button, and then click the **Page View** button 🖼.

The chart is positioned above the PivotTable in Page view as shown in Figure 4-43. The y-axis scale on your chart may differ depending on the size of the chart on the screen.

Figure 4-43	CHART AND PIVOTTABLE COMBINATION

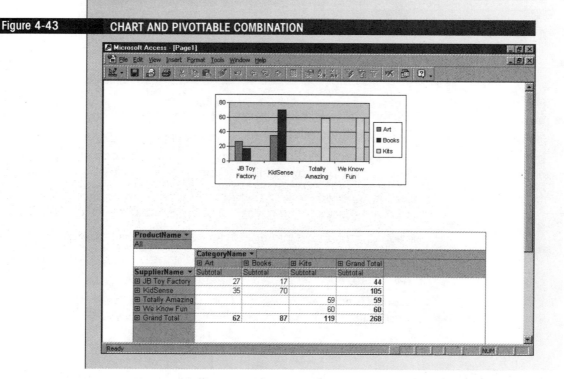

As you would suspect, any changes made to the PivotTable will be dynamically updated in the chart! For example, you may wish to hide the Art and Books categories.

To manipulate the data on a chart from a PivotTable:

1. Click the **CategoryName** list arrow in the PivotTable, click the **Art** check box to clear it, click the **Books** check box to clear it, and then click the **OK** button.

   As shown in Figure 4-44, the chart displays only what the PivotTable shows—data for the Kits category.

Figure 4-44	USING THE PIVOTTABLE TO CHANGE A CHART

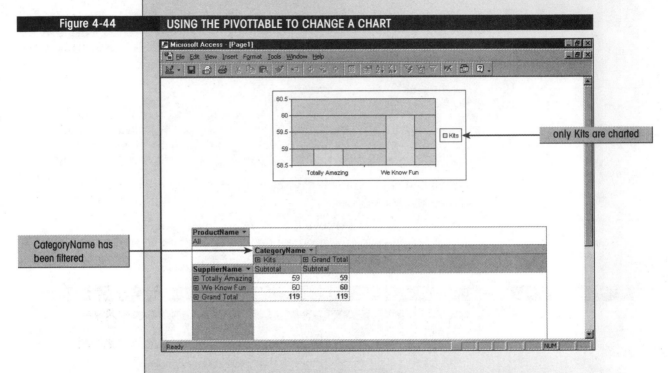

2. Click the **CategoryName** list arrow, click the **Show All** check box to check it, and then click the **OK** button.

   All three categories are now shown in the chart. You can change the chart by using the filter list arrows for the filter and row fields too.

3. Click the **SupplierName** list arrow, click the **Totally Amazing** check box to clear it, click the **We Know Fun** check box to clear it, and then click the **OK** button.

   Now the graph shows information for only the two remaining suppliers, JB Toy Factory and KidSense.

4. Click the **Save** button 💾 on the Page View toolbar.

   The chart is now saved as part of the page object. The PivotTable and chart are saved as they were last displayed in Page Design view.

Chart Properties

There are many formatting changes, such as changing color, size, or appearance, that you can make to various chart elements such as the titles, axes, gridlines, data labels, and legend. All of these types of formatting changes are available through the **Chart Property Toolbox**, just as formatting changes to the PivotTable list are available through the PivotTable Property Toolbox. Unlike the PivotTable list control, however, the Chart Property

Toolbox cannot be accessed from Page view. You must work in Page Design view to make these chart changes. Therefore, changes to chart structure are reserved for the developer/designer of the Web page, who has access to Page Design view, rather than provided to the user who may be viewing the Web page through Internet Explorer.

In order to understand how to format a chart object, you must understand the difference between the control's property sheet and the Chart Property Toolbox. The chart's property sheet contains properties that apply to the control *as a whole*. You open the chart's property sheet just as you would open the property sheet of any control on a page, form, or report— by double-clicking the control, single-clicking the control, and then clicking the Properties button 🖻 on the Page Design toolbar, or by right-clicking the control and then choosing the Properties option.

To open the Chart Property Toolbox to format the elements within the chart, such as the titles, bar colors, or axes, you must single-click the chart twice to open it for editing, and then right-click the chart and choose Property Toolbox from the shortcut menu. This is the same mouse clicking technique you used to open the PivotTable for editing. The chart control will display a hashed border when it is opened for editing, just like the PivotTable list control.

To examine the property sheet for a chart and PivotTable control:

1. Click the **Design View** button 📈 on the Page View toolbar, click the **Toolbox** button ✖ to toggle it off, click the **chart** once to select it, and then right-click the **chart** as shown in Figure 4-45.

| Figure 4-45 | RIGHT-CLICKING A SELECTED CHART |

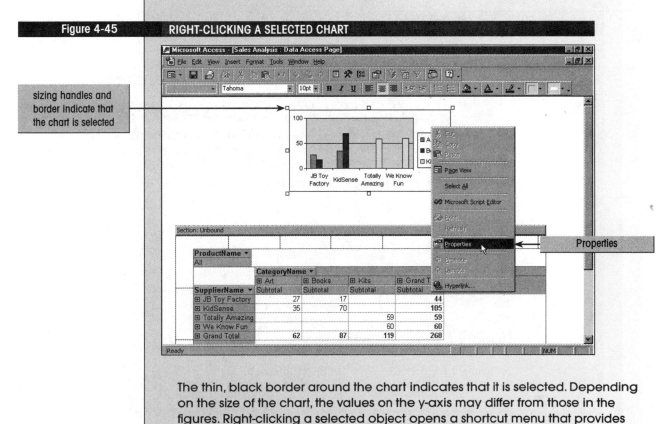

The thin, black border around the chart indicates that it is selected. Depending on the size of the chart, the values on the y-axis may differ from those in the figures. Right-clicking a selected object opens a shortcut menu that provides options available at that time.

2. Click **Properties** on the shortcut menu, then click the **All** tab on the property sheet to examine all of the properties of the chart.

The property sheet for Object: Chart0 opens as shown in Figure 4-46. The Id property contains the name of that particular control and the AlternateDataSource property identifies which data source supplies the data for the chart.

Figure 4-46	PROPERTY SHEET FOR CHART

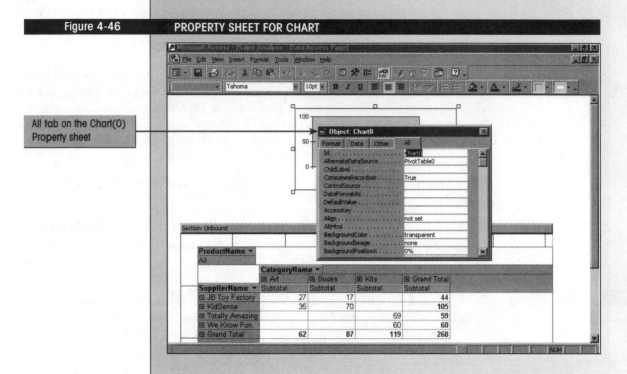

All tab on the Chart(0) Property sheet

This property sheet defines several characteristics for the chart control *as a whole* but does not allow you to modify the individual elements *within* the chart. Every control on a page, form, or report object has a property sheet. Once the property sheet is open, you can examine the properties of any control or section by single-clicking it.

3. Click the **PivotTable** control.

The title bar on the property sheet and the first property ID identifies the name of the selected control as PivotTable0.

4. Click the **Properties** button 🖼 on the Page Design toolbar to close the property sheet for the PivotTable.

Using the Chart Property Toolbox

Now use the Chart Property Toolbox to make formatting changes to items within the chart.

To format a chart using the Chart PropertyToolbox:

1. Single-click the **chart** to select it, and then single-click the **chart** again to edit it as shown in Figure 4-47.

Figure 4-47	EDITING A CHART

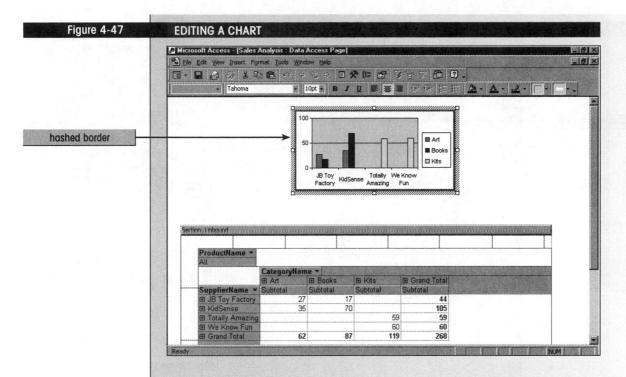

hashed border

The hashed border around the chart object indicates that you are editing the chart object and have access to the Chart Property Toolbox.

2. Right-click the **chart**, and then click **Property Toolbox**.

The Chart Property Toolbox window opens. It has several collapsible sections, including General, Chart, Format, and Options, which are similar to the PivotTable Property Toolbox's collapsible sections. Another way that the Chart Property Toolbox is similar to the PivotTable Property Toolbox is that the Chart Property Toolbox shows you the properties of only one item at a time, whichever item is currently selected. Click a number of chart items to observe the changes in the chart and Chart Property Toolbox.

3. Click the **top number** on the y-axis, click **JB Toy Factory** on the x-axis, click a **blue column bar**, click the gray **plot area**, click the horizontal **gridline** that crosses the middle of the chart, and then click the **legend**.

Each time you select a different element within the chart, the Chart Property Toolbox changes to display the items relevant to that item. The selected item on the chart is identified with a dark border.

You want to change the blue bars to royal blue and the maroon bars to bright green.

4. Click a **blue bar** on the chart, click the **Format** bar in the Chart Property Toolbox, click the **Interior color** list arrow, and then click the **Blue** sample box in the second row.

5. Click a **maroon bar** on the chart, click the **Interior color** list arrow, and then click the **Bright Green** sample box in the second to the last row.

Your chart should look like Figure 4-48.

Figure 4-48   CHANGING BAR COLORS

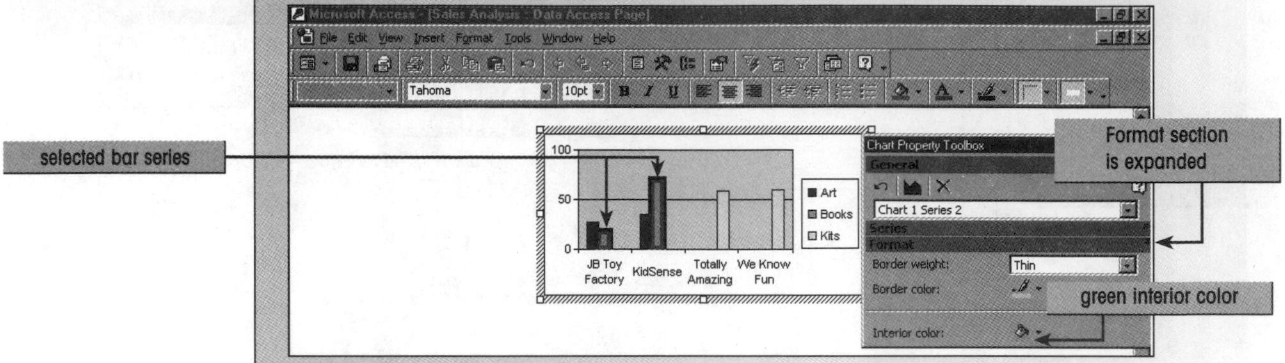

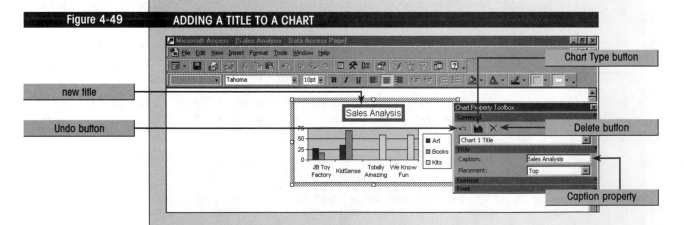

Now change the y-axis so that its gridlines appear at 25, 50, and 75.

6. Click **any value** in the y-axis, then click the **Scale** bar on the Chart Property Toolbox to expand that section.

7. Click the **Custom major unit** check box, double-click the current entry, and then type **25** in the Custom major unit text box.

Add a title to the chart.

8. Click the **white area** inside the chart border, click the **Chart** bar in the Chart Property Toolbox to expand that section, and then click the **Show title** check box to add a title to the chart.

Now that a title is added to the chart, edit the title's text so that it is a meaningful title for the chart.

9. Click **Chart Title** text on the chart, click the **Title** bar in the Chart Property Toolbox to expand that section, delete the **Chart Title** text in the **Caption** property, and then type **Sales Analysis** as shown in Figure 4-49.

Figure 4-49   ADDING A TITLE TO A CHART

Notice that throughout the chart formatting process, the Chart Property Toolbox has displayed three buttons at the top of the window that enable you to Undo the last action, change the Chart Type, and Delete the selected chart element. You decide that the chart is self-explanatory, and doesn't need the title.

10. Click the **Delete** button ❌ in the Chart Property Toolbox to remove the title you just added, and then click the **Page View** button 🔳 to view the final result in Page view as shown in Figure 4-50.

Figure 4-50   FINAL CHART

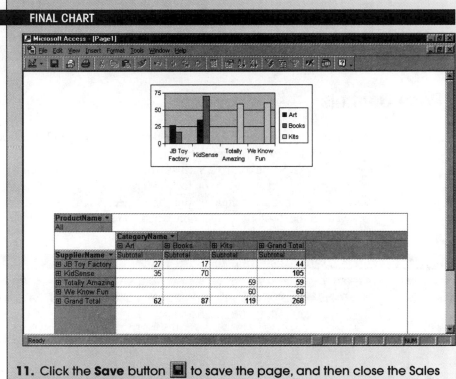

11. Click the **Save** button 🔳 to save the page, and then close the Sales Analysis page.

As the saying goes, "a picture is worth a thousand words." As the popularity of the World Wide Web has grown, the appetite for powerful multimedia presentations of information has risen as well. Charts often provide a much faster and easier way to comprehend numeric information than traditional reports. Certainly any time you need to present summarized information, you should consider how that might best be displayed in a chart. Charts are an extremely powerful business communication tool.

Session 4.2 QUICK CHECK

1. What chart type is the most common?

2. Which chart types are most often used to show trends, or changes over time?

3. What are three considerations to keep in mind when developing a pie chart?

4. When can a scatter chart be used to predict future values?

5. A chart can be created from what data sources?

6. What types of decisions does the Chart Wizard help you with?

7. After creating a chart, where would you look to determine what data source was supplying the data for the chart?

8. How can you make formatting changes to a chart?

9. Describe the steps to open the Chart Property Toolbox.

SESSION 4.3

In this session you'll learn about other controls that you can add to a page object, such as an Excel spreadsheet and a sound clip. You'll also learn more about page design and usability issues.

Other Page Controls

There are many controls that you can add to a page object in Page Design view. The PivotTable and Office Chart controls are definitely two of the most exciting, but several others deserve mention as well. Some controls, such as labels, text boxes, and command buttons, work the same way on a page object as they do on form and report objects. This session, therefore, will focus on those controls that are unique to the page object. Figure 4-51 describes the controls that are displayed on the Toolbox toolbar only when you are working in Page Design view.

Figure 4-51		TOOLBOX TOOLBAR BUTTONS UNIQUE TO PAGE DESIGN VIEW
BUTTON SCREENTIP	**BUTTON IMAGE**	**HOW THE CONTROL WORKS ON THE PAGE OBJECT**
Bound HTML		Reads HTML code and changes the field entry accordingly. By adding the field to the page through the bound HTML control (versus the more common text box control), you ensure that each field entry will be formatted according to any additional HTML coding within that field entry.
Scrolling Text		Displays text that scrolls across the page. Also called a **marquee**. You can customize the text, direction of travel, speed, and type of motion.
Dropdown List		Works in the same way as a combo box used on a form or report, but it is called a drop-down list when used on a page object.
Expand		Allows you to hide or show additional fields within a group of records.
Record Navigation		Allows you to add, delete, find, and move between records.
Office PivotTable		Presents data in a cross-tabular format. It also provides expand/collapse and data filtering capabilities.
Office Chart		Presents data in a graph format.
Office Spreadsheet		Provides a spreadsheet window into which you can enter raw data and build formulas similarly to how you would use an Excel spreadsheet.
Bound Hyperlink		Interprets the entry in a field with a Text data type as an Internet address. (*Note:* Giving a field a Hyperlink data type also indicates the entry is an Internet address.)
Hotspot Image		Creates a link between an image and another Web page.
Movie		Plays a video clip.

You have already experienced many of these controls in the previous tutorial when you were building pages using the Page Wizard. For example, the expand control is automatically added to pages that present grouped records. The navigation control (which displays the Web navigation toolbar in Page view) is automatically added to the bottom of all pages that are created through the Page Wizard. Hundreds of other controls are available if you click the More Controls button ⬚ on the Toolbox toolbar, and they help you build complex Web pages with content from other programs without requiring extensive programming skills. Two powerful yet easy-to-use controls include the scrolling text and Office Spreadsheet control.

The Scrolling Text Control

You have decided to add a multimedia dimension to your Web pages. A **multimedia** Web page can be narrowly defined as one that displays more than one type of medium. In this sense, the combination of a chart and text would create a "multimedia" Web page. Most Web page designers today, however, require some element of motion or sound to be present in order for a Web page to earn the "multimedia" label. One of the easiest ways to add motion to a Web page is with the scrolling text control. The **scrolling text** control adds a text marquee to your Web page.

To add a scrolling text control to a page:

1. Click the **Supplier Analysis** page, click the **Design View** button 🖉 to open the page in Page Design view, click the Toolbox button 🛠 to toggle the Toolbox toolbar if it isn't already visible, click the **Scrolling Text** button 🖼 on the Toolbox toolbar, and then click in the upper-middle portion of the page to add the control as shown in Figure 4-52.

   TROUBLE? If the control is positioned on the left edge of the screen, delete it and redo Step one, adding the scrolling text control a little higher on the page. By default, items placed at the top of the Web page are centered, but items placed just above the Section area are left-aligned.

| Figure 4-52 | ADDING A SCROLLING TEXT CONTROL |

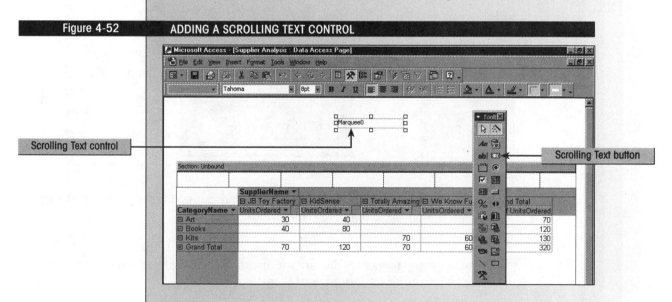

There is no wizard associated with the scrolling text control, so you have to modify its characteristics directly by using either its property sheet or the toolbar and menu commands.

2. Click the **Properties** button 🗐 on the Page Design toolbar.

   The InnerText property found on the Other tab controls the text within the marquee.

3. Click the **Other** tab, delete **Marquee0** in the InnerText property text box, then type **Supplier Analysis Pivot Table** in the InnerText property text box.

TROUBLE? If your marquee number differs, note that Marquee0 refers to the first marquee control that you created. The second will be Marquee1 and so forth.

To see how the control will appear to the user, you must view it in Page view.

4. Click the **Page View** button 🔳, read the marquee, and then click the **Design View** button 🔳 to return to Page Design view.

The marquee works, but it is small and difficult to read. You'll improve its appearance.

5. Click the **scrolling text** control to select it, click the **Font/Fore Color** list arrow 🔺▾ on the Formatting (Page) toolbar, click bright **blue** in the second row, click the **Font Size** list arrow on the Formatting (Page) toolbar, click **24**, and then drag the sizing handles on the control so that all of the marquee text is visible as shown in Figure 4-53.

Figure 4-53	FORMATTING A MARQUEE

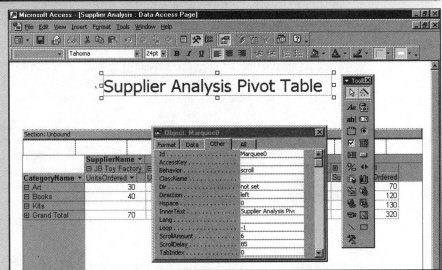

6. Click the **Page View** button 🔳, read the marquee, and then click the **Design View** button 🔳 to return to Page Design view.

There are many properties that are specific to the scrolling text control that change the scrolling action. You'll explore a few of them.

To change the action of a scrolling text control:

1. Click the **scrolling text** control to select it, click the **Behavior** property text box in the property sheet, click the **Behavior** list arrow, and then click **slide**.

This change to the Behavior property will cause the text to "slide" into and remain in the box rather than constantly scroll.

2. Click the **ScrollAmount** property text box, delete **6**, and then type **20**.

   The ScrollAmount property determines the speed of the action. The higher the number, the faster the text will appear.

3. Click the **Page View** button 🖼 to observe the marquee, and then click the **Design View** button 🖼 when the action is finished.

4. Click the **scrolling text** control to select it, click the **Behavior** property text box within the property sheet, click the Behavior **list arrow**, click **alternate**, and resize the control as necessary.

5. Click the **Page View** button 🖼 to observe the marquee, click the **Save** button 🖼, and then close the Supplier Analysis page.

Of course a little motion goes a long way. Be sure to test any multimedia element you add to a Web page with several users to make sure that it enhances rather than detracts from the task at hand. Adding motion through the scrolling text control compels your eyes to study that element, and therefore it has become a popular way for advertisers to gain your attention on the World Wide Web.

The Office Spreadsheet Control

The **Office Spreadsheet** control provides users with a spreadsheet window on the Web page into which they can enter raw data and build formulas similarly to how they would use an Excel spreadsheet. It is particularly handy if users have a need to do a quick calculation while they are working with a Web page. For example, you might want to add an Office Spreadsheet control that could be used to calculate a value that would be entered into the database.

To add an Office Spreadsheet control:

1. Double-click **Create data access page in Design view**, then click the **Properties** button 🖼 on the Page Design toolbar to toggle it off.

2. Click the **Office Spreadsheet** button 🖼 on the Toolbox toolbar, then click in the upper-left corner of the **Section:Unbound** section.

   The Microsoft Office Spreadsheet control appears in Page Design view. If you have prior experience with Excel, you will notice the similarities. First you decide to expand the control so that you have more room to work with it.

3. Drag the lower-right corner of the **Office Spreadsheet** control to the lower-right corner of the screen so that Column G and Row 10 are fully visible, and then click cell **A1** as shown in Figure 4-54.

Figure 4-54 ADDING AN OFFICE SPREADSHEET CONTROL

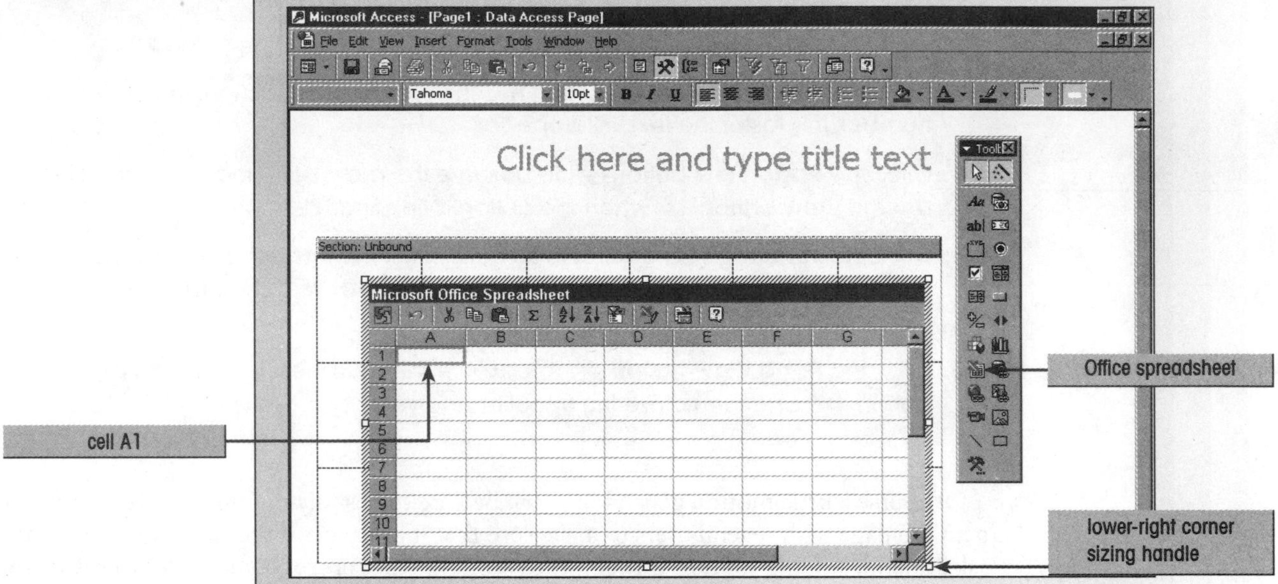

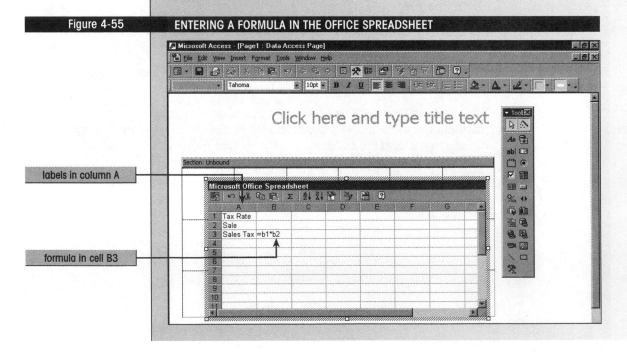

Now add three labels in column A to help identify the values that will be added later.

4. Type **Tax Rate**, press the **Enter** key, type **Sale**, press the **Enter** key, type **Sales Tax**, and then click cell **B3**.

Cell B1 is where the user will enter the tax rate percentage. Cell B2 will hold the total value of the sale, which is the amount to be taxed. Cell B3 will contain a formula that will automatically multiply the two to present the actual sales tax. All formulas in Excel start with an equal sign.

5. Type **=b1*b2** as shown in Figure 4-55.

Figure 4-55 ENTERING A FORMULA IN THE OFFICE SPREADSHEET

Test the new control in Page View.

6. Press the **Enter** key, click the **Page View** button , click cell **B1**, type **5%**, press the **Enter** key, type **3000**, and then press the **Enter** key.

Your screen should look like Figure 4-56.

| Figure 4-56 | USING THE OFFICE SPREADSHEET TO CALCULATE SALES TAX |

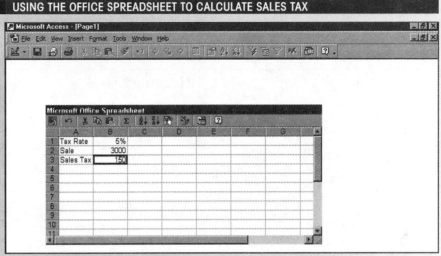

7. Click the **Save** button 🖫, navigate to the Tutorial\Solutions folder for Tutorial 4, type **Sales Tax Calculator** in the File Name text box, and then click the **Save** button.

Notice that the Sales Tax Calculator Web page responds by resetting itself with no values in cells B1 and B2. As you already know, the Web page does not save the activity of the user, but only the changes that the designer made in Page Design view.

8. Close the **Sales Tax Calculator** page.

Themes

So far, this tutorial has focused on aspects of the page object that provide connectivity to the underlying database and interactivity for the user. Once the basic functionality of the Web page has been established, however, you'll want to spend some attention on the beauty of the Web page as well. An appropriately formatted Web page will be easier to use and more professional. One of the easiest ways to format a Web page is to apply a theme. A **theme** is a complimentary collection of color schemes, images, lines, and font choices that are applied to the Web page in one process. A variety of themes are installed with Access, and more can be downloaded from the *www.microsoft.com* Web site.

To apply a theme:

1. Click the **Supplier Analysis** page object, then click the **Design View** button 🔍 to open the page in Design view.

2. Click **Format** on the menu bar, then click **Theme**.

The Theme dialog box opens with the (No Theme) option chosen as shown in Figure 4-57.

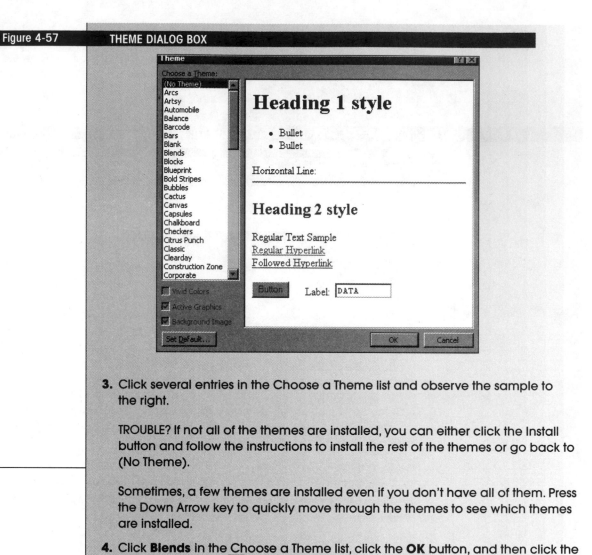

Figure 4-57 THEME DIALOG BOX

3. Click several entries in the Choose a Theme list and observe the sample to the right.

   TROUBLE? If not all of the themes are installed, you can either click the Install button and follow the instructions to install the rest of the themes or go back to (No Theme).

   Sometimes, a few themes are installed even if you don't have all of them. Press the Down Arrow key to quickly move through the themes to see which themes are installed.

4. Click **Blends** in the Choose a Theme list, click the **OK** button, and then click the **Page View** button to observe the new color scheme.

The more controls on your page, the more formatting changes you would change by applying a theme. You can always individually format a control, whether or not a theme is applied, and you can remove a theme altogether by choosing the (No Theme) option in the Theme dialog box.

Background

You may wish to add a background picture to a Web page (sometimes called a **watermark**) or a background sound that is played when the Web page loads. As with any multimedia element, you must be careful that these powerful additions truly add rather than detract from the clarity and the user's enjoyment of the Web page. You decide to experiment with sound clips.

To add a sound clip:

1. Click the **Design View** button , click **Format** on the menu bar, point to **Background**, and then click **Sound**.

> The Insert Sound dialog box opens, allowing you to choose the sound clip to add as a background control.
>
> 2. Navigate to the C:\Windows\Media folder on your computer, type ***.mid** in the File name text box, and then press the **Enter** key.
>
>   The Canyon.mid file should appear in the Insert Sound dialog box.
>
>   TROUBLE? If you do not have the canyon.mid file on your computer, use Explorer to search for any other .mid, .wav, or .au file to use as an alternative.
>
> 3. Double-click **Canyon.mid** to insert it as the background sound for this page.
>
>   The music starts playing, provided that you have appropriate hardware and volume settings.
>
> 4. Click the **Save** button on the Page Design toolbar, view the page in Page view, and then close the Supplier Analysis page object.

It's always a good idea to test all Web pages in Internet Explorer to make sure that they will work in IE just as you experienced them in Page view.

> ### To test the page in Internet Explorer:
>
> 1. Close the **AMToys-4** database.
> 2. Start IE, click **File** on the menu bar, click **Open**, and then click the **Browse** button in the Open dialog box.
> 3. Click the **Look in** list arrow to navigate to the appropriate Solutions folder, double-click the **Supplier Analysis** HTML file, and then click the **OK** button in the Open dialog box.
> 4. Sit back and enjoy the music (and your work), or use the PivotTable to analyze orders from suppliers. If the music stops and you'd like to hear it again, click the Refresh button to reload the page.
> 5. When finished, close **IE**.

As you can see, Access provides a number of extremely valuable tools to build interactive Web pages to analyze data, to format Web pages, and to present information in a multimedia format.

Session 4.3 QUICK CHECK

1. What control would you use if your field contained HTML code?
2. What other name is given to the scrolling text control?
3. What control would you use if you wanted to give the user the ability to interact with Excel formulas?
4. What's the purpose of using a theme rather than formatting a Web page on your own?
5. What types of items can be added to a Web page using the Background option on the Formatting menu?

REVIEW ASSIGNMENTS

You work in the business office of a graduate school, Adair Graduate School, that offers several master's degrees, including a Master of Business Administration (MBA), Master of Telecommunications Management (MTM), and Master of Information Systems Management (MISM). You have developed an Access database, called **AdairGS-4**, to help the faculty track students, classes, assignments, grades, and instructors. You'll use this database to build data access pages for data analysis.

1. Start Access and open the **AdairGS-4** database from the Review\Solutions folder for Tutorial 4.

2. You want to develop a data access page to analyze the average score attained among different students and among different classes. A PivotTable would work well for this. First, you'll build the query to collect the information you need. Click the Queries button on the Objects bar, then double-click Create query in Design view.

3. Add the Students, Results, Assignments, and Classes tables to Query Design view. Add three fields as follows. The first and third fields are calculated fields.

   Student:[FirstName]&" "&[LastName]
   ClassName
   Attainment: [Score]/[MaximumPoints]

4. Display the datasheet. There should be 70 records because there have been 70 assignments among all of the classes and students.

5. In Query Design view, summarize the records in the query by clicking the Totals button. Change the Group By function for the Attainment field to Avg to calculate an average attainment on all of the assignments for each student within each class.

6. Display and print the datasheet. There should be 15 records. On a piece of paper, explain why there are now only 15 records, when in Step 4 there were 70.

7. Save the query with the name **Attainment Comparison**, then close the datasheet.

8. Click the Pages button on the Objects bar, double-click Create data access page in Design view, and then maximize the window.

9. Open the Field List, then expand the Queries folder. Drag the Attainment Comparison query into the Section: Unbound section, click the PivotTable List option button, and then click the OK button. Close the Field List.

10. Single-click the PivotTable to open it for editing, right-click the Student field, and then click Move To Row Area. Right-click the ClassName field, and then click Move To Column Area.

11. Right-click the Attainment field, then click Property Toolbox. Expand the Format section, then choose Percent for the Number format option. Close the Property Toolbox.

12. Resize the control so that all of the classes and students are visible, and enter the text **Attainment Comparison-*Your Initials*** by clicking in the title area at the top of the page.

13. Display the page in Page view, and then use the ClassName filter so that only the telecommunications classes (they start with a TM prefix) are displayed in the PivotTable. Print the page.

14. The Grand Total row and column has no meaning, since the percentages represent average scores. Return to Page Design view, right-click the Student field, and then click Subtotal to remove that row. Right-click the ClassName field and then click Subtotal to remove that column. Resize the PivotTable control so it is as small as possible while keeping all classes and students visible.

15. Save the page with the name **Attainment Comparison** in the Review\Solutions folder for Tutorial 4, and then close it.

16. You have decided to add a filter field to the PivotTable list with the instructor's name. Open the Attainment Comparison query in Design view, open the Show Table dialog box, add the Instructors table to the Query Design view, and then add the following calculated field to combine the instructor's first and last names:
Instructor:[InstructorFName]&" "&[InstructorLName]

17. Save the query, display the datasheet to make sure that the new field works as intended, and then close the datasheet.

18. Open the **Attainment Comparison** page object in Design view, click the Field List button to open that window, click the expand button for the Queries folder, and then expand the Attainment Comparison query.

19. Drag the Instructor field from the list of fields in the Attainment Comparison query to the PivotTable. Right-click the Instructor field and click Move To Filter Area. Close the Field List.

20. Save the page, and then display it in Page view. Filter the PivotTable for Doug Brown's information, and then print that page. Save and close the **Attainment Comparison** page.

Explore ▶ 21. You want to build a data access page that displays a PivotTable and graph that help analyze student scores and determine their grades. Start by gathering the needed information in Query Design view with the Students, Results, Assignments, and Classes tables. Add the following four fields in the order shown to the query:

Student:[FirstName]&" "&[LastName]
MaximumPoints
AdjustedScore: IIf([Late]=Yes,[Score]*0.5,[Score])
(This calculated field determines if the assignment was late. If the Late field contains a Yes value, the score is multiplied by 50% to calculate the adjusted score. If the Late field contains a No value, the adjusted score equals the value in the Score field.)
ClassName

22. Save the query as **Student Scores**, and then view the datasheet to make sure that the calculated fields are working properly.

23. Return to Query Design view, then click the Totals button on the Query Design toolbar. Change the Group By function to Sum for both the MaximumPoints and the AdjustedScore fields. View the datasheet to make sure that the records were grouped and summarized properly. There should be 15 records that correlate to 15 different Student/ClassName combinations. Save and close the query.

24. You'll use a second query to calculate the ratio of the AdjustedScore field to the MaximumPoints field, as a percentage. Double-click Create query in Design View, click the Queries tab in the Show Table dialog box, double-click Student Scores, and then close the Show Table dialog box.

25. In the query grid, add the following fields in the order shown:

Student
ClassName
Percentage: [AdjustedScore]/[SumOfMaximumPoints]

26. Save the query as **Student Percentages**, view the datasheet to make sure that the calculated field is working properly, and then close the query. You might want to format the calculated field to appear as a percentage within the query. You could do this by right-clicking the calculated field and accessing its property sheet in Query Design view. Remember, however, that many field properties aren't applied to the field when viewed by the page object, so you'd also have to change the field on the page anyway.

27. Click the Pages button on the Objects bar, then double-click Create data access page in Design view.

28. Open the Field List window, and then click the expand button to the left of the Queries folder. Drag the Student Percentages query from the Field List to the Section: Unbound section, click the PivotTable List option button, and then click the OK button.

29. Close the Field List window, click the PivotTable control to edit it, right-click the Student field, and then click Move To Filter Area. Right-click the ClassName field, and then click Move To Row Area. Right-click the Percentage field, point to AutoCalc, and then click Sum. (Even though there is only one detail value to be "summed," this action is necessary in order for you to be able to create a chart from this PivotTable later. Charts can only graph summarized values on a PivotTable, not individual detail values.)

30. Right-click the ClassName field, and then click Expand to collapse all of the detail values. Right-click the ClassName field, and then click Subtotal to remove the Grand Total row from the PivotTable.

31. Click the Page View button, then use the Student field in the Filter Area to filter for Brad Smith's scores. This PivotTable shows the percentages for each student in each class.

32. Now you want to add a graph that helps evaluate the grade that a student would get based on a 90-80-70-60-50 (ABCDF) grading scale. Click the Design View button to return to Design view. Click the OfficeChart button in the Toolbox toolbar, then click to the right of the PivotTable.

33. Choose a Clustered Column chart in the first step, choose Microsoft Office PivotTable as the available data source and PivotTable0 in the second step. Click the Columns option button in the third step.

34. The graph is intended to show the percentage attainment for each class by student. Therefore, filter for a single student. Click the Student filter arrow, and then click Nancy Gray so that the chart responds by showing the percentage for only one student.

35. Modify the chart to more clearly show the grade cutoff percentages on the y-axis. Single-click the chart twice to open it for editing, right-click any value on the y-axis, and then click Property Toolbox to open that window.

36. With the y-axis still selected within the chart, click the Scale section in the Property Toolbox to expand it. Click the Custom maximum check box and change the entry in the corresponding text box to 1. Click the Custom minimum check box and enter .5 in the corresponding text box. Click the Custom major unit check box, and change the entry in the corresponding text box to 0.1. These changes will set the y-axis to these parameters instead of allowing it to automatically change as you filter for different students.

37. The legend with the Total entry doesn't mean anything on this chart. Single-click the legend, and then press the Delete key.

38. You want to add values above the bars on the chart so click any bar in the chart, then click the Series section in the Property Toolbox to expand it. Click the Add Data Labels button in the Add to series area so that the value that the bar is charting appears above the bar.

39. The values on the bars would look better if formatted as percentages. Click one of the numbers so that all of them are selected, and then click the Font bar in the Property Toolbox to expand the section. Click the Number format list arrow, and then click Percent.

Explore

40. As a final formatting embellishment, format the values on the PivotTable so that they appear as percentages rather than decimal values. Single-click the PivotTable twice to open it for editing, right-click Sum of Percentage, then click Property Toolbox. Click the Format section in the Property Toolbox to expand it, click the Number Format list arrow, and then click Percent.

41. Click the Save button on the Page toolbar. Save the page as **Student Grade Analyzer** to the Review\Solutions folder for Tutorial 4.

42. Add the text **Student Grade Analyzer – *Your Initials*** above the PivotTable and graph.

43. Add a scrolling text control to clarify the grade percentage cutoff information. Click the Scrolling Text button on the Toolbox, then click below the PivotTable control below the Section: Unbound section. Click the Properties button on the Page Design toolbar, then click the Other tab on the property sheet. For the InnerText property, type 90% = A, 80% = B, 70% = C, 60% = D. Close the property sheet.

44. With the marquee control still selected, click the Font Size list arrow on the Formatting (Page) toolbar, click 18, and then resize the control so that all of the text is clearly visible.

45. As a final formatting touch, click Format on the menu bar, and then click Theme. Apply whatever theme you wish. Save the page.

46. Click Format on the menu bar, point to Background, and then click Sound. Click the Look in list arrow, navigate to the C:\Windows\Media folder on your computer, and search for File names *.mid to locate and insert Passport.mid as the background sound clip. If Passport.mid is not available, substitute any appropriate.mid, .wav, or .au file.

47. Save the page, then display it in Page view. Click the Student filter arrow, then filter for Anne Peacock. Print that page, and then close the **Student Percentages** page object, close the **AdairGS-4** database, and exit Access.

CASE PROBLEMS

Case 1. Building DAPs for Premier Consulting You work for a Web hosting business called Premier Consulting that rents Web server space to small businesses as well as provides a variety of Web consulting services such as Web page design and creation, Web-enabled database development, and Web programming. You have developed an Access database called **PremierConsulting-4** that tracks clients, projects, payments, and employees. You'll use this database to build data access pages for data analysis.

1. Start Access and open the **PremierConsulting-4** database from the Cases\Solutions folder for Tutorial 4.

2. You want to build a page with a PivotTable and chart to analyze payments per project per client. First you'll build a query to gather the desired fields into one object.

3. Click the Queries button on the Objects bar, and then double-click Create query in Design view. Add the Clients, Projects, and Payments tables, close the Show Table dialog box, and then add the following fields in the order shown:

CompanyName (from the Clients table)
ProjectName (from the Projects table)
PaymentAmount (from the Payments table)

4. Save the query as **Payment Analysis** and view the datasheet. You should have five records. Close the datasheet.

5. Click Pages on the Objects bar, then double-click Create data access page in Design view. Click the Field List button on the Page Design toolbar, then click the expand button to the left of the Queries folder.

6. Drag the Payment Analysis query to the upper-left corner of the Section: Unbound section, click the PivotTable List option button, and then click OK. Close the Field List.

7. Click the PivotTable List control to open it for editing, right-click the CompanyName field, and then click Move To Filter Area. Right-click the ProjectName field and then click Move to Row Area. Right-click the PaymentAmount field, point to AutoCalc, and then click Sum. Right-click the ProjectName field, and then click Expand to collapse all of the details and view only the subtotals within the PivotTable.

8. Save the page to the Cases\Solutions folder for Tutorial 4 with the name **Payment Analysis**, then view PivotTable in Page view. You see that the Sum of PaymentAmount heading makes the control wide, so you'll modify that heading.

9. Return to Page Design view, click the PivotTable control to open it for editing, right-click the Sum of PaymentAmount heading, and then click Property Toolbox. Click the Total Caption section in the Property Toolbox to expand it, enter **Revenue** in the Caption text box, and then close the Property Toolbox.

10. Now use the Office Chart Wizard to add to the page an accompanying chart that changes as you use the PivotTable control. Click the Office Chart button in the Toolbox, and then click to the right of the PivotTable control. Choose the Clustered Column chart in Step 1, and choose the Microsoft Office PivotTable and PivotTable0 in Step 2. In Step 3, click the Columns option button, and then click Finish to complete the Microsoft Office Chart Wizard.

11. Click the Total legend in the chart, then press the Delete key to remove it.

12. Click above the Section: Unbound section and type **Revenue Analysis – *Your Initials*** to identify the page.

13. Click the Format menu, and then click Theme. Apply any theme that is installed on your system that you feel is appropriate.

14. Save the page, then display it in Page view.

15. Click the CompanyName filter arrow, then click Lazy K Kountry Store to filter for the revenue for that company.

16. Print that page, then save and close the **Payment Analysis** page object, close the **PremierConsulting-4** database, and then exit Access.

Case 2. Using DAPs for Data Analysis for the Dyslexia Support Organization You are the director of a charitable organization dedicated to providing education and support services for those who suffer from dyslexia. You have created an Access database called **Dyslexia-4** that currently tracks contributors and pledges. You wish to expand the database to also track events and expenditures. You'll use this database to build data access pages for data analysis, containing a line chart and an Office Spreadsheet control.

1. Start Access and open the **Dyslexia-4** database from the Cases\Solutions folder for Tutorial 4.

2. You wish to build a page with a chart that analyzes pledges over time. You'll start by building a query to gather all of the fields into one object.

3. Click the Queries button on the Objects bar, then double-click Create query in Design view.

4. Add the Pledges table to the query, and then add the following fields in the order shown:

AmountPledged
DatePledged
Mon: Month([DatePledged])

The calculated field Mon uses the Month function to extract the Month from the DatePledged field.

5. Display the datasheet to make sure that the calculated field works as intended, click in the DatePledged field, and then click the Sort Ascending button on the Query Datasheet toolbar to sort the 25 records in ascending order on date.

6. For your final chart, you'd like to show a total value by month, so you'll group and summarize the records in the query before graphing them in the page. Click the Query Design button, then click the Totals button on the Query Design toolbar. Change Group By to Sum for the AmountPledged field, and delete the DatePledged field, since it is no longer needed.

7. Display the datasheet showing the total value pledged for six months, then save the query with the name **Monthly Pledge Totals**. Close the query.

8. Click the Pages button on the Objects bar, then double-click Create data access page in Design view. Click the Office Chart button, and then click in the Section: Unbound section. Choose the Line chart type, and the first chart sub-type option in Step 1, choose the Monthly Pledge Totals query in Step 2, click the Entries for the legend are in one column option button in Step 3a, choose SumofAmountPledged for the Values and Mon as the Category (X) axis labels in Step 3b, and then click Finish.

9. Since there is only one line on the chart, click the legend element (it says **Series**) and then press the Delete key.

10. Expand the chart so that it takes up the entire left half of the Section: Unbound section.

11. Embellish the chart with some formatting improvements. Click the chart to open it for editing, right-click the line, open the Chart Property Toolbox, and then click the Series bar in the Property Toolbox to expand that section. Click the Add Data Labels button to add values to the chart. Click the Format bar in the Property Toolbox to expand that section, click the Line Color list arrow, and then click bright yellow in the second row from the bottom.

12. Click one of the data labels to select them all, then click the Data Label bar in the Property Toolbox to expand that section. Click the Position list arrow, then click Outside Bottom.

13. Click the Font bar in the Property Toolbox to expand that section. In the Text format area, click the Bold button, click the Font Color list arrow, and then click bright blue in the second row to make the data labels more prominent.

14. Click above the Section: Unbound section and then type **Monthly Pledge Totals – *Your Initials*** to identify the page. Save it to the Cases\Solutions folder for Tutorial 4 with the name **Pledge Analysis**.

15. Now you'll add an Office Spreadsheet control to the right side of the page that will give you an easy way to add up the cumulative pledges for the year. Click the Office Spreadsheet button on the Toolbox, and then click to the right of the chart in the Section: Unbound section.

16. With the active cell as A1, type Jan, and then press Enter. In cell A2 type Feb, in cell A3 type Mar, in cell A4 type Apr, in cell A5 type May, and in cell A6 type Jun. Resize the Office Spreadsheet control so that you can clearly see nine or ten rows.

17. Now enter the monthly values that have already been pledged. In cell B1 type 250, in cell B2 type 570, in cell B3 type 425, in cell B4 type 275, in cell B5 type 370, and in cell B6 type 200.

Explore   18. Enter the formula to add up the entire column in cell B7. Click in cell B7, click the AutoSum button on the Office Spreadsheet control toolbar, and then press Enter. Click the Page View button.

19. The real value of the Office Spreadsheet control is not that it was able to add a column of numbers. The real value of the Office Spreadsheet control is the fact that formulas automatically recalculate the values when raw data changes. For example, what if your goal was to increase the pledges by 15% for the second six months of the year? If you could accomplish that goal, how much money would you have? To answer this question, you need to work more with the Office Spreadsheet control. Click in cell D1 and type 15%. Click in cell C7, type =b7*(1+d1), and then press Enter.

Explore   20. The answer, 240350% should appear in cell C7. Obviously you didn't want this value to be formatted as a percentage, so click cell C7, and then click the Property Toolbox button in the Office Spreadsheet control. Click the Format bar to expand that section, click the Number format list arrow, click Standard, and then close the Property Toolbox. The answer 2,403.50 should appear in cell C7 (which is exactly 15% greater than the total in cell B7).

21. Click in cell D7, type =b7+c7, and then press Enter. The total, 4,493.50 should appear in cell D7.

22. The real glory of the Office Spreadsheet control becomes apparent when many formulas are dependent on the same variable. For example, you may decide to analyze what would happen if your second half pledges were 20% higher than the first half of the year. This is easy to analyze. Click cell D1, type 20%, and then press Enter. Both calculated numbers change to reflect the new value in cell D1. The annual total in cell D7 should be 4,598.

23. Print this page, then save and close the **Pledge Analysis** page. Remember that any changes that you made in Page view are not saved at the time you save the page. If you wanted those formulas to be a permanent part of the page, you would have to develop them in Page Design view and save them there.

24. Close the **Dyslexia-4** database and exit Access.

Case 3. Exploring Help for Ship Shape Health Club You work in the business office of a health club called Ship Shape. You have developed an Access database that tracks clients, workouts, and exercises. Explore the Help system for information on PivotTables, Office Charts, and other data analysis controls.

1. Start Access. You do not need to open a database to explore the Help system.

2. Click the Microsoft Office Help button on the database toolbar. In the Office Assistant, type Office Web Components and then click the Search button.

3. Click About Microsoft Office Web Components to view that page, and then print it. Circle the part of the page that identifies which three controls are available when Office Web Components are installed on your computer.

4. Click the Show button to display the tabs, and then click the Contents tab. Click the expand button to the left of the following topics to narrow your focus each time:

Working with Data Access Pages
Working with Microsoft Office Web Components
Microsoft PivotTable Component
Designing PivotTable Lists

5. Click the About designing and publishing PivotTable lists for the Web page.

6. Click the link for Terminology in PivotTable lists on the Help page, and then print and read the printout.

Explore   7. The information introduces you to a new acronym, OLAP (found in the Field drop-down arrow section). Click the Index tab and type OLAP in the Type keywords text box. Not finding any "hits," you decide to search for the term using the broader Answer Wizard tool.

Explore   8. Click the Answer Wizard tab, type **What is OLAP?**, and then click the Search button. Only one topic, Add fields to a PivotTable list, was found, and it is not a direct match, so click the Not sure which choice you want? link on the page to broaden the options.

Explore   9. The About adding fields to a PivotTable list page appears. Since you already know that OLAP has something to do with the source of the data from your printout in Step 6, click the source data for PivotTable lists link. Scanning the page, you see that OLAP is defined. Print this page and circle what OLAP stands for.

Explore   10. You have also recently heard about ActiveX controls and would like to find out more about them. Start by determining if the word is listed in the Index. Click the Index tab, and then type ActiveX in the Type keywords text box.

Explore   11. Click the ActiveX entry in the Or choose keywords list, and then click Search. In this case, you found many pages that have information about ActiveX controls, but none really appears to answer your basic question: What is an ActiveX control? You decide to see if you can find any general references to ActiveX in the Contents.

Explore   12. Click the Contents tab, scroll down the list of entries, then click the expand button to the left of the following topics to narrow your focus each time:

Microsoft ActiveX Data Objects (ADO)
Microsoft ActiveX Data Objects (ADO)
Microsoft ADO Programmer's References (the first one)
Getting Started with ADO

If these topics are not available, find and print a single page describing ActiveX Data Objects.

13. Click the Solutions for Local Data Access entry, and then print that topic.

14. Close the Help manual, and then exit Access.

Case 4. Using DAPs to Analyze Registration Data for Distinctive Meetings   Distinctive Meetings is an event management company that organizes corporate seminars for such areas as sales, communication, and computer training. They have developed an Access database called **DistinctiveMeetings-4** that tracks events, event registration, attendees, and internal employees. You'll use this database to build a data access page with a chart that analyzes registration fees for various events over time.

1. Start Access and open the **DistinctiveMeetings-4** database from the Cases\Solutions folder for Tutorial 4.

2. Before building the page object, you'll build a query that gathers the fields needed for the area chart into one object. Click Queries on the Objects bar, then double-click Create query in Design view.

3. Add the Events, Registration, and Attendees tables to Query Design view.

4. Add the following fields to the query grid in the order shown:

   EventName and EventFeeGoal from the Events table
   RegistrationFee from the Registration table
   Discount/Markup: [EventFeeGoal]-[RegistrationFee]

   The Discount/Markup field is a calculated field that calculates the difference between the EventFeeGoal field and the actual revenue recorded in the RegistrationFee field.

   Attendee:[AttendeeFirstName]&" "&[AttendeeLastName]

5. Display the datasheet to make sure that the calculated fields work properly, then save the query as **Fee Analysis** and close it.

6. Click the Pages button on the Objects bar, double-click Create data access page in Design view. Click the Field List button, click the expand button to the left of the Queries folder, and then drag the Fee Analysis query from the Field List to the Section: Unbound section.

7. Click the PivotTable List option button, then click OK. Close the Field List.

8. Resize the PivotTable so that all data is clearly visible, but move it as far left as possible to leave room for a chart on the right.

9. Now set up the PivotTable fields. Click the PivotTable List to edit it, right-click the EventName field and click Move To Row Area. Right-click the Attendee field and click Move To Filter Area. Right-click the Discount/Markup field, point to AutoCalc, and then click Sum. Delete the EventFeeGoal and RegistrationFee fields. Right-click the EventName field, and then click Expand to collapse the detail records.

10. Click the Office Chart button on the Toolbox, and then click just to the right of the PivotTable.

11. Working through the Office Chart Wizard, choose a Clustered Column chart type in Step 1, and choose the Microsoft Office PivotTable and PivotTable0 for Step 2.

12. Delete the legend.

13. Click the Columns option button in Step 3, then click Finish. Click above the PivotTable control and enter the title **Fee Analysis – *Your Initials*** to identify it.

14. Add a scrolling text control below the PivotTable with the following entry in the InnerText property: **If attendee is a full-time student, apply a $100 discount to all courses.**

Explore 15. Increase the size of the scrolling text control to 14 points, and format it with a bright red Font/Fore Color and a bright yellow Fill/Back color. Resize the control so that the entire message is visible at all times, and change the Behavior property to slide.

16. Click Format on the menu bar, click Theme, then add a theme of your choice.

17. Save the page as **Fee Analysis** to the Cases\Solutions folder for Tutorial 4, and then display it in Page view.

18. Close the **Fee Analysis** page, close the **DistinctiveMeetings-4** database, and then exit Access.

19. Open the **Fee Analysis** Web page in IE, use the Attendee filter arrow to determine which attendee received the largest Grand Total discount, and then print the Web page.

QUICK CHECK ANSWERS

Session 4.1

1. New sections within a page object include the record navigation section used to display the navigation toolbar and the caption section used to display text. Neither of these two new sections can contain bound controls.

2. The PivotTable list control on a page object is similar to the crosstab query in Access and a pivot table in Excel.

3. Typically, a PivotTable list control will be used to summarize *three* fields: a numeric field in the middle (data field) that is summarized according to two other fields. The two non-numeric fields are used as the row and column headings (row field and column field) and represent the categories by which the numeric information is summarized.

4. The benefit of learning how to analyze data using the PivotTable list control in Page view rather than opening the Web page within IE is that you have quick access to Page Design view, should you have to modify or otherwise change the page object.

5. You can use a PivotTable to analyze data in the following ways:
   - expand/collapse details
   - filter/hide data
   - sort data
   - subtotal rows and columns
   - create summary calculations

6. You must open the **PivotTable Property Toolbox** to format the individual fields and elements within the PivotTable list control.

7. To edit a PivotTable control in Page Design view, single-click it twice. If you double-click it, you will open the property sheet for the control.

8. Right-click the PivotTable and choose Refresh Data from the shortcut menu to make sure that all values are updated.

Session 4.2

1. The column chart is the most common chart type.

2. The line chart most clearly shows trends, or changes over time. The area chart shows cumulative changes over time.

3. Pie chart considerations include:
   - The pie chart only graphs one series of numbers at a time.
   - The wedges of the pie (the values that they represent) should add up to 100% of a whole.
   - Sometimes it is difficult to compare differences in wedge sizes.

4. When a high correlation is found between two measurements, the scatter diagram can be used to predict future values with a high level of confidence.

5. A chart can be created from a table, query, PivotTable, or external source of data such as an Excel spreadsheet.

6. The Chart Wizard helps you decide the chart type, the data source, the way the entries for the legend are organized, and specifications for the series, value data, and Category (X) axis labels.

7. The AlternateDataSource property in the chart control's property sheet (found on the Data or All tabs) contains the name of the table, query, or PivotTable that provides the data for the chart.

8. You make formatting changes to a chart through the Chart Property Toolbox.

9. To open the Chart Property Toolbox, single-click the chart once to select it, single-click it a second time to open it in edit mode, and then right-click it and choose Property Toolbox from the shortcut menu.

Session 4.3

1. If you had a field in the database that contained HTML code, you could use the Bound HTML control to read the stored HTML code and display the results on a Web page.

2. The scrolling text control is also called a marquee.

3. You would use the Office Spreadsheet control to create a control in which the user could interact and build formulas.

4. A theme is a collection of formatting elements that are applied altogether. A theme provides a more productive way to quickly format a Web page than modifying each element individually.

5. The Background menu option can be used to add color, sound, and picture elements.

DDWS 5.01

OBJECTIVES

In this tutorial you will:

- Learn about the relationship among the Web server, database, and user when sharing data access pages across the Web

- Learn about underlying technologies such as HTML, Web servers, Web folders, and shared databases necessary to support data-driven Web sites

- Install Personal Web Server and learn about its purpose

- Use the Home Page Wizard to set up and personalize your home page within Personal Web Server

- Publish Web pages developed by an Access database to the Personal Web Server

- Learn about the Web Publishing Wizard

- Discuss the skills needed by today's Webmaster

INSTALLING
A WEB SERVER AND PUBLISHING WEB PAGES

Publishing Web Pages for Aaron Michael Toys

CASE

Aaron Michael Toys

Now that you've developed dynamic Web pages that are used for data entry, interactive reporting, and data analysis, you're ready to publish the Web pages and make them available to others at the company. In this tutorial you will learn about Web servers and other technologies needed to publish Web pages for use over the Internet or a corporate intranet. You'll prepare your Access database to be used in a shared environment, and you'll set up and use Microsoft's Personal Web Server to demonstrate the steps and understand the considerations for publishing Access Web pages over an intranet or to the Internet. You'll also explore the Web Publishing Wizard and the HTML code behind the Web pages you've created. Finally, you'll look at some of the technical skills that are required for one of today's hottest job titles, Webmaster. The **Webmaster** is often considered the person most directly responsible for the success of the Web site.

SESSION 5.1

In this session you will learn about the Web Server and use various tools, such as Personal Web Server and the Web Publishing Wizard, to make the Web pages you created through Access available to other users at Aaron Michael Toys.

The Web Server

Making Web pages created through Access available over the Internet or a company intranet requires publishing your Web pages to a **Web server**, a computer devoted to storing and downloading Web pages. **Publishing** means to store the Web page files in a special folder on the Web server called a Web folder. A **Web folder** stores and organizes Web pages. Often, Web folders are protected with an additional level of security so that only certain people with a preestablished userID and password can read the files in the folder or publish files to the folder. Once your Web page files are stored appropriately, **clients**, computers with Internet Explorer and the necessary connectivity and security rights to the Web folder, may download, view, and use those Web pages.

Figure 5-1 illustrates how the Web server is organized in a typical company. Local clients access the Web server through a connection to their internal file server just as they would access any local resource. Remote clients access the Web server through a dial-up connection to an **ISP** (Internet service provider), just as they would access any other World Wide Web resource. Regardless of where the client is physically located, they can use Internet Explorer to locate and download the Web pages created by Access that are stored on the Web server. The dynamic connection between the Web page and the Access database allows the user to enter and analyze live Access data from any location.

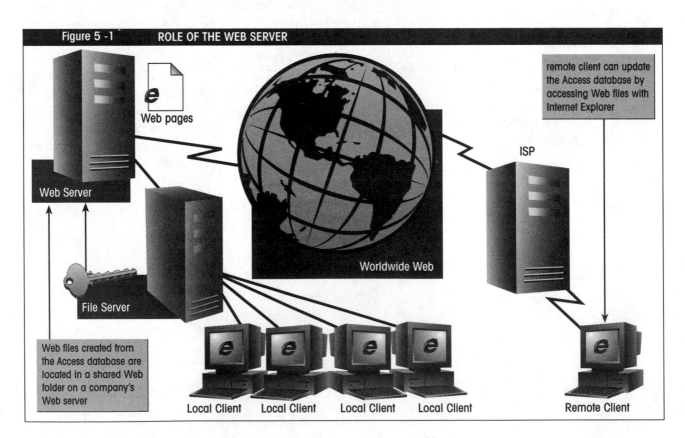

Figure 5 -1   ROLE OF THE WEB SERVER

Local clients, of course, would also have the option of working in the Access file through direct access to queries, forms, and reports in the database file. You can add a great deal of security to an Access database by using the Access workgroups feature to password protect the entire database or objects within the database. By giving users access to dynamic Web files, and not to the Access database file itself, however, you have added two additional levels of protection to the database.

First of all, if users interface with an Access database through Web pages and not by using forms and reports within the database file itself, there is no chance of them figuring out how to "get behind" the forms and reports you have provided. Users cannot modify a table, query, report, or form in Design view because they are working with Web pages, not with the objects themselves.

Secondly, by providing access to a Web-enabled database through a URL such as *http://www.amtoys.net/vendors.htm*, you have masked the physical location of the database file from the user. For example, although the user enters *http://www.amtoys.net/vendors.htm* into their browser, the Web pages may be physically stored at *\\AMTWEB\DB\vendors.htm*. The Web server handles this translation and does not provide information about the physical location of the Web pages to the user. In this example, AMTWEB is the name of the server where the Web pages are stored, DB is the name of a folder, and vendors.htm is the name of the Web page that the user is downloading through his or her browser, IE.

Publishing Access Web Pages to a Web Server

The general process that you must follow to publish Access Web pages to a Web server is outlined below:

1. Use Access to create the relational database with all of the necessary tables and query objects.
2. Store the Access database in a shared network folder on a file server.
3. Use the Access database to create dynamic HTML Web pages through the page object.
4. Save the HTML Web page files created through the page object in a shared network folder on a Web server.
5. Give the users the URL (uniform resource locator) to access the Web pages.
6. As users access the Web pages, the underlying Access database will be automatically updated.

In order to accomplish these steps, you should understand several important underlying concepts.

Shared Network Folders

On a network, most folders are not available to everyone. Therefore, you must be sure to put the Access database in a folder called a **shared network folder** that the appropriate people have permission to use. The network administrator, the person in charge of maintaining the computer network, grants permissions to files and folders. The network administrator grants rights to use files and folders to users and groups through utility programs provided by the server's operating system.

For example, if the file server or Web server's operating system were Microsoft Windows NT, the network administrator would use a program called **User Manager** to define each user with a name (**userID**), password, and membership in groups. The network administrator would then establish the appropriate rights to network resources such as shared network folders, individual files, printers, and modems. Obviously, if you want multiple users to be able to use Web pages to update an Access database, those same users must be given the appropriate rights to update the underlying database file. Since you automatically have unlimited permission to any file you create and store on your own personal computer, the issue of providing secure access to a database to a group of individuals in a shared folder over a network is sometimes underestimated. A document similar to the one in Figure 5-2 can help you communicate your database sharing needs with the network administrator.

Figure 5-2		SAMPLE RIGHTS TO SHARED NETWORK FOLDERS		
USER	TITLE	SHARED NETWORK FOLDER: \\SERVERNAME\FOLDERNAME	RIGHTS: F = FULL CONTROL R = READ W = WRITE X = EXECUTE D = DELETE	DESCRIPTION
Kathryn	Network administrator	\\AMT\DB	F	Can read, add, delete, execute, and modify files plus change permissions and take ownership of folders
		\\AMTWEB\DB	F	Can read, write, add, delete, execute, and modify files plus change permissions and take ownership of folders
Jacob	Database administrator	\\AMT\DB	RWXD	Can read, write, execute and delete files
		\\AMTWEB\DB	RWXD	Can read, write, execute and delete files
All		\\AMT\DB	WX	Can write new files in the folder and execute program files
		\\AMTWEB\DB	RWX	Can read, write, and execute program files

In the Rights Document to Shared Network Folders in Figure 5-2, there are two separate servers (AMT and AMTWEB) that provide the traditional file server and Web server needs for Aaron Michael Toys. The Microsoft NT naming convention places two backslashes before a file server name. AMT is the name of the company file server and it contains a folder named DB, hence \\AMT\DB. AMTWEB is the name of the company Web server and it also contains a folder named DB, hence \\AMTWEB\DB.

Once the appropriate Web folders are set up and permissions to use the files within the folders are established, nothing more needs to be done to the Access database file in order for multiple people to use it simultaneously. Access databases are inherently **multiuser** so that many people can enter and update information at the same time. Two people cannot, however, update the same record at the same time because of the **record locking** capabilities of Access.

Technically, you don't need a separate file server and Web server computer to implement this system. You could store both the database files and HTML Web files on the same machine that provides the services of both the file server and Web server. You could even store the database and Web files in the same folder. But, for security and performance purposes, you probably want to store the database and Web files on separate machines. You may not want to give users "read" permission to the database itself, but only "write" and "execute" permission. Also, it's always easier to manage security rights to folders (and therefore all files within them) than to go through each file in a folder individually, determining which users need which rights to that file.

Personal Web Server

As you can see, publishing Web pages involves more than just saving them to a Web folder. The appropriate infrastructure, including Web and file servers, Web folders, and user rights, needs to be established if the system is to be a success. Since you may not have access to a Windows NT file server or Internet-connected Web servers, you need a way to experience the activities of developing a Web site and publishing Web pages to that Web site using a single Personal Computer.

Fortunately, Microsoft Windows 98 provides a program called **Personal Web Server** that allows you to practice these activities using your own computer as if it were a server. If you are using the client version of Windows NT on your computer, you can download a version of Personal Web Server from *www.microsoft.com/windows/ie/pws* for that operating system as well. See Appendix C for more information on Web servers and Windows operating systems.

With Personal Web Server, you can go through the process of installing Web server software, setting up Web folders, and publishing Web pages to the Web folder. Although all of the activities occur on your own computer, they mimic the steps involved with publishing files on a large network. Therefore, you gain experience with Web server concepts and the activities involved in publishing Web pages to them. Obviously, a big benefit of Personal Web Server is that you don't have to rely on a preexisting network and the associated security clearances to learn about the steps and concepts of publishing Web pages.

Installing Personal Web Server

Personal Web Server is a product provided to all Windows 98 users, but by default, it is not installed. Often, when you install new software, you need to restart your computer in order for it to function properly, so it's always a good practice to save all work and close all open programs before installing a new program.

REFERENCE WINDOW | **RW**

Installing Personal Web Server
- Save all work and close all existing programs.
- Insert your Windows 98 CD in the CD drive.
- Click the Start button on the taskbar, click Run, click Browse, click the Look in list arrow, click the CD drive, double-click the add-ons folder, double-click the pws folder, double-click setup.exe, and then click the OK button in the Run dialog box.
- Follow the Installation Wizard steps. Choose a typical installation and default folder locations unless you have a specific reason to select other options.
- Wait while the Personal Web Server files are copied from the CD to your computer, and then restart your computer when prompted.
- Be sure to put your Windows 98 CD back in a safe location when finished.

To install Personal Web Server:

1. Save all work and close all existing programs.

   Your taskbar should be clear of all open programs and window buttons. You don't need to close virus checkers or other memory resident programs.

2. Click the **Start** button on the taskbar, point to **Programs**, point to the **Microsoft Personal Web Server** group, and then click **Personal Web Server.**

TROUBLE? The Personal Web Server may be installed within the Internet Explorer group.

The Welcome to Microsoft Personal Web Server Web page loads in your browser as shown in Figure 5-3.

Figure 5-3   **WELCOME TO MICROSOFT PERSONAL WEB SERVER**

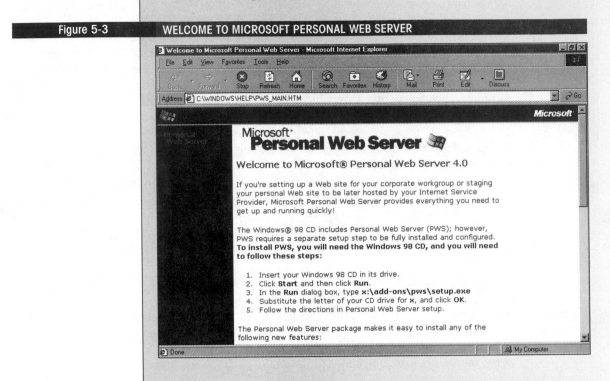

TROUBLE? If Personal Web Server is already installed, it may appear as a group entry within the Internet Explorer group as shown in Figure 5-4. If Personal Web Server is already installed and you see the Personal Web Manager option, skip the rest of the steps to install Personal Web Server and begin with the next section, Using Personal Web Manager.

Figure 5-4   **PERSONAL WEB SERVER GROUP**

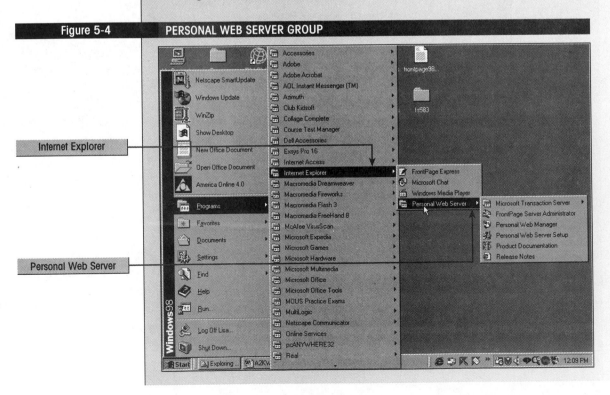

3. Read the page about Personal Web Server and the other features within the Personal Web Server package, and then close the browser window.

   Now you'll follow the steps in the documentation that you just reviewed to install Personal Web Server. If you are working on a shared or lab computer, of course you must have permission to install software on that machine. These steps assume that you are installing PWS on your own machine.

4. Insert your Windows 98 CD in the CD-ROM drive, click the **Start** button on the taskbar, click **Run**, click **Browse**, click the **Look in** list arrow, click the **CD drive**, double-click the **add-ons** folder, double-click the **pws** folder, double-click **setup.exe**, and then click the **OK** button in the Run dialog box.

   TROUBLE? If the automatic installation window opens, close it.

   TROUBLE? Depending on how Windows 98 and Internet Explorer were previously installed on your computer, you may be directed to double-click the setup.exe file found at the following path: c:\windows\options\cabs\pws\setup.exe. If your instructions differ from those in these steps, follow the specific instructions provided by your unique computer installation.

   The Microsoft Personal Web Server Setup dialog box appears as shown in Figure 5-5.

Figure 5-5	MICROSOFT PERSONAL WEB SERVER SETUP

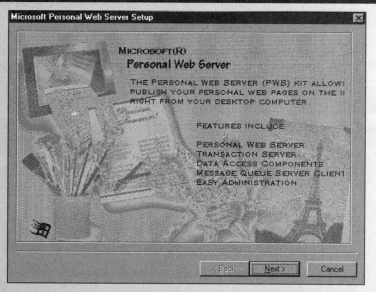

5. Click the **Next** button, click the **Typical** button, and then record the location for the default Web publishing home directory on a piece of paper.

   By default, the default Web publishing home directory is C:\Inetpub\wwwroot, and this home directory will be used for the rest of this tutorial.

6. Click the **Next** button.

   Wait while Personal Web Server files are copied to your computer. The Overall progress indicator will show how the installation is progressing and when the process is finished.

7. Click the **Finish** button to complete the Microsoft Personal Web Server Setup process, and then click the **Yes** button to restart your computer.

8. Remove your Windows 98 CD from the CD-ROM drive and put it back in a safe place after the installation is finished.

If you are installing Personal Web Server on a Windows NT workstation or on a Windows 2000 machine, please check the documentation at the *www.microsoft.com* site for specific installation instructions, and refer to Appendix C.

Using **Personal Web Manager**

Now that Personal Web Server is installed on your machine, you can use a part of the system called **Personal Web Manager** that manages the Web server, Web folders, and publishing process. Personal Web Manager comes with its own tutorial that helps you understand its capabilities.

To explore Personal Web Manager:

1. Click the **Start** button on the taskbar, point to **Programs**, point to the **Microsoft Personal Web Server** group, and then click **Personal Web Manager**.

   Personal Web Manager loads with a hyperlinked Tip of the day dialog box as shown in Figure 5-6.

   TROUBLE? The Personal Web Server group may also be installed within the Internet Explorer group.

Figure 5-6	PERSONAL WEB MANAGER AND TIP OF THE DAY

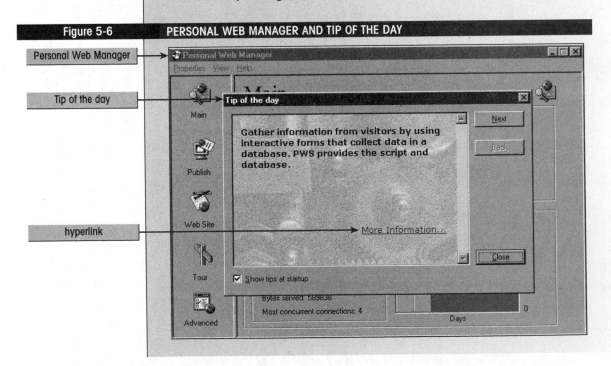

2. Read the tip of the day, and then click the **More Information** hyperlink. If you are connected to the Internet, you may need to click the **HELP** menu, and then click **Personal Web Server Topics**.

TROUBLE? If the Welcome to the Internet Connection Wizard opens on your screen, close it since you won't be using the Internet, but rather publishing files to your own computer.

3. Maximize the IE window.

A Web page with Personal Web Server Documentation loads within IE as shown in Figure 5-7.

| Figure 5-7 | PERSONAL WEB SERVER DOCUMENTATION |

URL does not reference the WWW

Personal Web Server Documentation

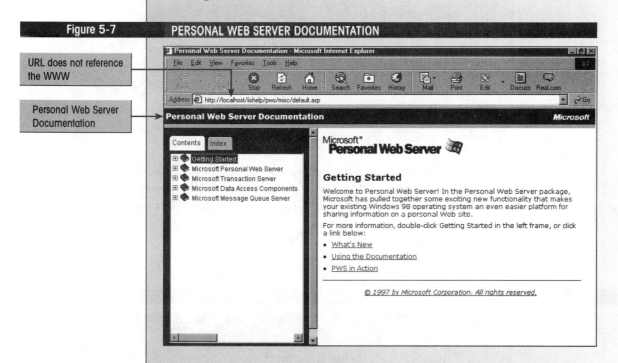

The entire Help manual for the Personal Web Server system is built as a set of hyperlinked HTML Web pages that can be opened and read within a browser such as IE. Note within the IE Address bar that the URL does not refer to the World Wide Web, but rather to a local resource.

The window on the left provides a navigation system for the documentation. Use it to learn about the different features within Microsoft Personal Web Server, including some information on the Microsoft Transaction Server, Data Access Components, and Message Queue Server. For now, however, you will exit the documentation system and return to Personal Web Manager.

4. Close the **IE** window, and then click **Close** in the Tip of the day dialog box if it is still open to view the Main window for the Personal Web Manager as shown in Figure 5-8.

Figure 5-8 | PERSONAL WEB MANAGER - MAIN

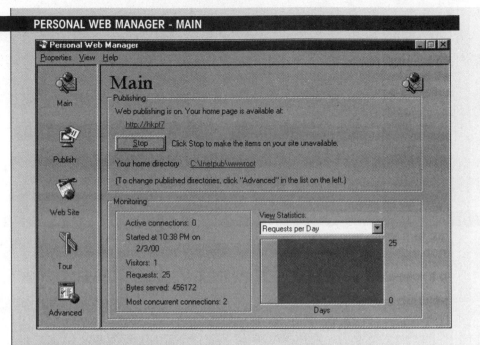

The Main section of the Personal Web Manager provides some general information about your home page, home directory, and site statistics. You'll come back to these items later as you learn more about Personal Web Manager. For now, explore the other areas of the program that are represented by the five large icons on the left side of the window.

5. Click the **Publish** button 🖳 as shown in Figure 5-9.

Figure 5-9 | PUBLISHING WIZARD

The Publishing Wizard appears; it will help you publish your Web files to the Web server.

6. Click the **Web Site** button 🎨 as shown in Figure 5-10.

Figure 5-10	HOME PAGE WIZARD

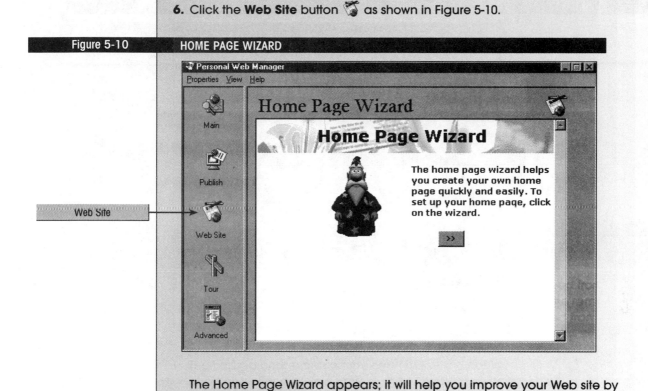

The Home Page Wizard appears; it will help you improve your Web site by building a home page. Right now, however, you want to take the Personal Web Server tour.

Taking the Personal Web Server Tour

Rather than exploring the program on your own or going through the hyperlinked Help manual, you've decided to continue exploring the program by taking the Personal Web Server tour.

To take the Personal Web Server tour:

1. Click the **Tour** button 🗡 as shown in Figure 5-11.

Figure 5-11   PERSONAL WEB SERVER TOUR

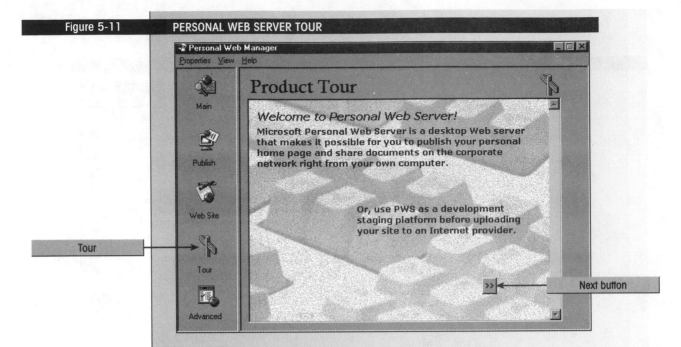

2. Read the **Welcome to Personal Web Server!** window to find out about the two uses for Personal Web Server.

   Personal Web Server is used to publish Web pages and share documents on your computer with others on your company intranet. It is also used as a staging platform (a simulation of a real Web server) before deploying Web pages to a live site.

3. Click the **Next** button `>>`, and then read the **What is a Web server?** window.

   A Web server can be a large computer with thousands of Web folders and Web pages, or a user's computer such as the one you are using now.

4. Click the **Next** button `>>`, and then read the **Create a Home Page Automatically!** window.

   As you have already seen, Personal Web Server contains a Home Page Wizard that will help you develop your home Web page.

5. Click the **Next** button `>>`, and then read the **Locate Documents Easily!** window.

   Through hyperlinked documents managed by Personal Web Server, you can make it easier for users to find and open files.

6. Click the **Next** button `>>`, and then read the **Publish Documents Quickly** window.

   You can restrict the rights of users to the files in your Web publishing folders. This protects the rest of the resources on your computer.

7. Click the **Next** button `>>`, and then read the **Share Documents Across Platforms** window.

   By converting files to an HTML format, you can minimize document-sharing problems caused by multiple versions of the same software.

8. Click the **Next** button `>>`, and then read the **Interact With Your Visitors** page.

Special Web page features, such as the Guest Book and Drop Box, allow you to Interact With Your Visitors.

9. Click the **Next** button $\boxed{>>}$, and then read the **Gather Information** page.

   Personal Web Server provides tools to create custom forms to gather information. In your case, you'll use Access to create these types of data-gathering Web pages.

10. Click the **Next** button $\boxed{>>}$, and then read the **Test Drive Your Internet Web Site** page.

    Personal Web Server can be used to build and test Web pages before publishing them to a production Web Server.

11. Click the **Next** button $\boxed{>>}$, and then read **Start Publishing Now!**

Using the Home Page Wizard

Now that you have had an overview of what the Personal Web Server software is capable of, you'll start building your Web site for Aaron Michael Toys. The next step is to create your **home page**, the first page displayed to visitors on your Web site. You can quickly create a home page by clicking the Web Site button 🖬.

To create a home page using the Home Page Wizard:

1. Click the **Web Site** button 🖬, read the **Home Page Wizard** window, click the **Next** button $\boxed{>>}$, and then click **Yes** if prompted about sending information on a Local intranet.

   You can choose from one of three templates to personalize your home page. In this context, **templates** are predefined color, formatting, and Web page layout definitions. The three template options available for your home page are named Looseleaf, Journal, and Gunmetal.

2. Click **Looseleaf**, then click the **Next** button $\boxed{>>}$.

   The **guest book** is a common element on a Web page where users can sign their names, leave a public message, and view other messages.

3. Be sure that the **Yes** option button for the guest book is selected, and then click the **Next** button $\boxed{>>}$.

   The drop box is another common element on many Web pages. The **drop box** provides a way for visitors to leave a private message for you.

4. Be sure that the **Yes** option button for the drop box is selected, click the **Next** button $\boxed{>>}$, and then click the **Next** button $\boxed{>>}$ at the Congratulations! Window.

   TROUBLE? If you receive an error message ceated by the VBA debugger, click No to continue.

   IE starts and displays a partially completed home page as shown in Figure 5-12.

Figure 5-12   YOUR HOME PAGE

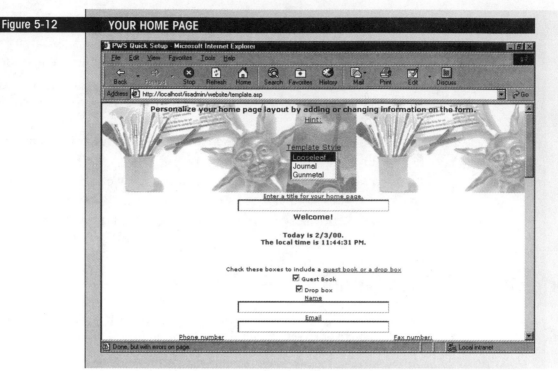

Your home Web page has now been created, but the process has created a page that you can continue personalizing—right within the Web page itself. You review the template that you selected and decide to make some changes. Your choice of a template is purely a matter of taste. For example, the Looseleaf template may not fit your personal style.

To personalize the home page created by the Home Page Wizard:

1. Click **Journal** in the Template Style list to view that template, and then click **Gunmetal**.

   You decide to stick with the Gunmetal template for now. Now you'll modify the title.

2. Click in the **text box** below the Enter a Title for your home page hyperlink, and then type **Aaron Michael Toys** to enter a title for your home page.

3. Fill out the rest of the fields in the upper portion of the form, as shown in Figure 5-13, typing your own personal information in the Name, Email, and other fields.

Figure 5-13 | PERSONALIZING YOUR HOME PAGE

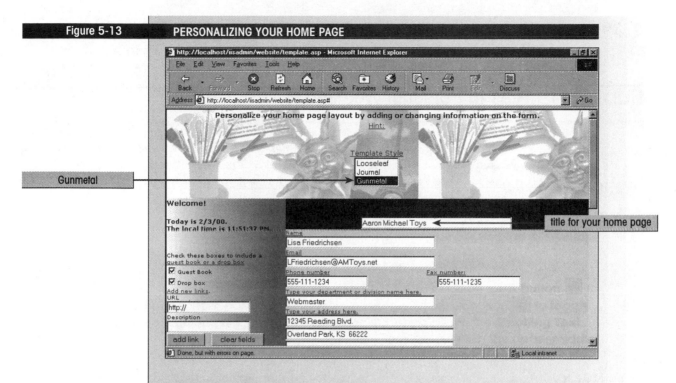

Gunmetal

title for your home page

4. Scroll down to the bottom of the page and click the **enter new changes** button.

The finished Web page is shown in Figure 5-14.

Figure 5-14 | THE FINAL HOME WEB PAGE

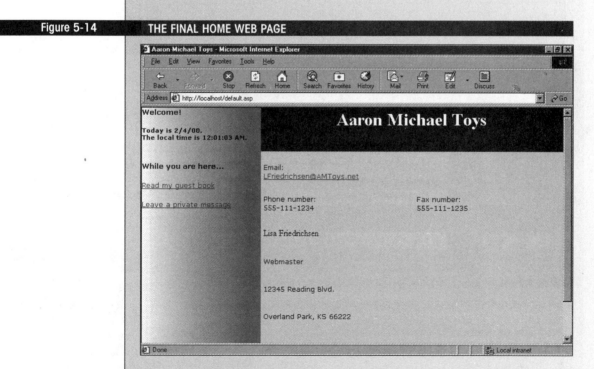

5. Close IE and the new Web page you just created, then click the **Personal Web Manager** button on the taskbar to return to that program.

Now that you've used the Home Page Wizard once, Personal Web Manager offers options to Edit your home page, View your guest book, and Open your drop box. You'll explore these options later.

Publishing Files to Personal Web Server

Now that the Personal Web server is set up and your home page is created, you're ready to start publishing additional pages to the Personal Web server, including those that are connected to your AMToys-5 Access database. You'll use the Publishing Wizard within Personal Web Server to accomplish this, but first you need to open AMToys-5 and create a Web page to publish.

To create an Access Web page to publish:

1. Start Access and open the **AMToys-5** database from the Tutorial\Solutions folder for Tutorial 5.

   You don't need to leave Personal Web Manager open when you are creating the Web page, but since you'll soon use it to publish the Web page, you will leave it running.

2. Click the **Pages** button on the Objects Bar, click the **New** button in the database window, click **AutoPage: Columnar** in the New Data Access Page dialog box, click the **Choose the table or query where the object's data comes from** list arrow, click **Suppliers**, and then click the **OK** button.

   The page opens in Page View.

3. Maximize the page in order to clearly see it, click the **Save** button, navigate to the Tutorial\Solutions folder for Tutorial 5, type **Suppliers** as the filename, and then click the **Save** button.

4. Close the Suppliers page, close the AMToys-5 database, and then exit Access.

Using the Personal Web Manager Publishing Wizard

To **publish** a file means to send (or upload) it to a particular Web folder on a Web server so that other users have access to it. Therefore, to publish means to make the files (Web pages and associated files) public to others.

REFERENCE WINDOW   RW

Using the Personal Web Manager Publishing Wizard
- Open Personal Web Manager.
- Click the Publish button.
- Follow the wizard prompts to browse for, select, and add the appropriate files to the list of those that you wish to publish.

To publish Web pages using the Publishing Wizard:

1. Click the **Personal Web Manager** button on the taskbar, click the **Publish** button 🖳, read the opening text, and then click the **Next** button `>>`.

   The next window prompts you for information about the current location of your files.

   TROUBLE? If you are presented with an additional window with the question "What do you want to do?" click the option button for Add a file to the published list, and then click the Next button.

2. Click the **Browse** button.

   You navigate for files within this window much as you navigate hyperlinks on a Web page. Each folder represents a link. Click the links to open them.

3. Navigate to the Tutorial\Solutions folder for Tutorial 5. Your screen will look similar to the one shown in Figure 5-15, but the directory (folder) path will be different, depending upon how you have named and set up the folders for the data files on your computer.

| Figure 5-15 | SPECIFYING THE PATH FOR FILES TO BE PUBLISHED |

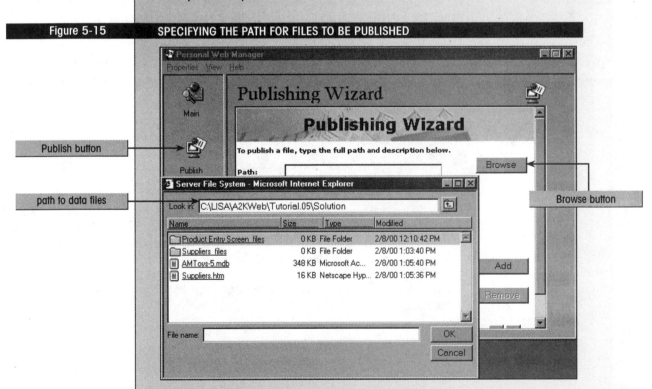

4. Click **Suppliers.htm**, and then click the **OK** button.

   The path to the file appears in the Path text box in the Publishing Wizard.

5. Click the **Add** button to add that file to the list of those to be published.

6. Click the **Next** button `>>` in the Publishing Wizard window.

   The Publishing Wizard window indicates that you added the Suppliers.htm file to your Personal Web server. All published Web pages are capable of being accessed through the home page that you previously created. You are now ready to view the published Web page as if you were another user of this Web server.

Now that you've published Web pages to your Personal Web server, you will use Internet Explorer to open them using **HTTP** (Hypertext Transfer Protocol) rather than opening them directly from a folder on your hard drive. This process will simulate the same activity that happens when you download a Web page into your browser from the server.

To open a Web page through HTTP that was published to your Personal Web Server:

1. In Personal Web Server, click the **Main** button.

   The Main page tells you the default name used for the first Web folder created on your machine (hkpf7 in this example). You can create new Web folders with more meaningful names on your machine by using PWS or by using the Add Web Folder Wizard within Explorer. Web folders appear within the My Computer group within Explorer. For now, you'll use the default Web folder.

2. Click the link where your home page is located to open your home page in IE.

   From the address on the Address bar, you can see that the Web page was delivered to the browser through the HTTP just like the Web pages that are delivered through Internet-based Web servers, even though you know that the page is physically stored on your local hard drive. You could have entered this URL into the IE browser itself or given it to another user on your local area network.

   TROUBLE? If a window opens to connect to the Internet, close it. You won't be going through the Internet to access these Web pages, even though you are using HTTP protocol.

3. Click the **View my published documents** link on the left side of the home page to view all of the files you have previously published to this Web folder.

4. Click **Suppliers.htm**, and then click **Yes** if prompted about accessing data on another domain.

   TROUBLE? If no data is displayed, you may have to lower the security level within Internet Explorer for your local intranet. Click Tools on the Internet Explorer menu bar, click Internet Options, click the Security tab, click Local Intranet, drag the slider to Medium-low, and then click OK in the Internet Options dialog box.

   The Suppliers Web page opens in IE through HTTP as shown in Figure 5-16.

Figure 5-16	THE SUPPLIERS WEB PAGE THROUGH THE PERSONAL WEB SERVER

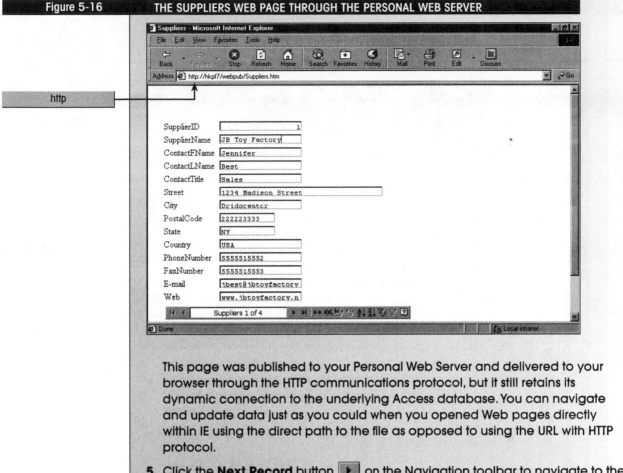

http

This page was published to your Personal Web Server and delivered to your browser through the HTTP communications protocol, but it still retains its dynamic connection to the underlying Access database. You can navigate and update data just as you could when you opened Web pages directly within IE using the direct path to the file as opposed to using the URL with HTTP protocol.

5. Click the **Next Record** button [▶] on the Navigation toolbar to navigate to the second record for supplier We Know Fun, click to the right of **Anne** in the ContactFName field, type **tte** to change the name from Anne to Annette, and then click the **Save Record** button [💾] on the Navigation toolbar.

6. Close **IE**.

Now check to make sure that the change updated the Access database file.

To verify changes to the underlying database:

1. Start Access and open the **AMToys-5** database from the Tutorial\Solutions folder for Tutorial 5.

2. Click the **Tables** button [📧] on the Objects Bar, and then double-click **Suppliers**.

   The Suppliers table should show the change in the ContactFName from Anne to "Annette" for SupplierID 4, as shown in Figure 5-17.

Figure 5-17	SUPPLIERS TABLE WITH UPDATE

Suppliers : Table

	SupplierID	SupplierName	ContactFName	ContactLName	ContactTitle	Street	
▶ ⊞	1	JB Toy Factory	Jennifer	Best	Sales Representative	1234 Madison Street	Brid
⊞	2	We Know Fun	Annette	Lang	Account Representative	987 Monroe Avenue	Des
⊞	3	KidSense	Kent	Lee	Marketing Representative	222 Sunset Drive	Am
⊞	4	Totally Amazing	Arno	Guth	President	987 Adams Street	Fon
*	(AutoNumber)						

Record: 1 of 4

updated ContactFName

3. Close the Suppliers table, close the AMToys-5 database, and then exit Access.

You have just explored three ways to update an Access database, two of which involve Web pages. First of all, don't forget that you can always use the tables, queries, and forms within the Access database itself to enter and update data, provided you have direct access to and proper security for the database file. The form object still provides the most flexible and easy-to-use data entry tool that you can create for a user.

When you want the additional security and accessibility benefits provided by Web pages, however, you can quickly create Web pages that are dynamically connected to the underlying database by using the page object. Web pages can be opened directly within IE by two methods. First, you can directly enter the path to the file, such as C:\AMTOYS\DB\products.htm, in the browser, or browse for the file by clicking the File menu and then choosing the Open option.

Or, you can open Web pages within IE by using HTTP and entering the Web page's URL. If you wish to use HTTP, you must publish the Web pages to a Web server that can translate the HTTP communications protocol to the physical path of the file. If you don't have access to a Web server, you can publish the Web pages to Personal Web Server located on your own machine. If you are connected to a LAN or WAN, PWS gives you an easy way to quickly give others access to these Web pages through HTTP too.

Exploring **Advanced Options within Personal Web Manager**

Now that you have published Web pages with Personal Web Manager, you'll want to explore the advanced options. These options will help you determine default settings, such as how home pages will work on your Personal Web Server, as well as how to set up activity logs and security.

To explore Advanced Options within Personal Web Server:

1. Click the **Personal Web Manager** button on your taskbar, and then click the **Advanced** button 🖳.

The Advanced Options window appears as shown in Figure 5-18.

Figure 5-18 | ADVANCED OPTIONS

virtual folders

Directory Browsing

Site Activity Log

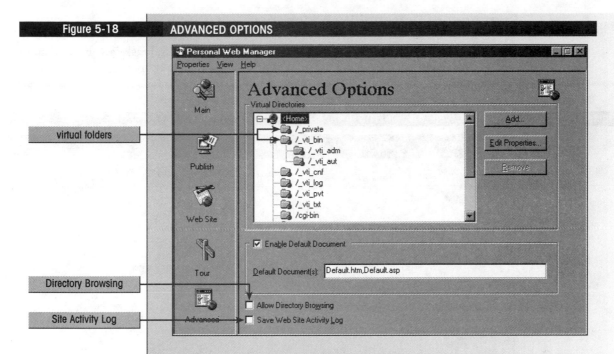

The folders displayed are **virtual folders**, which are directory names used in a URL address that correspond to a physical directory on the server. Virtual folders are also called **URL mappings**, since they map URL addresses to physical folders similarly to how network mappings map drive letters to physical folders on a local area network.

It is through these virtual folders that you control security to the Web pages within them.

2. Click the **/_private** virtual folder, and then click **Edit Properties**.

TROUBLE? If you don't have a /_private virtual folder, click any other folder that is presented and click Edit Properties to explore how the physical mapping and access permissions options appear.

The Edit Directory dialog box opens, allowing you to change the physical mapping to the C:\Inetpub\wwwroot directory, change the virtual directory name (alias), and change access permissions.

3. Click the **Cancel** button.

Other advanced options that you should consider include the **Directory Browsing** and **Activity Log** options. Both features are enabled through check boxes in the Advanced Options window. Directory Browsing enables visitors to your Web Server to view documents as a list of files in a directory as opposed to links from a home page. Activity Logs create a file that lists everyone who has visited your site and which files they accessed while they were there.

4. Close the Personal Web Manager window.

Summary of Personal Web Manager

Personal Web Manager is a great way to explore the concepts and tasks involved in publishing Web pages to a Web Server. Personal Web Manager's components are summarized in Figure 5-19.

Figure 5-19		PERSONAL WEB COMPONENTS
COMPONENT	**BUTTON**	**PURPOSE**
Main		■ Allows you to turn Web publishing on and off ■ Gives you the HTTP address for your home page ■ Documents your home directory ■ Provides connection information
Publish		Presents the Publishing Wizard that lets you: ■ Add files to the published list ■ Remove files from the published list ■ Refresh published files ■ Change file descriptions
Web Site		Presents the Home Page Wizard that helps you: ■ Edit your home page ■ View your guest box ■ Open your drop box
Tour		Gives you a guided tour of the features of Personal Web Server
Advanced		■ Helps you manage virtual directories and access permissions ■ Lets you set default document choices ■ Lets you set Directory Browsing options ■ Lets you set Web site activity logs

Understanding the Web Publishing Wizard

When you're ready to publish your Web files to an Internet Web server rather than the Personal Web Server, you can use the Web Publishing Wizard to help send the files to the site. The **Web Publishing Wizard** is an Internet tool bundled with Windows 98 that helps you publish files to an Internet Web site. The Web Publishing Wizard can be described as an easy-to-use file transfer program. Note that Web Publishing Wizard is a totally separate program from Personal Web Server. PWS has its own built-in component for publishing Web files to Personal Web Servers.

If you are already comfortable with file transfer programs, such as FTP Explorer or others, you could use one of those programs to send your Web pages to the Web server, and you wouldn't need to use the Web Publishing Wizard to help you with this process. Since the Web Publishing Wizard provides a step-by-step interface for this process and is available on a Windows 98 computer, it is handy tool to use for the publishing process.

Of course you cannot publish Web files to any Web server that you are not authorized to use, so the infrastructure and appropriate security levels that allow you to write files to the chosen Web server need to be in place before you can publish Web pages over the Internet. Therefore the most difficult aspect about publishing your Web pages to an Internet Web server isn't the publishing process, but rather, setting up the appropriate infrastructure, Web folders, and permissions to allow for Web page publishing ahead of time.

In this example, you'll explore the Web Publishing Wizard as if you were actually publishing Web pages to an Internet Web server. For the reasons stated above, you'll stop at the point at which you need to enter the Internet Web server address.

To use the Web Publishing Wizard:

1. Click **Start** on the taskbar, point to **Programs**, click **Web Publishing Wizard** or point to **Internet Explorer**, and then click **Web Publishing Wizard**.

TROUBLE? If the Web Publishing Wizard is not installed on your computer, you can install it using Add/Remove Programs within Control Panel. Click the Start button, point to Settings, click Control Panel and then double-click Add/Remove Programs. Click the Windows Setup tab, click Internet Tools, click the Web Publishing Wizard check box, click the OK button in the Internet Tools dialog box, click the OK button in the Add/Remove Programs Properties dialog box, and then close the Control Panel window.

The first page explains what the wizard will help you do and the type of information you need ahead of time in order to successfully publish Web pages.

2. Click the **Next** button.

The Select a File or Folder dialog box appears, prompting you for information about what you want to publish. You want to publish all of the files in the folder that contains the AMToys-5 database.

3. Click the **Browse Folders** button to open the Browse for Folder dialog box, click the drive that contains your Data Disk, navigate to the Tutorial\Solutions folder for Tutorial 5, and then click the **OK** button.

Your screen will look similar to Figure 5-20. The directory (folder) path will be different, depending upon how you have installed the data files on your computer. Note that you can publish all files in all subfolders if the Include subfolders check box is checked.

Figure 5-20	SELECT A FILE OR FOLDER

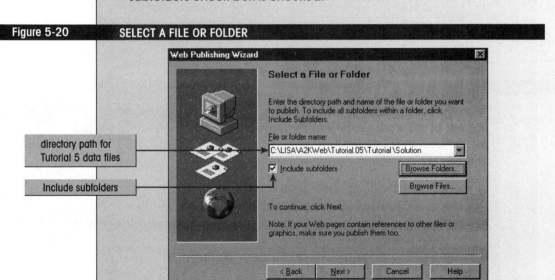

4. Click the **Next** button.

Now you are prompted to enter a name for the Web Server. The window further explains that this is simply a descriptive name to help you publish files to this location in the future.

5. Type **Aaron Michael Toys**, and then click the **Next** button.

The next wizard question, shown in Figure 5-21, prompts you for the location where you want your files to be published. This entry would have to be provided by your Internet service provider (ISP) or company Webmaster, depending on if you were using an ISP or your own company's Web servers to host the files.

Figure 5-21	SPECIFY THE URL AND DIRECTORY

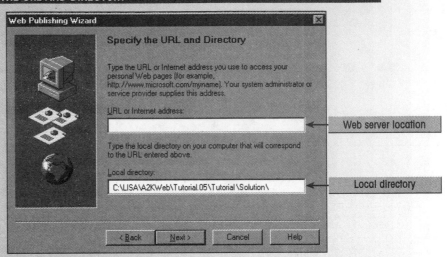

The responses to this dialog box establish a connection between a specific Web folder with a directory on your hard drive. Once this connection is established, you'll be able to publish additional files to the "Aaron Michael Toys" Web server instead of specifying the exact location again.

Figure 5-22 shows you a fictitious Web server URL, *www.jccc.net/amtoys/suppliers*, and the Enter Network Password dialog box that would appear, allowing you to continue this publishing process.

Figure 5-22	ENTER NETWORK PASSWORD DIALOG BOX

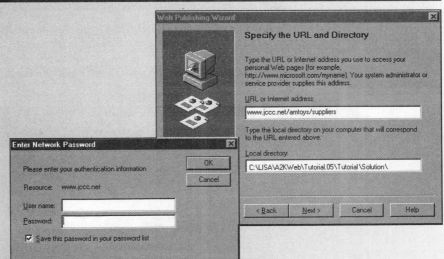

6. Click the **Cancel** button, and then click **Yes** to quit the Web Publishing Wizard.

As you can see, publishing to an Internet Web server really isn't difficult, but the proper infrastructure has to be in place before you can do it. The person who sets up your company's Internet Web server, creates Web folders for different publishing purposes, and administrates user IDs and passwords often has the title of **Webmaster**. Other common job titles for these people include network administrator, network manager, or if you are publishing to a local Web server, LAN manager.

Most public Internet service providers, such as The Microsoft Network and America On-Line, also allow you to publish a limited number of files to their Web servers. Generally, you can find an **FAQ** (frequently asked questions) document at their Web site that details the specific instructions on how and where to publish your files. These types of Web server locations, however, generally allow full public access to the files you publish. So if your files are for the internal uses of your business or not for public consumption, you'll either have to build your own Web server or rent private space from a Web hosting company that offers the additional security layers you need.

Exploring HTML

Each of the underlying technologies discussed in this tutorial could fill a book. Of special note, however, is **HTML**, Hypertext Markup Language. HTML is the programming code that describes the appearance of a Web page. A Web browser, such as IE, interprets HTML codes to display a Web page. There are several extensions to HTML (such as those used by Access) that expand what a Web page file can deliver to a client. HTML cannot, for example, provide a dynamic connection to an underlying database. Through extensions such as **XML**, Extensible Markup Language, however, the Web page "container" can act as the vehicle that delivers additional programming code, which can in turn create a chart, display a scrolling marquee, or provide a data entry screen.

Fortunately, with the page object tools provided within Access, you were able to create very powerful Web pages for data entry, interactive reporting, and data analysis without knowing anything about HTML, XML, or any of the other programming languages that Microsoft uses to put together a Web page. You used a **GUI** (graphical user interface) tool to quickly create a Web page that would have required hours of time and years of experience by programmers only a few years ago.

Although you may never wish to program a Web page by entering codes, it is helpful to know what the underlying code of a Web page looks like and how to view it.

To view the code of a Web page:

1. Right-click the **Start** button on the taskbar, click **Explore**, navigate to the Tutorial\Solutions folder for Tutorial 5, and then double-click the **Suppliers.htm** file.

   The Suppliers.htm file loads using IE. This time you opened it directly within IE rather than downloading it from Personal Web Server using Hypertext Transfer Protocol. For the purposes of viewing a Web page's code, it doesn't matter how your browser opens the file.

2. Click **View** on the menu bar, and then click **Source**.

   A window opens, displaying the code that created the Suppliers.htm Web page as shown in Figure 5-23.

Figure 5-23	SUPPLIERS.HTM CODE

Notepad

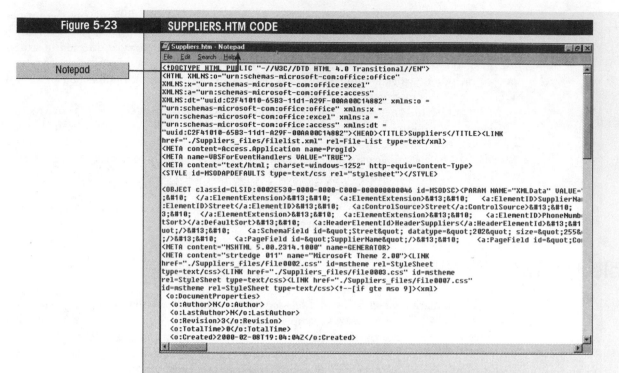

The HTML code opened in a Notepad window. **Notepad** is a simple text editor program included as a Windows 98 accessory program. Notepad allows you to directly enter HTML programming code without introducing extraneous formatting commands.

For example, if you knew the HTML to create a title for this Web page, you could quickly add it directly in this Notepad window rather than having to return to Access and add the title by adding a label control in Page Design view.

3. Press the **End** key to move the blinking insertion point to the end of the first line, press the **Enter** key, and then type **<H1> Supplier Entry Screen </H1>** as shown in Figure 5-24.

Figure 5-24	EDITING HTML CODE

new line of HTML

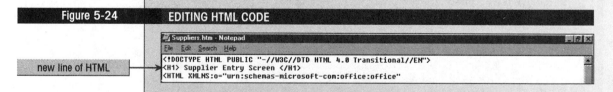

HTML is written using **tags** that the browser uses to interpret the code. Tags are always surrounded by a less than and greater than sign (also called angle brackets) as follows: <tag>. Some tags are **one-sided**, meaning that only a single tag is used. The first line of the Suppliers.htm code is an example of a large one-sided comment tag. The exclamation point indicates that everything else inside the tag is a comment used to document the Web page file and not something that is displayed on the Web page when it is opened with a browser.

Many tags, however, are **two-sided**, meaning that two tags, called an **opening tag** and a **closing tag**, are required for the code to be interpreted successfully. The <H1> and </H1> tags mark the beginning and end of Heading 1 text. The forward slash within the tag indicates that it is a closing tag.

4. Click **File** on the menu bar, click **Save**, and then close the Notepad window.

   To see the effects of the new line of code, you need to refresh the Web page within the browser window.

5. Click the **Refresh** button 🔄 on the Standard buttons toolbar.

   The text "Supplier Entry Screen" was added to the page in a "Heading 1" style as shown in Figure 5-25.

| Figure 5-25 | ADDING A HEADING TO A WEB PAGE |

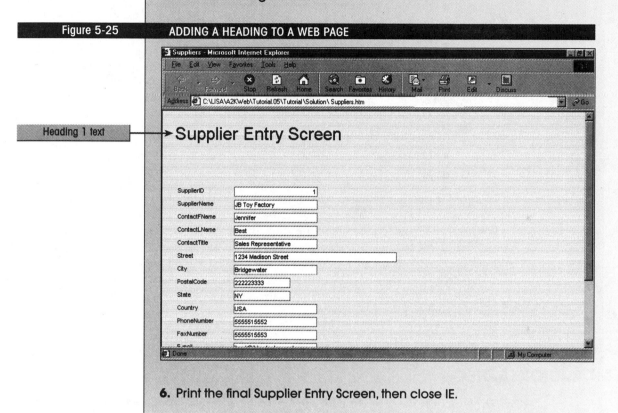

6. Print the final Supplier Entry Screen, then close IE.

Within Notepad, you can add and delete code as well as copy and paste it to other windows. Most Web page developers feel that it is necessary to have a solid understanding of HTML in order to troubleshoot problems that your Web pages might present. It is often difficult to understand why a Web page isn't working the way you had intended unless you can read and unravel each line of code. Even though you may not be an HTML or XML programmer, you now know how to view the code for a Web page, and also have some sense of how the tags work.

Webmaster Skill Areas

GUI Web page editors, such as the Page Design view in Access, or a traditional Web page development software package, such as FrontPage, are wonderful tools for creating sophisticated Web pages quickly. When it comes to fixing Web page problems, however, a solid understanding of HTML and XML can help you figure out why something isn't working as planned.

Similarly, the Personal Web Server and Web Publishing Wizards are great tools that enable you to quickly publish Web page files to Web servers. Setting up the necessary prerequisite infrastructure, however, requires significant (and sometimes expensive) hardware and networking skills.

The various skills required to "put it all together" are vast. The technologies discussed in this tutorial are only a subset of the skills required by today's Webmasters. The technical skills discussed include the following areas:

- Databases
- Web pages development tools
- Networking
  - Web server installation
  - Web folder management
  - UserID and password management
  - Folder and file security
  - Network communications protocols
- Publishing and file transfer tools
- Web programming languages
  - HTML
  - XML

It's rare for one individual to have a deep understanding of all of these technologies, but the more aware you are of how they all fit together, the more capable and valuable you'll be.

For now, you may decide to limit the scope of the Aaron Michael Toys database to internal needs. You decide to publish Web pages created from the database to Personal Web Server for internal use over your LAN. This is a great start, and is a good example of how a data-driven Web site can be established quickly, and without the need for expensive Webmaster resources. In the next tutorial, however, you'll learn more about some of the software programs and tools used to scale up databases for true e-commerce.

Session 5.1 QUICK CHECK

1. What is a likely job title for the person considered most directly responsible for the success of the Web site?

2. Explain the relationships between publishing, Web pages, Web folders, and Web servers.

3. What is a likely job title for the person who is in charge of maintaining a local computer network?

4. What types of user rights would you consider when publishing Web pages to shared Web folders?

5. What program allows you to go through the process of installing Web server software, setting up Web folders, and publishing Web pages to the Web folder all on your own computer?

6. What are the major components and the capabilities of each component within Personal Web Manager?

7. Identify two defining characteristics of HTML code.

8. Identify five categories of technical skills required for Webmasters.

REVIEW ASSIGNMENTS

You work in the business office of a graduate school, Adair Graduate School, that offers several degrees including a Master of Business Administration (MBA), Master of Telecommunications Management (MTM), and Master of Information Systems Management (MISM). You have developed an Access database called **AdairGS-5** to help the faculty track students, classes, assignments, grades, and instructors. You'll use this database to create and publish Web pages to your Personal Web Server.

1. Start Access and open the **AdairGS-5** database from the Review\Solutions folder for Tutorial 5.

2. Click the Pages button on the Objects Bar, and then double-click Create data access page by using wizard.

3. Choose all of the fields from the Classes table, remove all grouping levels, do not specify any sort orders, title the page **Class Entry Screen**, and open it in Page view.

4. Save the page with the name **Class Entry Screen** to the Review\Solutions folder for Tutorial 5, close the page, and then exit Access.

5. Start Personal Web Manager, read the tip of the day if presented, and then close the Tip of the day window. (*Note*: Personal Web Server must be installed in order for you to have Personal Web Manager on your computer. If you are unsure whether Personal Web Server is installed, refer to the steps in the tutorial on Installing Personal Web Server and Taking the Personal Web Server Tour.)

6. Click the Web Site button, and then click Edit your home page. (*Note*: If you have never created a home page, the Home Page Wizard will appear. Follow the steps in the tutorial on Using the Home Page Wizard, and then return to this step to continue.)

7. Click the Journal template style.

8. Click in the URL text box to add a link by typing **www.course.com**, press the Tab key, and then type **Course Technology home page** in the Description text box. (*Note*: The entire entry in the URL text box will be *http://www.course.com*)

9. Click the add link button to add the hyperlink.

10. Change the title to **Adair Graduate School**. Click in the Name text box and type your name. Fill in the other text boxes with your information, and then click the enter new changes button at the bottom of the template.

11. When the Welcome! page with the *http://localhost/default.asp* page loads, click View my published documents. The only published document should be the Suppliers.htm file that you published to your Personal Web Server in the tutorial. Click the Back button on the Standard buttons toolbar to return to your home page.

12. Click the Personal Web Server button on the taskbar, then click the Publish button.

13. If presented with the introductory Publishing Wizard information window, click Next. When presented with the What do you want to do? window, click Add a file to the published list option button, and then click the Next arrow button.

14. Click the Browse button, navigate to the Review\Solutions folder for Tutorial 5, click Class Entry Screen.htm, and then click the OK button.

15. In the Publish Wizard window, click the Add button to add the file to the list of Files to publish.

16. Click the Next arrow button to finish the publishing process, then click the Adair Graduate School IE button on the taskbar.

17. Click the View my published documents link on the left side of your home page, click the Class Entry Screen.htm link, and then click Yes to allow the page to access data from the underlying Access database.

18. In IE, change the ClassDescription for the first record from Global Diversity to **International Culture**.

19. Click the New Record button on the Navigation toolbar, and then start a new record with the following information by entering the minimum information. In the ClassName field, type **IS599**, and in the ClassDescription field, type **Data-Driven Web Sites**. Click the Save Record button on the Navigation toolbar. The ClassID field should have been automatically incremented to 15, and the Credits field defaulted to 0, since it is a Number field.

20. Close the IE window.

21. Start Access, open the **AdairGS-5** database, click the Tables button on the Objects bar, and then double-click Classes to view the datasheet.

22. Click File, and then click Page Setup to open the Page Setup dialog box. Change the page orientation to landscape, and then return to the datasheet.

23. Resize the ClassName and ClassDescription fields so that you can see all of the data within each column, but narrow the other fields so that you can print the datasheet on one page.

24. Save and print the datasheet, close it, and then close the **AdairGS-5** database.

25. Close Personal Web Manager.

CASE PROBLEMS

Case 1. Researching the Job of a Webmaster You are interested in a career as a Webmaster and want to find out more about opportunities and the requirements of the job. You'll use the Internet and World Wide Web to conduct a search for job salary and skill requirements information for Webmasters.

1. Connect to the Internet, start IE, and then type **www.about.com** in the Address text box.

2. Type **Webmaster** in the Find It Now text box, and then click Go.

3. Click the links to find information about Webmaster Certificates and/or Certification programs. Keep surfing the Web to find and print a list of skills required for a Webmaster Certification program. One such site that provides this information is *www.joinwow.org*.

4. Use *www.about.com* as a starting point to surf for Webmaster jobs and/or careers. Find and print a list of jobs for Webmasters in your area. One such site that provides this information is *www.hotjobs.com*.

5. Use *www.askjeeves.com* as a starting point to search for Webmaster Certification programs. Find a different certification program, and print the list of certification requirements.

6. Use *www.askjeeves.com* as a starting point to search for Webmaster jobs and/or careers. Find and print a list of jobs, including salary information for Webmasters in your area.

7. On a piece of paper, combine and summarize the certification requirements of both programs, listing the general areas of knowledge (e.g., Web design skills, business skills, and networking skills) and the specific items within each general area.

8. On a piece of paper, write down the salary range for the jobs you found for Webmasters.

Case 2. Exploring the Web Server Manager You want to become more familiar with some of the features available within the Web Server Manager, specifically the guest book and drop box. You'll explore these features from the standpoint of a user as well as a Web page developer.

1. Start Personal Web Manager, read the tip of the day if presented, and then close the Tip of the day window. (*Note*: Personal Web Server must be installed in order for you to have Personal Web Manager on your computer. If you are unsure whether Personal Web Server is installed, refer to the steps in the tutorial on Installing Personal Web Server and Taking the Personal Web Server Tour.)

2. Click the Web Site button. (*Note*: If you have never created a home page, the Home Page Wizard will appear. Follow the steps in the tutorial on Using the Home Page Wizard, making sure that you have chosen both the guest book and the drop box features, and then return to this step to continue.)

Explore 3. Click the View your guest book link, do not add any criteria, and then click the Submit Query button. If you have not had any visitors to your home page, the window will indicate that there are no entries in your guest book.

Explore 4. Click the Web Site button, and then click the Open your drop box link. Once again, if you have not had any visitors to your home page, the window will indicate that there are no entries in your drop box.

5. Click the Main button, and then click the link for your home page.

6. Your home page opens with links to both the drop box and guest book on the left side. Click Read my guest book, and then click Click here to sign the guest book.

Explore 7. Fill in the form with your actual name. Enter your e-mail address and home page address if you have one. Enter **Web Publishing** as the Message subject, and then enter a brief message about one thing you learned or would still like to learn about Web Publishing based on your experiences with this tutorial.

8. Click the Send message button at the bottom of the guest book, and then print the Thank you for entering your comments! Web page.

Explore 9. Click the Return to guest book link, click the link with your name, and then view the message. On your printout, write down who has access to the messages you enter in the Guest Book. (*Hint*: If you don't know for sure, you can use the Help system within Personal Web Manager to verify your answer.)

Explore 10. Click the Return to the home page link, and click the Leave a private message link.

11. Fill in the form with your actual name. Enter your e-mail address and home page address if you have one. Enter **Webmaster** as the Message subject, and then enter a brief message about whether or not you'd like to pursue a career as a Webmaster based on your experiences with this tutorial.

Explore 12. Click the Send message button at the bottom of the private message page, and then print the Thank you for entering your comments! Web page. One your printout, write down who has access to the messages you enter in the Leave a private message area. (*Hint*: If you don't know for sure, you can use the Help system within Personal Web Manager to verify your answer.)

13. Close IE. Click the Personal Web Manager button on your taskbar if that window is not visible on your screen.

14. Click the Web Site button, and then click the View your guest book link. Click the MessageDate, MessageFrom, and MessageSubject list arrows so that you can get a feel for how you submit a query to a guest box that contains a large number of messages. Click the Submit Query button without entering any criteria to see all sent messages.

15. Click the link that displays your name so you can view the message, and then click the Delete message button.

16. Click the Web Site button, and then click the Open your drop box link. Click the link that contains your name so you can view the message, and then click the Delete message button.

17. Close Personal Web Manager.

Case 3. *Exploring Personal Web Server Features* You want to learn more about the other components of Personal Web Server. You'll use the Personal Web Server Help system to familiarize yourself with some of the other features of the system.

1. Start Personal Web Manager, read the Tip of the day if presented, and then close the Tip of the day window. (*Note*: Personal Web Server must be installed in order for you to have Personal Web Manager on your computer. If you are unsure whether Personal Web Server is installed, refer to the steps in the tutorial on Installing Personal Web Server and Taking the Personal Web Server Tour.)

2. Click Help on the menu bar, and then click Personal Web Server Topics. Click the Contents tab in the left pane, and then click the expand button to the left of Microsoft Transaction Server entry.

3. Click the expand button to the left of the Quick Tour of MTS entry, and then click the link for What is Microsoft Transaction Server? Print that page.

4. Navigate back to the Quick Tour of MTS entry, and click and read each of the remaining five links from that page.

Explore

5. Click the collapse button to the left of Microsoft Transaction Server, and then click the expand button to the left of Microsoft Data Access Components. Depending on how your Personal Web Server was installed, you may not have the Help files for this section of Personal Web Server. If you have all of the Help files, print the page titled ADO Overview.

6. Click the collapse button to the left of the Microsoft Data Access Components entry, and then click the expand button to the left of the Microsoft Message Queue Server section. Again, depending on how your Personal Web Server was installed, you may not have the Help files for this section. If you have all of the Help files, expand the Administrator's Guide entry, expand the Microsoft Message Queue System entry, and print the page titled Introducing MSMQ.

7. If you were unable to print information in Steps 5 and 6, you can either reinstall Personal Web Server and request more components (see the section in the tutorial on Installing Personal Web Server) or look up more information at Microsoft's Web site.

8. Connect to the Internet, start IE, and enter **www.microsoft.com/windows/ie/pws** in the Address text box. Print this Web page, which has information on how to use PWS for Windows 95 and Windows NT.

9. Using the Microsoft site, click the Search button and search for **data access components** in the Product Information database. Find and print one article that further discusses this concept.

10. Using the Microsoft site, search for **Message Queue System** in the Product Information database. Find and print one article that further discusses this concept.

11. Close all windows and disconnect from the Internet.

Case 4. Learning More about HTML You want to become more familiar with some of the HTML codes used to develop a Web page. You'll build a small Web page from scratch using only a text editor and HTML code. It will not contain any XML or dynamic links to a database, but will give you more familiarity with HTML programming.

1. Start Notepad. (*Hint*: It is usually found in the Accessories group.)

2. Enter the following HTML code into the window that creates a Web page that documents two classes you are currently taking. Replace the text with information that is meaningful to you, but enter the HTML tags identified with the greater than and less than symbols <tag> exactly as shown.

```
<!Your Name's Web Page>
<HTML>
<head><B>Your Name's Masterpiece</B></head>
<P>These are my current classes</P>
<H1>Class Name</H1>
<H2>Teacher's Name</H2>
<H3>Meeting Time</H3>
<HR>
<H1>Class Name</H1>
<H2>Teacher's Name</H2>
<H3>Meeting Time</H3>
</HTML>
```

3. Click File, and then click Print to print the Notepad document.

4. Click File, click Save, navigate to the Cases\Solutions folder for Tutorial 5, enter *Your Name* **classes.htm** in the File Name text box, click the list arrow for the Save as type list, and choose All Files (*.*) so that the .txt extension used to identify text-only Notepad documents doesn't get appended to the filename. Click the Save button in the Save As dialog box.

5. Close the Notepad window and open an IE window.

6. Click File on the menu bar, click Open, click the Browse button, navigate to the Data Disk, double-click Your Name classes.htm, and then click the OK button. Click the Print button on the IE Standard buttons toolbar to print the Web page.

7. Using both printouts, cross-reference which line of code created each element on the Web page.

8. Now enter the URL for an Internet-based Web page in the Address text box, such as *www.webdatabase.org*, a Web site devoted to information on Web-enabled databases.

9. Print the Web page. Click View, and then click Source to view the underlying code. Print the code.

10. Using both printouts, cross-reference the first five lines of code with the elements on the Web page.

11. Exit IE and close other open windows.

QUICK | CHECK ANSWERS

Session 5.1

1. Webmaster

2. A Web server is a computer devoted to storing and downloading Web pages. Publishing means to store the Web page files in a special folder on a Web server called a Web folder. A Web folder stores and organizes Web pages.

3. network administrator or LAN manager

4. Common user rights include the following list:

   F = Full Control
   R = Read
   W = Write
   X = Execute
   D = Delete

5. With Personal Web Server, you can go through the process of installing Web server software, setting up Web folders, and publishing Web pages to the Web folder

6. The major components of Personal Web Manager and their capabilities are:

   Main
   - Allows you to turn Web publishing on and off
   - Gives you the HTTP address for your home page
   - Documents your home directory
   - Provides connection information

   Publish   Presents the Publishing Wizard that lets you:
   - Add files to the published list
   - Remove files from the published list
   - Refresh published files
   - Change file descriptions

   Web Site   Presents the Home Page Wizard that helps you:
   - Edit your home page
   - View your guest box
   - Open your drop box

   Tour   Gives you a guided tour of the features of Personal Web Server

   Advanced
   - Helps you manage virtual directories and access permissions
   - Lets you set default document choices
   - Lets you set directory browsing options
   - Lets you set Web site activity logs

7. A description of some of the characteristics of HTML code include the following:
   - HTML is the programming code that describes the appearance of a Web page.
   - A Web browser, such as IE, interprets HTML codes to display a Web page.
   - There are several extensions to HTML (such as those used by Access) to expand what a Web page file can deliver to a client.
   - HTML is written using tags that the browser uses to interpret the code. Tags are always surrounded by a less than and greater than sign as follows: <tag>.

8. Today's Webmasters need skills in each of these five technical categories.
   - Databases
   - Web pages development tools
   - Networking
   - Publishing and file transfer tools
   - Web programming languages

In this tutorial you will:

- Explore Web-enabling technologies on both the client and server sides

- Learn about different approaches to creating data-driven Web sites beyond Access

- Use the Microsoft Knowledge Base

- Use the MSDN Online Library

- Use FrontPage to create dynamic Active Server Page Web pages

- Publish ASP files to your Personal Web Server

- Learn about the various jobs in a data-driven Web site implementation

- Explore JavaScript and other Web-enabling scripting languages

- Explore Java and other Web-enabling programming languages

- Explore Microsoft's Internet Information Server and other Web-enabling networking software

USING
OTHER WEB-ENABLED DATABASE TECHNOLOGIES

Dynamically Updating Data in the Aaron Michael Toys Database Through Published Web Pages

CASE

Aaron Michael Toys

Now that you've seen how Access can build Web pages for data entry, interactive reporting, and data analysis, you're ready to explore related technologies and products. Using Access 2000 and Personal Web Server, you'll be able to share data internally using the AMT (Aaron Michael Toys) intranet, but as the uses for the Access database grow, you'll want to expand access to outsiders such as customers and vendors. Expanding access to your Web-enabled database to outsiders involves additional issues such as higher levels of performance and security. You'll also want to consider new e-commerce technologies such as a shopping cart interface, secure credit card authorization, and shipping lists.

In this tutorial you will learn about technologies used to expand a data-driven Web site to the rest of the world over the World Wide Web. You'll delve into some of the underlying technologies that make a data-driven Web site work that were hidden when you used the GUI Web page creation tools within Access and the wizards within Personal Web Server. You'll also explore supporting Web-enabling technologies such as JavaScript, Java, and Microsoft Internet Information Server.

SESSION 6.1

In this session you will learn about client-server computing and other underlying data-driven Web site technologies. You'll also learn about different approaches to building data-driven Web sites.

Defining Client-Server Computing

Inherent to your understanding of the technologies used to build data-driven Web sites is your understanding of client-server computing. **Client-server computing** (C/S) can be defined as two or more information systems processing cooperatively to solve a problem. Figure 6-1 gives the expanded meaning of each part of this client-server definition.

Figure 6-1	DEFINING CLIENT-SERVER COMPUTING
PHRASE	**EXPANDED MEANING**
two or more	C/S involves two or more computers. A stand-alone PC is not an example of C/S nor is a mainframe with "dumb" terminals. Examples of the latter are more difficult to find as Web-enabled applications and networks continue to become more commonplace. Web-enabled applications require an **intelligent client** (a PC with processing and memory capabilities) to process the delivery and presentation of the Web page. In order to find, download, and open a Web page, you must have a client PC loaded with the appropriate browser software to open files and execute instructions locally. In other words, the client must be "intelligent."
information systems	An information system consists of both hardware and software. A dumb terminal, such as an old mainframe CRT, an ATM machine, or a fixed function I/O (input/output) device, is used to send and receive data, but these are not information systems themselves. At a minimum, an information system must be able to manage files and process information. It must be capable of accomplishing work by itself. If not, it is considered a "dumb" device, dependent upon the capabilities of another information system to provide value.
cooperatively	"Cooperatively" refers to the fact that the client and server must be able to communicate electronically. For example, exporting a mainframe file to an ASCII format, copying that file to a floppy disk, and then opening the file from the floppy into an Excel spreadsheet on a PC isn't an example of C/S. When people talk of C/S systems, the two information systems must be able to request information of each other through an electronic connection. "Cooperatively" also means that both the client and server share the responsibilities for a process. A common example of cooperative processing involves a client computer storing database input forms on its local hard drive and the server computer storing the physical data. Both the client and the server must cooperate in the process of delivering the final screen (a form with up-to-date data) to the user.
processing	"Processing" refers to the fact that both the client and server have processor chips, and that both processors are required to accomplish the entire task. In a Web-enabled application, both the server's processor and client's processor are involved in the activities of downloading and displaying the requested Web page.
to solve a problem	C/S means that both the client and the server are working on separate parts of the same problem. Each works on the parts of the task that are best suited to that system.

What Is Emulation?

The term emulation is of special historical note. **Emulation** refers to a personal computer "acting" like a dumb terminal. Emulation is therefore not an example of C/S, even though there are two information systems involved. Emulation is becoming less common. In the early and mid-80s, when both mainframe applications and stand-alone PCs were prevalent, users searched for a way to eliminate the extra dumb terminal from their desks and use their PCs as both stand-alone devices and the device to connect to their mainframe applications. **Emulation boards** (sometimes called 3270 cards or IRMA cards) were added to PCs so that their keyboards and input signals would map to those of a dumb CRT. In this way, a PC could toggle back and forth, performing the functions of both a stand-alone PC and a dumb terminal. Since most mainframe applications have now been replaced with Web-enabled or other types of client-server applications, we see fewer PCs used to emulate dumb terminals.

If you ask 10 information systems professionals for their definition of client server computing, you are probably going to get 10 different answers, since there is no central "authority" that manages an information systems glossary. Even worse, the meaning of a term used in the information systems world can often change over time as technology changes (e.g., the original meaning of the word "floppy" obviously did not refer to today's 3.5-inch 1.44 MB diskette enclosed in a hard plastic case, as it does today).

Learning About Client/Server Computing on the Web

Since almost all new programs are Web-enabled, they are also C/S. Understanding which technologies and processes happen at the client and which happen at various servers in a Web-enabled database is absolutely essential to your ability to develop and manage a large-scale Web-enabled application. There are some good sources of current information on technical terms on the World Wide Web that you'll want to bookmark for easy access as you expand your understanding of these technologies.

To look up technical terms on the World Wide Web:

1. Connect to the Internet, load Internet Explorer (IE), then go to **www.whatis.com** as shown in Figure 6-2.

Figure 6-2   WWW.WHATIS.COM

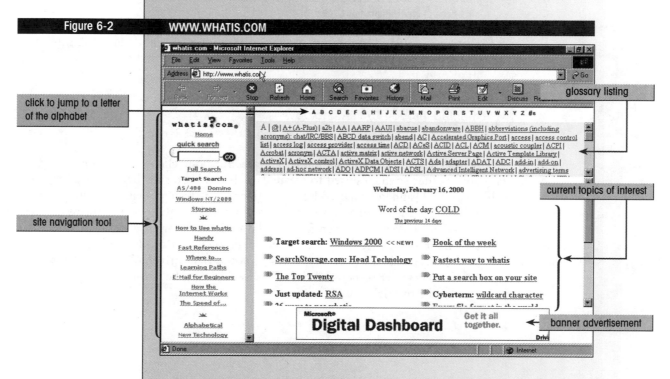

You can search for the definition of a specific technical term or read an article on a topic of interest at the *www.whatis.com* site. You wish to find their definition of client server computing.

2. Click **C** in the alphabet, scroll in the glossary listing area of the page (if necessary), and click **client/server**.

Scroll and read the entry on client/server computing. Note the appearance of hyperlinks within the definition that allow you to jump to other related definitions.

3. Scroll to the bottom of the client/server definition and click the Carnegie-Mellon University offers **Client/Server Software Architectures – An Overview** link.

TROUBLE? If that link is no longer available, feel free to explore other related links on the *www.whatis.com* site or go to the Carnegie-Mellon site directly by entering the following URL: *http://www.sei.cmu.edu/str/descriptions/clientserver_body.html*. The Carnegie-Mellon explanation of C/S is particularly good at comparing C/S to earlier mainframe-dumb terminal architectures. Now use the *www.about.com* portal to find information on C/S.

4. Go to **www.about.com**.

Drill down into the portal before entering your search criteria in an effort to eliminate extraneous links and improve the speed of your search.

5. Click the **computing/technology** link, type **client server definition** into the search box, and then click **Go**.

6. If available, click the link for **Network Architectures – 09/26/99** and read the article.

TROUBLE? If the link in Step 6 is not available, click another link that appears to provide a definition for C/S.

7. Continue surfing the Internet for information on C/S, click the **Back** button ⬅ as many times as necessary to return to your favorite article on C/S, and then print it.

Be sure that the article defines C/S as well as explains how the WWW is implemented through C/S technology.

Now that you have some additional knowledge about client-server computing, you'll learn about other strategies used to create data-driven Web sites beyond your experiences with Access 2000 and Personal Web Server. All of these strategies employ multiple software tools at both the client and server levels for various tasks in the overall process of developing a data-driven Web site. Therefore, a solid understanding of general C/S is necessary before diving into any specific type of implementation for a data-driven Web site.

Figure 6-3 expands the previous sketch of how a data-driven Web site is organized to show the various server responsibilities. These servers will be defined as they are discussed in the rest of the tutorial.

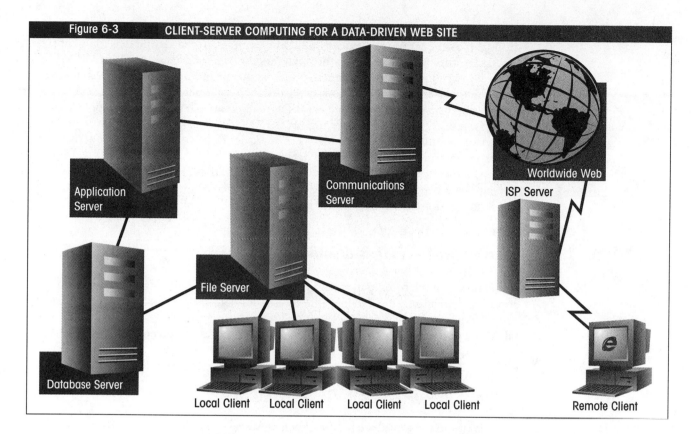

Figure 6-3 CLIENT-SERVER COMPUTING FOR A DATA-DRIVEN WEB SITE

Every data-driven Web site implementation involves each of these server functions, regardless of how many computers are used to support these functions. Whether the file, database, application, and HTTP server functions are all combined on one machine as you previously experienced using Personal Web Server or whether they are satisfied through separate computers is really a matter of the size and requirements of your data-driven Web site. Depending on the traffic and number of users, you may need more than one physical machine to work in each of these server roles.

Strategies for Creating Data-Driven Web Sites

There are many products that you can use to develop a data-driven Web site. Each product has its own strengths and weaknesses, and most of the products can be categorized into one of the four general software solutions as follows:

1. Database products with Web-enabling features

2. HTML editors with database features

3. Application server products

4. Programming languages

This book has focused on an all-Access 2000 solution that is representative of the first strategy, that of using a database product with Web-enabling features. But Access 2000 is primarily a microcomputer database software product, not a Web page development tool. Over time, Access 2000 may become the fastest, easiest, and most powerful way to develop a Web-enabled database for a large site. But right now, Access 2000 page objects are new to the Web development world, and there are several other strategies, products, and technologies that are being used to develop data-driven Web sites that you should be aware of.

Note that Access 2000 can be used in the role of a database management system, to support the other three strategies as well. For example, in the second development strategy, HTML editors with database features, you might use FrontPage 2000 (an HTML editor) to develop Web pages that dynamically pull data from an underlying Access 2000 database.

In the third strategy, application server products, you may use a product such as Allaire's ColdFusion or Microsoft's Active Server Pages to create Web pages at an application server level that pull data from an underlying Access 2000 database. In the fourth strategy, you may use a programming language such as Java or Visual Basic to create Web content that pulls data from an underlying Access 2000 database.

The following section, therefore, will review each of these four data-driven Web site strategies, and help you appreciate the issues involved in each of them. You'll also surf the Web for more information on some of the key terminology and products within each category.

Database Products with Web-enabling Features

As the power of microcomputers has grown, the power of microcomputer-based databases has improved dramatically too. No longer is Access considered a "personal" database. Entire departments and many small businesses rely on Access to manage their mission-critical activities. FileMaker Pro is another desktop database that offers built-in Web enabling features.

Considerations for Using a Database Product with Web-enabling Features to Build a Data-Driven Web Site

The reasons to use a database product, such as Access or FileMaker Pro, to build a data-driven Web site include the following:

- *Simplicity:* Access allows you to use GUI development tools such as the Page object to build a Web page. FileMaker Pro also allows you to make Web pages with an easy-to-use GUI interface.

- *Low cost:* The Web-page features of Access are not provided as a separate product or at additional cost. Once you've purchased Access 2000, you have everything you need to build dynamic Web pages that connect to the underlying Access database. Web page development and publishing tools are integrated into FileMaker Pro as well.

- *Speed of implementation:* Access's GUI interface and helpful wizards speed up the Web page creation process.

The downside to using such products as Access and FileMaker Pro include:

- *Compatibility:* One of the biggest problems with the dynamic Web pages created by Access 2000 is the fact that they are incompatible with browsers other than Microsoft's Internet Explorer. This item alone might be the "show stopper" that causes you to seek out other tools for Web page development. In addition, using Access requires that you use Microsoft operating systems (Personal Web Server or Microsoft Internet Information Server with Windows NT or Windows 2000) at the Web server level.

  Since FileMaker Pro is not a Microsoft product, this fact creates additional compatibility issues. You always need to research and test implementations that use products from multiple vendors because it is often difficult to find documentation on the interfaces.

- *Power:* Depending on the amount of traffic at your site and the size of the underlying database, Access and FileMaker Pro may not perform at acceptable levels. Important measures of performance include how fast the solution responds to a request, how many simultaneous users can access the site, and its ability to grow. You should also evaluate the maturity of the product. The "older" a product is, generally the more stable it is. If a solution is unstable, it obviously doesn't matter how fast or robust it claims to be.

■ *Advanced Features:* Examples of advanced features include the ability to integrate other technologies and the ability to apply advanced security controls.

Three Competing Forces Premise

One widely held premise is that many information systems decisions can be evaluated using a triangle of the three competing forces of "good," "inexpensive," and "fast," as shown in Figure 6-4.

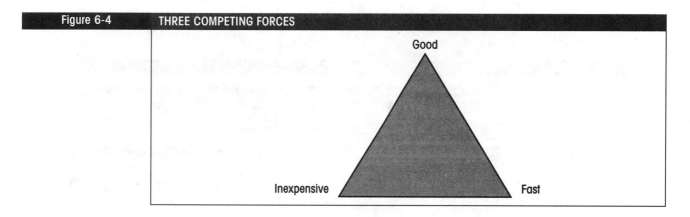

| Figure 6-4 | THREE COMPETING FORCES |

The theory is that if you cover any corner of the triangle, you can design an information system solution to achieve the other two goals, but that it is difficult to achieve all three corners of the triangle at the same time.

Using this rudimentary evaluation system, Access 2000 would probably be considered a fast and inexpensive solution. Of course any solution that meets *your* business needs is "good," however, regardless of the level of sophistication of the technology! That is why it is so important to define your business needs and goals before choosing the strategy and tools to address it.

Searching the Microsoft Web Site

In the following hands-on exercise, you'll surf the World Wide Web for more information on Access 2000 in order to gain a greater perspective on where and how Access 2000 Web-enabled databases are used. You'll start with the home page for Access at Microsoft's Web site.

To search the Access home page:

1. Go to **www.microsoft.com/access**, and then click the appropriate links to take the Access 2000 tour.

As you can see by the URL in your address bar, *www.microsoft.com/access* is really just an easy-to-remember alias for another Web site. Since the data access page is one of the biggest new features within Access 2000, Microsoft generally spends a lot of time discussing this feature in their promotional material about Office 2000.

2. Navigate back to the Access home page, and then click the **Downloads & Support** link to go to **http://www.microsoft.com/office/dlsupport.htm**.

   This site provides links to many valuable resource areas, including an extensive question-and-answer database in the Support Online section.

3. Click the **Downloads** link in the Self Support area or click the **Download Center** link.

   You can also find downloadable files such as clip art, sample solution files, bug fixes, and many third-party products. Take your time to surf this Web site; it will show you the variety of downloads available.

4. Click the **Product Name** list arrow, click **Access 2000**, click the **Operating System** list arrow, click **Windows 98**, and then click the **Find It!** button.

   Your screen should look similiar to Figure 6-5. The available downloads are constantly changing.

Figure 6-5 | ACCESS 2000 DOWNLOADS

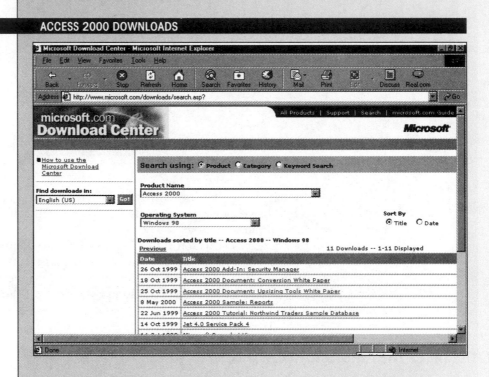

5. Print the Web page that displays the Access 2000 downloads.

There are many different resources available on the Microsoft Web site. You can download sample databases, white papers, and many handy add-in programs. A **white paper** is an article that gives background information about a technological subject. Sometimes white papers are written as the result of company research in order to support a new product by explaining the philosophy or design criteria. An **add-in** is a program that can be added to a primary program to extend its capabilities. Some add-ins are developed by Microsoft, and others are created by third-party developers.

The Microsoft Knowledge Base

If you develop solutions with Microsoft products, not only will you use the home page for each individual product to stay current on new features and downloads, but you'll also probably find yourself in a situation in which you need to ask an expert a specific question. The **Microsoft Knowledge Base** is a database of technical support information and tools for Microsoft products.

To use the Microsoft Knowledge Base:

1. Go to **www.microsoft.com** to display the home page for Microsoft itself as shown in Figure 6-6.

Figure 6-6	MICROSOFT HOME PAGE

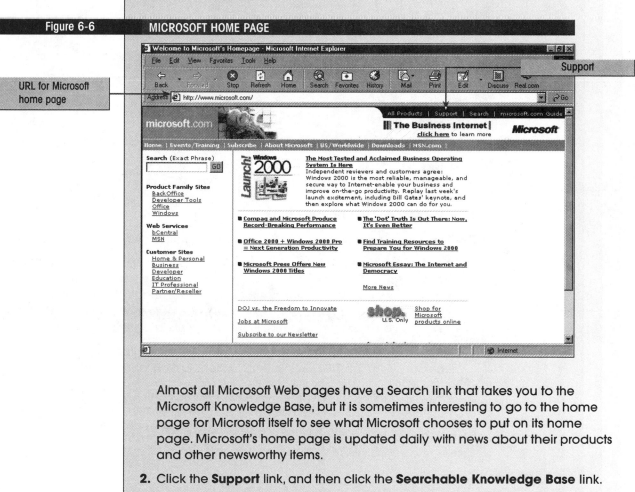

Almost all Microsoft Web pages have a Search link that takes you to the Microsoft Knowledge Base, but it is sometimes interesting to go to the home page for Microsoft itself to see what Microsoft chooses to put on its home page. Microsoft's home page is updated daily with news about their products and other newsworthy items.

2. Click the **Support** link, and then click the **Searchable Knowledge Base** link.

You are presented with the Knowledge Base Search screen that allows you to tailor your search request as shown in Figure 6-7.

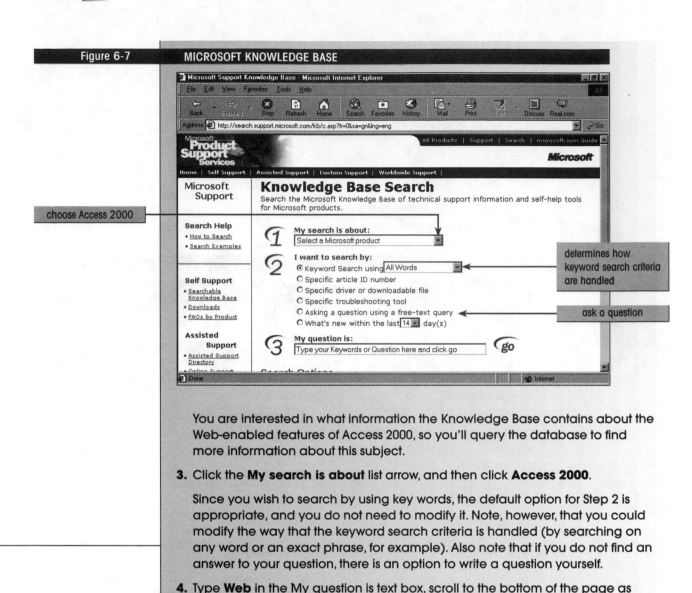

Figure 6-7 — MICROSOFT KNOWLEDGE BASE

choose Access 2000

determines how keyword search criteria are handled

ask a question

You are interested in what information the Knowledge Base contains about the Web-enabled features of Access 2000, so you'll query the database to find more information about this subject.

3. Click the **My search is about** list arrow, and then click **Access 2000**.

Since you wish to search by using key words, the default option for Step 2 is appropriate, and you do not need to modify it. Note, however, that you could modify the way that the keyword search criteria is handled (by searching on any word or an exact phrase, for example). Also note that if you do not find an answer to your question, there is an option to write a question yourself.

4. Type **Web** in the My question is text box, scroll to the bottom of the page as necessary, click the **Title only** Search Options button, and then click **Go**.

You'll start by searching titles only. If you don't find what you're looking for, you can always come back and research the database with a full text search.

Your search results should look similar to Figure 6-8.

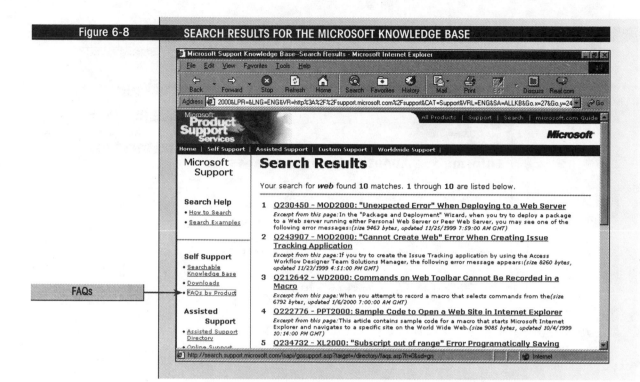

Figure 6-8   SEARCH RESULTS FOR THE MICROSOFT KNOWLEDGE BASE

FAQs

As you can see, the results are very specific and often address particular error messages that you may encounter when using the product. If your question is of a more general nature, you may wish to use the **MSDN** (Microsoft Developers Network) online library of **FAQs** (frequently asked questions) and other articles of general interest.

The MSDN Online Library

The **MSDN Online Library** (or simply MSDN Library) contains an enormous amount of technical information about the Microsoft products that are used to develop applications such as sample code, documentation, technical articles, and reference guides. If you wish to learn about the technical aspects of a product in general, rather than generate a specific question, the MSDN Library is the place to go.

To use the MSDN Library:

1. Click the **FAQs by Product** link, click the **Access 2000** link, click the **Show all** button, scroll, and then click the **Need Information About Using Data Access Pages** link.

The resulting page, shown in Figure 6-9, provides information on three important issues should you choose to deploy your data-driven Web site through Access.

| Figure 6-9 | FAQ INFORMATION ABOUT DATA ACCESS PAGES |

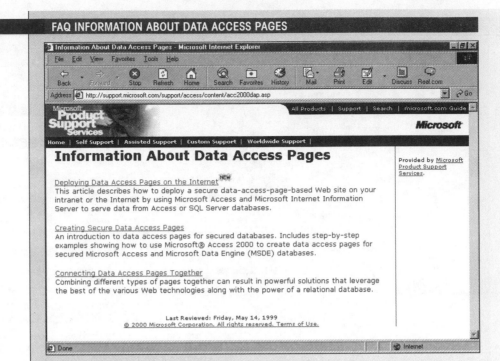

2. Click the link for **Deploying Data Access Pages on the Internet**.

An **MSDN** (Microsoft Developers Network) Online Library window opens and displays the page for Deploying Data Access Pages on the Internet or Your Intranet.

3. Resize the sections of the resulting window as shown in Figure 6-10 so that you can see more of the entries on the left.

| Figure 6-10 | MSDN ONLINE LIBRARY |

Deploying Data Access Pages on the Internet or Your Intranet

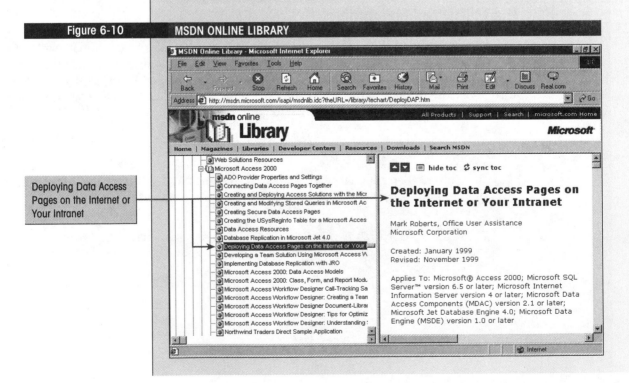

If you scroll through the article on the right and read the summary near the beginning, you will realize that this article is a treasure trove of information on how to build and secure a data-driven Web site using Access as the database and **IIS** (Internet Information Services) on the Web server. The article is 42 printed pages.

4. Scroll through the entries in the left section of the window, and then click the **Northwind Traders Direct Sample Application** entry.

5. Scroll through the article on the right to find the link titled **Click to view or copy the sample Web site discussed in this article**.

By clicking that link, you would be able to download a file, 5298.exe, to your local hard drive. After unzipping it, you would be able to experience a full-scale e-commerce Web site based on an Access 2000 database!

TROUBLE? Don't download the file now. Step-by-step instructions explaining how to download, unzip, and use the resulting Web-enabled database are provided in the Review Assignment at the end of this tutorial.

6. Click the **Cancel** button to cancel the download, take your time exploring the MSDN Library, and be careful about printing MSDN articles, since most of them are very long.

7. Close your browser and then disconnect from the Internet.

While the dynamic Web pages created by Access 2000 obviously have some shortcomings in terms of their compatibility with other vendors' products, Access 2000 also provides some tremendous benefits as a Web page development tool, including its ease of use, low cost, and vast Microsoft support structure. For small-to-medium deployments for intranet or low volume Internet data-driven Web sites, an all-Access solution is a good option.

There are other approaches to data-driven Web site development that you will also want to examine. One of the most popular ways to accomplish connectivity between a Web page and a database is to use the tools of existing HTML editors. In other words, instead of using the database to develop a Web page, you can also start with the Web page and connect back to a database.

Session 6.1   QUICK CHECK

1. What is the definition of client/server computing and why is knowledge of client/server computing important to data-driven Web sites?

2. What four types of products can be used to develop data-driven Web sites?

3. What is the Microsoft Knowledge Base?

4. What is the MSDN Online Library?

SESSION 6.2

In this session you will learn about HTML editors with database features. You'll use FrontPage to build a dynamic Web page connected to an underlying Access database.

HTML Editors with Database Features

An **HTML editor** is a software product that helps you write and edit HTML (Hypertext Markup Language) code. As you may recall from Tutorial 5, **tags** are the building blocks of HTML code and define how the Web page will appear when opened with HTML editors. Some HTML editors are very basic, such as the text editor **Notepad** that you used to add a heading to the Suppliers page in Tutorial 5. The Notepad text editor is available as a free accessory with Windows. Given a Notepad window, you could key in HTML codes and save the file with an HTM extension to create a Web page.

FrontPage

Most people prefer to use a more advanced HTML editor, such as Microsoft **FrontPage 2000**, that contains wizards, toolbars, and other features to make the process of developing Web pages faster and easier than entering tags into a text editor. FrontPage is a **WYSIWYG** (What You See Is What You Get) HTML editor because it allows you to see how the Web page will appear when viewed by a browser as you are developing it. In FrontPage, you don't have to write the specific HTML code (the tags). Instead, you create the page in much the same way that you create a Word document. FrontPage translates what you do in your design window into the HTML code.

You experienced a WYSIWYG Web page development environment when you worked in Page Design view within Access. Within Access, Page Design view is the GUI development tool, and Page View presents the Web page as if you had opened it from Internet Explorer. Behind the scenes, Access created all of the necessary code.

Even though it's a very good idea to get some HTML skills so that you can read and troubleshoot the HTML code that you create with any product, you don't have to be an HTML expert to create sophisticated Web pages with FrontPage, just as you didn't need to be a programmer to create data-driven Web pages using Access.

Furthermore, with FrontPage 2000, you can design a Web page that will dynamically present up-to-date data from the underlying Access 2000 database through a technology called Active Server Pages (ASP). **Active Server Pages** are HTML pages that contain scripts that can retrieve or update live data from a database. A **script** is a program that is embedded in another program to do a certain function. In this case, the "program" is a Web page, and the script is used to dynamically query or update a database each time the program is run (each time the Web page is downloaded).

FrontPage allows you to build ASP pages that can be used to enter, update, query, and report on data in an underlying database. Pages used to enter data into or query the database are called forms. Common uses for FrontPage forms include:

- Gathering customer information
- Recording requests for information
- Soliciting feedback
- Conducting a survey

In summary, FrontPage not only provides an easy-to-use graphical and WYSIWYG environment in which to develop static Web pages, but it also supports many robust features that provide dynamic connectivity to an underlying Access database.

Considerations for Using an HTML Editor with Database Features to Build a Data-Driven Web Site

The reasons to use FrontPage 2000 as the Web page development tool to develop a Web-enabled database and Access 2000 as the backend database can be summed up as follows:

- **Simplicity:** All of the required tools are part of the Microsoft Office suite and have GUI interfaces, wizards, and extensive Help systems. Extensive training in HTML and underlying technologies is not required.
- **Low cost:** Both Access and FrontPage are part of the Premium edition of the Microsoft Office suite.
- **Speed of implementation:** Since the products are easy to use, the Web pages can be built quickly.

The disadvantages of using these tools are:

- **Compatibility:** FrontPage 2000 makes use of Active Server Pages (ASP) technology to create dynamic Web pages that can be viewed by any browser. Although there may be some differences in how the page appears, this effectively negates the IE vs. Netscape browser compatibility problem for the client. The Web server, however, must still use Microsoft operating systems (Windows NT and Internet Information Server) to process ASP Web pages, which makes this solution somewhat proprietary and incompatible with other existing technologies.
- **Power:** Since performance is most directly affected by the backend database (and not by the Web page development tool), using FrontPage to develop data-driven Web pages doesn't directly affect the performance of your Web site. In fact, FrontPage Web pages can connect to any **ODBC** (Object Database Connectivity) compliant database. Because Access 2000 is part of the same Microsoft Office suite, it is the most common database resource used by FrontPage. As a microcomputer product, Access 2000 has both size and simultaneous user limitations that make it less powerful than some of the UNIX-based relational database products such as Oracle. Fortunately, Access 2000 databases can be easily upsized to Microsoft's SQL Server product, which is a relational database targeted for those users who outgrow Access.
- **Advanced Features:** FrontPage does not provide any database security beyond that which the database already provides, so this aspect of your evaluation would depend on the database you were connecting to. Since FrontPage is Microsoft's premier Web page development product, you will find many more Web page creation features, such as the ability to create tables, add graphics, and apply formatting changes, than you did when using the page object in Access 2000.

Using FrontPage 2000 to Build a Data-Driven Web Site

If you have FrontPage 2000 on your computer, you can use it to build a data-driven Web site by completing the next exercise.

To use FrontPage 2000 to view HTML code:

1. Click the **Start** button on the taskbar, point to **Programs**, and then click **Microsoft FrontPage**.

TROUBLE? If prompted with a message about making FrontPage your default HTML editor, press the Esc key to cancel the dialog box.

FrontPage loads and a blank Web page design window opens in which you can create Web pages. There are three views of the page: Normal, HTML, and Preview. Each view is available by clicking a tab at the bottom of the window. **Normal** view is the WYSIWYG design surface on which you will create the Web page. **HTML** view presents the corresponding HTML codes, and **Preview** presents the Web page as it would be viewed by a browser.

2. Type **Your first and last name** in the Normal view window.

   Normal view allows you to enter and edit your Web page similarly to how you would create a document in Word.

3. Click the **Preview** tab at the bottom of the window.

   This window shows you the Web page as it would look in a browser.

4. Click the **HTML** tab at the bottom of the window.

   You are now viewing the corresponding HTML code for the text you entered in Normal view, as shown in Figure 6-11.

Figure 6-11	FRONTPAGE HTML VIEW

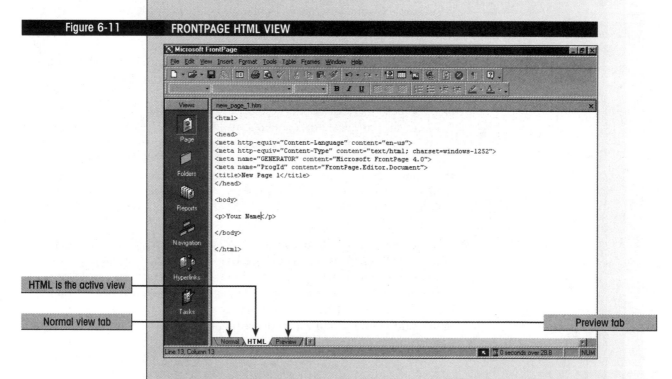

The HTML tags are in blue in the HTML window. Variable information to which the HTML tag is applied is called an **attribute**. Attributes appear in black.

Although you could spend a lot of time building beautiful Web pages with the vast capabilities of FrontPage and learning about the associated HTML code, you'll focus on the specific steps required to dynamically connect a Web page created within FrontPage to an Access database. You'll use a Web page created within FrontPage to connect to the AMToys-6.mdb database. You'll use this Web page to develop a Supplier report that is dynamically linked to the Supplier table in the AMToys-6 database.

Building a FrontPage Web and Establishing a Database Connection

Before you can connect a database to a FrontPage Web page, you must establish a Web within FrontPage. To FrontPage, a **Web** is a collection of files stored in a Web folder on a Web server or your computer's hard drive. The Access database must be in that folder too. A Web also contains files that support FrontPage-specific functionality such as the instructions and supporting programming code that support the connectivity of the Web page to an underlying database.

REFERENCE   WINDOW   **RW**

Creating a FrontPage Web
- Open FrontPage, click File on the menu bar, click Open Web, navigate to the folder that contains your database, click the Open button, and then click Yes if prompted to add information to this folder.

REFERENCE   WINDOW   **RW**

Establishing a Connection between a Web Page and a Database
- Once a Web is established, click Tools on the menu bar, and then click Web Settings.
- Click the Database tab, and then click the Add button.
- Click the Browse button to navigate to the database file name that contains the information for the Web page you are about to create, click the file, click the OK button in the Database Files In Current Web dialog box, and then click the OK button in the New Database Connection dialog box.
- Click the Verify button in the Web Settings dialog box to make sure that the open Web page is connected to the underlying database.

To create a FrontPage Web and connect to an underlying database:

1. Click **File** on the menu bar, click **Open Web**, click the **Look in** list arrow, navigate to the Tutorial\Solutions folder for Tutorial 6, click the **Open** button, and then click the **Yes** button to add information to the folder if prompted with this question.

   TROUBLE? In order for this exercise to work, the AMToys-6 database must be in the Web folder at the time the Web is established. If you are unsure, exit FrontPage, verify that the AMToys-6.mdb file is in the Tutorial\Solutions folder, start FrontPage, and then redo Step 1.

   The process of creating a Web adds special folders (e.g., _private, _vti_cnf, vti_pvt, and images) within the Solutions folder to organize the files that will be used to create the resulting FrontPage Web page. With the Web established, the Web Settings option on the Tools menu is available.

2. Click **Tools** on the menu bar, and then click **Web Settings**.

   The Web Settings dialog box opens. The Web Settings dialog box is where you'll create the database connection to this Web and change other Web default options.

3. Click the **Database** tab, and then click the **Add** button.

The New Database Connection dialog box opens as shown in Figure 6-12.

Figure 6-12 NEW DATABASE CONNECTION DIALOG BOX

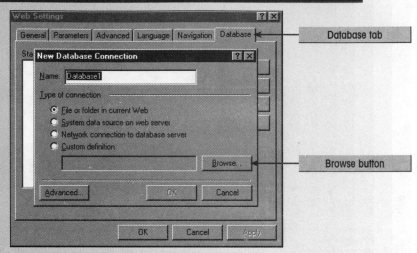

4. Type **AMToys** in the Name text box, make sure that the **File or folder in current Web** option button is chosen, and then click the **Browse** button.

You do not need to name the database connection with the same name as the database file, but using a descriptive name is always helpful. The Database Files In Current Web dialog box opens and presents you with the Access files in the current Web.

5. Click **AMToys-6.mdb**, click the **OK** button in the Database Files In Current Web dialog box, and then click the **OK** button in the New Database Connection dialog box.

TROUBLE? If you can't locate the AMToys-6.mdb database in the Tutorial\Solutions folder, close FrontPage, open Explorer, verify that the AMToys.mdb file is in the Solutions folder for Tutorial 6, start FrontPage, and repeat Steps 1 through 5.

The dialog box displays a connection name, AMToys, and a Status indicator. Currently the status indicator is a question mark.

6. Click the **Verify** button in the Web Settings dialog box.

The Web Settings dialog box should appear as shown in Figure 6-13. The question mark indicator changes to a green check mark, indicating that the connection to the AMToys database worked properly.

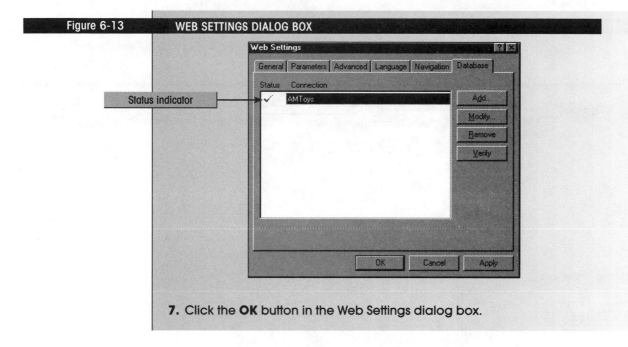

| Figure 6-13 | WEB SETTINGS DIALOG BOX |

7. Click the **OK** button in the Web Settings dialog box.

Now that you've established the FrontPage Web and made the database connection, you're ready to design the Web page itself.

Building a FrontPage Web Page with Connectivity to an Access 2000 Database

Now that the FrontPage Web page and Access database have been "connected," you can start to build within FrontPage your Web page that dynamically reports on information from within the AMToys-6 Access database. In this exercise you'll create a Suppliers Web page to dynamically report information from the underlying Access database.

To use FrontPage 2000 to create a Web page for data entry:

1. Select **Your Name**, type **Supplier Information Report** in its place, and then click the **Normal** tab.

Formatting text in FrontPage is very similar to formatting text in any of the other Microsoft Office products. You'll use the buttons on the Formatting toolbar to enhance the selected text.

TROUBLE? If the Folder list appears to the left of the Web page, click the Folder List button 🔲 to toggle it off.

2. Drag across **Supplier Information Report** to select it, click the **Font** list arrow on the Formatting toolbar, scroll the alphabetical list of font faces, click **Georgia**, click the **Font Size** list arrow on the Formatting toolbar, click **5 (18 pt)**, click the **Font Color** list arrow ▲·, click **Blue**, and then click to the left of **Supplier**. Your screen should look like Figure 6-14.

TROUBLE? If the Georgia font is not in your font list, pick another font such as Arial.

| Figure 6-14 | FORMATTING TEXT IN A FRONTPAGE WEB PAGE |

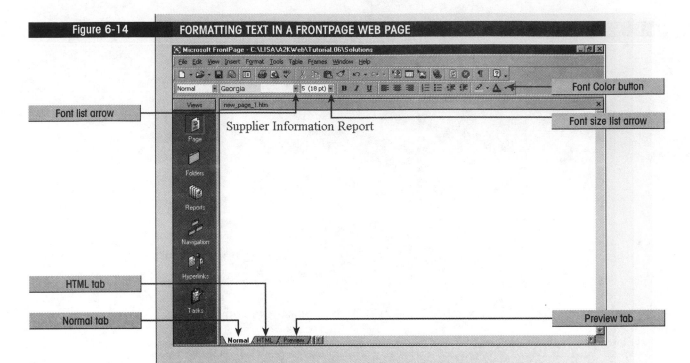

You can quickly take a look at the HTML code you just created.

3. Click the **HTML** tab at the bottom of the page.

   The code that was created is shown in Figure 6-15.

| Figure 6-15 | HTML CODE CREATED BY FRONTPAGE |

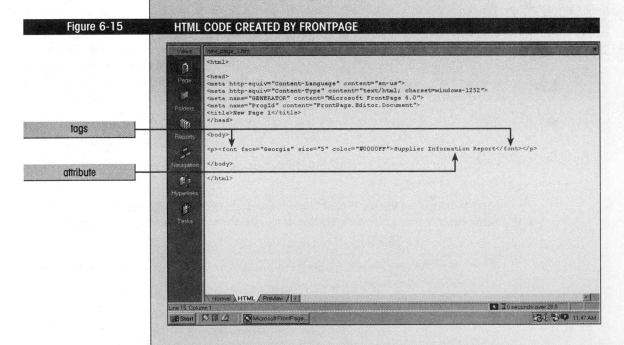

If you know HTML, you can add statements directly to the HTML window to build the page.

4. Double-click the word **Information**, and then press the **Delete** key.

   Now you have experienced editing a Web page in a non-GUI environment. You can use FrontPage to see how the Web page would appear in a browser.

5. Click the **Preview** tab at the bottom of the window, double-click **Report** to select it, and then press the **Delete** key on your keyboard.

   The Delete key has no effect in Preview view because you cannot modify your Web page in the Preview screen. The Preview screen is provided as a tool to help you visualize how the final page will appear in a browser window. You can only edit your Web page in Normal or HTML view.

6. Click the **Normal** tab at the bottom of the window.

Normally, you would spend a lot of time developing the background color, image, and navigation system for the Web page, but for now, you'll go ahead and add fields to create a dynamic Supplier report that shows the most up-to-date data from the AMToys-6 database.

Inserting Dynamic Database Components on a FrontPage Web Page

Now that the Web is created and the connectivity between the Web page and database is established, you're ready to determine what type of data the Web page will display from the AMToys-6 database. You wish to display all of the fields and records from the Suppliers table in the AMToys-6 database on this Web page. There are many ways to add this data to the Web page, but you'll use a handy wizard, the **Database Results Wizard** to help you through this process for the first time.

REFERENCE WINDOW **RW**

Adding Dynamic Database Components to a FrontPage Web Page
- Click Insert on the menu bar, point to Database, and then click Results.
- Follow the prompts of the Database Results Wizard to add the desired fields contained in database queries (views) or tables.
- View the Web page with the new database connectivity elements in Normal view.
- Click the Save button on the Standard toolbar, make sure that the Save in location is pointing to where you want to save the file, make sure that the Save as type lists Active Server Pages (*.asp), and then click the Save button to save the Web.

To add dynamic database components to a FrontPage Web page:

1. Press the **Down Arrow** key to place the cursor on the line below the **Supplier Report** title, click **Insert** on the menu bar, point to **Database**, and then click **Results**.

   The Database Results Wizard - Step 1 of 5 appears, as shown in Figure 6-16, indicating that you can use a sample database connection, use an existing database connection, or create a new database connection.

Figure 6-16   THE DATABASE RESULTS WIZARD - STEP 1 OF 5

You want to use the existing AMToys connection to the AMToys-6 database that you previously created.

TROUBLE? If another database connection is listed, click the list arrow and then click AMToys.

2. Click the **Next** button.

Step 2 of 5 may take a few seconds as the connection creates a list of tables and queries (called VIEWs) in the Record source list. Suppliers is the name of a table in the AMToys-6 database that you want to display on this Web page. If your database did not contain the fields and records you desired for this form in one object, you could also create a custom query at this time.

3. Click the **Record source** list arrow, click **Suppliers**, and then click the **Next** button.

Step 3 of 5 shows all of the fields in the chosen record source, the Suppliers table, as shown in Figure 6-17.

Figure 6-17   DATABASE RESULTS WIZARD - STEP 3 OF 5

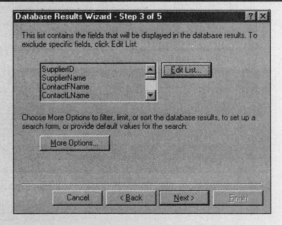

The Edit List and More Options buttons allow you to exclude fields, filter records, or set up a "search" form. For now, use the default options.

4. Click the **Next** button.

Step 4 of 5 asks you how you would like to format the records returned by the query. Use the default options so that the data is organized in a table with a header row and sized to the width of the page.

5. Click the **Next** button.

Step 5 of 5 asks you how you would like the records grouped and presented. You use the default options here as well to split the records into groups of five (which will reduce the amount of scrolling down the page required by the user when large groups of records are presented).

6. Click the **Finish** button.

The Web page with the new database connectivity element is shown in Normal view. See Figure 6-18. The field names in the Suppliers table appear in the first row of the table. The yellow section of the table gives you messages about the data connection. The field values will appear in the row below the message about the data connection. This presentation is similar to a form or report in Access, in which unbound label controls are used to present field names, and bound text boxes are used to present field values.

Figure 6-18	CONNECTING TO THE SUPPLIER TABLE THROUGH A FRONTPAGE WEB PAGE

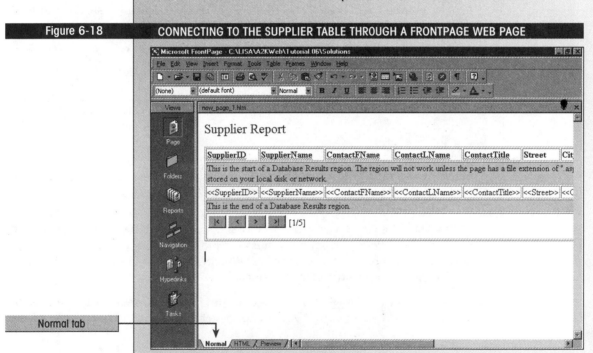

Normal tab

7. Click the **Save** button 🖫 on the Standard toolbar, make sure that the Save in location is pointing to the Tutorial\Solutions folder for Tutorial 6, make sure that the Save as type lists **Active Server Pages (*.asp)**, and then click the **Save** button.

The Web page has been named and saved as supplierid.asp. View the HTML code you created and Preview the page.

8. Click the **HTML** tab at the bottom of the page, and then scroll up and down the page.

If you didn't appreciate the power of a WYSIWYG editor and Microsoft wizards before, this is a great example of just how much work they do for you. Not long ago (before products like FrontPage were available), Web page developers had to enter all of this code themselves! Note that even though the file has an ASP extension, the first code in the page is <html> indicating that HTML tags follow. The ASP tags start and end with <% and %> tags. The attributes within the ASP tags describe the dynamic data connections.

9. Click the **Preview** tab at the bottom of the page as shown in Figure 6-19.

Figure 6-19   PREVIEWING THE SUPPLIER DATA IN THE WEB PAGE

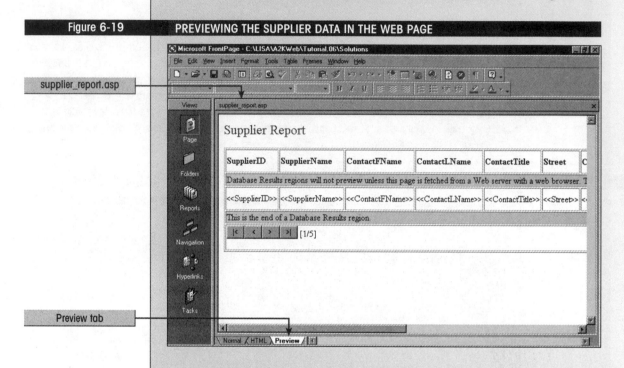

In this case, the Preview window cannot show you how the page will appear in the browser. Instead, it displays a message indicating that you cannot preview the database connectivity parts of this Web page unless the page is fetched from a Web server with a Web browser.

10. Click the **Save** button 🔲 to save the changes to supplier_report.asp. Be sure to leave this "Web" open so that you can publish these files in the next steps.

You used FrontPage to create a Web, explored the different views of a FrontPage Web page, established a connection with the AMToys-6 database, and added fields from the Suppliers table to the Web page. You still don't know how the page is going to look and work for the user, though, because the Preview window within FrontPage did not support the capability to process the ASP tags that pull the data from the AMToys-6 database. To see the finished product, you have to publish your Web page and view it with a browser.

Publishing a FrontPage Web Page

Publishing a FrontPage Web page with Personal Web Server is just like publishing any other file. Be aware, however, that the FrontPage Web pages require that special files called **FrontPage server extensions** are installed at the server in order to properly serve FrontPage-created Web pages. PWS is automatically configured with these server extensions, but if you plan to publish FrontPage Web pages to a non-PWS server, you should check to make sure that it can support FrontPage files. Microsoft supplies a program called **FrontPage Server Administrator** to help you install the FrontPage server extensions on Web servers. By default, it is located in the same Start menu location as is Personal Web Server. You might also want to check the **Microsoft Personal Web Server Setup** program. This program helps you see what PWS features (such as support for FrontPage Web pages) are installed with PWS.

There are many ways to publish a Web page to your Personal Web Server. One way is to use the Web Publishing Wizard by dragging the file from within an Explorer window to the PWS Publish icon on your desktop or you could use the Web Publishing Wizard within PWS itself. Another way is to use the publishing features within FrontPage. Throughout the rest of this tutorial, be sure that the Personal Web Server is running on your machine by starting Personal Web Manager. When you examine the Main area within the Personal Web you will see whether Web publishing is turned on or off.

REFERENCE WINDOW **RW**

Publishing a FrontPage Web Page
- Within FrontPage, open the Web that contains the files you wish to publish.
- Within FrontPage, click File on the menu bar, and then click Publish Web.
- In the Specify the location to publish your web to: text box, type the URL that you wish to publish your Web pages to. If you are publishing them to your own machine, use the http://localhost address.
- Complete the options in the Publish Web dialog box to choose whether you want to publish all of the files in the Web, or just those that have changed, and then click Publish.
- Click the Done button when prompted that your files have been published.

To publish a FrontPage Web page:

1. Start FrontPage, click **File** on the menu bar, and then click **Publish Web**.

   The Publish Web dialog box opens asking you for information about where you want to publish your web and which files you wish to publish.

   TROUBLE? You cannot publish successfully if the AMToys-6 database is open, so be sure to close it before completing Step 1.

2. Click to the right of http:// in the **Specify the location to publish your web to** text box, type **localhost**, and then click the **Options** button (if it is not already expanded) to expand the Publish Web dialog box as shown in Figure 6-20.

Figure 6-20	ENTERING THE DEFAULT NAME FOR YOUR COMPUTER'S WEB SITE

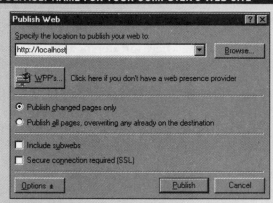

Localhost is the default name for your own computer's Web site. The specific name for your own computer is found by clicking the Main button within Personal Web Manager, but you can always use the default name of localhost to refer to the Web site hosted by your own computer.

3. Click the **Publish all pages, overwriting any already on the destination** option button, and then click the **Publish** button.

   FrontPage publishes all of the files in the web (your Solutions folder).

   TROUBLE? If an ISP dialer window opens, close it. You do not need to connect to the Internet to publish files to your own computer.

4. Click the **Done** button when prompted that your Web site published successfully.

5. Close FrontPage.

Depending on the other publishing activities that have been taking place at this computer, the "Click here to view your published Web site" link within the Microsoft FrontPage dialog box doesn't always work since it attempts to present the homepage at *http://localhost*. If that homepage file isn't working correctly, you get an error message. Now that the supplier_report.asp file has been published to your Web server, you can view it using IE.

To open the FrontPage Web page in IE:

1. Start **Internet Explorer**, and type **http://localhost/supplier_report.asp** in the Address bar as shown in Figure 6-21.

Figure 6-21	SUPPLIER_REPORT.ASP FILE OPENED IN IE

URL for
supplier_report.asp

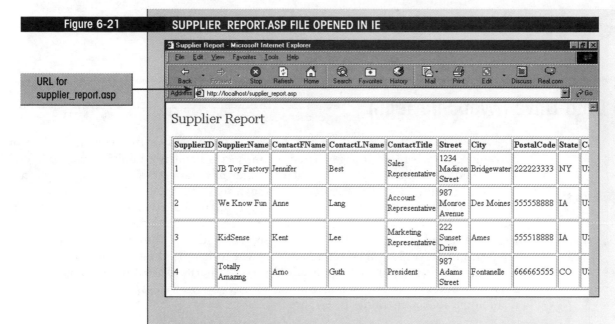

TROUBLE? If the Web page still doesn't appear correctly and you are sure
that you have typed the URL correctly, close all of your programs, restart
your computer, and redo Step 1.

In order to test the dynamic nature of an .asp file, open the underlying Access database,
make a change to one of the records, and then refresh the Web page within IE.

To test the dynamic nature of the .asp file:

1. Open the **AMToys-6** database from the c:\Inetpub\wwwroot folder.

   TROUBLE? C:\Inetpub\wwwroot is the default Web folder for *http://localhost*. If
   AMToys-6 is not found there, check the default Web folder location in the Main
   area of Personal Web Manager.

2. Click the **Tables** button 🔲 on the Objects bar, and then double-click
   Suppliers to open it.

   Jennifer Best has been promoted from Sales Representative to VP.

3. Select **Sales Representative** in ContactTitle field for Jennifer Best, and then
   type **VP**.

4. Close the **Suppliers** table, close the database, and then exit Access.

5. Click the **IE** button on the taskbar that contains the supplier_report.asp Web
   page, click the **Refresh** button 🔁 on the Standard Buttons toolbar, and then
   click the **Print** button 🖨 to print the Web page.

   The page is redisplayed with the new information in the ContactTitle field for
   Jennifer Best.

6. If you want to test the ASP Web page within Netscape, copy and paste the URL
   (in this case **http://localhost/supplierid.asp**) from the IE address bar to a
   Netscape location bar, and press the **Enter** key.

You'll see that ASP Web pages work well within Netscape too.

7. Close all open IE and Netscape windows.

The Data-Driven Web Site Team

The exercises in the Tutorials in this book were designed so that you could develop dynamic data-driven Web pages based on an Access database, publish them to a Web server, and open them in IE using one computer to demonstrate all of the steps in the process. In the real world, the computer on which the database and Web pages are developed is rarely the same machine as the one where the database and Web pages are published. In fact, the database is often stored on its own "database server," the Web pages are stored on their own "application server," and yet a third server, called a "communications server" or "HTTP server," is used to handle the communications traffic between the user and the application server where the Web pages are stored. Schematically, the various server computers used by the typical data-driven Web site team might look something like Figure 6-22.

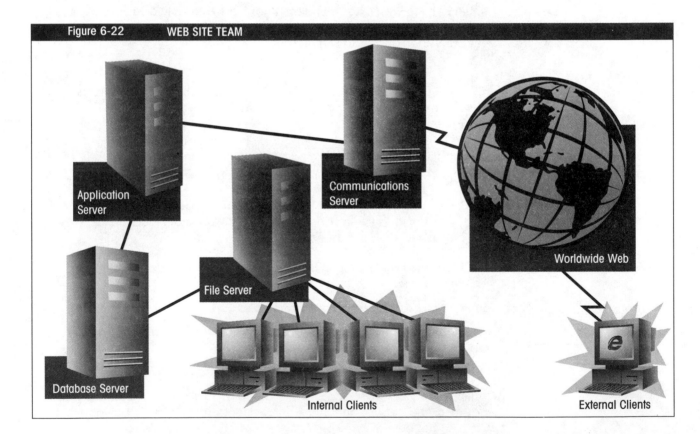

Figure 6-22   WEB SITE TEAM

Application Server

Communications Server

Worldwide Web

File Server

Database Server

Internal Clients

External Clients

In a real-world situation, not only are there multiple servers that divide up the processes of the data-driven Web site, but there are also usually multiple people with specialized skills who are responsible for various portions of the Web site. Figure 6-23 describes the typical role of each of the people on the data-driven Web site team. This is not an exhaustive list of people who may be a part of a data-driven Web site team, nor are these responsibilities mutually exclusive. In a small business, there may be only one person wearing all of these hats! As the size and complexity of the Web site grow, however, you'll need deeper and more specialized skills in each area.

Figure 6-23	RESPONSIBILITIES OF THE DATA-DRIVEN WEB SITE TEAM
TITLE	**TYPICAL DUTIES**
Network engineer	Handles the physical installation of the computers (both servers and clients) and operating systems; installs, tests, and supports the necessary communications hardware and software
Webmaster	Sets up Web folders, publishes Web files, secures Web resources, monitors Web site activity, and plans for growth; often serves as the liaison between business groups and users and the people who build the Web site such as the network engineers and Web page developers
Database administrator	Designs, maintains, and secures the database
Web page developer	Builds Web pages with a variety of software tools; generally very skilled in HTML and Web-enabling languages
Programmer	Writes code for either server- or client-side processing in such languages as Java, CGI/Perl, C++, Visual Basic, and JavaScript
Graphic artist	Develops images and other multimedia content displayed on Web pages, using a variety of software products, helps with overall theme, color, readability, and Web page navigation issues
Systems analyst	Monitors and analyzes the impact of new technologies, upgrades, and changes made to the system; helps tune the system to provide acceptable levels of performance and security

After the Web-enabled database site is up and running, the job of improving and maintaining the site never ends. For example, if the Web-enabled database and Web site for Aaron Michael Toys continued to grow and improve, a typical day in the life of their data-driven Web site team might go something like this:

1. A *graphic artist* creates an electronic animated cartoon with software products such as Shockwave and Macromedia's Flash to advertise a new toy and wants to add it as a new element on the home page.

2. The graphic artist gives the animated content to a *Web page developer* who is responsible for the site's home page. The Web page developer determines the proper placement of the animation on a Web page developed in Macromedia's Dreamweaver or Microsoft FrontPage and develops a new Web page to support the new content.

3. The Web page developer works with the *webmaster* to publish the page to the application server. Within hours, the ad creates such demand for the new toy that orders start pouring in. The webmaster receives 200 e-mails for more information on the product. (The webmaster's e-mail address has been conveniently provided as a link at the bottom of the home page.)

4. The webmaster turns to the *network engineer*, indicating that orders for the new toy and site activity is at an all-time high. Network availability statistics indicate that the communications server is close to its peak capacity.

5. The network engineer adds additional modems and communication servers to handle the additional capacity but informs the *database administrator* that with the additional communication capacity, the backend Access database may become bogged down.

6. The webmaster also informs the *database administrator* that, with the success of the new product, they are probably going to get a call from marketing indicating that the company is going to expand into new product lines and markets. And by the way, additional sales and customer demographic analysis will be needed as well.

7. The database administrator knows that with the increased traffic and information analysis needs, the company really needs to analyze how different technologies affect performance and calls the *systems analyst* and *programmer* for some help.

As you can see, it takes many diverse skills and types of experience to develop and support large-scale data-driven Web sites. By using Access 2000 and Personal Web Server, you were able to deploy a data-driven Web site without vast technical resources, using only one computer to play the part of all server roles as well as the client role. You were introduced to many of the same responsibilities and processes that are part of large-scale implementations. The exciting part about learning about data-driven Web sites using Access 2000 and PWS is realizing that not only does this approach serve the needs of many small-scale and internal data-driven Web sites, but it also provides an excellent introduction and education about data-driven Web site technologies in general.

Session 6.2 QUICK CHECK

1. What is an HTML editor?

2. What technology does FrontPage 2000 use to build a Web page with dynamic content from an Access 2000 database?

3. What are the titles of the individuals used to build and support a data-driven Web site?

SESSION 6.3

In this session you will learn about application server software as well as Web page programming languages.

Application Server Products

As discussed earlier, there are four strategies used to develop data-driven Web sites, and the strategies can be categorized into four major groups of software tools as follows:

1. Database products with Web-enabling features

2. HTML editors with database features

3. Application server products

4. Programming languages

The third category, **application server products**, sometimes called Web server products, are represented by such packages as Allaire's ColdFusion, EveryWare Development's Tango, and HAHTsite. These products provide a way for a developer to connect existing databases to Web pages to produce dynamic content by using GUI and WYSIWYG tools.

ColdFusion

If your corporate database was already developed in the Oracle database product, or if your corporation used UNIX Web servers (rather than servers that use Microsoft's operating systems), you'd need new and powerful tools to get the data-driven Web site project completed.

Application server software interacts with a relational database to create a dynamic Web page that is then sent to the client. This function exists in all data-driven Web site implementations, but is not readily apparent when using Access page objects or FrontPage ASP files. When you use these two Microsoft products to create dynamic Web pages, the dynamic connections between the database and Web page are coded for you by the wizards and features of the products. When you attempt to connect and combine the resources and services of various non-Microsoft products into one HTML Web page, however, application server products, such as **ColdFusion**, have become quite popular.

To explore application server products:

1. Connect to the Internet, load Internet Explorer (IE), go to **www.whatis.com**, navigate the **a** entries, and then click the link for **application server**.

The definition for application server should appear as shown in Figure 6-24.

Figure 6-24	DEFINITION OF APPLICATION SERVER

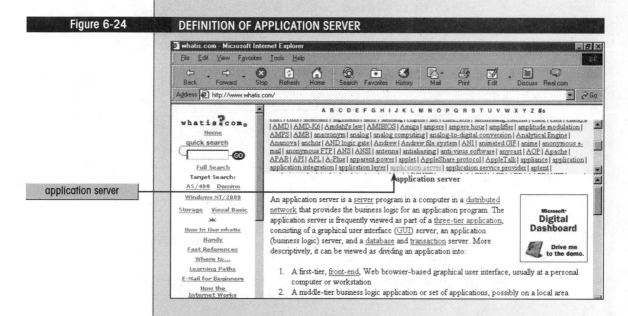

As of this writing, the definition for an application server is provided by *www.whatis.com* and uses the three-tier application model.

2. Click the **three-tier application** link and then read the page.

The three-tier application model is a common way for people to discuss the parts of a client/server application; it is an approach that encompasses all data-driven Web sites. Now surf for information on Allaire's ColdFusion.

3. Click the letter **C** at the top of the Whatis home page to move to the glossary words that start with the letter C, scroll down through the **www.whatis.com** glossary words, click the link for **ColdFusion**, and then read that glossary definition.

The bottom of the page shows you related selected links for ColdFusion.

4. Click the link for the **Allaire home page** or enter **www.allaire.com** into your browser, click the link for **Products**, and then click the link for the **ColdFusion** home page shown in Figure 6-25.

| Figure 6-25 | HOME PAGE FOR ALLAIRE'S COLDFUSION |

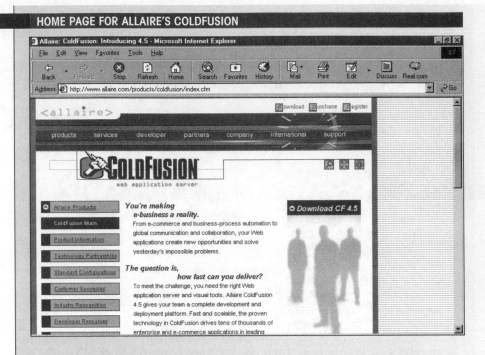

Surf through the site to find information about Allaire's products, free downloads, and tutorials

5. Go to **www.everyware.com** using your browser, and then surf through the site to find information about the Tango application server products.

6. Go to **www.haht.com** using your browser, and then surf through the site to find information about the Hahtsite application server products.

Evaluating the application server product strategy against the three competing forces of good, fast, and inexpensive, would give this approach high marks in the "good" category, since it gives you a way to create a data-driven Web site using many non-Microsoft products and resources. The problem with gaining improvements in compatibility, power, and advanced features, however, is that it makes this solution strategy more complex, expensive, and slower to implement. And so we return to the basic premise that your business needs should dictate the solution.

Programming languages

One final strategy for developing a data-driven Web site is that of developing the data-driven Web pages by using programming languages.

Java

Many languages are used to build data-driven Web sites such as C++, CGI (Common Gateway Interface) using Perl, and others. The one that is currently getting the most media attention, however, is Java. **Java** is a programming language, developed at Sun Microsystems in the 1990s whose characteristics make it particularly applicable to client/server and Web-enabled applications. Java is:

- *Platform-independent:* Java programs can be executed without changes on many different operating systems such as Windows, UNIX, and the Macintosh OS.

■ *Object-Oriented:* Java programs are faster, more efficient, and more consistent because of their object-oriented nature.

■ *Robust:* Java programs are capable of accessing data files by using various Internet communications protocols, Java has excellent security features, and Java is capable of developing a wide variety of applications. You could use Java to develop custom, in-house application programs (similar to how programmers used COBOL and C++ in the past), or use it to develop an **applet**, a Java program delivered through a Web page. For the purposes of this book, you would be most interested in Java applets that access data from a database and return them to the Web page.

It probably goes without saying that this solution is by far the most complex approach, requiring serious programming, database, and Internet technology skills. On the upside, the benefits of such a solution include the greatest degree of security, scalability, and compatibility among all of the four strategies. On the downside, this approach will probably be the most expensive as well as take the most time to implement. Companies with the largest and most complex data-driven Web sites gravitate toward this type of strategy not out of choice, but out of a need to provide the highest degree of functionality and sophistication.

To explore Java:

1. Go to **www.whatis.com**, click the letter **J** to move to the glossary words that start with the letter J, click the link for **Java**, and then read that glossary definition.

   Since Java was introduced by Sun Microsystems, you'll check out their home page to see what Sun has to say about Java.

2. At the bottom of the Java Web page, click the link for **Sun Microsystems' Java page** or enter **java.sun.com** into your browser.

   Just like the Allaire site for ColdFusion, Sun offers free information, support, tutorials, and downloads from their home site, as shown in Figure 6-26.

| Figure 6-26 | HOME PAGE FOR SUN'S JAVA |

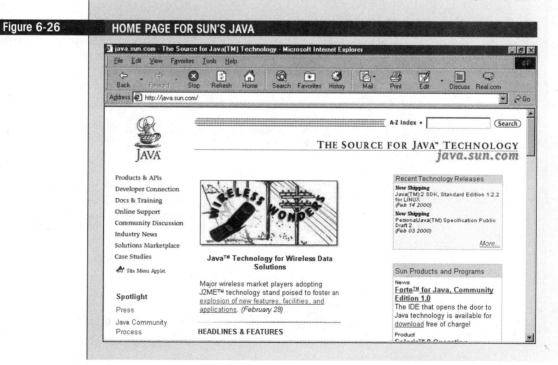

3. Scroll through the page and view the links. If the Shortcuts section is still available, click the option for **What Is Java...?**, and then click **Go**.

Try to find information on two of the most important technologies that make Java programs so popular: the Java platform and the sandbox.

The **Java platform** is what makes Java programs capable of being run on any operating system. The Java platform is software incorporated into current versions of browsers that translate Java programs into code that can be run on that machine. The **sandbox** is a concept that Java uses to secure and separate its programs. Using the sandbox, even if a Java applet (delivered through a Web page) bombs, the sandbox will keep it separated from the other resources and processes of your computer.

JavaScript

Not to be confused with Java, JavaScript is an entirely different programming language. JavaScript is a **scripting** language, which means that its commands are interpreted one at a time by a command interpreter which is part of the operating system. Interpreted programs are slower than compiled programs (such as Java programs). Compiled programs break the instructions down into lower-level statements that the processor can execute and that do not require the intermediate intervention of the command interpreter.

Because of its narrower role as a scripting language, JavaScript is less robust than Java. Also, the interpreted code created by JavaScript is carried line for line in the Web page, processed by the client, and is easily viewable. On the flip side, JavaScript is easier to use and learn than a programming language like Java, and more suited to small programming jobs.

In terms of how JavaScript is used for data-driven Web sites, it can be a handy tool to use for such functions such as creating user interaction messages, calculating field values based on entries in other fields, and building query strings.

To find out about JavaScript:

1. Go to **www.whatis.com**, click the letter **J** to move to the glossary words that start with the letter J, click the link for **JavaScript**, and then print that glossary definition.

2. Surf through the links or other **www.whatis.com** definitions.

3. Print two articles about any aspect of data-driven Web sites from Whatis.com.

4. Exit from Internet Explorer and then disconnect from the Internet.

Technology, Technology, Technology

There is really no end of topics, discussions, and technologies that could be explored when implementing a data-driven Web site. In reading this tutorial, however, you have been exposed to four separate types of software tools used to develop data-driven Web sites and some of the major business reasons that each is employed. You have also explored some of the specific software products used to implement a data-driven Web site within each of the four categories. Most importantly, however, you have been taught how to find information for yourself through online glossaries, tutorials, downloads, and reference libraries.

This book has focused on the creation of dynamic Web pages for data entry, up-to-date reporting, and interactive data analysis using Microsoft Access 2000. It has exposed you to the other activities involved in creating a data-driven Web site such as installing Web server software and publishing files to a Web server. Finally, it has tried to introduce you to products and technologies other than Access 2000 that you might use to create your data-driven Web site.

Session 6.3 QUICK CHECK

1. List three common application server products.

2. Why would you use an application server product such as ColdFusion as opposed to a FrontPage-Access combination of tools to develop a data-driven Web site?

3. What is the URL for a good glossary of information systems and technology terminology?

4. Identify three characteristics of Java that make it an excellent software language for developing Web-enabled applications.

5. Why might a company choose a programming strategy to develop their data-driven Web site?

6. What is the most fundamental technological difference between Java and JavaScript?

REVIEW ASSIGNMENTS

You work in the business office of a graduate school, Adair Graduate School, that offers several degrees including a Master of Business Administration (MBA), Master of Telecommunications Management (MTM), and Master of Information Systems Management (MISM). You have developed an Access database to help the faculty track students, classes, assignments, grades, and instructors called **AdairGS-6**. You'll use FrontPage to create and publish a data-driven Web page. Then you'll publish the Web page to your Personal Web server so that you can use HTTP to pull the files into Internet Explorer using a URL. You'll also explore the various folders on your hard drive that are used to store your development database, published database, and various FrontPage files.

1. Start Access 2000, and then open the **AdairGS-6** database from the Review\Solutions folder for Tutorial 6.

Explore
2. Click the Queries button, then double-click Enrollment Query to open it and view the data. This is the information that you wish to publish as a dynamic Web page using FrontPage. Note there are 15 enrollment records. Sort the database in ascending order by LastName as well as by ClassName to become familiar with the data within the query. Close the query without saving any changes and close the **AdairGS-6** database.

3. Start FrontPage 2000 and establish the Review\Solutions folder that contains the AdairGS-6 database as the FrontPage "Web" using the following instructions: Click File on the menu bar, click Open Web, and navigate to the Review\Solutions folder for Tutorial 6. When the Review\Solutions folder for Tutorial 6 is selected in the Look in list, click the Open button in the Open Web dialog box. If prompted to add FrontPage information to this folder, click the Yes button.

4. To identify your Web page when it is completed, type *Your Name* at the top of the Web page, press the Enter key, type *Your School's Name* **Enrollment Report** on the second line, and then press the Enter key.

5. Now establish the connection between the Web page and the database. Click Tools on the menu bar, click Web settings, click the Database tab, click Add, and type **Adair** as the name of the database connection in the Name text box.

6. Make sure that the File or folder in current Web option button is chosen for the type of connection, click the Browse button, click AdariGS-6.mdb, click OK in the Database Files in Current Web dialog box, and click OK in the New Database Connection dialog box.

7. Click Adair in Connection listings, and click the Verify button to make sure that the connection between the Web page and database is established. Click OK in the Web Settings dialog box to close it.

8. Now insert the contents of the Enrollment Query in the AdairGS-6 database as a dynamic data element on the page. Click Insert on the menu bar, point to Database, and then click Results.

9. In the Database Results Wizard – Step 1 of 5 dialog box, make sure that the Adair database connection is used, and then click the Next button.

10. In the second step of the wizard, click the Record Source list arrow, click Enrollment Query (VIEW), and then click the Next button.

11. In the third step of the wizard, accept all of the fields in the list by clicking the Next button.

12. In the fourth step of the wizard, accept all of the default formatting options by clicking the Next button.

13. In the fifth step of the wizard, accept the default options on how to split the records into groups by clicking the Finish button.

14. Now that the page is created that contains the appropriate code to link it to the Enrollment Query within the AdairGS-6.mdb database, it should be saved. Click the Save button on the Standard toolbar, make sure that the Save in folder is the same folder that was specified as the "Web" in Step 3, type **enroll** as the filename, make sure that the Save as type option indicates that the Web page will be saved as an ASP file, and then click the Save button.

15. Now you'll publish the ASP file to your local Web server that was previously established to Personal Web Server. First make sure that PWS is running by opening Personal Web Manager. (Click Start, point to Programs, point to the Personal Web Server group, which may be in the Internet Explorer group, and click Personal Web Manager. Click the Main button to find the start/stop button that allows you to start and stop publishing services. The Main section also shows you the default URL for your machine's Web server, which can also be identified as *http://localhost*, as well as the home directory to which all files will be published.)

Explore   16. If you have access to other Web servers, you may publish your files there. These instructions assume that you are publishing your Web pages to the default publishing directory of your local PWS Web server.

17. Within FrontPage, click File on the menu bar, click Publish Web, type **http://localhost** in the Specify the location to publish your web to text box, click the Publish all pages, over-writing any already on the destination option button, and then click the Publish button.

18. If dialer windows open (that help you connect to your ISP), close them because you do not need to connect to the Internet to publish files to your local Web server. When the Microsoft FrontPage dialog box opens, click Done.

19. Close FrontPage and start Internet Explorer. Type **http://localhost/enroll.asp** in the address bar of IE. It should load the **enroll.asp** Web page. Use the navigation buttons on the Web page to scroll through the 15 records. The records are presented in three sets of five records each, as specified by the Database Results Wizard within FrontPage. Print the Web page that shows the first five records.

20. Start Explorer, and then open the **C:\Inetpub\wwwroot** folder. By default, all files that are published to the *http://localhost* URL are published in this folder. You should see the AdairGS-6.mdb file in the file listings window on the right.

21. Double-click the **AdairGS-6.mdb** file to open it, click the Tables button, and double-click the Students table to open it in the datasheet view.

Explore 22. Change Nancy Gray's last name to **Nancy Lang**. Change Brad Smith's last name to **Brad Beetle**. Close the **Students** datasheet and close the database. By making these changes, you are changing the data in the database that the ASP Web page uses to create its dynamic reports. The original development database in the Review\Solutions folder has not changed.

23. Click the Microsoft Internet Explorer button on the taskbar, and then click the Refresh button on the Standard Buttons toolbar. Click the Retry button in the Microsoft Internet Explorer dialog box if prompted. Print the first Web page. Brad and Nancy should both have new last names based on the changes you made to the published database in Step 22.

24. Click the Exploring button on the taskbar, navigate to the Review\Solutions folder for Tutorial 6. You will see that extra FrontPage folders (_fpclass, _private, _vti_cnf, _vti_pvt, and images) were added to this folder in order to make it a FrontPage "Web." You will also see the original copy of the AdairGS-6.mdb file.

Explore 25. Double-click the **AdairGS-6.mdb** file in the Review\Solutions folder to open it, click the Tables button on the Objects bar, and double-click **Students** to open that table in datasheet view. You'll see that Nancy Gray and Brad Smith's names are in their original condition. This proves that the original "development" database and the "published" database are separate databases in separate folders. In most cases, these folders are on completely separate machines! In this exercise, however, you have used one machine to serve both the development and Web server roles.

26. To resynchronize the development database with the published database, you must republish it. You'll make one more edit to the Students table, however, so that you clearly track the process. Change the City from Tacoma to *your own hometown* for Brad Smith's record, close the **Students** table, and then close the **AdairGS-6.mdb** database.

27. Click the Exploring button on the taskbar, and then double-click the Enroll.asp file in the Review/Solutions folder. **Enroll.asp** will automatically open in FrontPage.

28. Click File on the menu bar, and then click Publish Web. Make sure that the **http://localhost** location is entered in the first text box, the Specify the location to publish your web to text box. Click the Publish all pages, overwriting any already on the destination option button, and then click the Publish button.

29. Once again, be sure to close any dialer windows that may appear, and click the Done button within FrontPage when prompted that your Web site published successfully.

30. Close FrontPage and click the Microsoft Internet Explorer button in your taskbar.

31. Click the Refresh button on the Standard Buttons toolbar and then click the Retry button if prompted.

32. The **enroll.asp** Web page should reload displaying the original last names for both Brad Smith and Nancy Gray. Brad Smith's City entry should display your hometown name since you made those changes to the production database, and republished it to c:\Inetpub\wwwroot.

Explore ▷ 33. Print the first page of the enroll.asp Web page from within IE one more time, and then close IE and Explorer.

CASE PROBLEMS

Case 1. Northwind Traders Database You may be familiar with the Northwind Traders sample database provided with Access 2000. Not only does the Northwind database provide examples of many different tables, queries, forms, reports, macros, and modules, but it also ties them together as a "total solution" for the order entry and inventory management needs of a small fictitious company, Northwind Traders. In this case, you'll explore the Northwind.mdb database. In Case 2 you'll find and download the Web-enabling files from the *www.microsoft.com* site that expand the capabilities of the Northwind database into a true e-commerce solution.

1. Start Access, double-click More Files in the Microsoft Access dialog box, and then open the **Northwind.mdb** file from the C:\Program Files\Microsoft Office\Office\Samples folder.

   Be careful not to open the NorthwindCS.adp file. If you do not have the Northwind.mdb file, you may have to install it from the Office 2000 CD or download it from *www.microsoft.com*.

2. The Welcome to Northwind Traders dialog box may appear. If so, read the welcoming message, and then click OK.

3. Click each button on the Objects bar to get an overview of the number of tables, queries, forms, reports, pages, macros, and modules that this database provides.

4. Click the Relationships button on the Database toolbar to get an overview of the relationship between the tables. Click the File menu, click Print Relationships, click the Print button on the Print Preview toolbar, and then close the report as well as the Relationships window without saving any changes.

5. You'll learn a lot by freely exploring the database, so open any object that appears interesting and study its Design view too. Try not to make any changes to the database, however, so that Northwind remains the same for the next user. At a minimum, observe the following interesting features of the Northwind database:

6. **Tables**:

   Open the **Employees** table in Design view and press the down arrow key to move through the field names. Observe the properties for each field in the lower section of the screen. Of special interest are the Format and Validation Rule properties on the BirthDate field, the Caption properties on each field, the fact that the Photo field is created with an OLE Object data type, and the Lookup properties for the ReportsTo field.

7. View the **Employees** table in Datasheet view, and then tab through the fields. Click the list arrow in the ReportsTo field to observe the effect of the Lookup properties. Close the **Employees** table without saving any changes.

8. **Queries**:

   Click the Queries button on the Objects bar to display the queries in the database. Note the Union query icon for the Customers and Suppliers by City and the Crosstab query icon for the Quarterly Orders by Product.

9. Click the Details button on the database window toolbar and observe the entries in the Description column.

10. Open the **Employee Sales by Country** query in Design view and notice the use of parameter criteria in the ShippedDate field. Also notice that the field lists contain both table and query objects (Employees and Orders are tables and Order Subtotals is a query).

11. Click the Datasheet View button and enter 1/1/96 and 1/1/97 in the parameter prompts. Close the query.

12. **Forms**:

    Click the Forms button on the Objects bar. Open the **Employees** form in Form view and move through the records. Observe the Photo field as you move through the records.

13. Click the Personal Info tab as well as the Title Of Courtesy combo box arrow to experience these powerful controls.

14. Click the Design View button and observe the calculated control in the upper-right corner of the form; this control appends the FirstName and LastName fields into one control. Close the **Employees** form without saving any changes.

15. Open the **Customer Orders** form to observe a form with two subforms. Move from company to company to observe the changes in the subforms. Click in any value in the Order subform to observe the change in the Order Details subform.

16. Close the **Customer Orders** form without saving any changes.

17. **Reports**:

    Click the Reports button on the Objects bar. Open Products by Category in Print Preview to observe a three-column report.

18. Click File on the menu bar, then click Page Setup to open the Page Setup dialog box. Click the Columns tab to observe where the number of columns information is specified. Cancel the Page Setup dialog box.

19. Click the Design View button to open the report in Design view. Observe the calculated control in the Report Header section that formats the current date. Observe the labels and text box controls in the CategoryName Header. If you do not know which controls are labels and which ones are text boxes, open the Property Sheet, and single-click each control, observing the title bar of the property sheet.

20. Click the Sorting and Grouping button to observe the group properties for the CategoryName. Click the various Group Properties while observing the explanation of the property in the lower-right corner of the dialog box. Remember that you can press F1 any time you are working with a specific property to open the Help manual for that specific topic.

21. Close the Sorting and Grouping dialog box and close the **Products by Category** report without saving changes.

22. **Pages**:
    Click the Pages button on the Objects bar. You should explore each of the page objects individually. Each provides a wonderful example of advanced Web page development using Access 2000. The following list represents a few of the exciting things you will notice.

    - Analyze Sales: Read the explanatory text at the top of the pivot table. Note that the pivot table both counts and subtotals orders by customers. Use the ShipCountry field in the filter position to analyze the data. Use the Expand and Collapse buttons to view and hide detail information.

    - Review Orders: Read the explanatory text at the top of the combo box. Use the combo box to retrieve the records for a particular company. Notice the modified image on the Expand and Collapse buttons. Click the Expand and Collapse buttons to view the details of an order. Note the modifications on the Navigation toolbar (fewer buttons and modified text).

    - Review Products: Note the Expand and Collapse button image. Note the horizontal layout of the text boxes and the large Description text boxes. Expand a category and note the discontinued check box control. Also note how the Navigation toolbars are presented.

    - Sales: Read the explanatory text above the pivot table. Work with the filter arrows to modify the data in the pivot table and watch how the chart responds to each change.

    - View Products: Move through the records and test the combo boxes for Supplier and Category. Try not to make any changes to the actual data.

23. Based on what you have experienced exploring the Northwind database, print one example of each object type from which you learned something. On the back of the paper, write two or three sentences indicating why you chose that particular example, and what you learned from it.

24. Once you are finished exploring the Northwind database, close all objects without saving changes, close **Northwind**, and exit Access.

Case 2. Web-Enabled Northwind Traders Database Microsoft has developed the files necessary to expand the Northwind Traders database to a true e-commerce application. You can download the files from the *www.microsoft.com* Web site and learn a great deal about the capabilities of Access to provide Web-enabled solutions. Once you find the zipped **5298.exe** file on the Microsoft Web site that contains the Web-enabling files for the Northwind Traders database, you'll download the file and unzip it. Then you'll explore the Web-enabling features of the Northwind Traders database.

1. Go to **http://support.microsoft.com/directory/** to go to the home page for Microsoft support. (You should be able to get to this page by going to *www.microsoft.com* and clicking the Support link as well.)

2. Click the MSDN for developers link because the file you wish to download is part of the Microsoft Solution Developers Network area.

3. Click the Downloads link and then click the Samples link. (*Hint*: This area may have moved to the Code Center or another location on the Microsoft Web site.)

4. Explore the many sample downloads in the Code Center. The site is changing constantly, and specific instructions on how to find a particular resource can be frustrating. If you don't find the Northwind Traders Direct Sample Application, don't worry! Microsoft provides such vast resources at their Web site, it's impossible to master the site after only a few visits.

5. Click the Search MSDN link, enter **Northwind Traders Direct Sample Application** into the search box, clear all of the check boxes except for MSDN Library, and then click Search.

6. Click the Northwind Traders Direct Sample Application link. Click the Click to view the complete article and download the sample application link.

7. Print the page, then click the Click to view or copy the sample Web site discussed in this article.

8. A File Download dialog box should appear indicating that you are about to save the **5298.exe** file to your disk. Make sure the Save this program to disk option button is checked, then click OK.

9. Click the Save in list arrow, and navigate to your desktop so that the downloaded file will be easy to find later, and then click Save in the Save As dialog box.

10. Once the file download is complete, double-click the **5298.exe** file on your desktop. A WinZip Self-Extractor window should open indicating that the files will be unzipped into the C:\Windows\TEMP folder. Click the Unzip button. If you do not have WinZip on your computer, you can use other decompression programs to unzip this file. If you do not have any decompression programs and would like to use WinZip, please refer to Appendix A.

11. Click OK in the dialog box that indicates that 290 files unzipped successfully, and click Close in the WinZip Self Extractor dialog box.

12. Start Explorer, then navigate to the C:\Windows\TEMP folder in the folder tree. Click the **Northwind Traders Direct** folder to open it (it may be located in the C:\Windows\TEMP\Temp folder), and then double-click the default.htm file to open it in Internet Explorer. The Welcome to Northwind Traders Direct page appears.

13. Explore the site by using the navigation buttons on the left. Click the large Browse button on the left, and then click the link for Meat/Poultry. Click the link for the Perth Pasties item from the G'day Mate company, and click the shopping cart icon to add this item to your order.

14. Enter **5** into the VBScript dialog box, indicating that you want to place 5 Perth Pasties in your shopping cart. Click OK, and then navigate back to the product categories page. *Hint*: You can click the Back button or you can click the Return button on the Web page to return to the previous page as well.

15. From the Seafood category, add a quantity of **10 Boston Crab Meat** to your shopping cart.

16. Click the large Search button in the left side of the Web page, click the Category check box, choose **Confections** from the Category list box, enter **Scones** into the Product Name box, and click Search.

17. You should have found one "hit" for Sir Rodney's Scones. Add 20 of them to your shopping cart.

18. Click the large Recipes button on the left side of the Web page, and print that page. Click the link for Aniseed Syrup, and add a quantity of **1** to your shopping cart.

19. Click the large Shopping Cart button on the left side of the Web page to review your order, and print that page.

20. Click the Register button at the bottom of the page to register as a new customer, and fill out the information for a New Customer. Print that page so that you can remember your 5-character CustomerID, and then click the Submit button.

21. Click the Confirm Purchase button, and then click Home.

22. Continue to play with the Northwind Traders Direct Web-enabled database, and when you are finished, close IE.

23. If you are working on a shared computer, you may want to delete the files from the C:\Windows\Temp folder.

Case 3. Building a Customer Feedback Database Using FrontPage 2000   FrontPage 2000 can be used to develop very simple data-driven Web sites regardless of whether the database is developed or not. In this case, you'll use FrontPage 2000 to build a small user feedback form. The data entered by the user will be stored in a backend database created by FrontPage.

1. Start FrontPage 2000 and click No if presented with a FrontPage dialog box that presents a question about whether or not you want FrontPage to be your default HTML editor. Click File on the menu bar, and then click Open Web. Click the Look in arrow, and then navigate to your \Cases\Solutions folder for Tutorial 6. Remember that you need to establish a FrontPage Web before you can use the database connectivity features within FrontPage. Click Open in the Open Web dialog box, and then click Yes when prompted to add information to your folder.

2. Click File on the menu bar, point to New, and then click Page.

3. The New dialog box presents you with many different types of predeveloped Web page templates, which you can use as the basis for your Web page. Some of the templates have built-in database connectivity such as the Feedback Form.

4. Single-click the Feedback Form, read the description information, and then click the OK button.

5. The Web page is presented along with some clarifying information at the top of the page on what happens to the data that is entered by the user. Since you would like the data to be placed in an Access database rather than in a text file, you'll modify the form's properties. Right-click the form (inside the dashed line), and then click Form Properties.

6. Click the Send to database option button, click OK in the Form Properties dialog box, and then click Yes to edit the settings for the form.

7. Click the Create Database button to allow FrontPage to create an appropriately structured database to store the information from this survey, note the name of the database (so that you can open the database later to view the data it contains), click OK in the message box that tells you where the database is located and what connection to use with the Database Results Wizard, and then click OK in the Options for Saving Results to Database dialog box.

8. Click the HTML and Preview tabs. In the Preview screen, click the radio buttons and list arrow to get a feel for how this Web page will appear to a user.

9. You decide that the Complaint and Problem option buttons are so similar, you might as well delete the Complaint option button. You'd also like to add Service as an option to the list of items that the user can provide feedback about.

10. Click the Normal tab, click and drag through the Complaint text and option button, and then press Delete on the keyboard to delete that option.

11. Right-click the Web site Combo box, and then click Form Field Properties. In the Drop-Down Menu Properties dialog box, click the Add button, type **Service** in the Choice text box, and click OK.

12. Click the Move Up button three times so that Service is located between Products and Store in the list, and then click OK in the Drop-Down Menu Properties dialog box.

13. Save the page with the name **FeedbackForm** to the \Cases\Solutions folder for Tutorial 6, and print the Normal view of the form. The page is automatically saved as an ASP file.

Explore ▶ 14. If desired, complete the rest of the steps in this case to publish this to your Personal Web Server in order to view it from within IE. This requires that you have Personal Web Server running on your machine, or access to another Web server where you are allowed to publish files.

Within FrontPage click the Publish Web button on the Standard toolbar. Type **localhost** after http://. Click Options to expand the dialog box if it is not already expanded, click the Publish all pages overwriting any already on the destination option button, and then click Publish.

15. Close any dialer windows that may appear since you are publishing this to your Personal Web Server on your local machine. (If you do not have Personal Web Server installed, please refer to that section within this tutorial.)

Explore ▶ 16. Click Yes if prompted to replace any files, and then click the Done button. Open IE, and enter the HTTP address for this Web page. If you don't remember your default HTTP address (the machine name specified in the Main section of PWS), you can use the alias localhost. Therefore, enter the URL **http://localhost/feedbackform.asp** into the Address box of your browser to open the form you just created in FrontPage.

Explore ▶ 17. Enter one **Praise** comment into the Web page. Be sure to click the Submit Comments button at the bottom of the page. Print the Form Confirmation page, click the Return to the form link, and then close IE.

Explore ▶ 18. In Explorer, navigate to your PWS published files folder, (by default, C:\Inetpub\wwwroot), and then find and open the database that was created by FrontPage. (*Hint*: The database is probably called new_page.mdb or something similar. It will probably be in an fpdb (FrontPage database) folder within the C:\Inetpub\wwwroot folder.)

Explore ▶ 19. Double-click the **Results** table to open it in datasheet view, adjust the columns so that they are no wider than necessary, and then print it in a landscape orientation.

20. Close the **new_page** database, exit Access, and close any open IE or FrontPage windows.

Case 4. Connecting a Database to a Web Page by Using HTML As you become more familiar with various tools, you'll naturally become more technical. Even if you can solve your business's e-commerce needs with WYSIWYG HTML editors such as FrontPage and GUI application development tools such as Access, if you make a career out of building Web-enabled databases, you'll eventually want to "get behind" the glamour of these tools and get directly into the programming code that makes it all work. That requires a solid foundation in both the de facto Web page markup language, HTML, Hypertext Markup Language and the de facto database access language, SQL, Structured Query Language. In this exercise you'll return to the World Wide Web to search for and take tutorials on these two importantly underlying technologies.

1. Connect to the Internet, go to **www.searchengineshowdown.com**. This site compares many aspects of various search engines and should assist you in conducting general research on the Internet such as finding an HTML or SQL tutorial.

2. Take your time exploring the site. If you've ever been frustrated with the number or lack of relevancy of the hits you receive when using a search engine, you'll find the "Features" and "Search Strategies" sections of this Web site useful. Of special interest are the comparison charts that show statistics on which search engines have the largest databases. Once you find the search engine with the largest database (according to *www.searchengineshowdown.com*), go to that search engine site (*www.alltheweb.com* was ranked as having one of the largest databases at the time of this writing), enter the words "HTML SQL tutorial" as the search phrase, and search for the three terms.

3. Your goal is to find and take three separate online tutorials that address HTML, SQL, and the use of the two languages together. For each tutorial, print the home page of the site, and write up a one-page report about your experience. Summarize what you learned from the tutorial as well as what remains unclear or what you still want to learn.

4. If you're having trouble finding online tutorials, try these sites:

   www.etute.com
   www.webmonkey.com
   www.whatis.com
   www.zdnet.com

5. Disconnect from the Internet, and then exit IE.

QUICK | CHECK ANSWERS

Session 6.1

1. Client/server computing can be defined as two or more information systems cooperatively processing to solve a problem. Web-enabled applications, including those that incorporate data-driven Web sites, are inherently client/server. Understanding which technologies and processes occur on the client, and which on the server is fundamental to building a data-driven Web site. As your site grows, multiple servers will be introduced to handle various parts of the process. A firm understanding of C/S in general is fundamental knowledge for deploying or managing a large-scale data-driven Web site.

2. 1. Database products with Web-enabling features

   2. HTML editors with database features

   3. Web server database products

   4. Programming languages

3. The Microsoft Knowledge Base is a database of technical support information and tools for Microsoft products.

4. The MSDN Online Library (or simply MSDN Library) contains an enormous amount of technical information about the Microsoft products that are used to develop applications, such as sample code, documentation, technical articles, and reference guides.

Session 6.2

1. An HTML editor is a software product that helps you write and edit HTML (Hypertext Markup) code, the tags that define how the Web page will appear when opened with a browser.

2. With FrontPage 2000, you can design a Web page that will dynamically present up-to-date data from the underlying Access 2000 database through a technology called Active Server Pages.

3. network engineer

   webmaster

   database administrator

   Web page developer

   programmer

   graphic artist

   systems analyst

Session 6.3

1. Allaire's ColdFusion, EveryWare Development's Tango, and the HAHTsite

2. When attempting to connect and combine the resources and services of various non-Microsoft products into one HTML Web page, application server products, such as ColdFusion, are often used.

3. *www.whatis.com*

4. Java is:

   ■ *Platform independent:* Java programs can be executed without changes on many different operating systems such as Windows, UNIX, and the Macintosh OS.

   ■ *Object-Oriented:* Java programs are faster, more efficient, and more consistent because of their object-oriented nature.

   ■ *Robust:* Java programs are capable of accessing data files using various Internet communications protocols, Java has excellent security features, and Java is capable of developing a wide variety of applications.

5. The benefits of using a programming language for developing a data-driven Web site through Java include the greatest degree of security, scalability, and compatibility among all of the four possible strategies for doing so.

6. Java creates programs that can be compiled. JavaScript is a scripting language whose programs must be interpreted by the operating system.

WINZIP

Appendix A will help you manage the data files you will be using and creating as you work through the Tutorials, Review Exercises, and Case Problems in this book. This information is not required to do these exercises in the book. If you work on multiple computers and transport files from one to another either by using floppies or by attaching them to e-mail messages, you will become more productive if you learn to use compression software such as WinZip.

Today's standard 3½-inch floppy disks provide approximately 1.44 MB of storage space. While this provided ample room for many data files only a few years ago, this isn't enough room to complete the exercises in this book for many reasons:

- The size of Access database files can become quite large because all objects are stored in one MDB file. The database will grow very quickly if you add graphics to your forms and reports, or use OLE Object fields. OLE Object fields allow you to embed information such as pictures, sound clips, or Word documents into the Access database, which increase the size of the database quickly.

- If you use the Compact on Close feature, a temporary file is created in the background while the database is closing that requires as much space as the database itself. So while the Compact on Close feature keeps the final size of the database as small as possible, the process requires that at least half of your diskette remain empty to deal with the temporary file used in the compact process.

- The process of creating page objects within Access creates external HTM, XML, GIF, and CSS files. These are used in the definition and creation of the final Web page as it appears within Internet Explorer. Although these external files usually aren't large files, they do require some additional storage space beyond the requirements of the database file itself.

- The demand for multimedia elements, such as sound, animation, and graphical elements on Web pages, quickly drives up storage space requirements.

Therefore, for speed and storage reasons, we recommend that you copy all of the Data Files provided with this book to Solutions folders on your computer's hard drive. The recommended structure is explained in the Read This Before You Begin section at the beginning of the book. If you work from a hard drive, you will not encounter disk storage problems as you complete the Tutorials and exercises.

If you need to transfer the data files from one computer to another, you could always copy the data files on multiple floppies (provided that each file is 1.44 MB or less). However, we recommend that you use a popular compression software program such as WinZip to help automate the process. WinZip is an extremely popular program that allows you to compress (zip) one or multiple files into one smaller file. In many cases, zipped files are reduced to 10% to 20% of their uncompressed size. Even if you don't want to compress programs for archival or transfer purposes yourself, you'll want to have a copy of WinZip on your computer to decompress (unzip) files that you will inevitably download from the Internet or receive from other people.

Downloading WinZip

Before downloading WinZip, check to see if your computer already has a current copy by clicking the Start button and pointing to programs. Within WinZip, click the Help menu option, and then click About WinZip to find out what version you are currently using. If your copy of WinZip isn't current (in the year 2000, WinZip had both 7.0 and 8.0 versions available), you may want to download a current version of the software so that you have all of the latest features.

To purchase or download a free evaluation version of WinZip, go to *www.winzip.com*. The WinZip home page provides links to the pages that allow you to download WinZip, some general information about the product, and a list of frequently asked questions.

Installing WinZip

If you download the WinZip software or WinZip upgrade from *www.winzip.com*, you'll receive one executable file with a name such as winzip70.exe. To install WinZip, double-click the winzip70.exe file and follow the prompts to install WinZip on your computer.

Compressing and Decompressing an Entire Folder and Subfolders

Once you have WinZip installed, you may want to learn how to compress and decompress an entire folder so that all of the data files are zipped into the same WinZip file. After compressing all of your data files into a single WinZip file, you can copy the WinZip file to a floppy, carry the floppy to a different machine, and decompress the files there. In this way, you can work on the same data files in two locations using a single floppy to carry them back and forth. Of course this requires that WinZip be installed on both computers to compress and then decompress the files. These steps assume that you are not using the Wizard interface, but rather, the Classic interface.

To compress an entire folder and its subfolders into one WinZip file:

1. Start **WinZip**. Read and close the Tip of the Day dialog box if it is presented and close the Wizard if it automatically appears.

2. Click the **New** button on the Large Buttons toolbar.

3. Click the **Create** list arrow, navigate to the folder where you wish to store the new WinZip file, type the name of the new WinZip file in the File name dialog box, for example *YourName***Tutorial01**, and then click **OK** in the New Archive dialog box.

4. Click the **Add** list arrow, navigate to the folder that you wish to compress, and then click it to select it.

5. Verify that the **Include subfolders** check box is checked, and then click the **Add with wildcards** button in the Add dialog box to create the final *YourName*Tutorial01.zip file.

6. If you are transferring the *YourName*Tutorial01.zip file to a floppy, use Explorer to make sure that its size is less than 1.44 MB, and then transfer it to a clean floppy.

You'll see the name of the zip file in the title bar of the WinZip program, for example *YourName*Tutorial01.zip. Within the WinZip window you'll see which files have been compressed in the zip file.

To decompress an entire folder and its subfolders using WinZip:

1. Copy the file that you wish to decompress from your floppy to the hard drive of the computer where you wish to decompress it. The desktop is a handy location for temporarily storing WinZip files.

2. Double-click the **YourNameTutorial01.zip** file to open it in WinZip.

3. Click the **Extract** button on the Large Buttons toolbar.

4. Click the **All files** option button, make sure that the **Use folder names** check box is checked, choose the appropriate Extract to folder, and then click **Extract**.

Be sure to read the title bars of the dialog boxes that are presented by WinZip. The title bars will prompt you for the information needed at that point.

More Information about WinZip

To get more information about WinZip, click Help on the menu bar, and click Brief Tutorial for some basic information on how to use the product. Also, WinZip provides a "wizard" interface that many people prefer because it provides additional prompts regarding the processes of zipping and unzipping files. Click the Wizard button on the Large Buttons toolbar to start the WinZip Wizard.

Be sure to always label your floppies carefully and delete any old data files that you won't need from existing floppies or hard drives. The easiest way to manage the data files for this textbook is to use a single computer for all of the exercises, but if you need to carry the data files with you, or work on the exercises from multiple computers, WinZip can be a valuable tool.

ASSOCIATING
HTML FILES WITH INTERNET EXPLORER

As you work though the Tutorials, Review Exercises, and Case Problems in this book, you will see that many of the activities require that a file be opened in a browser window. If Internet Explorer is not your default browser, Appendix B will give you the instructions to change that setting so that IE automatically opens any file with an HTM extension.

If your computer has both the Netscape Navigator and Internet Explorer browsers loaded, only one of the programs will be considered the default browser. The default browser is the program used to automatically open HTML files. For example, when you click a URL within Access or double-click a file with an HTM extension in Explorer, one of your browsers will be used to display the Web page that is being accessed. Since the Web pages created by Access 2000 do not appear properly in Netscape Navigator, you may want to make IE your default browser instead. To change which program automatically opens a file, you have to change the file type association in Windows Explorer or My Computer.

To associate HTML and HTM files with IE:

1. In **My Computer** or **Windows Explorer**, click the **View** menu, and then click **Folder Options**.
2. Click the **File Types** tab.
3. In the list of file types, click the one that represents the HTML and HTM extensions. (*Note*: The HTML and HTM extensions may be listed as "Netscape HTML document".)
4. Click the **Edit** button in the Folder Options dialog box.
5. In the **Actions** list, click **Open**, and then click the **Edit** button in the Edit File Type dialog box.
6. Click the **Browse** button in the Editing action dialog box, and navigate to the Iexplore.exe file that represents Internet Explorer (*Note*: By default, Iexplore.exe is found in the C:\Program Files\Internet Explorer folder path.)
7. Click the **Iexplore.exe** file, and then click the **Open** button in the Open With dialog box.
8. Click **OK** in the Editing action for type dialog box.
9. Click **Close** in the Edit File Type dialog box.
10. Click **Close** in the Folder Options dialog box.

Now HTM files should appear with an IE icon instead of a Netscape Navigator icon. When you open HTM files by double-clicking the file or clicking on an htm hyperlink, the files should automatically load in IE instead of Netscape Navigator.

Note that these settings can be overridden by options within the programs themselves. The first time you use Internet Explorer after changing the file type association, you should be prompted with a message asking you whether you wish to make Internet Explorer 5 your default browser. Be sure to answer "Yes" to this question. If you are still having trouble associating HTM files with IE, go into IE and take these additional steps:

1. Click the **Tools** menu, and then click **Internet Options**.
2. Click the **Programs** tab.
3. Click the **Internet Explorer should check to see whether it is the default browser** check box to check it.
4. Click **OK** in the Internet Options dialog box.
5. Close **IE**.
6. Start **IE** and click **Yes** when prompted to make IE your default browser.

WEB
SERVERS AND WINDOWS OPERATING SYSTEMS

This textbook has been written for the Windows 98 operating system. If you are using the Windows 95 or Windows NT workstation operating system, you will need to modify the Personal Web Server installation instructions to handle the differences between the operating systems. If you are using Windows 2000, you have many Web-enabling features built right into the operating system. Specific information for each version of Windows is listed below.

Windows 95

Windows 95 users will need to download and install Microsoft Personal Web Server for Windows 95 found at *http://www.microsoft.com/windows/ie/pws/*

Windows NT Workstation

Windows NT users will need to use **Microsoft Peer Web Services for Windows NT Workstation 4.0** instead of Microsoft Personal Web Server. To install Microsoft Peer Web Services for Windows NT, insert the Windows NT Workstation CD and add the Microsoft Peer Web Services through the Network option in the Control Panel program. Information about Microsoft Peer Web Services can be found at *http://support.microsoft.com/support/kb/articles/Q163/7/75.asp*.

Windows 2000

Windows 2000 users have Internet Information Server 5.0 (IIS) integrated into the operating system which automatically gives them Web Folders and support for FrontPage Server Extensions. Windows 2000 users will not need to install Personal Web Server. A good summary of the Web-enabling Windows 2000 features can be found at *http://www.microsoft.com/WINDOWS2000/guide/server/features/web.asp*.

GLOSSARY

A

action queries

Used to update or change data. There are four types of action queries: make-table query, append query, delete query, and update query.

active server pages (asp)

HTML pages that contain scripts that can retrieve or update live data from a database.

add-in

A program that can be added to a primary program to extend its capabilities.

aggregate calculation

A calculation that uses the field values of several records to create a calculation such as a subtotal or average for that group of records.

aggregate function

The type of calculation performed within an aggregate calculation such as Sum, Avg, Min, Max, Count, Stdev (standard deviation), Var (variance), First, and Last.

alias

A URL that translates one address into another; one method companies are using to funnel more "hits" to their Web sites.

applet

A Java program delivered through a Web page.

application server software

Software devoted to creating dynamic Web pages. Also called Web server products, they are represented by such packages as Allaire's ColdFusion, Everyware Development's Tango, and HAHT.

ASP

See active server pages.

AutoPage tool

A tool that automatically creates a new page object. The only question presented to the user is what table or query the page should be based upon. The AutoPage tool makes all of the other design choices.

B

body

The basic design surface of the data access page.

bound control

In a form, report, or page object, bound controls are used to display data from the underlying record-set. Examples include the text box and combo box. Bound controls change as you move from record to record through the object.

bound HTML control

A control you can add to a page object that reads HTML code and changes the field entry accordingly.

bound hyperlink control

Interprets the entry in field with a Text data type as an Internet address on a page object.

bound object frame

A bound control used to display the contents of an OLE field.

browser

Software such as Netscape Navigator and Microsoft Internet Explorer, which provide an easy-to-use graphical user interface (GUI) by which to locate, find, and display Web pages connected by hyperlinks.

C

calculated controls

In a form, report, or page object, calculated controls are used to contain an expression such as page numbers, dates, or other calculated values based on data from other controls.

calculated field

A field created within a query, form, or report that evaluates an expression to produce a single value for each record.

category

In a chart, each item on the x-axis.

category axis

In a chart, the x-axis.

chart

One of twelve types of business graphs including area, column, line, pie, and XY (scatter).

Chart Property Toolbox

A toolbox window used to format and modify the individual items within a chart control in a page object.

Chart Wizard

A wizard that helps you through the process of creating a chart.

check box

A bound control used to display a "yes" or "no" answer for a Yes/No field in the form of a checked or unchecked box.

client

On the Internet, the client is the user's computer with Internet Explorer and the necessary connectivity and security rights to the Web folder. The client may download, view, and use those Web pages.

client-server computing

Two or more information systems cooperatively processing to solve a problem.

Clipboard toolbar

A toolbar that saves the last twelve items that have been cut or copied, so that you can selectively paste any of these twelve items within or between application windows.

collaboration tools

Features within the Office 2000 suite of products that allow multiple people to be actively working with the same data at the same time, such as online meetings, shared workbooks, and document discussions.

column field (within a PivotTable)

A field in the column area (the top edge of the PivotTable).

combo box

A bound control that is a combination of both the text box and list box controls. The combo box provides a list of field entry choices plus the ability for the user to enter a new value for the field from the keyboard. A field such as city that contains a group of common entries but cannot be limited to a single list is a good choice for a combo box.

command button

An unbound control that appears as a button on a form or page object. When clicked, it initiates a macro or other action.

comparison operator

An entry such as <, >, or Like that is entered before a criteria entry in the query grid to further specify how the criteria is to be evaluated. The default comparison operator is = and therefore does not need to be entered. Other comparison operators include: >, >=, <, <=, <>, Between...And, In, Null, Is Not Null, Like, and Not.

control

Each item on a form, report, or page object.

cookie

A small file stored on your hard disk that stores information about your interaction with a particular Web site.

criteria

In a query, criteria determine which records will appear on the datasheet and are entered in the lower half of the design grid.

crosstab query

Creates a pivot table arrangement of data using at least one field in the column heading area, one in the field heading area, and one in the middle upon which a calculation such as a subtotal, is being applied.

DAP

See page.

data access page (DAP)

See page.

data marker

In a chart, an individual bar.

data series

In a chart, a set of bars that graph the same type of data across all categories.

data type

A characteristic of the field that determines the type of data that the field will accept.

database

A broad collection of data associated with a topic.

database administrator

A person who designs, maintains and secures the database.

Database results wizard

Within FrontPage, a wizard that allows you to add database connectivity to a Web page.

datasheet

A logical view of the fields and records of a single table or query in which a field appears as a column and a record as a row.

Design view

The view of an object in which you create and modify the object's structure.

Detail (section)

Appears in the middle of the report (or between the group header and group footer sections).

Detail area (within a PivotTable)

The part of a PivotTable that shows detail (nonsummarized) data.

Detail field (within a PivotTable)

A field that is placed in the intersection of the column and rows, and contains individual or summary values from the underlying recordset.

docked (toolbar)

A toolbar that is positioned at the edge of the screen and is not "floating."

domain name

See Web server address.

drill down

To click on a category heading (or click subcategories within categories) before you enter search criteria in a Web page search engine.

drop box

A feature on a Web page that gives visitors a way to leave a private message for you.

dropdown list control

A bound control that works in the same way as a combo box used on a form or report, but is called a dropdown list when used on a page object.

e-business

Internet-based business activities such as providing customer support, advertising, or conducting market research.

e-cash

Electronic cash.

e-commerce

See electronic commerce.

EDI

See electronic data interchange.

e-form

Electronic form.

EFT

See electronic funds transfer.

electronic commerce (e-commerce)

Conducting business using the Internet.

electronic data interchange (EDI)

Electronic transmission of data from one company's computer to another company's computer.

electronic funds transfer (EFT)

Electronic payment sent from one company to another through a bank.

e-mail

Electronic mail.

emulation boards

Circuit boards added to personal computers so that their keyboards and input signals would map to that of a "dumb" CRT. Also called 3270 cards or IRMA cards.

Enforce Referential Integrity

An option you can choose within the Edit Relationships dialog box that helps you maintain the accuracy of your data by imposing certain rules preventing a value from being entered into the foreign key field that isn't first entered into the primary key field of the related table.

e-shopping

Electronic shopping.

e-tailing

Electronic retailing.

expand control

On a page object, a control that allows you to hide or show additional fields within a group of records.

expression

A combination of fields, values, functions, and mathematical operators that calculates to a single value.

Extensible Markup Language

See XML.

e-zine

Electronic magazine.

F

FAQ

Frequently asked questions.

field

A category of information about an item in the database.

Field filter arrow (within a PivotTable)

The arrow at the right side of each field in a PivotTable that, when clicked, presents a list of entries for that field from which you can choose to selectively hide or display in the PivotTable.

field list

In Form, Report, or Page Design view, the list that opens inside a small window that contains all of the fields available for that object.

field selector

In the query grid, the short gray bar just above the field name that is used to select, move, and delete the field.

file locking

Excel spreadsheets and Word documents are file locking because they allow only one person to update a file at the same time.

file server

A powerful microcomputer that stores data files and software shared by multiple users.

File transfer protocol (FTP)

A protocol that describes the rules for electronic transmission of a file from one computer to another over the Internet.

Filter field (within a PivotTable)

A field in the filter area (the upper-left corner of the PivotTable).

floating (toolbar)

A toolbar that is positioned in the middle of the screen, has a title bar, and can be resized.

foreign key field

The field in the table on the "many" side of a one-to-many relationship.

form

Provides an easy-to-use data entry screen that generally shows only one record at a time.

Form Design view

The view of a form used to modify the structure and formatting of the form object.

Form view

The view of a form object used to enter and update data.

FrontPage Server Administrator

A program used to install and manage the FrontPage server extension files on Web servers.

FrontPage server extensions

Special files added to a Web server to correctly process and serve Web pages created with FrontPage.

FTP

See File Transfer Protocol.

G

graphic artist

A person who develops images and other multimedia content displayed on Web pages using a variety of software products. The graphic artist helps with overall theme, color, readability, and Web page navigation issues.

graphical user interface

See GUI.

Group By

In an aggregate calculation, Group By is the aggregate function used for the field that will determine which records are "grouped" together.

Group Footer (section)

Appears at the end of each group of records.

Group Header (section)

Appears at the beginning of each group of records.

grouping

To sort records and create a section on the report that prints before and after the group.

guest book

A common feature of a Web page, in which users can sign their names, leave a public message, and view other messages.

GUI (graphical user interface)

An interface in which the user may use menus, buttons, toolbars, icons, and other "graphical" means by which to communicate with the computer (as opposed to typing commands).

H

home page

The first page displayed to visitors when they visit your Web site.

hotspot image

An unbound control that is available for the page object. It looks like a piece of clip art but behaves like a hyperlink.

HTML

See Hypertext Markup Language.

HTML editors

Software programs used to create Web pages, such as Microsoft's FrontPage or Macromedia's Dreamweaver.

HTML file

Web page.

HTML view

Within FrontPage, the view that presents the corresponding HTML codes.

HTTP

See Hypertext Transfer Protocol.

hyperlink

A control in the form of a label, button, or image placed on a form that when clicked, automatically opens another object, document, e-mail message, or Web page.

hyperlink data type

Used to indicate that a field entry is either a URL (Uniform Resource Locator), more commonly known as a Web page address, or a UNC (Universal Naming Convention).

Hypertext Markup Language (HTML)

The programming language used to create Web pages that consist of a set of tags and attributes.

Hypertext Transfer Protocol (HTTP)

A communications protocol used to find and route Web pages over the Internet.

 I

IIS

See Internet Information Services.

image

An unbound control used to add a clip art image.

intelligent client

A PC with processing and memory capabilities.

interactive reporting

A term that applies to a Web page in which the user can interact with the data using such techniques as sorting, filtering, or expanding grouped records.

Internet

A public global network of computer networks that pass information from one to another using common computer protocols.

Internet Information Services (IIS)

Software used on a Windows NT or Windows 2000 server to provide Web server capabilities.

Internet Network Information Center (InterNic)

The organization that maintains and assigns server addresses on a first-come, first-served basis.

Internet service provider (ISP)

A company whose purpose is to connect computers to the Internet.

Internet software suite

Collections of Internet software bundled together. A common bundle might include a browser, chat program, HTML editor, and e-mail package.

InterNic

See Internet Network Information Center.

ISP

See Internet service provider.

 J

Java

A programming language, developed at Sun Microsystems whose characteristics make it particularly applicable to client/server and Web-enabled applications.

JavaScript

A scripting language that is a separate language from Java.

junction table

A table that is established between two tables with a many-to-many relationship. The junction table contains foreign key fields that link to the primary key fields of each of the original tables, and thus establishes separate one-to-many relationships with them with the junction table serving as the "many" side of each relationship.

 K

key field

See primary key field.

 L

label

An unbound control used to add descriptive text.

LAN

See local area network.

Leszynski naming convention

A popular object and field naming convention that uses a three-letter tag to identify the object type or field data type.

line (control)

An unbound control used to insert a line.

list box

A bound control used to provide a lengthy list of mutually exclusive choices for a field such as a State field. The user clicks the choice for the field from the list.

local area network (LAN)

Computers networked together in a single room, department, or building.

localhost

The default name for your own computer's Web site; *http://localhost* is the URL for your own computer.

macro

Stores a collection of keystrokes or commands to automate a task such as printing several reports or displaying a toolbar when a form opens.

main form

When a form is created that shows fields from more than one table in a one-to-many relationship, it will often attempt to organize the fields into a main form – subform arrangement. The main form contains the fields from the table on the "one" side of the one-to-many relationship between the tables.

many-to-many relationship

A record in Table X has many records in Table Y and a record in Table Y has many records in Table X.

marquee

See scrolling text control.

mathematical operators

Symbols such as add (+), subtract (-), multiply (*), divide (/), and exponentiation (^) that you can use within an expression to define how the expression will be calculated.

Microsoft Developers Network (MSDN)

A comprehensive online library with technical information about the Microsoft products that are used to develop applications such as sample code, documentation, technical articles, and reference guides.

Microsoft Knowledge Base

A database of technical support information and tools for Microsoft products.

Microsoft Personal Web Server Setup

A program that helps you manage which features of Personal Web Server are installed on your computer.

module

Stores Visual Basic programming code that extends the functions and automated processes of Access.

More Buttons button

A button at the end of a toolbar that provides users with a way to customize their toolbars to display those buttons that they most frequently use.

movie control

Plays a video clip on a page object.

MSDN

See Microsoft Developers Network.

multimedia

Consisting of more than one media (text) such as clip art, sound, or motion.

multiuser

Files that are multi-user, such as Access databases, allow many people to enter and update information at the same time.

Navigation bar

A toolbar placed upon the page object that is used to find, filter, sort, delete, edit, and move between records.

network administrator

A person who installs and maintains computers and software associated with a local or wide area network.

network engineer

A person who handles the physical installation of the computers (both servers and clients) and operating systems. Installs, tests, and supports the necessary communications hardware and software.

Normal view

Within FrontPage, the view that provides the WYSIWYG design surface on which you will create the Web page.

normalization

The process of designing a relational database, which involves determining the appropriate fields, tables, and table relationships.

Notepad

A simple text editor program included as a Windows accessory program.

objects

In an Access database, there are seven object types: tables, queries, forms, reports, pages, macros, and modules.

Office Chart control

A bound control within the page object that allows you to create interactive charts that are dynamically updated when underlying data in the Access database changes.

one-sided tag

HTML tags in which only a single tag is necessary.

one-to-many relationship

The most common relationship between tables, in which the common linking field is the primary key field in the table on the "one" side, and is the foreign key field in the table on the "many" side of the relationship.

one-to-one relationship

A record in Table X has no more than one matching record in Table Y.

option button

To provide the mutually exclusive choices within a bound option group. For example, option buttons within an option group bound to a gender field would provide a male or female field entry.

option group

A bound control used to organize the options available for a field with a few possible entries such as a Gender field.

orphaned records

Records in a "many" table that do not have a matching record in the "one" table of a one-to-many relationship. Enforcing referential integrity will prevent this condition.

page

An Access object that creates Web pages that are dynamically updated by an Access database.

Page Footer (section)

Appears at the bottom of each page.

Page Header (section)

Appears at the top of each page, but below the report header on the first page.

Page Wizard

A wizard that is used to quickly create a page object, allowing the user to make some basic choices about the design of the page.

path

The folder, drive, and server location of a desired file such as \\server\sharedfoldername or c:\amtoys\databases.

Personal Web Manager

A program within Windows 98 that manages the Personal Web Server, Personal Web Server folders, and Personal Web Server publishing process.

Personal Web Server (PWS)

A program within Windows 98 that allows you to develop a Web site and publish Web pages to that Web site using your own computer as a server.

PivotTable list control

A powerful bound control used in a page object that summarizes data within an interactive table.

PivotTable Property Toolbox

A toolbox window used to format and modify the individual fields and elements within the PivotTable list control in a page object.

portals

Search engines that are customized and indexed to provide categories of high quality information.

positioning

A description of how the items on a page object are located with respect to one another. By default, the positions of text, sections, and other elements in the body of a page are relative to one another (determined by the preceding content on the page).

Preview

Within FrontPage, the view that presents the Web page as it would be viewed by a browser.

primary key field

A field that contains unique information for each record and is used as the "one" field when linking tables in a "one-to-many" relationship.

programmer

A person who writes code for either server or client-side processing in such languages as Java, CGI/Perl, C++, and JavaScript.

properties

Characteristics that further define a field, control, section, object, or any other customizable element within a database.

protocol

Rules that dictate the structure of data and computer-to-computer communication.

publishing

To store the Web page files in a special folder on the Web server called a Web folder.

push technology

Technology that "pushes" information (in the form of Web pages) to you at the interval you define rather than waiting for you to actively "pull" or request the Web page.

PWS

See Personal Web Server.

query

Creates a datasheet that displays a subset of fields and/or records from one or more tables. Queries are created when a user has a "question" about the data in the database. Queries can also be used to create calculated fields and summarized information.

query grid

The lower half of query design view that displays the fields that will appear in the resulting datasheet and is used to specify sort orders and criteria.

read-only page

A page that presents data, but from which you cannot enter or update data. Pages that present grouped records are read-only.

record

A group of related fields for an item.

record locking

Access databases are record locking because they allow multiple people to simultaneously update the same database, but not the same record at the same time.

record navigation control

A control that allows you to add, delete, find, and move between records in a page object.

recordset

A subset of fields and records from one or more tables produced by a query.

rectangle (control)

An unbound control used to insert a rectangle as a graphic design element on a form, report, or page.

referential integrity

See enforce referential integrity.

relational database

A collection of related tables that share information.

report

Provides a professional printout of data that may contain enhancements such as headers, footers, and calculations on groups of records. Mailing labels can also be created from report objects.

Report Footer (section)

Appears after the last detail record or group footer section in the report.

Report Header (section)

Appears at the top of the first page.

Row field (within a PivotTable)

A field in the row area (the left-most edge of the PivotTable).

S

Sandbox

A concept that Java uses to secure and separate its programs.

script

A program that is embedded in another program to perform a certain function.

scrolling text control

Displays text that scrolls across the page and is also called a marquee.

search engines

Web sites devoted to indexing and finding other Web sites.

section

The area of the report that determines where and how often a control will print.

select query

The most common type of query, which selects fields and records to display in a datasheet.

shared network folder

A folder that stores and organizes files that many people need to use in a local area network.

sizing handles

In Form, Report, or Page Design view, sizing handles are black or gray boxes in the corners and middle edges of selected controls that, when dragged, change the size and shape of the object.

sort

Putting records in ascending or descending order based on the value in the specified sort field.

spreadsheet control

A control that provides a spreadsheet window into which you can enter raw data and build formulas similarly to how you would use an Excel spreadsheet on a page object.

SQL (Structured Query Language)

The programming language that is written within a query and is used to request from the specified tables.

Structured Query Language

See SQL.

subform

When a form is created that shows fields from more than one table in a one-to-many relationship, it will often attempt to organize the fields into a main form – subform arrangement. The subform contains the fields from the table on the "many" side of the one-to-many relationship between the tables.

subform (control)

A bound control used to insert a subform that displays the fields and records on the "many" side of a one-to-many relationship for the recordset on which the form is based. The data in a subform is usually organized as a datasheet.

Summary area (within a PivotTable)

The part of a PivotTable that shows summarized data.

surfing

Browsing from Web page to Web page for general Internet research.

systems analyst

A person who monitors and analyzes the impact of new technologies, upgrades, and changes made to the system. Helps tune the system to provide acceptable levels of performance and security.

T

tab control

An unbound control used to create a three-dimensional aspect to a form so that other controls can be organized and displayed in Form View by clicking the tabs.

table

Contains all of the raw data within the database organized by fields and records in a spreadsheet-like view called a datasheet. A table is the collection of records for a single subject. Tables can be linked with a common field to share information and therefore minimize data redundancy.

tags

HTML codes that the browser uses to determine how the Web page should appear. Tags appear in <angle brackets>.

TCP/IP

See Transmission Control Protocol/Internet Protocol.

Telnet

An Internet protocol that allows users to log into computers from remote sites.

template

A predefined color, formatting, and Web page layout definition.

text box

A bound control used to display the contents of a Text, Number, Currency, Memo, or Date/Type field.

theme

A complementary collection of color schemes, images, lines, and font choices that are applied to the Web page in one process.

three-tier application

A common way for people to discuss the parts of a client/server application; an approach that encompasses all data-driven Web sites.

toggle button

A bound control used to display a "yes" or "no" answer for a Yes/No field in the form of a toggled button.

Toolbox toolbar

The toolbar that contains buttons for the different types of controls that you can add to a form, report, or page object.

Transmission Control Protocol/Internet Protocol (TCP/IP)

A communications protocol for sending information across the Internet.

two-sided tag

HTML tags in which both an opening and closing tag are needed such as <H1> and </H1>. The forward slash within the second tag indicates that it is a closing tag.

unbound control

In a form, report, or page object, unbound controls are used to clarify or enhance the appearance of the object. Examples include lines, labels, and clip art. Unbound controls do not change as you move from record to record.

unbound object frame

An unbound control used to add a sound, movie, spreadsheet, document, or other type of object from another application to a form.

UNC

See Universal Naming Convention.

Uniform Resource Locator (URL)

The address used to locate a Web page.

Universal Naming Convention (UNC)

A naming convention to locate a file on a local area network. The structure of a UNC is \\server\sharedfoldername\ filename.

URL

See Uniform Resource Locator.

URL mappings

See virtual folders.

User Manager

A program within Windows NT that allows the network administrator to define each new user, their password, and their security rights.

user ID

The name given to each user in a local area network, often used in conjunction with a password to log on to different parts of the network.

value axis

In a chart, the y-axis.

virtual

Being in essence or in effect, though not in fact.

virtual auction houses

Web sites in which you can submit competitive bids at an auction to buy items and services.

virtual folders

Directory names used in a URL address that correspond to a physical directory on the server. Also called URL mappings.

virtual malls

Web sites in which you can browse from many stores.

virtual stores

Web sites in which you can make a purchase.

W

watermark

A background picture added to a Web page.

Web

Within FrontPage, a Web is a collection of files stored in a Web folder on a Web server or your computer's hard drive.

Web folder

A folder that stores and organizes Web pages.

Web hosting company

A company whose job it is to administer a Web server and out-source that service to others.

Web page developer

A person who builds Web pages with a variety of software tools. Generally very skilled in HTML and Web-enabling languages.

Web Publishing Wizard

An Internet tool bundled within Windows 98 that helps you publish files to an Internet Web site.

Web server

A special type of file server dedicated to managing Web pages.

Web server address

Also called domain name. Examples include *www.ibm.com*, *www.whitehouse.gov*, or *www.redcross.org*.

Webmaster

A person who installs and maintains Web servers and is often considered the person most directly responsible for the success of the Web site.

white paper

An article that gives background information about a subject.

wildcard

When entering criteria in the query grid, a wildcard character can be used to expand the capabilities of the criteria. The asterisk (*), for example, can be used within criteria to represent any number of characters. The question mark (?) wildcard can be used to represent a single character.

World Wide Web

A technology for linking files located on different Web servers located throughout the Internet evolved to provide an easy-to-use hypertext navigation system to retrieve Internet resources.

WWW

See World Wide Web.

WYSIWYG

What you see is what you get; the ability for software to show you how a page will appear while you are still editing it.

XML (eXtensible Markup Language)

A programming code that acts as an extension of HTML. XML provides enhanced features such as the ability for your Web page to dynamically interact with a database.

TASK	PAGE #	RECOMMENDED METHOD
Access home page, open	DDWS 6.07	In IE, go to *www.microsoft.com/access*.
Access objects, create	DDWS 2.07	Click the appropriate object button on the Objects Bar, then click the New button on the Database window toolbar for a list of ways you can create that object.
Access objects, delete	DDWS 2.07	Right-click the object you wish to delete in the Database window, and then click Delete.
Access objects, Design view	DDWS 2.10	Right-click the object you wish to work with in Design view, and then click Design View.
Access objects, open	DDWS 2.02	Click the appropriate object button on the Objects Bar, and then double-click the object you wish to open.
Access objects, view	DDWS 2.02	Click the appropriate object button on the Objects Bar, and then click one of the View buttons (Large Icons, Small Icons, List, or Details) on the Database window toolbar.
Aggregate calculations, create	DDWS 2.29	In Query Design view, click the Totals button Σ, and then choose the appropriate aggregate function for each field included in the query.
Background (picture or sound), add	DDWS 4.52	In Page Design view, click Format on the menu bar, point to Background, and then click Picture or Sound.
Calculated fields, create	DDWS 2.28	In Query Design view, click a new field name cell, and then enter the calculated field using the following format: newfieldname:expression.
Charts, create	DDWS 4.35	*See* Reference Window: Creating a Chart
Charts, modify	DDWS 4.42	In Page Design view, click the chart once to select it, click it again to edit it, right-click it, and then click Property Toolbox.
Controls, add	DDWS 2.40	In Form or Report Design view, click the control you wish to add on the Toolbox toolbar, and then click on the object where you wish to place the new control.
Controls, change properties	DDWS 2.46	Click the control to be changed, and then click the Properties button on the Form or Report Design toolbar.
Controls, modify	DDWS 2.46	In Form or Report Design view, click the control you wish to modify, and then make the appropriate change using mouse actions, toolbar buttons, menu choices, or by making changes in the control's property sheet.
Data Access Page, create	DDWS 3.05	*See* Pages, create
Data Access Page, open	DDWS 3.05	*See* Pages, open
Data Access Page, save	DDWS 3.06	*See* Pages, save
Datasheet, sort	DDWS 2.21	*See* Records, sort
Datasheet, filter	DDWS 3.10	*See* Records, filter
Domain names, check availability	DDWS 1.14	In IE, go to *www.internic.net* to find a list of accredited registries, or go directly to a domain name registry site such as *www.register.com*.

TASK	PAGE #	RECOMMENDED METHOD
Favorites (Web sites), create	DDWS 1.21	In IE, drag the IE icon 🗗 that is to the left of the Web page address on the Address bar to the top of the Favorites window.
Favorites (Web sites), delete	DDWS 1.24	In IE, right-click the entry in the Favorites window, and then click Delete.
Favorites (Web sites), display	DDWS 1.21	In IE, click the Favorites button 🗄 on the Standard Buttons toolbar.
Favorites (Web sites), rename	DDWS 1.23	In IE, right-click the entry in the Favorites window, and then click Rename.
Fields, add to a query	DDWS 2.20	In Query Design view, drag a field from the field list to the appropriate column in the query grid.
Fields, add to a form or report	DDWS 2.45	In Form or Report Design view, drag the field from the Field List to the appropriate location on the object.
Fields, create	DDWS 2.10	In Table Design view, type the new field name in an empty field name cell, specify the Data Type, and then modify properties for that field as necessary.
Fields, delete from a query	DDWS 2.21	In Query Design view, click the field selector above the field name, and then press the Delete key.
Fields, navigate	DDWS 2.03	Press the Tab key or the Enter key to move from field to field within a record.
Fields, set primary key	DDWS 2.02	In Table Design view, click the field you wish to designate as the Primary Key field, and then click 🔑 on the Table Design toolbar.
Field list window, toggle on	DDWS 2.44	In Form or Report Design view, click the Field List button 🗉 on the Form Design or Report Design toolbar.
Filters, apply	DDWS 3.10	*See* Records, filter
Filters, remove	DDWS 3.11	Click the Remove Filter button 🔽 on the Table, Query, Form, or Page Navigation toolbar.
Form section, size	DDWS 2.37	Position the mouse pointer at the bottom edge of the section until it changes to the ➕ pointer, click, and then drag.
FrontPage Web, create	DDWS 6.17	*See* Reference Window: Creating a FrontPage Web and Establishing a Connection between a Web Page and a Database
FrontPage Web page, add database connectivity	DDWS 6.21	*See* Reference Window: Adding Dynamic Database Cmponents to a FrontPage Web Page
FrontPage Web page, connect to a database	DDWS 6.17	*See* Reference Window: Creating a FrontPage Web and Establishing a Connection between a Web Page and a Database
FrontPage Web page, publish	DDWS 6.25	*See* Reference Window: Publishing a FrontPage Web Page
Help, open	DDWS 3.11	Click the Help button ❓ on the Database or Navigation toolbar.

TASK	PAGE #	RECOMMENDED METHOD
Hotspot image control, add	DDWS 3.26	In Page Design view, click the Hotspot Image button 🖳 on the Toolbox toolbar, and then click on the page where you want to add the control.
Hyperlink control, add	DDWS 3.24	In Page Design view, click the Hyperlink button 🖳 on the Toolbox toolbar, and then click on the page where you want to add the control.
Hyperlink data type, specify	DDWS 2.11	In Table Design view, click the Data Type list arrow for the field you wish to specify with a Hyperlink Data Type, and then click Hyperlink.
Join properties, change	DDWS 2.15	Double-click the link line between the two tables in the Relationships window and then click the Join Type button to open the Join Properties dialog box. In Query Design view, double-click the link line between the two tables to open the Join Properties dialog box.
Label, create on a form or report	DDWS 2.40	Click 🄰🄰 on the toolbox. Click where you want to add the label.
Link line, modify	DDWS 2.15	*See* Join properties, change
Office Spreadsheet control, add	DDWS 4.49	In Page Design view, click the Office Spreadsheet button 🖳 on the Toolbox toolbar, and then click on the page where you want to add the control.
Pages, create	DDWS 3.05	Click Pages on the Objects bar of the Database window, then double-click Create data access page by using wizard.
Pages, create with AutoPage tool	DDWS 3.04	*See* Reference Window: Creating a page object using the AutoPage tool
Pages, create with Page Wizard	DDWS 3.12	*See* Reference Window: Creating a Page Object using the Page Wizard
Pages, open	DDWS 3.05	Double-click the page icon in the database window.
Pages, save	DDWS 3.06	*See* Reference Window: Saving a Page Object
Personal Web Manager, Publishing Wizard	DDWS 5.16	*See* Reference Window: Using the Personal Web Manager Publishing Wizard
Personal Web Server, install	DDWS 5.05	*See* Reference Window: Installing Personal Web Server
PivotTable, change calculations	DDWS 4.18	Right-click the field that you wish to base the calculation on, point to AutoCalc, and then click the appropriate calculation function.
PivotTable, collapse	DDWS 4.09	Click the collapse button to the left of the expanded PivotTable field.
PivotTable, create	DDWS 4.05	*See* Reference Window: Creating a PivotTable List Control on a Page
PivotTable, expand	DDWS 4.09	Click the expand button to the left of the collapsed PivotTable field.
PivotTable, filter	DDWS 4.10	Click the filter list arrow to the left of the appropriate PivotTable field.
PivotTable, format	DDWS 4.22	In Page Design view, click the PivotTable control once to select it, click it a second time to open it for editing, right-click it, and then click PivotTable Property Toolbox.

TASK	PAGE #	RECOMMENDED METHOD
PivotTable, modify structure	DDWS 4.12	Right-click the PivotTable control in either Page or Page Design view (you must be editing the PivotTable), and then click the appropriate choice.
PivotTable, show (and hide) elements	DDWS 4.25	In Page Design view, click the PivotTable control once to select it, click it a second time to open it for editing, right-click it, and then click PivotTable Property Toolbox. Expand the Show/Hide area of the PivotTable Property Toolbox and then toggle on or off desired elements.
PivotTable, sort	DDWS 4.17	Right-click the PivotTable field that you wish to sort by, and then click the appropriate sort menu option.
PivotTable, subtotals	DDWS 4.08	Right-click the PivotTable field that you wish to subtotal, and then click the Subtotal option to toggle it on or off.
Properties window, toggle on or off	DDWS 2.45	In Report or Form Design view, click 🖼 on the Report Design or Form Design toolbar.
Query, add criteria	DDWS 2.23	In Query Design view, click the Criteria cell for the field you wish to modify, then type the criteria entry.
Query, change Query Type	DDWS 2.33	In Query Design view, click ▦ ▾ .
Query, open datasheet	DDWS 2.21	In Query Design view, click ▦ .
Query, sort	DDWS 2.22	*See* Records, sort
Relationship, create between tables	DDWS 2.14	Click the Relationships button ⛁ on the Database toolbar, add the appropriate tables to the Relationships window, then drag the linking field from one table and drop it on the linking field of the other.
Relationships, print	DDWS 2.16	Click File on the menu bar of the Relationships window, then click Print Relationships.
Records, add	DDWS 3.09	In Table datasheet, Query datasheet, Form view, or Web page, click the New Record button ▸∗ and then enter the new data.
Records, filter	DDWS 3.10	In a datasheet, form, or Web page, click the field value to use for the selection criteria, and then click the Filter By Selection button ▽⁄ .
Records, group on a report	DDWS 2.45	In Report Design view, click the Sorting and Grouping button ▤ on the Report Design toolbar. To group records, change the Group Header and/or Group Footer properties to Yes.
Records, navigate	DDWS 2.03	Press the Up or Down arrow keys, press the Page Up or Page Down keys, or use the navigation buttons on the Navigation toolbar.
Records, sort in a datasheet or form	DDWS 2.21	In a datasheet or form, click the Sort Ascending ⥮ or Sort Descending ⥯ buttons on the Table Datasheet, Query Datasheet, or Form toolbars.
Records, sort on a report	DDWS 2.45	In Report Design view, click the Sorting and Grouping button ▤ on the Report Design toolbar.

TASK	PAGE #	RECOMMENDED METHOD
Referential integrity, enforce	DDWS 2.15	Double-click the link line between two tables in the Relationships window, and then click the Enforce Referential Integrity check box in the Edit Relationships dialog box.
Scrolling text control, add	DDWS 4.47	In Page Design view, click the Scrolling Text button [icon] on the Toolbox toolbar, and then click on the page where you want to add the control.
SQL, view	DDWS 2.31	In either Query Design or Datasheet view, click the View button arrow and then click SQL View.
Subdatasheet, display related records	DDWS 2.04	Click [+] to the left of the record.
Subdatasheet, hide related records	DDWS 2.04	Click [−] to the left of the record.
Terminology, define	DDWS 6.03	In IE, go to *www.whatis.com*.
Theme, apply to data access page	DDWS 4.51	In Page Design view, click Format on the menu bar, then click Theme.
Toolbox toolbar, toggle on or off	DDWS 2.40	In Form or Report Design view, click the Toolbox button [icon] on the Form Design or Report Design toolbar.
Web pages (dynamic), create	DDWS 3.05	*See* Data Access Pages, create
Web pages (static), create	DDWS 3.29	Right-click an object in the database window, click Export, and then specify HTML Documents as the Save as type option.
Web pages, open in IE	DDWS 3.18	In IE, click the File menu, click Open, and then browse for the appropriate .htm file.
Web pages, save	DDWS 3.19	Save the Data Access Page. Saving a page object automatically saves both the page object icon in the database file as well as the Web page (.htm) file.
Web sites, find	DDWS 1.05	In IE, go to *www.about.com* (or another general search engine such as *www.yahoo.com*) and then search for Web sites by entering key words and clicking the Search or Go button.

Folder path/structure on hard disk:

C:*YourName*\A2Kweb\Tutorial.0x\Tutorial
C:*YourName*\A2Kweb\Tutorial.0x\Review
C:*YourName*\A2Kweb\Tutorial.0x\Cases

C:*YourName*\A2Kweb\Tutorial.0x\Tutorial\Solutions
C:*YourName*\A2Kweb\Tutorial.0x\Review\Solutions
C:*YourName*\A2Kweb\Tutorial.0x\Cases\Solutions

File Finder		
Location in Tutorial	**Name of Data File**	**Student Creates New File**
Tutorial 1		
	No Data Files.	
Tutorial 2		
Session 2.1	AMToys-2.mdb	
Session 2.2	AMToys-2.mdb	
Session 2.3	AMToys-2.mdb	
Review Assignment	AdairGS-2.mdb	
Case Problem 1	PremierConsulting-2.mdb	
Case Problem 2	Dyslexia-2.mdb	
Case Problem 3	ShipShape-2.mdb	
Case Problem 4	DistinctiveMeetings-2	
Tutorial 3		
Session 3.1	AMToys-3.mdb	Suppliers.htm
Session 3.2	AMToys-3.mdb	Products within Categories.htm New folder created by Access: Suppliers_Files has many files.
	Suppliers.htm	
	Block.bmp	
Review Assignment	AdairGS-3.mdb	New folder created by Access: Students_Files has many files.
	Teaching.bmp	Students.htm Instructor Assignments.htm
Case Problem 1	PremierConsulting-3.mdb	Project Activity.htm Employee Update Screen.htm
Case Problem 2	Dyslexia-3.mdb	Pledges.htm Contributors.htm
Case Problem 3	ShipShape-3.mdb	
Case Problem 4	DistinctiveMeetings-3.mdb	Summary Sales.htm Attendees.htm
Tutorial 4		
Session 4.1	AMToys-4.mdb	New folder created by Access: Supplier Analysis_files has many files. Supplier Analysis.htm
Session 4.2	AMToys-4.mdb	
Session 4.3	AMToys-4.mdb	Sales Tax Calculator.htm
Review Assignment	AdairGS-4.mdb	New folder created by Access: Student Grade Analyzer_files has many files. Student Percentages.htm Student Attainment Comparison.htm Student Grade Analyzer.htm
Case Problem 1	PremierConsulting-4.mdb	New folder created by Access: Payment Analysis_files has many files. Payment Analysis.htm

File Finder

Location in Tutorial	Name and Location of Data File	Student Creates New File
Tutorial 4 *(Continued)*		
Case Problem 2	Dyslexia-4.mdb	Pledge Analysis.htm
Case Problem 3	ShipShape-4.mdb	
Case Problem 4	DistinctiveMeetings-4.mdb	New folder created by Access: Fee Analysis_files has many files. Fee Analysis.htm
Tutorial 5		
Session 5.1	AMToys-5.mdb	New folder created by Access: Suppliers_files has many files. Suppliers.htm c:\Inetpub\wwwroot (PWS published files)
Session 5.2	AMToys-5.mdb	Suppliers.htm
Review Assignment	AdairGS-5.mdb	ClassEntry.htm
Case Problem 1		*YourName*Classes.htm
Case Problem 2		
Case Problem 3		
Case Problem 4		*YourName*Classes.htm
Tutorial 6		
Session 6.1	C:*YourName*\A2Kweb\Tutorial.06\ Tutorial\AMToys-6.mdb	supplier_report.asp
Session 6.2	C:*YourName*\A2Kweb\Tutorial.06\ Tutorial\solutions\AMToys-6.mdb	
Session 6.3		
Review Assignment	C:*YourName*\A2Kweb\Tutorial.06\ Review\AdairGS-6.mdb	
Case Problem 1	C:\Program Files\Microsoft Office\ Office\Samples\Northwind.mdb	
Case Problem 2	www.microsoft.com: 5298.exe	Downloaded from Microsoft site: 5298.exe Unzips 5298.exe to C:\Windows\Temp
Case Problem 3		feedback_Form.asp
Case Problem 4		